How Christ Said the First Mass, or, The Lord's Last Supper

James Luke Meagher

bibliolife

old books. new life.

HOW

CHRIST SAID THE FIRST MASS,

OR

The Lord's Last Supper.

THE RITES AND CEREMONIES, THE RITUAL AND LITURGY,
THE FORMS OF DIVINE WORSHIP

CHRIST OBSERVED,

WHEN HE CHANGED THE PASSOVER INTO THE MASS.

*The Beginnings of the Mass with its Ceremonies foretold in the
Patriarchal Worship, in the Old Testament, in the He-
brew Religion, in Moses' Tabernacle, and in the
Temple of the Days of Christ.*

BY

REV. JAMES L. MEAGHER, D.D.

PRESIDENT OF THE CHRISTIAN PRESS ASSOCIATION PUBLISHING COMPANY,

SECOND EDITION.

NEW YORK
**CHRISTIAN PRESS ASSOCIATION PUBLISHING
COMPANY**
26 BARCLAY STREET
1908.

CONTENTS.

1

III. THE BREAD, WINE, WATER, OIL AND INCENSE IN THE TEMPLE.

THE SECOND PART: HOW THE MASS WAS FORETOLD IN THE PASSOVER.

IV. THE HISTORY OF THE HEBREW PASSOVER.

V. THE TALMUD ON THE LAST SUPPER OR PASSOVER.

VI. THE FEAST OF UNLEAVEN BREAD AT THE PASSOVER.

Why the feast lasted for a week. Why they asked Pilate to
deliver Barabbas in place of Christ. Ceremony of the
Omer " first fruits " foretelling Christ's arrest. The minor
feasts during Passover week. Why the Jews would not
enter Pilate's hall. How the victims were sacrificed on
Passover week. The evening banquet. The bath and
washing the feet images of baptism. The architriclinus.
The tables. Positions of guests. When the couch was introduced. Why they washed their hands. Origin of

THE THIRD PART: HOW THE MASS WAS FORETOLD IN THE CENACLE.

VII. THE HISTORY OF MELCHISEDECH, SION AND THE CENACLE.

VIII. THE SYNAGOGUE SERVICES IN THE CENACLE.

THE FOURTH PART HOW CHRIST AND THE APOSTLES SAID THE FIRST MASS.

X. HOW CHIRST AND THE APOSTLES PREPARED FOR THE FIRST MASS.

XII. THE PRAYERS AND CEREMONIES OF THE CANON OF THE
FIRST MASS.

Why the bishop lays by his crosier and miter before going
up to the altar How the tables were arranged at the Last
Supper. The Triclinium, "Three Beds." Origin of the
assistant priest, deacon and subdeacon. Peter, James and
John. What they represented in the Church. Why they
said Mass facing the people in the early Church. Origin of
the clergy seats in our sanctuary. How John could lay his
head on Jesus' breast Why Christ used the words "This is
my Body." The lamb eaten in the Old Law prophesied
"the Lamb of God" in the New. Communion image of the
Incarnation. Mystic and prophetic meanings of the Passover. The great Chalice Christ used. The paten with the
three altar breads. Origin of the credence table and cruets
of wine and water. Why the ministers put wine and
water in the chalice for the celebrant at Mass. Origin of the
Canon, why it is said in a low voice. The Passover Seder
and meanings of its sections. Why the clergy say the Mass
with the bishop while being ordained. Why the celebrant
leans over the altar table beginning the Canon and saying
the words of Consecration. Why the Gospels do not give the
details of the Last Supper. The Ritual of the Last Supper
the foundation of the Church Liturgies. Prayers at the
first chalice of wine. Why the celebrant washes his hands at
Mass. The parsley. The "Bread of affliction." The questions John asked, and the replies. The history of Abraham.
The delivery of the Hebrews from Egyptian slavery at
Passover imaged the delivery of the world from demonic
slavery. How the Divine Son delivered the Hebrews.
The plagues on Egypt. The paschal lamb foretelling the
crucifixion, and the bread and wine prophetic of the
Mass. The Little Hallel. The bitter herbs. Who was
Hillel? Judas' treason foretold. The Real Presence in the
Eucharist. End of the first Supper, thanksgiving prayers.
The washing of the feet. Christ consecrates the apostles
bishops. The ordination rite he followed. How the high
priest, priest, Rabbi, king and judge were ordained and
consecrated. Why three bishops consecrate a bishop.
Origin of consecrating the holy oils on Thursday. The
first bishops of the Church. How bishop and priest bind
Christ. The betrayal. Warnings against pride and vanity.
The three orders essential to the Church. Origin of the
religious orders. How the table was set for the feast of
unleaven bread. The rite Christ followed when he gave
Communion. Why the bread and wine are raised, lowered
and offered with a cross at Mass. Why the deacon touches

PREFACE.

WORLDLY people look with wonder at the Mass, and often say: "What is the meaning of this form of divine worship? Where did these ceremonies come from? Why are candles lighted during daytime? Why do the priests wear such peculiar robes? Why don't they say the service in a language the people can understand?"

The Catholic sometimes says to himself: "The Mass came from the Last Supper. But did Christ or the apostles say Mass as priest or bishop of our time? Did Christ that night follow any form of worship? If he did, where is it found? From ancient days the Church used the Ordinary of the Mass, but we do not know its origin."

Many questions rise in people's minds to which they find no answer. A common opinion holds that Christ said the First Mass at the Last Supper according to a short form of blessing and prayer, then consecrated the bread and wine, gave the apostles Communion, and preached the sermon John's Gospel gives. When the apostles said Mass, they recited some Psalms, read the Scriptures, preached a sermon, consecrated the bread and wine, recited the Lord's Prayer and then gave Communion. In the apostolic age the saints added other prayers and ceremonies. Afterwards Popes and councils still more developed the rites, composed new prayers, and that during the Middle Ages the Mass grew and expanded into the elaborate Liturgy and Ceremonial of our day.

But these opinions are wrong. From the beginning the Mass was said according to a long Liturgy and with ceremonies differing little from those of our time. No substantial addition was made after the apostolic age—what the early Popes did was of minor importance—revisions and corrections. Little addition was made to the Ordinary of the Mass handed down from the days of Peter, founder of our Latin Liturgy.

11

No pagan ceremony ever formed a part of the Mass. Through holy men of the Old Testament, God Himself revealed the forms, rites and ceremonies of divine worship, and these were all combined and summed up in the Last Supper. But what was this Supper? The four Gospels mention the feast, but do not enter into the matter. The Bible, Hebrew writers, and histories of that time tell us that the night He was betrayed the Lord held with His apostles the feast the Hebrews called the Passover, mentioned a hundred and seventeen times in Holy Writ as the Pascha, Phase, Azyme, Unleaven Bread, etc.

Every Jew from his youth celebrated the feast each Easter; even Heathens could have learned its history and meanings, and the Gospel writers did not think it seemly to fill their writings with its details. They mention only words, acts and incidents of the Last Supper, which did not properly belong to the Passover.

Round the lamb foretelling the crucifixion, and the bread and wine prophetic of the Mass, from times immemorial, the Holy Spirit, by and through the prophets, had gathered a long series of ceremonies and numerous objects recalling the history of God's people. The consecration of the bread and wine changed these shadowy forms, emblems, types and sacramentals of the Hebrew religion into the substance they had so wonderfully foretold. The apostles therefore saw nothing new or strange when Christ changed the ancient Passover into the Mass.

We will begin with the religion of the patriarchs, describe the tabernacle, the Temple, their ceremonial, give the history of the Passover, of the Feast of Unleaven Bread, and show how the Mass was foretold in the Hebrew religion. Then we will pass to the Cenacle wherein the Lord held the Passover, describe the Synagogue services they carried out before the Supper, the vestments they used that night, and give a translation of the Form of Prayer or Liturgy of the First Mass. This Passover service of the Last Supper was the foundation of the Liturgies of the Mass.

We will show that the ceremonies seen to-day in the Mass came down from the Hebrew rites God established through Moses and the great men of the Old Testament. We will cite many Jewish and non-Catholic writers who will not be suspected of favoring the Church. We cannot quote all without filling the work with notes. Many translations from the Talmuds will show that the lamb, as a type of Christ, was sacrificed, during these long ages of waiting, for the sins of the offerers, for their friends, the sick, the absent, and the dead as to-day He is offered in the Mass.

No work could be found in any language treating in a complete way the Last Supper, and the writer had to rely on his own resources regarding matter and form. A subject so vast was beset with many difficulties, for it is hard to lay before the reader minute details, descriptions and scenes of a world which passed away two thousand years ago.

The writer studied the Jewish authors of ancient and modern times, was present during synagogue services in different cities of the world, consulted learned Rabbis, searched libraries, read the lives of Christ by famous authors, lived for weeks in Jerusalem, talked with Palestine Jews, was present while they held the Passover on Sion, and the result of his investigations are laid before the public. We hope that it will clear up many questions the laity ask regarding the origin of the Mass and its ceremonies.

We do not hold that every statement is absolutely exact, but is about as correct as we can reproduce the First Mass "Small men" may find some things to criticise, they would have written in a different way, but we hope our humble efforts will draw sincere human hearts nearer in love to their Saviour when they see how He established the great Christian Sacrifice.

THE FIRST PART.

HOW THE MASS WAS FORETOLD IN THE TEMPLE.

I.—THE SIGNS, SYMBOLS, AND CEREMONIES OF THE MASS IN THE TEMPLE.

The Catholic Church, its divisions of porch, nave, and sanctuary, its ornaments, vestments, and ceremonial, came from the Jewish Temple and the synagogue of the time of Christ. The Passover service was modeled on the Temple worship. Thus the Last Supper combined in one ceremonial the patriarchal worship, the tabernacle, the Temple, the synagogue, all united in one feast the Hebrews called the Passover, which Christ fulfilled and changed into the Mass. Let us therefore see first the Temple, its divisions, its rites, its ceremonies, and its sacramentals, that we may better understand the ceremonies Christ followed when he said the first Mass.

To teach truth by visible objects is an instinct of our nature. Words, spoken or printed, represent ideas. But we love to show our thoughts by actions. Even animals make-believe a fight in play ; with her doll the girl images her motherly instinct ; boys amuse themselves with toys ; men speak in figure, type, parable ; tone of voice, shade word meanings, show hate, anger, fear or sorrow, and smile, tear, and sob tell our feelings.

We love to see the actor in the play represent, not himself but a celebrated personage. Therefore, before the dawn of history, the theater was found in civilized lands,

15

where on its stage tragedy, comedy, and history were imaged before delighted audiences.

God made use of these representative instincts through which to foretell the future Tragedy of Calvary, to prophesy the Last Supper and the Mass. This was the best way to teach mankind, in that age when Adam's children were ignorant, when words were few, when language was hardly formed, when ideas were crude, when books were unknown, when few could read or write.

From the gates of Eden the Redeemer was revealed, the woman's Seed who was to come and conquer the serpent-demon who had enslaved mankind. But how was the revelation to be handed down in that age of the childhood of our race? God made use of this representative instinct of our nature, and told the life of the foretold Christ in the ceremonial of sacrifice, in the rites of the tabernacle, and in the ceremonies of the Temple. We will, therefore, first see the Temple. its ceremonies, for these we will later find in the Last Supper.

To Jew and unbeliever the Temple has ever been a riddle, and they have written countless books to explain its mysteries. The Catholic Church alone has the key which unlocks the mysteries of that maze of vast bewildering building, with its Holy of Holies, Holies, Priests' Court, Court of Israel, Women's Court, Chel, Chol, Cloisters, some roofed, others open to the sky, with various chambers, each at the time of Christ having its own proper use.

The wonderful building, with its rites and ceremonies, was a divine poem written by God to reveal present, past and future. In the past, the Jew saw God his Creator, mankind in original innocence, the Temptation and the Fall, the condemnation on our race, woman's deeper wound, the promise of the woman's Seed, sinners drowned when the world was baptized by the flood, the call of Abraham, the blessing on his race, the revelation given the Hebrews, their delivery from Egyptian slavery, the manna their food for forty years, their miraculous preservation and struggles, the whole world plunged into darkest idolatry, the glory of their judges, and the splendors of David and Solomon.

The Temple was the very heart and soul of the Jewish

Church, in which alone Jehovah was then adored in days of deepest paganism. But beyond, deep into the future, the Temple story and worship carried their minds, down to the days of Christ, to his Last Supper, to his atrocious death, to the New Testament, to the Catholic Church [1] with her Pontiff, her bishops, her priests, her sacraments and her millions of redeemed souls.[2]

The Temple and its vast ceremonial formed a book within and without written by God's eternal hand, not in dead lifeless letters as man writes, but in warm, living signs, symbols, types and figures. Amid the multitudes of Temple emblems, let us take those relating to our subject, and read the lessons of this Divine Poem, this heavenly poetry, this drama of Calvary, transcendent above all others—God its author here taught the future death of the only Begotten Son.[3]

The Holy of Holies closed by a veil represented heaven closed to mankind because of the sin of our first parents. The Holies with its glittering golden altar and walls foretold the church building—especially our sanctuary with its altar on which now the Mass is offered. The Courts with the ministering priests, the sacrificed victims, prefigured the Jewish priests who later were to kill the Saviour.

The words then of God's wonderful book had two meanings:—one, what the objects showed in themselves; this now alone the Jew can see; and the other meant the God-Man, the Church, the Eucharistic Sacrifice, and this the Christian with his faith can see. Patriarch, prophet, the holy ones of Israel, filled with faith of the foretold Messiah saw this sacred drama of the future, and read between the lines and behind the objects the story of the redemption of mankind; thus they walked in the faith, hope and love of Him who was to be born of their race. Thus the holy ones of old saved their souls.

Cenacle and church building were modeled after the Temple. We will therefore give a rapid glance over this great building, famed in all the earth, visited so often by the Lord, itself being copied from the tabernacle.

---

[1] S Augustine, De civit Dei, L xviii. c. 48.
[2] S Augustine, In Epist Joan, ad Parthos, Tracts 11, n. 111.
[3] S. Thomas, Sum Theo. I. a, 2æ 102 , S. Augustine, The Fathers, etc.

2

The tabernacle God directed Moses to make while wandering in the vast deserts of Arabia, "the Sandy," leaving no permanent resting-place, represented mankind in this world of trials—tired, weary, wishing ever for something higher, better.[1] The Temple Solomon built to replace the tabernacle, permanently resting on Moriah "Jehovah provides," within the city of Jerusalem "Possession of Peace," was the emblem of heaven where in beatific vision our souls will rest in everlasting peace.

"When it was building, it was built of stone hewed and made ready, so there was neither hammer, nor ax, nor any tool of iron heard in the house, when it was building "[2]

The Temple Solomon "the Peaceful" built imaged the Universal Church[3] the Son of God, the "Prince of Peace," built, while the tabernacle represented the Hebrew religion. Whence the Hebrews alone built the tabernacle, but pagan Sidonians and Tyrenians aided Solomon to build the Temple, to foretell that pagan converts would help Christ and his apostles to build the Universal Church.

God revealed to Moses the model of the tabernacle, and the plans and specifications of the Temple came from heaven; the Eternal Himself being its architect, for the Divine Son planned and founded the Catholic Church. "And David gave to Solomon his son a description of the porch, and of the Temple, and of the treasuries, and of the upper floor, and of the inner chambers, and of the house for the mercy-seat. All these things, he said, came to me written by the hand of the Lord that I might understand the works of the pattern."[4]

Sole Temple of the Lord of hosts, amid the thousand temples of pagan gods, resting on Moriah's top, within the sacred City "Vision of heavenly Jerusalem," terrace upon terrace towered the Temple at the time of Christ, dominating high over all the city, except Sion, a loftier hill, the latter emblematic of the Church and her Eucharistic Sacrifice.

---

[1] S. Augustine, Enar. in Psal xiv , S Thomas, Sum I, 2, q : 102 4, ad 2, etc.
[2] III. Kings 6-7.   [3] S Thomas, Sum ii. 2. q : 102, 4 ad 2.
[4] See I. Par. xxii. xxviii. 19.

Cedar-roofed and richly carved, enclosed by cloisters grandest ever built, its walls of white marble, the sacred fane dominated the city. Copied after the tabernacle of desert wanderings, the Temple was divided into four parts —the Holy of Holies, the Holies, the Hebrew Courts and the Court of Gentiles—each with its own symbolic and prophetic meanings, this was the sacred sanctuary Christ called " His Father's House," [1]

The inner fane of the holy sanctuary, called by Jewish writers : " The Gold House," was seven stories high, and 150 feet square, but within and without was covered with plates of purest gold, bought with money received from the sale of millions of paschal lambs' skins. Each plate was a yard square and as thick as a twenty-five cent piece. Not only walls and sides were gold covered, but even the roof, and it bristled with gold spikes about four inches long, to prevent birds settling on and soiling. This " Golden House," was seven-storied, emblematic of the sacred number seven, the word in which the Gospels were later written, and the seven sacraments

In the center was a room thirty feet square, the Holy of Holies its walls covered with gold plates, this was the resting-place of the Holy Ghost of tabernacle and first Temple. There, visible as a cloud by day, a fire at night, He spoke to Moses, to the prophets and revealed to them the Old Testament. They called him the Shekina " The Holy Presence."

The Holy of Holies was closed by a great veil, sixty by thirty feet, so thick and heavy it took 300 priests to hang it.[2] It was woven of seventy-two colored strands—white, representing waters of baptism ; violet, emblematic of penance ; red, martyr's blood ; and green, youthful innocence. The closed Holy of Holies, dwelling-place of the Holy Spirit, represented heaven closed by Adam's sin to all the members of the seventy-two nations born of Noe's grandsons, except they pass through baptism, penance, martyrdom, or youthful innocence regained.[3] Josephus and Jewish writers say the colors typified water, sky, fire and earth.[4] The colors are now seen in the Church vestments.

---

[1] John ii. 16   [2] Edersheim, Sketches, p. 197   [3] See S. Augustine, De civitate Dei, L. xvi. c. 3 n. 2 ; c. 6 n. 2   [4] Antiq. lii. 7. 7.

Once a year, the Day of Atonement, the high priest, typifying Jesus Christ in his death and ascension, his hands dripping with blood of victims he had sacrificed in the Priests' Court, emblematic of the Jewish Church which killed Christ, entered alone that secret place, holiest sanctuary of earth, and there sprinkled the blood to foretell Christ entering and opening heaven to mankind.

In the center of the Holy of Holies of tabernacle and Solomon's Temple rested the ark of the covenant, sign of God's contract[1] with the Hebrews. It was a box of sweetly smelling sitim wood, the acacia of Arabia, about three feet long, two wide and high, and covered within and without with plates of purest gold. The cover was edged around with a gold rim, forming the "Mercy Seat of God," the Shekina.[2] That ark was an emblem of Christ in heaven and on earth, in whom burned the Holy Ghost, with his fire of love moving him to die for the race.[3]

In a gold cup, like a ciborium, was preserved some of the miraculous manna which fell from heaven during the forty years of the wanderings of the Hebrews through Arabia. It reminded them of the food with which the Lord had fed their fathers, and it foretold the Eucharist preserved in the ciborium on our altars with which Christ now feeds Christian souls. Let us see the story of the manna, for one of the cakes of the bread of the Last Supper was named after it.

During the desert wanderings, 15,000 pounds of manna a week fell from heaven to feed the Hebrews. One morning they found the ground covered with little grains like hoar-frost, and when they saw it the first time they exclaimed in Hebrew, "Manna?" "What is this?" For forty years God fed them on this miraculous food, till they entered the Promised Land, to foretell the Eucharist nourishment of our souls during the wanderings of this life.

Every morning, except the Sabbath, the ground was found covered with manna, which had to be gathered before the heat of the sun corrupted it; if a family gathered

---

[1] S. Augustine De civitate Dei, liber x 1   [2] An explanation of the Shekina will be found towards the end of this chapter   [3] See S. Augustine, De genes ad litteram, iv 17, Enarratio in Psalm cxxxi, Talmud, Yomah, 107.

more than wanted for food during the day it became offensive; but the double portion found Friday morning for that day and Saturday did not corrupt. They made the manna into thin cakes[1] like those of the Passover and of the Mass. The third cake Christ consecrated was called the Aphikoman "The heavenly manna." A gold ciborium filled with the miraculous manna was placed in the ark to remind them of the miracle, and down the ages it lasted unchanged till Solomon's Temple was destroyed; it was a type of the Eucharist reserved on our altars.

The Orientals still gather a kind of manna, which has not the qualities of that of Scripture. It is not a food but a purgative medicine; it does not fall all the year, but only from May to August; it is found only in small quantities; it keeps for a long time without corruption; a double portion does not fall on Friday; it does not suddenly cease as the miraculous manna did when the Hebrews entered Palestine, when they began to raise their own food.

Burkhardt, who traveled extensively through Arabia in 1812, says "Manna in our day is found on the ground, leaves, etc., must be gathered mornings for the sun melts it, and it is found only during wet seasons, rarely in dry weather. Strained through a cloth, it is spread on bread like butter or honey, but it is never made into cakes like the Hebrew manna, and in leather bottles will keep for years." The Arabian physician Avicenna says, "Manna is collected from the tarfa or tamarisk shrub *Tamarix gallica*, it is a dew which falls on stones and bushes, becomes thick like honey and can be hardened so as to be like grain."

In the ark was also the blooming rod of Aaron showing forth his priesthood, and shadowing holy orders in the Church. It was a type of Christ's eternal Priesthood blossoming forth into bishop and priest of every age. Beside the rod lay the two stone tablets, having engraved on them the Ten Commandments, the foundations of law and order in every civilized land. Thus the manna was emblematic of food sustaining life; the rod, priestly wisdom, and the two tables of the law faith and morals—

[1] Babyl Talmud, Yomah, p. 115.

belief and practice of the future religion of the Crucified. These were preserved to recall to the Hebrews the wisdom, power, and goodness of God leading them from Egyptian paganism, nourishing them in the desert, and preserving them in the Promised Land.

Over the mercy-seat of God, above the ark, brooded the great gold images of the Cherubim " Holding fast," or "Those grasped." They represented the highest heavenly spirits, holding fast purest and highest truths streaming down into their minds from the Divine Son, as their wills grasp the Good of God the Holy Spirit. They recalled to the Hebrew mind the Cherubims the Eternal placed at the gates of Paradise after the Fall, " with flaming sword turning every way to keep the way of the tree of life." [1]

In ancient religions they come from Eden's gates, as winged female sphinx of Egypt, as composite creature forms of Persia, as winged bulls of Assyria and Babylonia, as Chimera of Greece, as Gryphon of Assyria, as Griffins of Northmen, and as grotesque emblems of fable and heraldry. They are still seen on coins, in sculpture, and art.

There, between the gold wings of the cherubim, on the mercy-seat rested the Shekina, the visible Presence of the Holy Spirit, a cloud by day, a fire at night, who spoke to the prophets, and gave mankind the Old Testament. Why were these golden images placed in the Holy of Holies? To image the millions of supernal spirits ever adoring the Eternal in His heavenly sanctuary, and to foretell images of Christ, of his Mother, of angels and of saints in the sanctuary of our churches. No member of our race was then in heaven, for it was closed till Christ opened it to us, therefore no image of saint was there. The custom of placing images, paintings and statues of Christ in the church comes down to us from the Apostles,[2]

Temple and church are images of heaven, dwelling-place of God. " And they shall make me a sanctuary and I will dwell in the midst of them."[3] Here the word " dwell" is in the Hebrew "I will shekina." Israel's greatest prophet in vision saw the Lord on his high

---

[1] Gen. iii 24. See S. Augustine's Question, in Exod L ii 2, cv. etc.
[2] St. Thomas, Sum iii. q. 25, 3 ad 4   [3] Exod. xxv. 8.

eternal throne, his court of heavenly beings filled the celestial Temple, while the Seraphim " The Burning " with knowledge and love, forming two choirs, sang the tresagion, " Holy, Holy, Holy is the Lord God of hosts." [1] The words formed a part of the synagogue service sang at the Last Supper, and is now a part of the Preface of the Mass. The beloved Apostle saw the four living creatures in apocalyptic vision [2] who sing the same before the Eternal's throne.

Next to and east of that Holy of Holies, most sacred fane of earth, was the Holies, Jews called "the Holy Place," typifying the future Universal Church, the Jew or unbeliever cannot see. Therefore it was closed by a great veil woven of white, green, red, and purple strands, behind which twice daily entered the priest chosen to offer incense on its altar, to prophesy Christ praying in his Church. [3]

There were thirteen veils in the Temple—they gave rise to the veils now covering the tabernacles of our churches, behind which, in the ciborium, dwells Jesus Christ under the veils or species of bread, as under the form of the Shekina, the Holy Spirit brooded over the mercy-seat in the Temple.

The Holies not only represented the Universal Church, but also the sanctuary of our Church. Three things in the Holies also typified, in a still more striking way, what the cup of manna, Aaron's rod, and the tables of the Ten Commandments represented in the Holy of Holies.

In the middle of the Holies rose the altar of incense, which the Jews called the "Golden Altar," because it was made of pure solid gold, and to distinguish it from the great sacrificial altar outside in the midst of the Priests' Court. That gold altar was the image of Jesus Christ. At nine in the morning, and at three in the afternoon, the priest spread on it burning coals to image the burning Shekina in the inner sanctuary. On them he sprinkled incense, the ceremonial foretelling Christ, burning with fire of the Holy Ghost, offering the prayers of the Mass on our altars in our sanctuary by the ministry of his clergy. The altar in our Church is a type of Christ,

---

[1] Isaias vi. 1 to 4.   [2] Apoc. iv. 7.   [3] Apoc. viii. 3, 4.

and for that reason the altar is incensed at solemn services, as was the golden altar of the Temple.[1]

No animal was sacrificed on that golden altar, to foretell that in the Church, on our altar, Christ is not sacrificed in a violent, bloody or painful manner, but in the mystic ceremonial of the Mass. But on the Day of Atonement, the high priest reddened the four corners of that altar with the blood of the sacrifices, held out over it his hands dripping blood, to foretell the cross of Christ reddened with his blood, and to foreshadow that the sacrifice of Calvary and of the Mass are one and identical.[2]

At the north of the gold altar of the Holies, at your right, stood the gold table[3] with the twelve loaves of proposition bread, which Jewish writers call the "Bread of the Face," and twelve flasks of wine. They represented the twelve tribes of Israel, God had fed with manna in the desert. They foretold the bread and wine resting on our credence table at a High Mass, changed into the body and blood of Christ, with which he now feeds the souls of the members of his Church. Only Temple priests could eat this bread or drink this wine with the flesh, to prophesy that the clergy of the Church live on its revenues. In memory of these breads, in Greek, Russian, and Oriental Rites, they cut the bread for the Mass into twelve pieces in honor of the twelve Apostles, having one for John the Baptist, a large one for the Blessed Virgin, and a still larger piece for the Sacrifice.

Oriental Christians build their altar the same shape and size of the gold altar of incense in the Holies. They allow nothing to rest on it but the liturgical books, not even candles. Thus the Holies, with its altar in the middle, the credence table on your right, and the great candlestick on your left, foretold the altar, credence table, and Easter candlestick in our sanctuary.

The candlestick of Herod's Temple at the time of Christ was of solid gold, weighed 100 pounds, and had been presented by Queen Helen of Adiabne of Assyria, a convert to Judaism.

The middle shaft of the candlestick ended with a gold

[1] S. Aug., Question in Exod. L. ii. Qu. cxxxiii et cxxxiv.
[2] For a description of the altar of incense, see Edersheim, Temple, 133, 134, 377 ; Migne, S Scripturæ, 11, 169, 170, 1301 ; 6, 446, 447, etc.
[3] Migne, Cursus Comp. S. Scripturæ, ii 1300, vi. 305.

cup, having at each side a straight row of three cups of the same shape and size, making seven lamps. The central lamp burning day and night bent towards the Holy of Holies. The others were always lighted from it, which, with striking ceremony, foretold that while Christ's life was taken, his Divinity lived, and that he was to rise from the tomb.[1]

This great solid gold candelabrum, purest metal offered to God alone, was six feet high, Christ's stature. It could not be cast, but was made by being beaten, to foretell the flagellation. Its seven lamps, Josephus says, typified the the seven planets, but they foretold the seven gifts of the Holy Ghost: wisdom, understanding, counsel, fortitude, knowledge, godliness and the fear of God poured out on Christ.[2]

While the stone tables having the engraved Ten Commandments were within the ark and showed Christ resting in heaven after teaching mankind religion, the candlestick showed him "The light enlightening every man who cometh into the world,"[3] glorified in heaven, while his Church preaches the light of his Gospel. The lamps were lighted each morning and extinguished at night.[4]

The Rabbis wrote before the Incarnation, that the candles and lights of Temple and Passover, especially the great candlestick, with its seven lights, foretold the Messiah, who would come and kindle for them "The Great Light." They wrote that he was "The Lord our Righteousness," "The Branch," "The Comforter," "The Enlightener," "The Light of the nations," etc. For that reason, when presented in the Temple, Simeon took the Child-Christ in his arms, and filled with the Holy Spirit burst forth into the prophecy and poetry written in this candelabra.

> Now thou dost dismiss thy servant,
> O Lord, according to thy word, in peace;
> Because my eyes have seen thy salvation,
> Which thou hast prepared,
> Before the face of all peoples,
> A Light to the revelation of the Gentiles,
> And the Glory of thy people Israel.[5]

[1] Lightfoot, Works, II 399.   [2] Isaias ii 2, 3; Migne 2, 168–1018.   [3] John i. 9.
[4] Migne, Cursus Completus, S. Scripturæ ii. 168.   [5] Luke ii. 29–32.

This was why John wrote: "And the Life was the Light of men, and the Light shineth in darkness, and the darkness did not comprehend it."[1]   The Holies was emblematic of this world with Christ burning with the fire of the Holy Ghost, filling men with the light of his teachings, enlightening souls with faith and heavenly truth.

It foretold the church building.   In the center of the Holies was the gold altar from which twice a day rose the smoke of incense ascending before the Lord, as from our altar, resting in the center of our sanctuary, ascends the Liturgy and prayers of the Mass.

Each of the seven branches of the golden candlestick ended in an olive oil lamp with wicks of worn-out priestly vestments; about a wine-glass of oil was poured into each every day by a priest chosen by " lot " for the function; the lamps were lighted from the central lamp turned toward the Holy of Holies ; thus it represented the Messiah the Christ—Hebrew and Greek words meaning " The Anointed "—by the Holy Ghost who was represented by the oil ; thus the candelabrum foretold God made man through the Spirit of God illuminating the world, enlightening men's minds by his teachings.

This is the meaning of numerous words and figures found in the Old Testament and Temple ceremonial. Many lamps of olive oil, hundreds of beeswax candles, burned during Temple worship, and before the Torah, " the Law," the first five books of the Old Testament, in Temple and synagogue hung an ever-burning lamp and this lamp and these candles have come down to us in the Church.

What became of the golden candlestick ?   That of Solomon's Temple was carried away into Babylonia when the first Temple was destroyed and was never heard of more.   That of the Temple of the time of Christ was carried away to Rome, after Titus took the city in the year A. D. 70, and was borne before the conqueror in his triumphal entry into the Eternal City.[2]   Its image is still seen on his triumphal arch, with the incense chests still standing in the upper part of the Roman Forum.

The candlestick was deposited in the Roman temple of

---

[1] John i 4-5   See Edersheim, Life of Christ, i. 198–200.
[2] Josephus Jewish Wars, VII, v. 5.

Peace. One writer says it was thrown into the Tiber from the Milivial bridge during Maxentius' flight from Constantine, but another account says it was carried by Genseric to Carthage in A. D. 455, recovered by Belisarius, brought to Constantinople in 533, and placed in a church, but it has never been heard of since.

The great gold candlestick of tabernacle and Temple representing Christ is still seen in our churches [1] in the Easter candlestick. It is lighted with long ceremony on Holy Saturday, and used during High Mass, till the Ascension, when it is quenched after the Gospel, to signify at the Ascension Christ finished his work of teaching the world religion.[2]

The candelabrum, bearing seven or more burning candles during our services, were copied from this famous Temple candlestick. The thirteen candles used while chanting the Tenebræ during Holy Week, are quenched as the Psalms are sung, while the highest is hidden behind the altar to signify the prophets the Hebrews killed, and the one hidden for a moment and brought forth represents Christ buried and risen from the dead.

Each Jewish synagogue has many seven-branched candelabrum, which they light during the services to remind them of the great candlestick of the Temple. But they do not light the central one, burning only six lights. It seems singular, for the central light foretold the Messiah in Temple ceremonial. The priest chosen each day trimmed and lighted the great candlestick. The Jewish laity never entered the Holies—only a priest, chosen day by day, burned the incense on its golden altar, prototype of the priest now offering in the Mass the prayer of Christ on our altar.[3]

The candlestick lighting up the Holies, emblematic of Christ the Light of his Church also foretold the bishop, light of his diocese.[4] Therefore the Pontiff places his episcopal throne on your left, where the candlestick stood in the Temple Holies, and there he sits "a light to the revelation of the Gentiles," reflecting the light which shines on him from the Fisherman's Throne. The Son

---

[1] See S Augustine, Sermo in cereo Paschali ; Sermo—182 de Verb Ap 1 ; Joan. 4, n x ; Sermo 317. de S Stephano, ix. [2] See S Aug Sermo. 338 n. 1.
[3] See Augustine, Enar in Psal cxxxviii. 15 in Psalm cix n 1.
[4] See S Augustine, Sermo 1, De cereo Pashah.

of God told John his beloved Apostle to write to the seven Churches of Asia, that if they did not do penance he would remove their candlesticks—that is, their bishops. We have seen the sad state of these cities where now Moslem fanatics rule.

The priest is placed as a light to the congregation.[1]

Where in the Holies the candlestick stood, on the side where now the Gospel is read in our churches, there rises the pulpit from whence is preached the sermon. Down from the Catholic Church, of which he is an officer, comes the bishop to his diocese, bringing with him all the lights and glories of the Universal Church. Down from the society of the priests of the diocese, comes the priest into the church bringing with him the Mass, Bible, sacraments, and wealth of doctrine. He is, in teaching and example, as a lamp for the people, a candlestick with the seven lamps of the Holy Ghost, with his seven-fold gifts of salvation for the members of the parish.

Ten gold candelabra, each with seven gold cups of olive oil, each forming a lamp, divided the Priests' Court from the Holies. They were united by gold chains, and they formed a railing for the sanctuary, like our sanctuary railing, to which they gave rise. These lamps were lighted on great Hebrew feasts.

Thus stood the Temple at the time of Christ, which he so often visited,—his " Father's house," where he so often worshiped when he came to the feasts of his people. Gold-walled within and without as well as roofed, every object of purest massive gold, adorned with religious objects, it was a sacramental emblem of the foretold glories of the Catholic Church. The Temple Herod had spent forty-six years building was famed in all the earth for its worship, its holiness, its glories and its wealth.

People of our day, when money-making has become a craze, when the whole object of this life is to get rich, find fault because they are asked to support religion, and grumble when they see our churches adorned with costly altars, statuary and works of art. Let them go back in thought to that time of dying David, who inspired of God prepared the means for his son Solomon to build the Temple, and they will find that he gave $19,349,260, be-

[1] See S Augustine, Enar. iv. in Psalm ciii, Sermo iv. n. 2.

sides other treasures of almost equal value to erect a building which was but an image of one of our churches.[1]

Directly east of the Holies, the three Courts of the Priests, of Israel, and of the Women—formed one great Court, divided as the names suggest. In the middle of the Priests' Court, now called the Es Sakhra "the Rock", where Abraham offered his son Isaac, rose the great sacrificial altar foretelling Calvary and its Victim the priests were to sacrifice that fatal Friday. To still more precisely typify Calvary, this altar was made of unhewn stones, built into four walls on the outside, the stones being held together by leaden bands, and the interior filled with earth.

The altar was fifteen feet high and forty-eight feet square, the exact dimensions of Calvary. It was in two terraces, the first forty-eight feet, the next thirty-six; the latter having a pathway, along which the ministering priest walked. The top was thirty feet square, on which burned three fires. To the south was an inclined plain forty-eight feet long by twenty-four wide, leading up to the altar. Each corner of the altar had a hollow bronze "corner" rising about eighteen inches high, to typify the arms of the cross. The one at the southwest had two openings with silver funnels, into which they poured the wine and water on the feast of Tabernacles, foretelling the Mass.[2]

This ever-burning fire, which had come down from heaven, in these three places on the sacrificial altar imaged the Shekina as fire and cloud on the mercy-seat.[3] One fire was to burn the flesh of the animals, the other was for the incense, the third to light the other fires if they went out. The roasted flesh was removed each day; but the bread and wine on Saturday were taken from the Holies and laid on a table for the priests to eat and drink. At the north of the altar stood the incoming priests chosen by "lot," and on the south stood the outgoing clergy, who had finished their duties for that week, the latter took their portions of bread and wine; in the center stood the high priest, and as the outgoing priests passed, they gave him half their portion of the proposition bread. The bread could be eaten and the sacred

[1] 1 Par. xxii. 14, etc.   [2] Edersheim, Temple, 32, 33.   [3] Mach. i. 22.

wine partaken of only on Saturday by priests in a state of Levitical purity, to foretell that only priests free from mortal sin must partake of Communion.

A red line ran round the middle of the altar ; above, the blood of the victims to be eaten was thrown, and below, the blood of the holocausts " entirely consumed." [1]

At the north of the altar rose six long rows of stone pillars, each about nine feet high, having near the top four rings to which they tied the bodies of the victims while removing the skins. Near-by were eight lower stone pillars, with hooks on which they hung the pieces of sacrificial flesh. Near-by were a marble table for laying out the pieces, a gold table for sacrificial vessels after the service, and another silver table on which they laid the victims before the services.

The Temple places we have described called the Chel "The Sacred Place," was surrounded by the Chol "The Profane." There the Gentiles could worship. But they were forbidden under pain of death to enter farther in. Greek, Latin and Hebrew bronze tablets on the surrounding marble balustrade, some of them found in the ruins in our day, told them the penalty of entering beyond. This Profane Place represented the Heathen nations not yet called to the Church till the Apostles went to preach to them. This is the reason every Catholic Church has a porch representing the heathens and infidels.

Now let us see the origin and history of these sacrifices of the Jewish Church. The grand liturgy of the Temple, the sacrifices of the Hebrew Courts have passed away, for the Sacrifice of the cross they foretold has been accomplished, while the sacrifice and ceremonial of the Holies, foretelling the Mass, still continues in the Eucharistic sacrifice.

When God condemned our parents for their sin, He foretold that from the woman would be born a Personage who would crush the serpent's head.[2] Then was revealed a person more powerful than the demon; the Seed of a virgin, a father is not mentioned ; suffering is in the prediction that his heel would be bruised ; and victory in the words that he would crush the serpent's head.[3]

---

[1] Edersheim, Temple, 33 ; Talmud, etc.   [2] Gen. iii 15.
[3] Edersheim, Temple, 97.

But ages of education and revelation were wanted that mankind might understand the cross and Mass. When the world was young, divinely directed patriarchs formed the ancient Passover, unfolding mystic rites, which Moses developed into the tabernacle ceremonial, which David and Solomon augmented into the Temple service, which the Jews introduced into the synagogue, and all these Christ fulfilled, finished and changed into the Eucharistic Sacrifice at the Last Supper.

In these ceremonies and prophecies, most minute details of the Incarnation, the life of Christ, the history of his sufferings and death, were written by the finger of God, that the Apostles might know him, and that the nations might enter his Church.

In the infancy of our race God taught our fathers as you would teach a child. Words were few, writing was not known. But religious truths might be seen in surrounding objects.

Whether God revealed the nature of sacrifice to Adam or if he knew it in his state of innocence we know not. But in the infancy of our race, they offered animals and first-fruits to God, to whom all belong, in place of their own life. The father priest might tell his children the story of creation, of the fall, of the foretold Seed of the woman, who was to come and restore mankind to innocence lost in Eden, but the words would be soon forgotten.

The father chose a lamb as the chief sacrifice, representative of the Redeemer in his passion and death,[1] that the gentle innocence and purity of the animal might foretell the same in Christ. Whence down the pages of the Old Testament, and in the Temple sacrifices, the lamb immolated morning and evening was the chief sacrifice—all others were only accessory.

What more impressive scene and prophetic type could have been given, than the young lamb, sinless, mute, chosen from the flock and condemned to die? The father, head and priest of the family, leads the victim to the altar, while round gather in prayer, wife, children, servants. Its feet are tied, it is thrown on the ground, its throat is cut, its warm blood flows, its skin taken off, its

[1] S. Thomas, Sum. 3, q. 23.

body roasted on the fire, its flesh is eaten while flame and prayer ascend up before the Lord. There was a prophecy of Christ's arrest, flagellation, crucifixion.[1] It was a sacred poem, written not in cold words, but by the Holy Ghost in acts, signs, symbols, and mystic movements, teaching in striking ceremony truth to minds of men when the world was young.

But people say, Who were these children of Adam? For the Bible mentions only his two sons, Cain and Abel. Jewish writers tell us that thirty-two times Eve brought forth twins, a boy and girl at each birth, and the twins married. The names of only two are given, for these related to Christ. They say Cain "Acquisition," married his twin sister Ripha "The Wanderer,"[2] and that Abel "Passing away," born without a sister never married. These statements of Jewish writers are to be taken with great care, but we give them and let the reader judge for himself.

How often Adam and his sons sacrificed we know not.[3] But in the year 129 or 130 after the fall, Holy Writ says Abel, a shepherd, offered the firstlings of his flocks, the lambs, for he was liberal and generous with his Creator. Cain, a farmer, was close and stingy, and loving worldly things, he offered the poorest and the most worthless of his farm products. For these reasons God received Abel's sacrifices and rejected Cain's.

Jealousy, the fiercest passion, human or demoniac, rose in Cain's soul, and he killed his brother. Talmudic writers say, that filled with frenzy, he hacked his brother all over, covering him with wounds, in his ignorance trying to make a hole through which, his soul might pass out of his body.

Abel the innocent priest lying dead, covered with wounds after his sacrifice, was an image of Christ[4] dead after his sacrifice of the cross, all wounded by the scourges. Condemned for the murder of his brother, Cain with Ripha, his wife, wandered over the world with a mark on him, lest his brothers might kill him.[5]

---

[1] S. Augustine, Sermo xxxi De Pasch 1 11, 111, xxxu. etc.   [2] Dutripon, Concordantia, S Scripturæ, word Cain, who quotes S Chrysostom.
[3] S Thomas Sum. Theo , 2 2 q 85, 1 ad 2
[4] S. Augustine, De civit Dei , L xv , c. vii , L xviii , xvii.
[5] S. Augustine, contra Faustum, L xii n. ix x. etc.

Because they killed their brother, Christ, the Hebrews have been an outcast people, living in cities, engaged in trade, never farming, for the earth yields not its harvests to them. Shunned by all people, they wander among the nations with a mark on them : " He is a Jew." Now they fulfil the prophesy God uttered in the case of their famous prototype Cain.[1]

" The voice of thy brother's blood crieth to me from the earth. Therefore, cursed shall thou be upon the earth, which hath opened her mouth to receive the blood of thy brother at thy hand. When thou shall till it, it shall not yield to thee its fruit; a fugitive and a vagabond shalt thou be upon the earth. And the Lord set a mark upon Cain, that whosoever found him should not kill him. And Cain went forth from the face of the Lord and dwelled as a fugitive on the earth."[2] The names and history of the other sixty-two children of Adam are not given, because they did not relate to Christ.

Sacrifice was revealed to acknowledge God, as Creator and Master of life and death, to recall blessings on their fathers, to excite their devotion, to keep the people from idolatry, and to foretell the future sacrifice of Christ. Its historic meaning was the creation, its literal meaning the worship of God, and its typical meaning the death of Christ.[3]

Every offering of the Hebrew religion foretold Calvary and the Eucharistic sacrifice, as St. Paul says : " Every priest standeth daily ministering the same sacrifice, which can never take away sin. But he, Christ, offering one sacrifice, forever sitteth on the right hand of God."[4] " Christ was offered in a lamb to show his innocence, in a calf because of the merits of his cross, in a ram to foretell his government, in a goat for he bore our sins, in a pigeon and dove because of his two natures, or in a pigeon because of purity, and in a dove because of his love of man."

The lamb with bread and wine were sacrificed from remotest history, all other offerings were secondary—one

[1] S Augustine, Enar Ps. xxxix, n xiii , Ps lviii , Ser ii n xxi ; Ps. lxxxii. n xxii. , De civitate Dei, 1 xv. c xiii [2] Gen iv 10-16 [3] See Migne, S. Scripturæ, ii. 1329 to 1346, etc. [4] Heb. x. 11, 12.

3

foretold the crucifixion, the other the Eucharist; they were always intermingled, mixed in mystic ceremony foretelling Christ's one sacrifice, of Calvary and the Mass which form not two, but one act of divine worship. Before he came they foretold his coming in the future. After he came the Eucharistic sacrifice points back to him. One majestic sacrificial ceremonial went before him in patriarchal, tabernacle, and Temple worship, telling that at a future age he would come to fulfil their meaning. Another still more magnificent ceremonial, the Liturgy of the Church, coming from the Last Supper, shows that He came. One pointed in the future, the other to the past, to the Tragedy of Calvary. Let us see what is a sacrifice.

The word comes from the Latin words *sacra faciens*: "doing a holy act." In a wide sense any religious act, as prayer, loss, suffering for God's sake, ourself, or for others, is a sacrifice. But strictly speaking sacrifice is the destruction of a valued sensible thing, which a priest offers to God in worship, to show forth His almighty power. It is the highest act of adoration, and must be only offered to the Deity. Reason demands the worship of God, but tells not the time, place or ceremonial—only revelation could determine these.[1]

Abraham, Isaac and Jacob built altars, offered sacrifices with the bread and wine of the Passover worship. Jacob with his sons went down into Egypt, became slaves in the Nile land, dwelled there till God, in the form of the Shekina, called Moses from the burning bush to be their deliverer. For forty years he led them through the vast deserts of Arabia, "The Sandy." Amid the fearful thunder and lightning of Sinai, while the earth quaked and the Shekina covered the mount, God gave the Ten Commandments, foundations of all laws of civilized countries. The Lord then developed the patriarchal Passover into the elaborate ceremonial of the tabernacle and Hebrew religion.

The tabernacle and its ceremonial came from God himself. "And they shall make me a sanctuary, and I shall dwell "—in the original it is " I shall shekina "—" in the

---

[1] See Goldhagen, De Religione, Hebreorum Dissert. Prop. lii ; Migne Cursus Comp. S. Scripturæ, ii. 1041 to 1348 ; vi. 609 ; xii. 177 to 181 etc.

midst of them, according to all the likeness of the tabernacle, which I will show thee." [1]

Down to the days of Moses the father was the priest and offered sacrifices for the family. Thus, in patriarchal days, fathers, heads of tribes, princes, kings, revered, feared and loved of subjects, offered sacrifices that their personality might excite reverence, devotion and religion in their subjects. Thus monuments of Assyria, Persia and ancient nations show us the priest-king in sacerdotal vestments offering sacrifices for the nations they ruled.

But when the Hebrews became a nation, a more special priesthood of the family of Aaron "The Enlightened", and ministers descending from Levi "Joined", were chosen to offer the sacrifices of the Hebrew nation, for these were later to kill the foretold Christ.[2]

Only beasts of the "clean" species, as the sheep, cow, and goat, with birds not younger than eight days, nor older than three years, without blemish, were sacrificed; the sick, castrated, lame, blind, etc., being rejected, for they foretold their great Antitype, the sinless Christ sacrificed in the fulness of his mild and gentle manhood.

Day by day at nine in the morning, and at three in the afternoon, the chief sacrifice was a lamb [3] offered with holy Psalms, canticles and prayers, sung by a choir of 500 priests and another choir of Levites—a magnificent ceremonial, image of a pontifical High Mass. The high priest pontificated, served by the Segan as assistant priest, with twelve priests, six each side of the pontiff, Aaron's heir, like the bishop or Pope in our days. They robed in the most costly and magnificent vestments the world could furnish.[4]

On great feasts after the sacrifice of the lamb countless animals were immolated, the blood of each splashed on the four "horns" of the great altar. The Temple was a vast shambles, a great slaughter-house of innocent victims, to shadow forth the awful, terrific sufferings of the Victim of Calvary. The blood was poured at the base of the altar, and flowed down through an underground

---

[1] Exod. xxv. 8, 9. [2] See Migne, iii 845 to 847, etc. See S. Thomas, Sum i, 2, q. 102-4; iii 983, etc [3] S. Thomas, Sum. iii q. 22. 3 5, etc. [4] Edersheim Temple, *passim.*

passage into the Cedron " the Black Valley," thus named because of the blood.

While the bloody sacrifices foretold the crucifixion, the unbloody offerings, the Jews call " flour " and " drink offerings," pointed to the Mass, where in an unbloody manner from the rising to the setting of the sun he is offered now among the nations. Wheat, barley, flour, chalices of wine, cakes of unleaven bread, azymous " thin," were offered with every sacrifice.

To get the animals for the sacrifice, Temple guards, led by priests, went out the Sheep Gate, and down into the Cedron Valley, as they went out that fatal night, led by Judas, when they arrested Christ. With money from the Temple treasury, they bought the victims, as they gave money to Judas. The high priests had stretched a bridge across the Cedron stream near Gethsemane, and across that bridge they led each victim tied and driven, as they led Christ, tied, the night of his arrest. To the priests they brought the animals, as later they brought the Lord.

They led the animals into the Temple, to the north of the great sacrificial altar.[1] The Jew saw in the cold dark north a figure of Lucifer, who had deceived Adam, and plunged the nations into unbelief and paganism. They sacrificed the victims towards the north as against the demon and sin resting on the world. At Mass, when the altar is in the eastern end of the church, the Gospel is read towards the north as against the demon of infidelity.

They washed the animal to foretell the Passover bath taken by Christ and his Apostles. They poured perfume over it to typify the odor of good works, words and miracles of the God-man. With a rope they fastened the right forefoot to the left hind-foot, and the left forefoot to the right hind-foot, the cord making a cross, emblematic of Christ fastened to his cross.

The bread and wine of the Mass is first raised up, offered the Eternal Father, lowered, moved to form a cross, and then laid on the altar. This comes from the Temple, and from the Last Supper. To foretell the Crucified they raised up every Sacrifice in the Temple,

[1] Edersheim, Temple, 84, 85.

offered it to God, holding it as high as their heads, the action being called the Terunia. Then they lowered it, and "waved" it to the north, south, east and west, this being the Tenupha, foretelling Christ raised up in the air on his cross, and his dead body taken down for burial. The Rabbis write that the actions meant that the sacrifices were offered for the nations living in the four quarters of the world.[1]

Ten classes of sacrifices thus formed a cross before being killed in the Temple. The bread and wine at the Passover were offered with the identical ceremony as the bread and wine of the Mass in our day. The animals to be sacrificed were offered with a cross, the bread and wine were not offered in the Temple with the same ceremonial, for the animals foretold his sufferings, and the bread and wine then typified the Mass, where he is not immolated in a cruel bloody manner but in mystic meaning in memory of the crucifixion. Sin sacrifices were sacrificed with a cross, but were not offered to God in the Temple, for God did not receive sin with the sacrificed victims. The following the Jews called the Menachot will explain our meaning.

THE MENACHOT TABLE.

Passover Barley Sheaf	were	Raised lowered and formed a cross.
Living animals		" " "
Barley flour of jealousy		Raised lowered but did not form a cross.
Libations of wine		" " "
Proposition bread		" " "
Leper's Log of oil		" " "
Pentecost Bread		" " "
Sin Offerings		Offered but did not form a cross.
Unleaven Cake		" " "
The Five voluntary Offerings		" " "
Initiation Sacrifice		" " "

[1] See Edersheim, Temple, *passim.*

The high priest with his assistant, the Sagan, at his right, and the twelve priests, all vested in magnificent priestly robes of cloth of gold, embroidered in the four colors of the sanctuary, spread out their hands between the animal's horns,[1] thumbs crossed, palms down and placed their sins and the sins of all the people on the animal, as the sins of the whole world were placed on Christ, and said a prayer we will give when we describe the ceremony when Christ and his Apostles offered the Passover lamb the day before his death.[2]

Two long lines of vested priests stand between the victim, one line having gold, the other silver chalices in their hands ready to receive the blood. The victim's throat is cut, the blood caught in the chalices, and passed along each line with arms crossed in form of a cross and splashed on the four horns of the altar, marking each with a bloody cross.[3] A choir of 500 priests and another of the same number of Levites, one surrounding the great altar, the other standing on the steps of the Nicanor Gate, sing the psalms. The Temple worship offered at nine in the morning and three in the afternoon was a striking image of a pontifical High Mass. We will describe it more in detail later when we come to the ceremony of offering the Passover lamb Christ brought to the Temple.

Down the ages from Solomon's day millions of people worshiped the God of their fathers in their Temple Courts, their backs turned to the east, for the pagans worshiped the rising sun, moon and stars facing the east. As a protest against idolatry, the Israelites faced the west towards the altar and the Holy of Holies.[4] They put their sins on the victims with outspread hands, sacrificing them as images of the future Victim they prayed for to come and fulfil these types. A line drawn through the center of the Temple, passing through the center of the altar and the Holy of Holies, towards which they faced, looking for the future Victim, and continued about 1,000 feet, passed through the center of Calvary. Thus every ceremony and victim faced the cross with its agonizing dying Sufferer.

They did not understand the reason God chose this

<hr>

[1] Edersheim, Temple, p. 87.   [2] Numb. xxviii. 18-28 ; Levit. iv. 15, 16-21 , II Par xxix 23, etc   [3] Edersheim Temple, p. 90   [4] Edersheim, Temple, 127.

place for the sanctuary. Rabbi Moses says it was lest Gentiles might there build a pagan shrine, destroy the sanctuary, or lest each Hebrew tribe might have its own place of worship. Therefore they had no Temple till a king was chosen, who could settle disputes about the place of divine worship.

Jewish writers say there was no forgiveness without blood, that the offerer, putting his hands on the victim's head, showed that he put his sins on the animal; that the beast bore the sins of the offerer and the people; that those who touched it, touched sin; this, Maimonides says, was why they were unclean. The sins were not forgiven, but "covered up" till the Messiah came. Let us give some of the words of Hebrew writers.[1]

" Properly speaking the blood of the sinner should have been shed, and his body burned as those of the sacrifices. But the Holy One, blessed be He, accepted our sacrifices, for us as a redemption and an atonement. Behold the full grace which Jehovah, blessed be He, has shown to man. In his compassion and in the fulness of his grace, he accepted the life of the animal instead of man's soul."

" While the altar and the sanctuary were still in their place, we were atoned for by the goats designated by lot. But now for our guilt, if Jehovah be pleased to destroy us, he takes from our hand neither burnt offerings nor sacrifices." " Bring us back in jubilee to Sion, thy city, in joy, as of old, to Jerusalem, the house of thy holiness. Then shall we bring before thy face the sacrifices that are due."

Alas for the children of Israel! The spiritual deep blindness which fell on them the night they sentenced their Messiah to death has not yet lifted. All their sacrifices are now centered in the Mass.

The prophets and Old Testament say, that these sacrifices were in themselves worthless, if separated from Christ the Antitype to whom they pointed, who at a future time was to die to fulfil their shadowy meanings. The Passover lamb, the bread and wine, filled up, combined in one the vast details of the Temple. The burning words of Hebrew prophets all down Old Testament

[1] Edersheim, Temple, 92.

history, find expression in these words of Messianic Passover prayer,

> Haste, my Beloved, come, ere ends the vision's day.
> Make haste Thyself, and chase the shadows all away
> " Despised " is He, but yet " extolled " and " high " shall be.
> " Deal prudently, " sprinkle nations," and " Judge " shall He."

While establishing the ceremonial of sacrifices foretelling the crucifixion, Moses wrote the Five First Books of
the Old Testament. He gathered up the traditions of
the patriarchs, which had been handed down from father
to son, from Noe to Sem and to Abraham, relating to
creation, the fall of man, the flood, the separation of the
seventy-two families, which developed into the tribes,
and which became the great nations of antiquity. We
will give a rapid glance over the Hebrew Scriptures, and
give some of the names in which God revealed the future.
These are lost in translations of the Bible.

God's first name given in the beginning of Genesis as
the Creator is Elohim, who made heaven, earth, and formed
Adam, " man," " the reasoning being."   Elohim is God in
justice, author of nature, unbending as the physical forces,
rigorous in righteousness, punishing Adam for his sin,
destroying the wicked down the pages of the Old Testament. The word was spoken for the last time by the
dying Son of God on the cross atoning the justice of his
Father for the sins of all men, when he quoted the Psalm
using the word Eloi Eloi, etc., " My God, my God, why
hast thou forsaken me ? " [1]

When man because of sin was doomed to hell like the
demons, Elohim–Jehovah appears to Adam, curses the
serpent, and promises that the Seed of the woman would
conquer. Here was first revealed a new name of the
Deity, Jehovah, " The Existing One " But the name has
another meaning : " The God of Mercy." Jehovah the
Divine Son, had mercy, took pity on fallen man, and
promised to redeem the race. While Elohim treated
man with the rigors of his justice, destroying the world
with the flood, burning Sodom and Gomorrah, killing the
wicked, in dealing with the Hebrews, the justice of Eloi,
the eternal Father, is tempered with the mercy of Jehovah,

---

[1] Mark xv 34, Psalm xxi 1.

" God of mercy," the Son, foretold as the Redeemer. " I appeared to Abraham, to Isaac and to Jacob by the name of God Almighty, but by my name Jehovah, I was not known to them." [1]

Down Hebrew history Elohim the Father is justice, Jehovah the Son is mercy. Acting with the Holy Spirit, called the Shekina—these three Persons of the Trinity carry on the preparation for the Incarnation, the Church, the Mass. They are often called in the original Hebrew Adon or Adonai, " Lord " or " Lords."

Filled with religion, animated with devotion, feeling the aurora of coming Christianity, the Hebrews called objects, places, and their children by names bearing the roots of these names of God to show forth his power and attributes. Elohim was shortened to El, Jehovah to Ja, Jo, or Je, while Adonai is often found unchanged. If the reader will examine the Bible words with these roots, he will find almost enough names with them to fill this book. Each is a revelation of God, of his attributes, or a prophecy of the coming Christ.

Let us take the words Jesus Christ as an example. Jesus is the Greek form of the Hebrew Josue, or Joshua, meaning " Jah Saves," " Jehovah Saves," or " The God of Mercy Saves." The name was first borne by Josue, that leader who succeeded Moses, and led the Hebrews into the Promised Palestine. Moses only saw it from afar, led them in sight of it, did not enter, and died on Nebo, for the law of Moses brought the Hebrews only in sight of the Church. Jesus or Josue led them into Palestine, as the one he foretold, Jesus Christ led mankind into the Church. Christ is the Greek for Messiah " The Anointed." Therefore Jesus Christ means, " The Anointed God of Mercy Will Save." How appropriate then the angel's words to the Virgin: " And thou shalt bring forth a Son, and thou shalt call his name Jesus. For he shall save his people from their sins." [2]

But a visible sign of the Almighty Guide was necessary during the existence of the Hebrew religion, to win them from the striking pagan rites of Egypt, to keep them from the paganism of surrounding nations, to foretell the Holy Spirit guiding the future Church. For that reason

[1] Exod. vi. 3.   [2] Luke i. 31, Matt. i. 21.

God appeared to them in visible form, spoke first to
Adam, to patriarchs, to Moses on Sinai, in the tabernacle,
taught their leaders, gave the revelations to their prophets, and appeared to holy men in the days of Christ.
This visible appearance of God the Jewish writers call
the Shekina. Let us see what they say, that the reader
may better understand the meanings of the Temple.

In the original language of the Old Testament and
later Hebrew writings, in hundreds of texts and passages,
we find the word Shekina, from the Hebrew word: " to
appear," " to dwell," meaning the " Majesty of God,"
" The Divine Presence." It was a cloud by day and a fire
by night. Hebrew writers represent it as a visible appearance of the Deity, God the Holy Ghost accommodating
himself to man's eyes, so that he might see the invisible,
Eternal Spirit.[1]

First before the fall, under this form of the Shekina,
God walked with Adam in Paradise, blessed marriage,[2]
gave them the world with its plants and animals for
food, and the law regarding the tree of good and evil, for
society cannot exist without laws.[3] Under this form of
a cloud, or fire, God spoke to Adam after the fall, condemned him and his race for eating the forbidden fruit
and promised the Redeemer.[4]

To the patriarchs, the Shekina appeared, revealed the
future and blessed them and their race. He told Noe how
to build the ark, called Abraham out of Ur of the Chalde-
ans into Palestine, blessed him and his race—in hundreds
of these passages of Scripture where the word God or
Lord in the translation is given, in the Hebrew it is the
Shekina.

For nearly four hundred years it spoke not till it appeared to Moses in the burning bush. " And the Lord
appeared to Moses in a flame of fire out of the midst of
the bush." That "bush" was the Rhamnus, from which
was made Christ's crown of thorns [5]

The Shekina directed Moses how to deliver the Hebrews
from Egypt, went before them as their guide, opened the
Red Sea, and led them for forty years through the Arabian deserts. It was a pillar of cloud by day, and a pillar

---

[1] See Geikie, Life of Christ, ii , 612, etc.; Edersheim, Life of Christ, i 166, 168.
[2] Gen. i. 28.   [3] Gen ii. 17.   [4] Gen iii. 15   [5] Exod iii 2.

of fire at night. When it moved, the hosts of Israel followed; when it rested, they camped; and when the fierce desert sun burned them, it spread over the whole camp, tempering the heat. It covered Sinai as a great cloud which Moses alone penetrated amid thunders and lightnings: it gave the law and commandments, told Moses to form the priesthood, the ceremonial, and build the tabernacle. "And they shall make me a sanctuary, and (I will shekina) I will dwell in the midst of them."[1]

In this visible form of fiery cloud, the Holy Spirit rested in the tabernacle, on the mercy-seat, over the ark of the covenant, between the gold wings of the cherubim. He spoke face to face with Moses, Josue, the Judges, Samuel, Nathan, David, Solomon and all the prophets. Through them He revealed to mankind all the prophecies of the Old Testament. God the Shekina was the King of the Hebrews; their government was a Theocracy: "God-ruled." The synagogue prayers coming down from this time have everywhere the words: "O Lord our King." "We have no King but Thee," etc.

They tired of God's government, asked for a king similar to the rulers of the nations round them. Samuel, filled with sorrow, consulted the Shekina. "And the Lord said to Samuel. . . They have not rejected thee, but me, that I should not reign over them."[2] God warned them of the troubles a king would bring on them. The people persisted, and the Shekina told Samuel to anoint Saul, who, rejected for his sins, David was chosen in his place.

His son Solomon built his famous Temple. The day of its dedication the Shekina filled its sanctuary so the priests could not minister.[3] On the Mount of Offence Solomon built temples for his wives' gods;[4] as a punishment[5] ten tribes rebelled and only the Jews and Benjamites remained faithful to David's family. Wicked kings led the Jews into idolatry, in the very Temple of Jehovah idols were adored,[6] and as a punishment the Babylonians destroyed the city, burned the Temple and carried the people away into captivity.

God told Jeremias to hide the ark of the covenant in a

---

[1] Exod. xxv 8.   [2] I. Kings viii 7.   [3] III Kings viii. 11.   [4] III Kings xi.
[5] III. Kings xii.   [6] Ezech. viii.

cave on Nebo where Moses died.[1] The covenant or con-tract with God was broken, the Shekina spoke no more, prophets ceased to teach; Rabbis, Scribes, Pharisees and Sadducees misled the people. For many centuries the Jews were left without a Divine oracle, and the narrow peculiar teachings and practices of Judaism, of Scribes and Pharisees, rose, which ended in the crucifixion of their Messiah.

But it was revealed that when the Messiah would come, the Shekina would appear and speak to them again. In far-off Persia, three high priests of Zoroaster's religion, coming down from Elam "The Youth", Sem's eldest son, saw the Shekina under the form of a star which led them to the manger of the infant Saviour.[2] The night Christ was born He appeared as a bright cloud to the shepherds on Bethlehem's hills, while angels sang the hymn of "Glory be to God in the highest, and on earth peace to men of good will.[3]

When John the Baptist baptized the Lord at Gilgal, the Shekina, in the form of a dove, overshadowed Christ. At the Transfiguration, in the form of a cloud, He covered Thabor's height. When preaching in the Temple He spoke in testimony of the Saviour. When he died He left the Holy of Holies as a mighty wind, saying, "Let us go hence." He rested on the western walls of the Temple, according to Jewish writers. The day of the Ascension He surrounded the ascending Christ. "And a cloud received him out of their sight." The day of Pentecost the fiery cloud, the Holy Ghost,[4] filled the Cenacle and rained down tongues of fire on the Apostles, giving each the language of the nations he was to convert.

Jewish writers tell us, the Shekina took up its abode on the summit of Olivet, for three and a half years, day and night they heard His voice in pleading words: "Come back to me, O my people, O come back to me!" The Presence never spoke again.[5]

In numerous places the Talmud has the words "Holy Spirit" having the same meaning as in Christian writings. The Old Testament, the Talmuds, Targums, Philo and Rabbinical writers use words which in translations of the

---

[1] II. Mach. ii   [2] Matt. ii. 1   [3] Luke ii 14   [4] S. Augustine Sermo, lxxi, de Verb, Mach xii n, xix.   [5] Shemoth, R 2 Ed. Warsh. 7 b. 12, etc.

Bible are rendered as Lord, God, etc., which show they had
a dim idea or knowledge of the Trinity. As all translations
are weak, our English Bible loses these peculiar terms.

The Hebrew Word Yaqara "The excellent Glory,"
found especially in Exodus, Leviticus, Numbers and
Deuteronomy, means God the Father in the act of re-
vealing, while the term Memra "the Logos," "The
Word," is the Divine Son revealed. Hundreds of times
Memra will be found in Moses' five books. The Targum
Onkelos gives it 179, the Jerusalem Targum 99, and that
of Pseudo Jonathan 321 times. Yaqara is God in his
divine majesty; Memra is God in his wisdom; the
Shekina is God revealing himself to man.

We give an example of the Targum Onkelos. "God,
Yaqara, spoke to Abraham." [1] "God, Yaqara, rested at the
top of Jacob's ladder," [2] and later spoke to the patriarch. [3]
Moses uses the word when he says God called to him
from the bush, [4] promised the manna, [5] when the Hebrews
defeated Amalec, [6] when Jethro visited Moses, [7] and when
the Lord, Yaqara, gave the Ten Commandments. [8] There
are hundreds of terms in the Hebrew Bible which are
dim revelations of the Persons of the Trinity.

The first foundations of the Hebrew religion was laid
by the Eternal Father Yaqara. The forms of nature, the
knowledge of divine things, were given by Memra, the
Word of God, the Wisdom of the Father, the Son of God.
The ceremonial, law, tabernacle, Temple and Hebrew
Church were founded by the Shekina the Holy Spirit.
The Apostles and converts were then, by reading the Old
Testament, ready to receive the belief in the Trinity, first
clearly revealed when Christ said, "Baptizing them in the
name of the Father, and of the Son, and of the Holy
Ghost." [9]

These words were applied to the Persons of the Trinity
in the times of the patriarchs, and continued down
through Moses' writings. When God called Moses from
the fiery bush to develop the patriarchal religion into the
tabernacle and Temple ceremonial and found the Hebrew
nationality, he revealed himself by a new name, " I am

[1] Gen xvii. 22   [2] Gen xxviii 13   [3] Gen xxxv. 13   [4] Exod. iii. 1--6.
[5] Exod xvi 7--10.   [6] Exod. xvii. 16   [7] Exod. xviii. 5.   [8] Exod. xx.
[9] Matt. xxviii. 19.

who am," [1] which was rendered by the Hebrew Jehovah "The Existing One" or Adonai, "Lords," from adon, "Lord," "sir."

While Elohim, from Eloi, "My God," represents the Eternal as creating and governing the universe, Jehovah shows him in his relation to man as the "God of mercy" revealing himself to the world, forming the covenant, giving the Law, forgiving sin, and promised as the Redeemer. Elohim is the God of justice punishing the wicked—the Eternal Father to whom sacrifices are offered by directions of Jehovah the Divine Son, with whom the Shekina acts, enlightening patriarchs and prophets.

After writing the Law and sprinkling the people with blood, "Moses, and Aaron, and Nadab, and Abiu, and the seventy ancients of Israel went up, and they saw the God of Israel." [2] Here the original Hebrew has the word Yaqara, as also in verses 11 and 17.

When God established the daily sacrifice of tabernacle and Temple for perpetual oblation [3] the word is Yaqara, as it is when Moses asked to see His glory. [4] The same word is used when God filled the tabernacle with his glory. [5]

The bullock and ram for peace offerings are sacrificed before Yaqara, [6] the Lord, Yaqara, commanded [7] them when He appeared to the multitude. [8] When the ark was set down, Moses said, "Return, O Lord, to the multitude of the house of Israel." [9] God as Yaqara spoke to Aaron and Mary, promised to appear to the prophets in vision and dream, and he spoke to Moses, who saw the Lord Yaqara. [10] Moses prayed to the Yaqara not to destroy the Hebrews, and the Yaqara was not with them when they wanted, against his wish, to go to the Promised Land. [11]

[1] Exod. xiii 14   [2] Exod. xxiv 10   [3] Exod. xxix 43   [4] Exod. xxxiii 18, 22, 33   [5] xi. 32-36   [6] Levit. ix. 4   [7] Ibidem   [8] Ibidem 23.   [9] Yaqara, Numb. x. 36.   [10] Numb. xii. 8   [11] Numb. xiv. 14-42.

II.—HOW THE HEAVENLY MYSTERIES OF THE MASS WERE UNVEILED IN THE TEMPLE.

Leaving not the supernal glories he had with the Father and the Holy Spirit before the world was, the Eternal Son was made man, suffered death to redeem us, then with our nature united to the Divinity, he went back into the spirit world unseen, where he ever offers sacrifices from our altars.

Day by day, at every Mass, he returns from these eternal, boundless, spaceless, timeless realms, hides his body, soul, and Divinity under forms of bread and wine, is sacrificed in Eucharistic offering, in Communion feeds our souls, and then enters again his eternal sanctuary. Thus every Mass is like a renewal of the Incarnation and an entry into heaven. Communion is an image of God made man in the Person of the Divine Son united to each soul who receives him, and the feasts of the Incarnation and birth of Christ intermingle with feasts of the Eucharist in all Church Liturgies.

Every year the Hebrews held a most holy and mysterious Temple rite, foretelling Christ's death and his entry into heaven at his Ascension and after every Mass. God himself told Moses how to establish the ceremonies of this the Day of Atonement, so celebrated in Jewish writings. But only thirty-four verses are all we have in the Old Testament relating to this great day.[1] The ancient world has vanished, the priesthood ceased centuries ago, and not a stone remains on a stone of the Temple. But fortunately, a work hardly ever seen by Christian eye has most minute details of this the most striking of all the Temple ceremonies of the time of Christ.

One Part of the Babylonian Talmud Tract Yomah: "Day of Atonement," is filled with descriptions of the rites and ceremonies of that day. We will first see the ori-

[1] Levit. xvi.

gin of this remarkable product of the Jewish people, which they revere next after the Old Testament. Then we will lay before our readers details picked out here and there from this work, at the same time giving explanations of the text as we go along. This is the first time, we think, that this work has been given to Christian readers in this form. For the Talmud has been looked on as a vile product of the Jewish mind, written to deceive, and perhaps prejudice has prevented its study. We will first give the origin and history of the Talmud.

The year 3,428 of Adam's creation, 128 of Rome's foundation, 626 before Christ, reigned in Babylon Nabu-chonosor II. " Nebo protects the landmarks." Nebo comes from *nibach*, " to teach," " to prophesy." Because of their idolatry, God allowed this monarch's armies to capture Jerusalem, destroy Solomon's Temple, carry away the Hebrews as slaves and scatter them over the plains of Babylonia.

There they began to better study their religion. With the Torah " The written Law," in Moses' five books, they claimed, came down also the Talmud " The Teachings "; that these traditions were as old as Holy Writ; that they were equally revealed to Moses with the law, and that they are the explanations and the supplement of the written word and Temple ceremonial.

The New Testament mentions these traditions thirteen times.[1] The Scribes and Pharisees had carried them to excess, which Christ reproved. In their foundations these Talmud traditions are correct. Many traditions come down to us from apostolic days, always existed, came from no Pope or counsel, and found everywhere. Such universal customs or teachings give us an idea of the Talmudic Jewish traditions, when stripped of fanciful, or distorted exaggerations.[2]

In the year A. D 70, the Jews rebelled against the Romans. Vespasian marched down from the north to invade Judea. Elected emperor by the army, his son Titus became commander, took Jerusalem, destroyed the Temple, carried the captive Jews to Rome, where they worked building the Colosseum. A few years later the

---

[1] Matt xv 2, 8, 6 ; Mark vn 3, 5, 8, 9, 13 , Acts vi 14 ; Gal. i 14 , Col ii. 8, II Thes. u. 14 , I. Pet. 18.   [2] See Geikie, Life of Christ, u. 193, etc.

Jews again rebelled, and Hadrian captured the sacred city, left it a heap of stones and forbade a Jew to enter the sacred city under pain of death, except once a year to celebrate the Passover.

On the site of an old cemetery, Herod Agrippa had founded Tiberias, nestling on the shores of the Lake of Galilee. The leading Jews made this their religious capital, where they founded a flourishing college, to which wealthy Jews from all the nations sent their sons to be educated, especially if they were destined to become rabbis or preachers of the synagogue.

None but a Jew would be received; the Gentiles were, they held, doomed to hell because they did not know the Torah or written law, and the Talmud or traditional Law, which were only for the Jew. St. Jerome tells us he could not find a Jew in Jerusalem or Bethlehem who dared teach him Hebrew, and he went down to Tiberias, where he says "his teacher feared for his life like another Nicodemus."

In the second century after Christ, the famous Jehudah Hansi, heir of a wealthy family, and honored as a patriarch, was president of this college. He began to write the traditions in the year 150 after Christ [1] which they claimed could be traced back as far as Josaphat, [2] David's recorder, and which they contend God had given to Moses with the written word.

These writings of Jehudah form the Mishna "Study," the first part of the Talmud. His successors at the Tiberias school wrote the part called the Gemara "Explanation" or "Commentary," on these traditions given in each Mishna. Later learned Jewish sages added further explanations, and opinions of different schools of thought which flourished before the destruction of the Temple under Titus, were added. In later ages still other opinions were incorporated till the work becoming unwieldy, a decree of the Sanhedrin forbade any other additions. This is what is now called the Jerusalem Talmud.

In the year B. C. 490, the great Persian king issued the decree that the Jews could return and rebuild their

---

[1] Zanolini, De Fide Jud. Cap. 1.
[2] II. Kings, viii. 16, 20-24; III. Kings iv. 3; I. Par. i. 18-15.

4

city and Temple.   But many Hebrews engaged in trade remained in Babylonia, and at the time of Christ numerous Hebrew colonies there flourished.   These also had their traditions coming down, as they held, from Moses. They also began to write them down in the same form as the learned rabbis of Tiberias.   Their labors come down to us under the name of the Babylonian Talmud.

The Talmuds, most peculiar products of an age when Christ walked the earth, throw a bright light on the Old Testament, Hebrew customs, Temple ceremonial, public and private prayers, and show the Jew of that epoch in his religious belief and practice.

Living in Palestine before the Babylonian Captivity, the Hebrew kept himself separated from all nations, for he was of the chosen race, of whom the Messiah was to be born.   Of brightest mind, glorying in being a son of Abraham, he kept secret from pagans his religion, and it was almost impossible to penetrate the secrecy of his belief and practice.   Religious right thinking and living, faith and morals, were only for the Jew.   All Gentiles were condemned to hell, because of their ignorance of the Law or Torah and of the Talmud, and they would not teach the Gentiles, for the Law was for the Jews—this was the prevailing idea of the Scribe and Pharisee in the days of Christ.

Mutual suspicions caused the persecutions of the middle ages, the Jew was prescribed in every Christian country, the Hebrew mind became exceedingly acute because of adversity and poverty.   But amid all their miseries they held with a death-grasp to their religion— perhaps there is a Providence in this, for they show that the Old Testament is true.

In the middle ages all Jewish books were condemned to be destroyed, the Talmud was ordered burned; but they saved a few copies.   A Jew learned in Talmudic lore was converted to the Catholic Church, and explaining to the Pope the contents of this work, the Pontiff forbade any further destruction of this product of antiquity.

This decree saved the Talmud from utter destruction.

The Talmud is divided into six sections : " Seeds," " Festivals," " Women," " Jurisprudence," " Holiness," and " Purity," making sixty "Tracts," each treating of different matters—both Talmuds forming sixty volumes in quarto.[1]

These Talmuds show you the Jewish mind before and during the time of Christ. There is little in them to be condemned, as many hold who never saw them, except that the Jerusalem Talmud, contains some scandalous attacks on Christ's character. But the Babylonian Talmud hardly alludes to Him.

You pass page after page of weary waste of discussion, disputes of learned sages, and their opinions of what the Torah "the Law," means reminding you of disputed points of moral theology. The oldest part, called the Mishna, the purest and best, is rich in information, for it comes down perhaps from beyond the Babylonian Captivity, when Israel was led by the prophets guided by the Holy Spirit.

The Gemara, coming after the Captivity, shows minds absolutely without faith, devoid of a spark of the supernatural. All is founded on the Torah, "the Law," as they call the Books of Moses,—the first five books of the Bible. The prophets are seldom quoted; the beautiful Temple service is explained, but they never look beyond and behind it to see the Christ it foretold.

They looked for two Christs—one to be born of David's family who was to establish a kingdom of matchless splendors, trample on his enemies, and wade through rivers of blood to his throne in Jerusalem, where he would make the Jews rulers over all the earth. Borrowing these ideas from the Jew, Mohammed and his successors spread their empire by the sword The other Christ or Messiah, to be born of Joseph's tribe, was to be a suffering Christ to come and die; why, they do not explain.

Bible and Talmud, both written by Hebrews, differ in a striking degree—one is the product of inspired men, through whom God spoke to the world, the other was written by men of an outcast nation, spiritually dead, absolutely divested of every spark of supernatural faith. One pulsates with life; in every page you see, in the original, the foretold Redeemer, the face of the Holy Ghost; the other, the Talmuds, show the heart of a race

[1] See Edersheim, Life of Christ, i. 47, 103, 104, 175.

punished for idolatry by the Babylonian Captivity, and for the crime of killing their Messiah driven by the Romans into all the earth fulfilling these words. " We will not have this man rule over us." " His blood be on us and on our children."

We do not always realize what an Oriental tradition is. To us a tradition is a story, more or less true, changing from one generation to another, vague, or exaggerated, founded on truth, but developed by time.

But a tradition among the Jews was a religious truth coming down from their forefathers, told and repeated in the synagogues, in the Temple, at feasts, by family firesides, given exactly word for word as they had heard it. If it were not given as handed down, in almost the very same words, if a word were added to it, or left out, the whole company cried out, the relator was execrated and driven away. This was the way the patriarchs taught their children the story of the creation, the fall of man, the religious belief of ancient days. In this way they claim religion and history were handed down till Moses wrote them in Genesis.

Adam died in the year 930 when Mathusala was ninety-four years old. The latter lived till Sem, called also Melchisedech, was in his fiftieth years. Sem, or Melchisedech, died on Sion when Isaac was thirty-three years of age, and the latter lived till he was 180,—2288 years after the creation of Adam, and but a short time before the birth of Amram, Moses' father. Thus history came down from Adam and the patriarchs to Moses the great Lawgiver, Founder of the Hebrew nationality and writer of the first five books of the Bible.[1]

In the same way, they claim, the teachings they called the " traditions " of the Jews, passed down till written in the Talmud. In the schools of Babylonia and Judea, the scholars received only what was taught, no deviation was allowed, not a word was changed. From his high seat, like a pulpit, the learned Rabbi gave the sayings of their fathers, the traditions of the elders held as sacred as the written word, sometimes more so, and the pupils learned them by heart and treasured them as the breath of their nostrils.

[1] De Religione Hebræorum n 68.

Living in Babylonia since the days of the Captivity, the Hebrews were not there disturbed by the Christ's life, his teachings, the tragedy of his death and the preaching of the apostles, The Talmud contains little relating to Christianity. We find in it Hebrew rules and customs of the Passover, as it was celebrated in the days of the Jewish kings.

We will describe the Temple worship on the Day of the Atonement, because we wish to lay before the reader the minute details of how God was worshiped in the days of Christ, because the Temple ceremonial was introduced into the synagogue and was followed by Christ on the night of the Last Supper, and because atonement of sin is the very foundation of every Old Testament offering fulfilled in the Last Supper and is now continued in the Mass.

The Temple high priest in the ceremonial, and the celebrant to-day offering the Mass, image Him, the High Priest of eternity who came into the world, offered his life and sufferings as a sacrifice, then passed back again into his heavenly sanctuary. Therefore ascending the altar steps, beginning Mass the celebrant recites these deep words of the Church's Liturgy :

" Take away from us, we pray thee, O Lord, our sins, that with pure minds we may be made worthy to enter into the Holy of Holies. Through Christ our Lord. Amen." [1]

To link every offering with Christ and the Holy Spirit burning in him, following God's orders, every sacrifice was consumed or roasted on the altar with a fire which had come down from heaven [2] But Nadab and Abiu, Aaron's sons, sacrificed with a strange fire, which did not typify the Holy Ghost or relate to the foretold Redeemer. For that awful sin God struck both dead. [3] Then the Eternal ordained the ceremonial the Hebrews were to follow each year on the Day of the Atonement. [4]

The Bible does not go into the details of that sacred, holiest and most striking of all the Temple ceremonies. But before us is the Tract Yomah " Day of Atonement," of the Babylonian Talmud. We will go over the whole volume, search in the rubbish for the pure untarnished

---

[1] Roman Missal   [2] Levit. ix. 24   [3] Levit. x 2   [4] Levit, xvi 16.

gold of the days before Christ, and lay before the reader these interesting details. As we go along we will give explanations of the Hebrew texts that the reader may better understand how Christ and the Mass were fore-told.[1]

The high priest, representing Christ for the Hebrew nation, alone performed all the ceremonies of this solemn day which always fell on the tenth day of Tishri. In fear and trembling, he bore the sins of Israel behind the veil in the gold-walled room, the Holy of Holies, image of heaven, where the Shekina, the Holy Spirit, dwelled as a cloud by day and a fire by night, in the tabernacle and first Temple. Before the ceremonial of this day, priest and people, even the very sanctuary, were unclean, and without this ceremonial the services of the following year could not be carried on. The Law laid down numerous details,[2] but we will give the more minute descriptions of the Talmud.[3]

"Seven days before the Day of Atonement, the high priest moves from his house, lest his wife might defile him, and takes up his abode in the Palhedrin Chamber, called in Greek Paraderon, (the Lord's Chamber), near the Nicanor Gate. Another priest, generally the Sagon, his substitute, is chosen and instructed to take his place if he becomes unclean.[4] Out of his own pocket he must buy all the animals for the sacrifice."[5]

Thus he foretold the sinless Christ atoning for the iniquities of the world, and foreshadowed the unmarried clergy entering our sanctuary to offer Mass.

"Why was he separated six days before the feast? When God gave the Law on Sinai, he called Moses up the mountain. 'And the glory of the Lord dwelled on Sinai, covering it with a cloud six days, and on the seventh day he called him out of the midst of the cloud.'[6] During all these six days of preparation, they sprinkled the high priest with the ashes of all the red cows offered."

---

[1] The words of the Old Testament in the Talmud are not the very same as those found in the translations Christians use, but the sense is the same. No two persons will give the same terms when translating from another language. [2] Levit. xvi [3] See Geikie, Life of Christ, i. 95. [4] Levit. viii 34
[5] Babylonian Talmud, Tract Yomah "Day of Atonement," Chap 1; Mishna and Gamaras. [6] Exod. xxiv. 16.

These animals, were sacrificed outside the walls of the city, led over the bridge spanning the Cedron, built by the high priest out of his own pocket. Across that same bridge they dragged Christ the night of his arrest. The red cows foretold Christ, red with his blood, offered in sacrifice for mankind. The high priest was sprinkled with water mixed with their ashes, to typify that the pontiff was typically in spirit sprinkled with the Redeemer's blood to clean him from sin to offer the sacrifice and enter the sacred sanctuary. Sprinkling the high priest foretold our holy water.

"Aaron was separated seven days, during which time Moses instructed him regarding the services of this day. During these days two men of the Beth Din 'The Court of Law' taught him (the high priest) the ceremony as it was written, as at this present it hath been done, that the rite of sacrifice might be accomplished.' [1] Moses ascended into the cloud and was sanctified in the clould, in order that he might receive the Torah 'The Law,' for Israel in a state of holiness." [2]

"This happened the day after the Ten Commandments were given, which was the first of Moses', fast of the next forty days.' The high priest the Day of Atonement has not the gold plate with the engraved words; 'Holiness unto Jehovah' on his brow " for he represented our High Priest Christ "who his ownself bore our sins in his body on the tree." [3]

"The chamber where he took up his abode was first called the 'Chamber of the Lords,' but after the high priests bought their office with money, after the Roman occupation of Palestine, it was called the Hall of the Palhedrin, ' Officers.'"

All houses, chambers, etc., had hangings on the door-posts boxes of leather, in which on parchments were written the morning and evening prayers. "Hear, O Israel, the Lord our God is one Lord. Thou shalt love the Lord thy God, with thy whole heart, and with thy whole soul and with thy whole strength," etc. "And thou shall write them in the entry, and on the doors of thy house." [4] Did they give rise to the holy water founts

[1] Levit viii. 34   [2] Talmud, Tract Yomah, " Day of Atonement " p. 4
[3] I Peter ii 24.   [4] Deut. vi. 4-9.

of our churches and houses, that by taking the water, and blessing ourselves we may remember our baptism and redemption through Christ?

"No chamber of the Temple had these Muzuzahs except the Palhedrin Chamber, because for seven days it was the high priest's abode, and the Nicanor Gate through which the people entered the Temple.

"First he clothed himself in the eight vestments God prescribed for Aaron and his sons, went with the gold basin turned over the sacrifices burning on the altar to make it burn better. Every day he sprinkled the blood of the victims, offered the incense in the Holies, trimmed the lamps of the seven-branched candelabrum, and takes for his own use a part of the first offerings, which he eats. Incense he offers first, then he trims the lamps, and sacrifices the lamb morning and afternoon. (Incense typified the prayers of Christ offered to his Father before he was sacrificed.)

"They drew lots to choose the priests to wait on him. The first lot was to select the priests to clean the ashes from the great altar, called the Ariel, 'Lion of God,' the second, for those who would kill the victim, sprinkle the blood, clear the ashes on the altar of incense in the Holies, trim the lamps and carry up the members of the sacrifices. The third lot was to choose the one among the nine priests to offer the incense in the Holies."

The incense was offered first, and that is the reason the candles are first lighted and the celebrant of the Mass first incenses the altar at the beginning of Mass. "And Aaron shall burn sweet-smelling incense upon it in the morning When he shall dress the lamps, he shall burn it." [1]

Then follow directions to mark the horns of the great altar with the blood of the victims in the form of a cross which we will describe later.

"Four chambers were in the heating-house, like small rooms opening into a great hall, two belonged to the sanctuary (the Priests' Court in the middle of which stood the great altar of sacrifice), and two were profane, and small wickets parted the sacred ones from the profane. The southwestern was for the lambs for the sacrifice.

[1] Exod xxx. 7, 8, etc.

The southeastern was for the showbreads (the proposi-tion bread in our Bible).   In the northeastern the Mach-abees, the Asmoneans, had hidden the stones of the altar profaned by the Greeks.   The northwestern was used as a passage to the bath-house.   The chamber at the northeast was the place where the wood was kept, and blemished priests examined the wood there, as moldy wood was unfit for the altar.   The northwestern chamber was the place for the cured lepers, who came to the Temple to be sprinkled.   Wine and oil for the offerings were kept there, and it was called the chamber of oil.

"The altar stood in the middle of the court, and was in size thirty-two ells, ten ells opposite to the door of the Temple, twenty ells wide, eleven ells toward the north, and eleven ells to the south, so that the altar was oppo-site to the Temple, and its walls."

This altar stood on the summit of Mount Moriah, where Abraham offered his son Isaac, who carried the wood of the sacrifice up the mount, foretelling Christ carrying his cross.   At the present time the Mosque of Omar, called the "Dome of the Rock," covers the rock summit of Moriah, which rises about fifteen feet over the floor of the eight-sided building, it being within covered with beautiful faince or delf ware, mostly colored white and blue, and ornamented with passages from the Coran. The rock is now inclosed with an iron railing.   In the southeastern part of the rock is a round hole about two feet in diameter, through which the blood of the victims flowed down and was carried by underground pipes below the city to the Cedron "Black Valley," thus called because of the blood.   The great rock, irregular like the top of a mountain, never leveled off, shows the groves where the blood flowed, and is colored by age.   To Mo-hammedan eyes this holy place is second to Mecca, be-cause of Abraham from whom the Arabians descended through Ishmael.   Under the rock is a kind of cave, and there they showed shrines, where they told the writer Abraham, Christ and Mohammed prayed.

"During these six days the elders of the Beth Din, judges and learned lawyers of the supreme court, instruct the high priest, read to him out of Leviticus xvi., and

say to him, 'My lord the high priest, say it aloud lest
thou hast forgotten or not studied this.'   On the morning,
preceding the Day of Atonement, he comes to the eastern
gate and the bulls, rams and sheep are placed before him,
that he might get a knowledge of the service.   All the
seven days he is free to eat and drink, but the eve of the
Day of Atonement he is not permitted to eat much.

"The elders of the Beth Din left him to the elders of
the priesthood, who took him up into the house of
Abtinas, and made him swear: 'My lord the high
priest, we are the delegates of the Beth Din, and
thou art our delegate, and the delegate of the Beth Din,
we conjure thee by Him who hast made his abode in this
house, that thou shalt not alter one thing about which
we have spoken to thee.' "

"They made him take an oath that he was not a Sadducee, for the Sadducees believed not in the future life.
He took farewell, weeping, and they wept, he because he
might be suspected of being an infidel, they lest they
might suspect an innocent man.   He read day by day the
Scriptures, especially the Books of Job, Esdras, Chroni-
cles and Daniel.

"He lived in two chambers, one on the north, the other
on the south, the Palhedrin to sleep in, and the Abtinas
as a study.   He used to take a handful of incense so as
not to spill any, and practised with the censer, the sacrificial knives, took five legal baths, and ten times washed
his hands and feet in the brazen laver." [1]

These baths were shadows of baptism.   The night before the great day, he slept not, for the night of his passion Jesus did not sleep   "The chief priests sang to him
Psalm cxxxvi., and talked among themselves and with him
all night.   About the midnight hour, they cleaned the
great altar of ashes, beginning at the crowing of the
cock, in Hebrew the *geber*, while the courts and the
Temple were filled with Israelites, for no one slept in the
Holy City that night.

"Bezeleel 'God in protection' made three arks, the
middle one was of wood nine spans high, the one inside
was of gold eight spans high, that outside was of gold
ten spans high, and a span and a trifle over to hide it.

[1] Exod xxx, 18,

The gold on the top was a span thick, that it might seem like a small crown on the top of the ark under the mercy seat.

"There were three crowns, one of the altar, one of the ark, and one of the table of proposition for the bread and wine. Of the altar called the 'Crown of the Priesthood' Aaron received; that of the table called the 'Crown of Royalty' David received; that of the ark called the 'Crown of Learning is yet to be bestowed on the Messiah." (That foretold the Crown of Thorns on Jesus).

Then follows a long description of the way God spoke to them through the Urim and Thummin with their twelve precious stones, each having the name of one of the twelve tribes of Israel, which became bright so they read God's oracles and thus wrote his reply.

"In the Urim and Thummim were only the names of the tribes, the names of Abraham, Itz'hak, and Jacob, likewise the words Shibtei Jeshurun 'The Tribes of Israel,' we have learned that a priest on whom the Shekina does not rest, and is not inspired by the Holy Spirit, need not be inquired through. The Holy Spirit enabled him to perceive the letters.

"Five things were missing in the second Temple. What are they? The ark, the mercy-seat, the cherubim, the heavenly fire, the Shekina, 'the Holy Spirit,' and the Urim and Thummim."

"Formerly, whoever desired to clear the altar of ashes did so. When there were many priests, they ran on the staircase leading to the top of the altar. Whoever came within four ells, merited it. One of two who were running up the staircase, pushed his companion so he fell and broke his leg. Another time one stabbed a priest to death. The Beth Din made a reform, that the altar should be cleared by lot—there were four lots. If a layman should sprinkle the blood, offer incense, water and wine, he would be put to death.[1]

"The second lot was to choose thirteen priests to slaughter the victim,[2] sprinkle its blood, clean the gold altar in the Holies of ashes, trim the lamps, take up the members of the victim to the great altar, the head, right hind leg, two fore legs, tail, left hind leg, windpipe, two

[1] See Yomah, chap. xi 33.   [2] Yomah, chap xi. 35.

flanks, entrails, fine flour, things in pans ; and the third lot
was to select priests who had never offered in the Holies,
and the fourth lot was to choose priests to take up the
members of the animal from the staircase to the altar.
The daily sacrifices were offered by nine, ten, eleven and
twelve priests, according to the feast. The ram was
offered by eleven priests, the flesh by five, the entrails,
fine flour and wine by two "

The services began when the sunlight illumined the
tomb of Abraham. When Sarah died, in her 127th year,
Abraham bought of Ephron, the Hethite, the double cave
of Hebron, with argument and talk, just as to-day the
Arabs will haggle with you in making a contract. It is
a specimen of Oriental agreement, showing how little the
people of that country have changed for thousands of
years.[1]

A good carriage road leads south from Jerusalem to
Hebron, twenty miles away, winding through Bethlehem,
and south by Solomon's Pools. On the side of the hill,
surrounded with ancient reservoirs, and other marks of
extreme antiquity, in the midst of the city of Hebron
rise the walls of a mosque once a Christian church.
Moslem fanatics fill the streets scowling at you. Your
life is hardly safe from those who guard with jealous
care the burial-place of the patriarchs and their wives.
The Prince of Wales, later Edward VII., with his suite,
having the Sultan's firman, was allowed to enter the upper
parts of the building, where six silk-covered cenotaphs
cover the places, where down beneath, in the " double-
cave," rest the remains of the fathers of Hebrew and
Arabian races.

On the walls of the upper church, a bronze Greek
tablet tells you that below is the tomb of " Abraham the
Friend of God." Some years ago the building was re-
paired under the direction of an Italian architect,
Farenti, who one day followed the keeper down the
stone steps, although kicked and rebuffed, he persisted,
and tells us, he saw on the floor of the cave the six white
marble sarcophagi of the patriarchs, Abraham, Isaac,
Jacob, and their wives.

" The lots to choose the ministers of the Temple took

[1] Gen. xxiii.

place either the evening before or at dawn. Before the break of day the Superintendent said: [1]

"Go out and see whether the time for sacrificing has come."

"They ascended the Temple tower at the southeast corner of the area, and the one who saw the light first said:

"Barquai, It becomes light. The East is bright."

"As far as Hebron? Is the whole East bright as far as Hebron?"

"Yes, Baraq Barquai, the light has risen."

"Then each went to his work. Why this ceremony? Because the patriarchs Abraham, Isaac, Jacob, Joseph and their wives were buried at Hebron. Abraham began the Mincha prayers of the morning, when the walls began to throw dark shadows, according to the words, "Abraham rose up early in the morning.'[2]

When the disc of the sun rose over the far-distant Nebo whence Moses saw the Promised Land, where he died and was buried, its shadows in the forenoon stretching across the mirrored waters of the Dead Sea, a band of priests, stationed in the tower on Olivet, blew blasts on their silver trumpets. The priests stationed on the Temple tower took up the strain and blew three blasts, the first reminding them of the prophecies of the coming of the Messiah and his kingdom, the second God's providence over the world, and the last the General Judgment. All the people in the sleeping city rose, each Jew put on his Phylacteries, stood beside his bed and recited his "Shema" and morning prayers. But this great Day of Atonement, all Jewry gathered in the Temple or went to the synagogue if they lived in distant lands.

The pontiff rose from his couch at the trumpet tone, clothed himself and went to take a bath showing forth the baptismal innocence required of the celebrant entering the sacred sanctuary of our church to sacrifice the Lamb of God.

"Undressing he went down and dived into the water of the great bath over the Beth Haparva, a screen of linen byssus being placed between him and the people. Five

[1] Yomah, chap. iii 40-41   [2] Gen. xxii. 3.

times the high priest bathed, and ten times he washed his hands and feet. Each time he dived into the water he said :

"Let it be thy will, O God, my Lord, that thou causest me to come in and to go out in peace, that thou causest me to return to my place in peace, and save me from this and from like danger, in this world and in the world to come."

The danger he feared was lest he might die within the Holy of Holies, as God struck with death the two wicked sons of Aaron.[1]

"The high priest ministers in eight vestments, a common priest in four—in linen breeches, cassock, girdle and miter; to the high priest are added the breastplate, the ephod, a coat, and the tists, the gold fillet on the forehead with the words "Holy to Jehovah."[2] The Urim and Thummim "Learning and Virtue" were inquired of only when he was thus vested, but inquiries were not made for a common man, only for the nation, the king, the chief of the Beth Din. (the chief justice of the Supreme Court), and for a public official.

"The vestments should be made, according to the Bible, of linen six times twisted. Where twisted linen is prescribed, it should be eightfold twisted. The material of the high priest's cassock was twelve times twisted, that of the veil twenty-four times twisted, and that of the breastplate and ephod twenty-eight.[3] They made on the lower hem of the robe pomegranates of blue, and purple and red yarn, twisted. "And thou shalt make the rational of judgment, with embroidered work of diverse colors, according to the workmanship of the ephod, of gold, violet and purple and scarlet twice dyed, and fine twisted linen."[4] Four times each sixfold is twenty-four, and the gold thread four times makes twenty-eight.

"Cleanliness is next to godliness" was the rule in the Temple. The frequent bathing of the whole body, the washing of the hands and feet required before ceremonies of the Temple and the bath taken before the Passover, foretold Christian baptism. For without this sacrament, the Eucharist cannot be received. When John the Baptist came to the banks of the Jordan at Galgal, where the

---

[1] Levit. x 2.   [2] Exod. xxviii. 36.   [3] Exod. xxxix. 28.   [4] Exod. xxviii. 15.

Hebrews crossed to take possession of the Promised Land, preaching penance and baptizing he followed the Temple teachings. Following the customs of Jewish bathing, the Mohammedan washes himself at the mosque before entering the house to him so holy.

In the morning, while the vast crowds are filling the Temple courts, and 1,000 priests and Levites are preparing for the service, the high priest again takes a bath saying the prayer we have given. While the high priest sacrifices the ordinary morning lamb the priests and Levites sing the Temple Liturgy, the Psalms, the Canticles and the prayers. Surrounded by twelve priests, at his right hand the Segan, ready to take his place if he became unclean, at his right and left the heads of the " course " of priests serving that week, like the assistant priest, deacon and subdeacon of the Mass, with twelve other priests around him he carried out the service.

" In the morning, he clothed himself in vestments of Pelusian linen costing $189, in the evening, Hindoo linen worth not less than $100; sometimes they were more valuable, and they were paid for from the Temple treasury. But he could use still more costly vestments bought from his own funds.[1]

" After the service of the congregation was finished, if the high priest had a linen vestment made by his mother at her own expense, he might put it on and perform the service for a private person, but not for the congregation, carry out the spoons for the frankincense, and incense from the Holies of Holies, but after taking it off he must give it to the congregation.

" His mother made for R. Ishmael ben Phabi,[2] who was the high priest, a linen vestment worth $9,000. He used to put it on, perform the services for private persons, and mentally give it to the congregation, but brought it home. R. Eliezer ben Harsum's mother made him a linen vestment worth 20,000 minas. (It seems hard to believe this, for as the former vestment cost $9,000 that is 100 minas, what did this cost? But we are giving the statements just as we find them in the Talmud, Tract

[1] Yomah, chap. iii 47   [2] He was very wealthy, dressed in the height of fashion, decked with gold lace and jewels. He seized the property of widow and orphan. He was one of the judges of the Sanhedrin, was bitterly opposed to Christ and with the others condemned him to death.

Yomah.)   His brethren the priests did not let him put it on, as in it he seemed to be naked, so delicate was its texture"

If priests of Jehovah's Temple vested in such magnificent and costly vestments, when sacrificing animals to foretell the Victim of the cross, how beautiful and spotless should be our vestments, when we offer in the Mass the real Lamb of God.

"The high priest Ben Katin made twelve cocks to the laver, which had only two. He also made a machine for the laver to take it down into the well at will, that its water might not become unfit by being kept overnight. The King Monobaz made all the handles of the utensils used on the Day of Atonement of gold. Helen, his mother, made the gold candlelabrum over the temple-gate. She likewise made a tablet of gold whereon was inscribed the section about a woman who goes aside."[1]

This Queen Helen, a convert to Judaism, carefully followed its tenets, took the vow of a Nazarene three times and practised it for twenty-one years. Her family tombs, called the "Tombs of the Kings" are now shown at the north of Jerusalem. They are very extensive, being rooms excavated out of the solid rock to the north of what was once a deep quarry. The steps leading down were cut so the rain water is conveyed into cisterns under the rock to the south. The door to the tombs was closed by a round flat stone like the stone which closed the door of Christ's tomb.

"The high priest bathed. Coming out, he wiped himself with a sponge, his vestments of cloth of gold were brought him, which he put on, and then again he washed his hands and feet. They brought him the daily sacrifice, the lamb offered morning and evening at nine o'clock and three P M. He cut the lamb's throat, another priest finished the sacrifice in his presence.

"He took up the blood, sprinkled it on the horns of the great altar. He went into the Holies and there offered the incense, trimmed the seven lamps of the gold candelabrum, and coming out he offered the head and members of the lamb, the things in pans and the bread and wine.

[1] Numb. v. 12.

" This day there were five services. The daily morning sacrifice in vestments of cloth of gold, the service of the day in linen vestments, his ram and the people's ram in vestments of cloth of gold, the spoon, and censer in linen vestments, and the daily offerings in cloth of gold. Between each service, he had to change his vestments, and dive deep into the bath, washing his hands and feet before and after the bath, according to the words of the Lord to Moses regarding his brother Aaron.[1]

" He made an incision in the throat of the next victim. How much? Says Ulla: The greater part of the windpipe and the gullet. Abyi ordered the services according to a tradition he had, and it agrees with that of Abbu Saul. The first great arrangement of wood precedes the second arrangement of wood on the southwestern corner of the altar, as will be explained in the Tamid. This preceded the two measures of wood, and they preceded the removal of the ashes from the inner altar, and this preceded the trimming of the five lamps. This preceded the sprinkling of the blood of the morning daily offering, and this preceded the trimming of the two lamps, and this preceded the offering of incense, which came before the offering of the members, this was before the flour-offering, and this was before the things baked in pans. This preceded the drink offering (the bread and wine), and this preceded the additional offerings for Sabbath or festival, and these were before the spoonfuls of frankincense. From the word Hashlamin, ' Peace-offerings,' it can be inferred that they complete the service of the day."

Now they lead the bullock into the priests' court, facing his body north and south, as he stands at the north of the great altar, they turn the animal's face to the west. For so faced Christ on the cross away from the city which killed him towards the western nations which would later receive his Gospel. The high priest stood towards the east, his face to the west. He placed his two hands, palms down, thumbs forming a cross, on the head of the victim, between the horns. " On this sin-offering he confessed the sins for which the sin-offering was brought, on the trespass-offering the sins corresponding to it, and on a burnt-offering sins of preventing the poor

---

[1] Levit. xvi. 23, 24, etc   See, Tract Yomah, p. 45, for details, etc.

5

to gather, for forgetting the poor and not leaving corners." [1]

"He put his two hands on him and confessed his sins in the following words:

"I beseech Thee, O Jehovah, I have committed iniquities, I have transgressed and have sinned before Thee, I and my house I beseech Thee, O Jehovah, forgive, I pray, the iniquities, the transgressions, and the sins I have committed, transgressed before Thee, I and my house, as it is written in the Law of Moses thy servant, "Upon this day shall be the expiation for you and the cleansing from all your sins, that you shall be cleansed from all your sins." [2]

With a mighty sound the whole congregation reply, "Blessed be the name of His kingdom's glory for ever."

The lust of money was on them. Families had monopolies of Temple duties, which brought them large revenues, and they would not tell the secrets of their crafts.

"And the memories of the following were mentioned with blame: those of the house of Garmo, they were unwilling to teach the art of making the showbreads (the proposition bread foretelling the altar bread); those of the house of Abtinas, who did not want to teach the art of preparing the incense; Hogros ben Levi who knew something in music, in which he was unwilling to instruct others. Ben Kamstar did not want to teach the art of writing.

"The house of Garmo was skilled in making the showbreads. The sages sent for workers from Alexandria, and they could bake it well, but could not take it from the oven for it got broken. They heated the oven from the outside, while the house of Garmo heated it from the inside. The showbreads of the Alexandrian bakers used to become mouldy, and that of the former never became so. So the Beth Garmo had to be invited to resume their post. The sages inquired of them : 'Why are you unwilling to instruct others?' 'Our family knows by tradition that this Temple will one day fall, and then if we should have taught it to an improper person, he may go and serve idols.'"

"The house of Abtinas was skilled in preparing in-

---

[1] Levit. xix. 9, 10.   [2] Levit. xvi 30, Yomah, vi. 9.

cense, and were unwilling to teach it. The sages sent for workers from Alexandria, who could prepare the incense, but could not make it so the smoke would ascend. R. Ishmael said, 'I was once on the road, and I met one of their grandchildren, and said, 'Your ancestors wished to increase their own glory, and diminish that of the Lord.' R. Ishmael b. Luga said: 'I and one of their grand-children went out into the fields to gather grass, and he wept, saying: "I see the herbs we used to put in the incense to make it smoke." "Point it out to me." "We are under an oath not to show it to any one." R. Johanan b. Nuri met an old man of the family of Abtinas with a scroll, on which was a list of the names of the spices for incense. I said: 'Show it to me.' 'As long as our family lived, they did not show it any man. But now when they have all died, and the Temple no longer exists, I can give it to thee, but be careful with it.'[1]

" Now the high priest comes to the front of the altar, and a priest holds out to him the gold box, wherein are the 'lots,' on one is written: 'For Jehovah,' on the other 'For Azazael.'[2] The Segan is on his right, the head of the family of priests serving that week on his left. If that of Jehovah was taken out by his right hand, the Segan says to him: ' My Lord the high priest, raise thy right hand.' If that of Jehovah was taken out by his left hand, the head of the family says: 'My lord the high priest, raise thy left hand.' He placed the lots on the two goats saying: 'To Jehovah, a sin offering.' 'For Azazael the scapegoat.' The whole assembly responded with a mighty voice: 'Blessed be the name of His Kingdom's glory forever.'

" The Segan always walked or remained at the pontiff's right hand, that if he became unfit for the service he might take his place. He tore the scarlet cloth in two, tied one half to the rack and the tongue of crimson wool to the head of the goat that was to be sent away, the scape-goat, and placed him opposite the gate, through which he was to be led, and the one to be sacrificed opposite the place of its slaughtering."

Formerly the crimson wool became white as a sign

---

[1] Yomah, chapter iii. 53-55. [2] Azazael means " Almighty Eloi," the Eternal Father; for Christ, foretold by the scape-goat, offered himself on the cross to his Father, with the sins of mankind on him.

that God had forgiven their sins; the western lamp always burned, and remarkable miracles happened showing their sacrifices were received.

"The Rabbis taught: Forty years before the Temple was destroyed, the lot never came into the right hand, the wool did not become white, the western light did not burn, the gates of the Temple opened of themselves, till the time that R. Johanan ben Zakki rebuked them, saying: Temple, Temple, why alarmest thou us? We know that thou art destined to be destroyed. For of thee hath prophesied Zacharias ben Iddo, 'Open thy gates, O Libanus, and let fire devour thy cedars.' "[1]

These prodigies took place the moment Christ died. Then the veil was torn from top to bottom, the earthquake shook down the two pillars sustaining the veil, shattered the walls, the dead rose and came into city and Temple. God showed that the services had fulfilled their mission in pointing to the Redeemer, and that he would receive no more the services of the Deicide nation. Another sacrifice, the Last Supper—the Mass fulfilling all these had been established the night before in the Cenacle as foretold. "I have no pleasure in you, saith the Lord of hosts, and I will not receive a gift of your hands. For from the rising of the sun, even to the going down thereof, my name is great among the Gentiles, and in every place there is sacrifice, and there is offered to my name a clean oblation. For my name is great among the Gentiles, saith the Lord of hosts."[2]

"Six times the high priest pronounced the name Jehovah during the Day of Atonement, three times in the first confession, and three times in the second confession, and the seventh time when he had drawn the lot. He went to the bull the second time, putting his hands on him and confessing in the same words given in the first confession. And all Israel responded as before."

Then began the preparations for the sacrifices. A layman killed the animals; for lay Romans crucified Christ delivered up by the priests.

"Every day he scooped up the incense with a silver spoon, and emptied it into a gold vessel, but this day he

---

[1] Zach. ii 1. Yomah ix 43-39-59. See Josephus, Wars, B. vi., x. 3, Antiq. iii., vi. 7; Edersheim, Life of Christ, ii. 610.   [2] Malachy i. 10-11.

used gold vessels. He gathered up the live coals from the altar of ever-burning fire, filling a vessel holding 3 Kabs, and poured them into one holding 3 Kabs. Every day he filled one holding a Seah—6 Kabs, but on this day he filled one of 3 Kabs. Every day it was a heavy vessel of yellow gold, but this day it was light made of red gold with a long handle.

" Every day he used to offer half a Mina, fifty Dinars in weight of incense, half in the morning, and half in the evening, but this day he added a handful more. Each day it was finely pounded, but this day it was of the finest.[1] Each day the priests went up the eastern staircase of the altar, and came down on the western, but this day the high priest went up and came down the middle. Every day the high priest washed his hands from the laver, but this day from the golden pitcher the cyanthus. Every day there were four fires on the altar, but this day there were five.

" When the bull was slaughtered, he received in a gold basin his blood, gave it to a priest, standing on the fourth row of marble steps, to be stirred. He took the censer, mounted to the top of the altar, cleared the coals on either hand. Taking a censerful of the glowing coals, he came down again, and placed the censer on the fourth row of stones in the forecourt."

Although five hundred priests and five hundred Levites vested in Temple robes stand by in the Priests' Court and at the Nicanor Gate, while thousands of people throng the Temple, the high priest alone must carry on the service in the Holies; no one must be with him; to typify that the apostles ran away when Jesus alone passed through in his Passion, his atonement, when he opened the Holy of Holies of heaven to mankind.

" They brought him the gold spoon and censer; he took two handfuls of incense, and filled the spoon with it. He took the censer in his right hand and the spoon in the left."

He is about to enter that holiest place of earth, image of that heaven closed by Adam's sin. Let the celebrant of the Mass learn the baptismal innocence, the purity of soul and the sinless life required to enter the sanctuary

[1] Levit. xvi. 12

to offer prayer and sacrifice the Lamb of God from the following:

" It once happened on the Day of Atonement that the high priest spoke in a public place with an Arab whose saliva was sprinkled on the high priest's vestments. He became unclean; this high priest was R. Israel, son of Qim'hith. Then his brother Jeshohab entered and took his place, so his mother saw two high priests of her sons the same day. Another day the high priest spoke with a Gentile nobleman, the same happened, then his brother Joseph took his place. [1]

" He bent his three middle fingers on his palm, and removed with the little finger and thumb the incense found outside the three, one of the most difficult service in the Temple He took the handle of the spoon with his fingertips, and moved his thumbs up the handle, being thus able not to spill the frankincense, till the handle fell near his armpits, and the head of the spoon was above his palms. He then overturned the spoon, thus emptying the frankincense into his hands, heaped the frankincense on the censer and spread it out upon the burning coals.

" He walks through the Temple, holding the censer in his right hand, hanging from its chains, till he reaches the place between the two veils separating the sanctuary from the Holy of Holies—one ell wide."

They did not know whether the veil of Solomon's Temple was on the inside or outside of the wall dividing the Holy from the Holy of Holies, so in the second Temple, they put up two veils one within the other without the dividing wall; the space between the two veils being called Debir.

" The outer one was raised and looked to the southern wall, and the inner one to the northern. He walked between them till he reached the northern wall, where he turned his face to the south, walked back with his left hand to the veil and reached the ark, which was on his right in the Holy of Holies. Coming there he placed the censer between the staves, heaped the incense on the top of the coals so the whole place was filled with smoke of incense. He departed in the same way as he had come, facing the Holy of Holies walking backward, and said a

[1] Yomah, iv. 69-70.

short prayer in the Holies, but not making it long, so as not to alarm the Israelites about his delay lest they might think he had been killed by God." [1]

A rope was tied to him so that if God struck him dead, they might pull his body out, for no one could ever enter that gold-walled room, with its dim religious light, where once God, the Shekina, the Holy Spirit, alone dwelled, showing forth that no member of mankind was in heaven.

" The ark, with the cup of manna,[2] the flask of oil for anointing priests and kings, Aaron's rod, with its almonds and buds, and the box the Philistines sent as a gift to the God of Israel with the gold vessels were not in the Holy of Holies." [3]

Under Solomon Israel broke the covenant their fathers made with God agreeing to adore him alone, and worshiped the idols of King Solomon's wives on the Mount of Offense, where he built temples to them. In the time of the prophets they worshiped idols in the very Temple of Jehovah.[4] God directed the prophet Jeremy, and he took the ark of the covenant with its great winged cherubim, the mercy-seat of God, and hid them in a cave on Mount Nebo, where Moses died and was buried. They could not find the place and there they still rest, and will remain till Israel returns to the Messiah their fathers killed [5] when they shouted, " Crucify him." The magnificent Temple Herod spent forty-six years building, was not entirely finished when Christ adored his Eternal Father within its holy Courts. Its Holy of Holies was empty. The Shekina dwelled not in it. The nation had fallen from the supernatural state of grace of the days of Moses and the prophets. Scribes, Pharisees, Rabbis and infidel Sadducee priesthood had deceived them. But they lived in hope of the Messiah foretold to visit this Temple.[6]

" When the ark was taken away there was a stone from the time of the first prophets, Shethia " Foundation ", three fingers high above the ground. Thereupon he placed the censer. Going out, he took the blood from the one who stirred it, went back and stopped, where he had stopped in the Holy of Holies, and sprinkled from his position once upward and seven times downward,[7]

[1] Yomah iv 73. [2] Exod. xvi 33 [3] Deut xxviii ; II. Par. 85. [4] Ezechiel vi.
[5] II. Machabees ii. [6] Malach iii 1 [7] Levit xvi 14.

holding the palm open, counting one, and one, downwards, one and two, one and three, one and four, one and five, one and six, one and seven.

"Bowing deeply he departed backward, and placed the basin on the gold stand in the Temple. They brought him the he-goat. When he was killed, he received its blood in a basin, he went to the former place, stopping where he stopped, and sprinkled once upwards and seven times downwards, holding his palm open counting one, one and two, etc. He came out, and placed the basin on the second stand in the Temple. He took up the bull's blood, and put down the he-goat's blood. He sprinkled the blood thereof at the veil, which was opposite to the ark outside, once upwards and seven times down, thus counting he lifted the blood-filled basin of the he-goat, and put down that of the bull's blood, he sprinkled it on the veil opposite the ark outside, once upward and seven times downward. He emptied the bull's blood into the he-goat's blood, mixing them and transferred the contents into the empty basin."[1]

In mystic meaning the one sprinkling downward foretold the Son of God in his one Personality, coming down from heaven and made man, the seven sprinklings showed him filled with the seven gifts of the Holy Spirit[2] pouring out his blood on the earth and showing it to his Eternal Father in the supernal sanctuary of heaven. Mixing the blood of bull and goat typified his double nature in the one Person of the divine Son, God and man united. The ark mentioned was the ark called "the Aaron," wherein the Scrolls of the Law were kept in the Temple as in the synagogue. The blood was sprinkled toward the ark, foretelling that the synagogue would later kill Christ.

"When he sprinkled toward the veil, he sprinkled not upon it, but opposite to it, so the blood fell on the ground. R. Eliezer ben Jose said. "I have seen the veil in Rome with the marks of the blood of the bull and goat of the Day of Atonement. Then he went into the Holies through which he had passed each time he entered the Holy of Holies.

"He then went out to the altar, which is before the Lord, which is the golden altar, and began to clean it

<hr />

[1] Yomah, ix. 76, 77, 79, 81.　　　[2] Isaias ii. 1, 2, 3.

downward. Whence does he begin? From the north-eastern corner or horn to the northwestern, southwestern, southeastern, where he begins to clean the outer altar, at that spot, he finishes cleaning the inner. Everywhere he sprinkled from below upward, except at the spot where he stood, thereat he sprinkled from above downward.

"He sprinkled on the clean place of the altar, where the gold was to be seen, seven times; what remained of the blood he poured out at the western base of the outer altar, and what remained of the blood of the outer altar, he poured at the southern base. Both kinds of blood mingled in the trench, and flowed out into the brook Cedron.

"It holds true of all the rites of the Day of Atonement, whose order is prescribed by the Bible, and stated in the above Mishnas, that if they are performed in the wrong order, one has done nothing, but of the ceremonies per-formed in white garments outside, that is the lots, emptying the remaining blood, or confessions, it is true, if he has done them out of order they are valid. 'And this shall be an ordinance for ever, that you pray for the children of Israel, and for all their sins once a year.'[1]

"Both he-goats for the Day of Atonement shall be equal in color, size and price, and both bought at the same time. If one die before the lots are drawn another is bought to make up the pair, if after the lots one die, another pair is bought, and the lots drawn again, the one belonging to the first pair is allowed to graze till it gets a blemish, when it is sold, and the money becomes a gift offering, for an animal designed to atone for the congre-gation is not put to death."[2]

The two goats now stand before the altar in the sight of that vast congregation of Hebrews from all the nations. The high priest comes to the scapegoat, spreads out his hands over his head between the horns, and confesses his sins and the sins of all the people, using the words we have given over the bullock, closing with : " For on that day shall he make an atonement for you so that ye may be clean from all your sins before Jehovah."[3]

"And the priests and people who stood in the fore-courts hearing the name of God, that is, Jehovah, issuing from the mouth of the high priest, used to kneel, prostrate

[1] Levit xvi. 34 ; Yomah, iv 82-84   [2] Yomah, vi. 87 , [3] Yomah, vi. 9.

themselves, fall on their faces and say : "Blessed be the name of His Kingdom's glory for ever."

"They delivered the scapegoat to the pagan man who was to be his conductor. All were fit to perform this function. But the Israelites were not permitted to do it. An elevated walk had been constructed for the he-goat, for the Babylonian and Alexandrian Jews used to pull him by the hair saying : "Take the sins. Take and go."[1]

There stood the scapegoat on the high platform with the sins of Israel on him foretelling Christ delivered up to pagan Pilate when Jesus stood on the high platform of the Pretorium, the real Scape-Goat delivered up to death by the Temple priests with the sins of mankind on him when they cried: "Crucify him."

"Even if the conductor becomes unclean he may enter the Temple and take the goat," to foretell that Pilate was not as guilty of the death of Christ as the members of the supreme court who sentenced the Saviour to the cross.

"With shouts and imprecations, the vast crowds followed the goat led by his pagan conductor through the Shushan Gate, across the arched bridge built over the Cedron by the high priest." That was the very bridge they led Christ across the night of his arrest. Later the multitude followed Him down the Via Dolorosa, out the gate, and up the little hill of Calvary that fatal Friday of the crucifixion.

"Some of the prominent men of Jerusalem used to accompany the goat as far as the first booth of the ten supplied with refreshments for the conductor. There were ten booths between Jerusalem and Tsuk, "the rock," of its destination, a distance of ninety Ris (twelve miles). At each booth they said to the conductor : "Here is food and here is water." And the persons of the booth accompanied him from booth to booth, excepting the last of them, for the rock was not reached by them, but they stood at a distance looking on what he, the conductor, did with the goat."

The Jews did not nail Christ to the cross, but stood by looking on while the Romans crucified Him. The conductor foretold Pilate and the Roman soldiers, while the multitudes looking on from a distance at the goat

---

[1] Yomah. xl. 94.

prophesied the leading Jews, high priest and Levites, around Calvary, not allowed to enter Roman ranks while the Son of God was sacrificed.

"The conductor divided the crimson wool tied between his horns" for they divided the purple garments worn by the Lord among them. "The half he tied to the rock, and the second half between the goat's horns," as David foretold of Christ: "They parted my garments amongst them."[1]

"He pushed him down backward. He went rolling and falling down, he did not reach halfway down the mountain, before he became separated limb from limb."[2]

Bloody, torn, mangled, smashed on the rocks far below, lay the sinless victim with the sins of Israel on him, a striking image of the bloody body of the dead Christ with the sins of all mankind on Him

"The conductor returned to the last booth, under which he sat till dark," image of Pilate in his palace, after his death sentence on the Christ had been put in execution. Before the death of Christ, each year the scarlet cloth on the rock and in the Temple after the death of the goat became white, and swift runners ran back to the city to tell the joyful news to the people. But after the crucifixion it changed no more. Jewish writers try many ways to explain the reason.

"Formerly the tongue of crimson wool used to be tied to the door of the porch of the Temple outside, so all could see it. When it became white, all rejoiced. When it did not become white, all became out of spirits and ashamed. Then it was changed so that it was tied to the door of the porch inside. They used to look at it even then. It was then re-formed that half should be tied to the rock, another half to the horns. They had another sign. A tongue of wool used to be tied to the gate of the Temple, and as the goat reached the desert, the wool by a miracle became white, as it is said: "If your sins be as scarlet they shall be made white as snow, and if they be red as crimson they shall be white as wool."[3]

When runners brought the news to the Temple that the goat was killed, they began the morning services, the image of a pontifical High Mass we have described in a former work (The Tragedy of Calvary, chapter viii).

[1] Psalm xxi. 19.   [2] Yomah, vi 92   [3] Isaias i 18 ; Yomah, vi. 95-97.

The high priest vests in his magnificent vestments. His Sagan, as assistant priest stands at his right, the twelve priests, images of the twelve sons of Jacob, fathers of the twelve Hebrew tribes, range, six on either side of the pontiff, as during the ceremonies morning and afternoon each day This was the number of assistant priests in all Temple ceremonies, and this was the reason Christ chose apostles to the number of twelve.

Five hundred vested priests and as many Levites took part in the services. First the priest chosen by "lot," assisted by two priests, like the deacon and subdeacon of the High Mass, entered the Holies and incensed the gold altar, as now we incense the altar at the beginning of Mass. Then the lamb is sacrificed, his blood thrown on the horns of the altar in the form of a cross, and his flesh placed to burn on the everlasting fire burning on the great sacrificial altar.

Before the porch of the Holies was an ornamental ark called the "Aaron," in which reposed the five first books of the Old Testament. With the ceremonial we will give when we describe the synagogue, the holy Scrolls are taken out mid prayer, chant and anthem.

" The high priest came to read. If he desired to read dressed in linen or white byssus vestments, he did so, otherwise he read in a white stole of his own. The Hazzan, "servant" or attendant, of the congregation takes the Scrolls of the Law from the ark and presents them to the president of the congregation, he gives them to the Sagan, and the latter presents them to the high priest." [1]

This ceremony, modified but little, is seen when the the Gospel is sung at a High Mass. But when the bishop pontificates it is carefully followed The altar boy or one of the clergy hands the Missal to the subdeacon, who reads from it the Epistle, after which he gives it to the deacon, who lays it on the altar, as the scrolls were in the ark, and kneels in prayer. He takes it, and kneeling presents it to the celebrant, who blesses him The book is carried by the deacon, the clergy going before him till they come to the place where the Gospel is sung. The Jews in their synagogues of our day carry the Scrolls of the Law with the same ceremonies.

[1] Yomah, chapter xii 98

" The high priest rises and receives the Scrolls standing. He reads the section. (The celebrant at a high Mass, standing at the altar, touches the Mass-book in the hands of the kneeling deacon.) "After the death of the two sons of Aaron, when they were slain for offering strange fire, etc.,[1] and the section : 'Upon the tenth day of this seventh month shall be the Day of Atonement,' etc.[2] Then he rolls the Scrolls together, and keeps them on his knees and says: 'More than what I have read to you is written here.'

" The section " Upon the tenth," etc., he reads by heart, and pronounces over it the eight blessings, namely over the Law, over the service, over the thanksgivings, the atonement of iniquity, the Temple by itself, Israel by themselves, Jerusalem by itself, the priests by themselves and the rest of the prayers. He who sees the high priest reading does not witness the burning of the bullock and the he-goat, not because it was not allowed, but because a great distance intervened, and both were done at the same time."

The Temple with its great cloisters, its courts open to the sky, its halls, chambers and rooms covered an area of about 1,000 feet square. It was the largest religious edifice perhaps ever built, and was so thronged with people that they could not all see every service.

"If he read in linen garments, he washed his hands and feet, stripped himself and went down to bathe, came out and dried himself with a sponge. Vestments of cloth of gold were brought him, he put them on, washed his hands and feet ; he went out and performed the rites over his ram, the ram of the people, and the seven unblemished lambs of one year. They were offered with the daily sacrifice of the morning, and the bullock for the burnt-offering, and the he-goat used outside, were offered with the daily sacrifice of the evening."[3]

" He washed his hands and feet, undressed, went down to bathe, came up and dried himself. White vestments were brought him, he put them on, washed his hands and feet, he went in to fetch the spoon and censer. He washed his hands and feet again, stripped himself, went down to bathe, came out and dried himself. Vestments

[1] Levit xvi.   [2] Levit. xvi 29, 80, 31, 32   [3] Yomah xii. 102.

of cloth of gold were brought to him, he put them on,
washed his hands and feet, and went in to offer the incense of the evening and to trim the lamps. He then
washed his hands and feet, took off his vestments, put on
his own clothes, which had been brought to him, and was
accompanied to his own house. He used to keep the day
as a holiday with his friends, when he came away from
the Holy of Holies unhurt.

"It is known to us by tradition that the high priest
bathed five times and ten times washed his hands and
feet. When the conductor of the scapegoat returned, if
he met the high priest in the street, he said to him:
'My lord the high priest, we have done the commission
of Him, who giveth life to all living. May he who
giveth life to all the living give thee a long, good and
orderly life.'"

What did this elaborate ceremonial of the destroyed
Temple of Jehovah signify? It pointed to the future,
the atonement of the Cross, the entry into the heaven of
heavens, of the Scape-Goat Christ with the world's sins
on him, first after his sacrifice of the Last Supper and of
the cross, and his entry again after each Mass.

This world and all in it images the unseen spirits, and
the abode of bliss beyond the skies where the Eternal
dwells in glory. When the priest says Mass or when
the bishop pontificates, as high priest of the newer and
more perfect Church, surrounded by his ministers,
clothed in purple, gold and fine linen, offering, not bloody
victims, but the "Lamb of God slain from the foundations
of the world," we look beyond the veil of this magnificent
ceremonial and image that supernal sanctuary shown
us thus in visible forms. St. Paul beautifully refers to
the Day of Atonement, telling that the ceremonies foretold Christ to the Jew, and now recalls him to the
Christians.

"For the first tabernacle was made, wherein was the
candlestick, and the table, and the setting forth of loaves,
which is called the Holy. And after the second veil, the
tabernacle, which is called the Holy of Holies. Having
the golden censer, and the ark of the covenant covered
about on every part with gold, in which was the golden
urn that had the manna, and the rod of Aaron that had

blossomed, and the tables of the Testament. And over it were the cherubims ('Those grasped' 'Held fast') of glory overshadowing the propitiatory, of which it is not needful to speak now particularly.

"Now these things being thus ordered, into the first tabernacle, the priest indeed always entered, accomplishing the offices of the sacrifices. But into the second, the high priest alone entered once a year, not without blood, which he offered for his own and the people's ignorance, the Holy Ghost signifying that the way into the sanctuary was not yet made manifest, while the former tabernacle was yet standing, which is a parable of the time then present, according to which gifts and sacrifices are offered, which cannot as to the conscience make him perfect, that serveth only in meats, and in drinks, and diverse washings, and justifications of the flesh laid on them until the time of correction.

"But Christ being present, a high priest of the good things to come, by a greater and more perfect tabernacle not made with hands, that is, not of this creation, neither by the blood of goats and of calves, but by his own blood entered once into the sanctuary, having obtained eternal redemption.

"For if the blood of goats, and of bulls, and the ashes of a heifer, being sprinkled, sanctify such as are defiled to the cleansing of the flesh, how much more shall the blood of Christ, who through the Holy Ghost offered himself without spot to God, cleanse our conscience from dead works to serve the living God?

"And therefore he is the Mediator of the New Testament, that by means of his death for the redemption of those transgressions, which were under the Old Testament, they who are called may receive the promise of eternal inheritance. For where there is a testament (that is a will dividing property after death), the death of the testator must of necessity intervene. For a testament is of force after men are dead, otherwise it is not yet of force whilst the testator lives. Whereupon neither was the first indeed dedicated without blood.

"For when every command of the Law had been read by Moses to all the people, he took the blood of calves and goats, with water, and scarlet wool, and hyssop, and

sprinkled both the book itself and all the people, saying :
'This is the blood of the Testament, which God hath en-
joined unto you.' The tabernacle also, and all the
vessels of the ministry, in like manner he sprinkled with
blood. And almost all things according to the Law are
cleansed with blood, and without the shedding of blood
there is no remission.

"It is necessary therefore that the patterns of heavenly
things should be cleansed with these, but the heavenly
things themselves with a better sacrifice than these. For
Jesus hath not entered into the Holy Places made with
hands, the patterns of the true, but into heaven itself, that
he may appear now in the presence of God for us."[1]

Let us look beyond the ceremonial of Temple and Mass
to that heavenly sanctuary, where God reigns in glory
mid millions of saints bought by his blood. Church
chancel, copied from Temple Holy of Holies, has now no
veil. The great veil closing the Holy of Holies was rent
from top to bottom the moment Christ died, to tell how
he opened heaven by his death. The Jewish high priest,
that day in the Holy of Holies, holding out his hands
dripping with blood, arms and body forming a cross, foretold our High Priest Jesus in the heavenly Holy of
Holies, holding out his bloody pierced hands before the
throne of his Eternal Father, offering there the Masses
said by all his ministers on earth.

For the agent binds the one who sends him to act for
him. The ministers bind the governments who send
them as representatives. In ordination the priest receives
the power to act for Christ in the business of saving souls
and offering sacrifice. Standing at the altar, sitting in the
confessional, administering the sacraments, Christ acts
through and by the priest. The priest may be learned or
not, good or bad, cultured or crude, homely or handsome,
but the Mass and sacraments are the same, for the Pontiff
of mankind does all these through him, the same as
though He in visible form performed the function.[2]

Now let us see our High Priest in heaven and the
Liturgy of that celestial Church, of which that of the
Temple, was, and ours is the image. John, born of Aaron's
family, priest of the Temple, most beloved of the twelve,

[1] Hebrews ix.   [2] See S. Augustine, Tract VI. in John.

so dear as to lay his head on Jesus' breast, John was saved from martyrdom by a miracle, and banished to Patmos by the cruel emperor Domitian. As the steamer passes you see that rocky isle, bleak, barren, desert, rising from the Grecian Sea. He tells us that he saw the heavenly Sanctuary from which Temple and Church buildings were copied.

In sensible forms and images the last of the apostles saw the vision, but far below the reality of the spirit world: "Eye hath not seen, nor ear heard, neither hath it entered into the heart of man what things God hath prepared for them that love him." [1] No one while living here can see the three Persons of God, angels or disembodied souls of men. For as with the light we see material things, so the light of glory streaming down from God the Son in beatific vision, shows us the world of spirits only after death. Under visible forms acting on his senses the beloved Apostle saw the opened heavens.

On the high heavenly throne was the Eternal Father, before Him rose the altar with the souls of martyrs under it. There were the four writers of the Gospels in forms of animals Ezechiel saw.[2] The twenty-four ancients, the great men of both Testaments sat on seats of glory. Because of her higher powers over the other dioceses, from apostolic times the Roman diocese formed her presbytery of twenty-four priests, now the College of Cardinals, while the other diocese had only twelve members of the senate. There was the woman clothed with the sun, crowned with twelve stars—the apostles—while the heavenly hosts sang the celestial Liturgy. There was spread the table of the Lord, the great Eucharistic Banquet to which were invited all the nations. The Son of man and Son of God, as High Priest of mankind, the Lamb of God, "The Angel,' stood at the heavenly altar offering to his Eternal Father the Masses his ministers said on earth.

For these reasons, at every Mass the priest with closed hands resting on the edge of the altar prays, that Christ may offer the Oblation on the heavenly altar, before the throne of his Eternal Father, amid the vast unnumbered angels and saints of that heavenly Jerusalem, saying:

[1] I Cor. ii. 9.   [2] Ezechiel i.

6

"We humbly beseech Thee, O Almighty God, that thou wouldst command these gifts to be carried by the hands of thy holy Angel to thy altar on high, before the sight of thy Divine Majesty, that all of us, who by partaking of this altar, shall receive the most holy Body ✠ and Blood ✠ of thy Son, may be enriched by every heavenly blessing and grace. Through the same Christ our Lord. Amen."

"I was in Spirit on the Lord's Day, and heard behind me a great voice. And I turned to see the voice that spoke with me, and being turned, I saw seven golden candlesticks, and in the midst of the seven golden candlesticks, one like unto the Son of man, clothed with a garment down to his feet, and girded about the breasts with a golden girdle.[1]

"After these things I saw, and behold a door opened in heaven. And behold there was a throne set in heaven, and one sitting on the throne. And he that sat was like to the jasper and the sardine-stone; there was a rainbow round about the throne, in sight like unto an emerald.[2]

"And round about the throne were four and twenty seats, and upon the seats four and twenty ancients, clothed in white garments, and golden crowns on their heads. And from the throne proceeded lightnings, and voices, and thunderings. And there were seven lamps burning before the throne, which are the seven Spirits of God. And before the throne there was, as it were, a sea of glass, like crystal, and in the midst of the throne, and round about the throne, were four living creatures, full of eyes before and behind. And the first living creature like a lion, and the second living creature like to a calf, and the third living creature, having the face, as it were of a man, and the fourth living creature was like to an eagle flying.

"And the four living creatures had each of them six wings, and round about and within, they are full of eyes. And they rested not day and night, saying, "Holy, Holy, Holy, Lord God Almighty, who was and who is and who is to come. And when these living creatures gave glory, and honor, and benediction to Him that sitteth on the throne, who liveth forever and ever, the four and

[1] Apoc. i. 10-14   [2] Apoc. iv.

twenty ancients fell down before Him that sitteth on the throne, and adored Him that liveth for ever, and cast their crowns before the throne, saying : 'Thou art worthy, O Lord, our God, to receive glory, and honor, and power, because thou hast created all things, and for thy will they were and have been created' "

In the right hand of the Eternal Father was a book written within and without, sealed with seven seals— the whole revelation the Holy Ghost gave man contained in the Bible of which Christ is the key. He shines forth from every page of both Testaments. Take him out, and no one can understand the Bible.

" I saw, and behold in the midst of the throne and of the four living creatures, a Lamb standing, as it were, slain, having seven horns and seven eyes, which are the seven spirits of God, sent forth into all the earth. And he came and took the book out of the right hand of Him that sat on the throne. And when he had opened the book, the four living creatures and the four and twenty ancients fell down before the Lamb, having every one of them harps, and golden vials full of odors, which are the prayers of the saints. And they sang a new canticle, saying: 'Thou art worthy, O Lord, to take the book and to open the seals thereof because thou wast slain and hast redeemed us to God in thy blood, out of every tribe, and tongue, and people, and nation, and hast made us to our God, a kingdom and priests, and we shall reign on earth.'

"And I saw and heard the voice of many angels round about the throne, and the living creatures, and the ancients, and the number of them was thousands and thousands, saying with a loud voice: 'Worthy is the Lamb that was slain to receive power, and divinity, and wisdom, and strength, and honor, and benediction.' And every creature, which is in heaven and on earth, and under the earth, and such as are in the sea, and the things that are therein, I heard all saying : 'To him that sitteth on the throne, and to the Lamb, benediction, and honor, and glory, and power, for ever and ever.' And the four living creatures said, Amen. And the four and twenty ancients fell down on their faces, and adored Him that liveth for ever and ever.

" After this I saw a great multitude which no man can number, of all nations, and tribes, and peoples, and tongues, standing before the throne, and in the sight of the Lamb, clothed in white robes, and palms in their hands. And they cried with a loud voice saying: ' Salvation to our God and to the Lamb.' And all the angels stood round about the throne, and about the ancients, and about the four living creatures, and they fell before the throne upon their faces, and adored God, saying: ' Amen. Benediction, and glory, and wisdom, and thanksgiving, and honor, and power, and strength to our God for ever and ever. Amen.' These are they who have come out of great tribulation, and have washed their robes, and made them white in the blood of the Lamb. Therefore they are before the throne of God, and serve him day and night in his Temple, and he that sitteth on the throne shall dwell over them. They shall not hunger, nor thirst any more, neither shall the sun fall on them, nor any heat. For the Lamb, which is in the midst of the throne, shall rule them, and shall lead them to the fountains of the waters of life, and God shall wipe away all tears from their eyes.

" And when he had opened the fifth seal, I saw under the altar the souls of them that were slain for the word of God, and for the testimony which they held. And they cried with a loud voice saying : ' How long, O Lord, holy and true, dost thou not judge and revenge our blood on them that dwell on earth ? ' And white stoles were given to each of them one, and it was said to them, that they should rest yet for a little time, till their fellow servants their brethren, who were to be slain even as they, should be filled up [1]

" And there appeared a great wonder in heaven, a woman clothed with the sun, and the moon under her feet and on her head a crown of twelve stars. And I saw and behold a Lamb stood on mount Sion and with him a hundred and forty-four thousand having his name, and the name of his Father written on their foreheads. And I heard a voice from heaven, as the voice of many waters, and as the voice of great thunder, and the voice which I heard was as of harpers harping on their harps.

[1] Apoc. vi, 9, 11.

And they sang as it were a new canticle before the throne, and before the four living creatures, and the ancients. And I saw as it were a sea of glass, mingled with fire, and them that had overcome the beast and his image and the number of his name, standing on the sea of glass, having the harps of God, and singing the canticle of Moses and the canticle of the Lamb, saying : 'Great and wonderful are thy works, O Lord God Almighty, true and just are thy works, O King of ages. Who shall not hear Thee, O Lord, and magnify thy name. For thou only art holy, for all nations shall come and shall adore in thy sight because thy judgments are manifest.'

"I heard as it were the voice of many multitudes in heaven saying, 'Alleluia. Salvation, and glory, and power is to our God. For true and just are his judgments, who hath judged the great harlot, which corrupted the earth with her fornications, and hath revenged the blood of his servants at her hands.' And again they said, 'Alleluia.'

" And the four and twenty ancients and the four living creatures fell down and adored God that sitteth upon the throne, saying, 'Amen, Alleluia,' And a voice came out from the throne saying. 'Praise ye our God, all his servants and you that fear Him little and great.' And I heard as it were the voice of many waters, and as the voice of great thunders saying ; ' Alleluia. For the Lord our God, the omnipotent hath reigned. Let us be glad and rejoice and give glory to Him, for the marriage of the Lamb has come, and his wife has prepared herself. And to her it hath been granted, that she should clothe herself with fine linen, glittering and white. For the fine linen is the justifications of saints."[1]

[1] Apoc. xix. 4.

III.—THE BREAD, WINE, WATER, OIL, AND INCENSE, IN THE TEMPLE.

THE Jewish Temple was filled with numerous objects reminding the Hebrews of their religion, exciting them to prayer and devotion. These objects did not of themselves give grace. But aroused at the sight of them they performed their acts of religion in the faith, hope, and love of their foretold Redeemer. These religious objects were the sacramentals of the Old Law. At the Last Supper Christ raised the Jewish sacramentals, bread, wine mixed with water, and oil, with the imposition of hands, into the dignity of being the materials of the Eucharistic Sacrifice and of holy Orders. The general impression is that when Christ did this he took materials never used before in worship. But he did not make any sudden change. From prehistoric time, in days of patriarchs, of Moses and of the prophets, the Holy Ghost had chosen bread, wine, water, oil, and incense, and in Passover and in Temple they came down in rite, history and religion of the Hebrews to the days of Christ. Let us see these images of the Mass and of the sacraments with their histories, for we will later find them in the Last Supper.

First we will begin the story of bread, " the staff of life." When at the dispersion of the seventy-two families of mankind from the plains of Mesopotamia, when the language of our race was changed, the white men retired to the southern shores of the Caspian Sea, where they found growing the wheat, *triticum vulgare* a species of the *hordeicae* or barley family. There soon after the flood but long before they emigrated to settle Europe, they cultivated this wheat, whence it spread over the world. It is mentioned as flourishing in Egypt in the days when the Hebrew captive Joseph became the Pharaoh's prime minister.[1]

[1] Gen. xli

86

Palestine produced great quantities of a superior wheat as soon as the Hebrews took possession of their " Promised Land." You will still find the hills of Palestine terraced to the tops. Long winding narrow fields, sometimes but a few feet wide, look like great steps, the soil upheld by stone walls, the labor of nearly 4,000 years, on which the wheat was grown in those days when the Holy Land was densely populated. Thirty-five times the wheat is mentioned in the Old Testament. Why did the Holy Ghost inspire the patriarchs to bake unleaven cakes of wheaten flour for the Passover? Why did the priests offer them in the Temple every Sabbath, and why did Christ change this bread into His Body? Let us see the deep reasons shown in the investigations of our day.

According to scientific research, wheaten bread is the most nourishing of all foods. The human body requires heat to supply energy, and nourishment to repair the losses. Life could be sustained longer on bread alone than on any other food, its only deficiency being want of nitrogenous matters. A pound of bread is more nourishing than a pound of meat. A man could live on two pounds of bread a day for an indefinite time, but not on any other one kind of food. Sugar is the next most valuable food, and this explains why children like bread with sweets. The sweets in wine, or grape sugar, supply what is wanting in bread. For that reason bread and wine are the most nourishing foods known to man. The patriarchs, directed by the Holy Spirit, chose for their sacrifices, and the Passover, a food and drink founded on strictly scientific principles.

People first ate grain without grinding. Passing through the fields, they rubbed the heads in their hands, separating the chaff and ate the grains, as the apostles did on the Sabbath.[1] In ancient times Hebrews ate grain this way.[2]

Later it was ground in a wooden or stone mortar, the flour was mixed with water and made into cakes and baked on the fire. They laid them on the live coals, as Abraham did when the Lord with two angels visited him.[3] In Moses' demands to let the Hebrews go, we first

[1] Matt xii 1, 2. [2] Levit xiv 23 ; Ruth ii 2, 3, 17, 18 ; II Kings, xvii. 28 etc.
[3] Gen. xviii. 6

find the mill mentioned [1] and seven times the Old Testament mentions the flour mill.

This ancient mill called in Hebrew *rechayim*, still used in Palestine and the Orient, is made of two flat stones, about two feet in diameter. The upper, called the *pelach*, rested on a lower, the *receb*, united by a spindle through a hole in the middle; women sitting on the ground turned the upper stone, the right hand grasping a handle, putting in the grain with the left. The stones were roughened on the lower and upper sides.[2]

In Christ's time, they sometimes used large stones turned by animals.[3] Kings and nobles had special bakers.[4] The law forbade one of the stones to be pledged for a debt, for then the family could not grind their grain.[5] They ground all kinds of grain in these little mills, but as flour of wheat was used to make the Temple proposition bread of the last Supper, we will confine ourselves to wheaten bread.

The word bread comes from the Hebrew *barah* "to eat," "to feed," "to nourish"; in this sense God told Adam after his sin that he would eat his bread with the sweat of his brow all the days of his life,[6] and many Bible texts show that bread meant all kinds of food.

After the wheat was pounded or ground in the mill, the flour was mixed with water made into a dough, rolled into thin cakes and baked on live coals. The patriarchs thus made the unleaven cakes of only flour and water; these were the Passover cakes, and in this way the breads have since been made for Mass in the Latin Church.

In the account of the flight from Egypt, we first find mentioned fermented bread. This is made by mixing the dough with yeast, "to foam," "to give off gas." The yeast is a microscopic fungus plant which feeds on the sugar and gives off gas, which makes the bread "rise." Numerous kinds of this fungus are used in the fermentation of wine, bear, etc, we find that the Egyptians made beer, and perhaps from them the Hebrews learned to make fermented bread. In Greek and Oriental Churches fermented bread is used for the Mass, but this is not ac-

---

[1] Exod. ii 5   [2] Deut. xxiv 6; Job xli 15, 16, II Kings xv. 21   [3] Matt. xviii. 6 [4] Gen xl 2, Jer. xxxvii. 21, Osee vii 4 [5] Deut xxiv.6. [6] Gen. iii.19.

cording to the strict rules of the Hebrew Passover, the Last Supper, and the patriarchal custom.

In the deserts wood is scarce, and Arabs now use dried dung, on which they lay the flattened unfermented cakes which they turn to bake both sides : the crust smells of the dung but the taste of the inside is pleasant.

Large ovens were established in each town and village of Judea where the people brought the bread to be baked. Going over Mount Olivet, a little below the place of the Ascension was seen a round dome, about ten feet in diameter and six high, in which was a fire of dried dung. A woman inside, surrounded with smoke, was making cakes and placing them on the fire. She offered one, but it was declined with thanks. Such ovens may be still seen in all parts of the East, especially among the common people, who have not been changed by modern methods.

The housewife prepared and baked the bread.[1] Later this became the servants' work.[2] After David's time, when the Hebrews began to devote themselves to business, each rich family had a baker.[3]

They used a wooden platter in which they mixed the dough made of flour and water, but later they put yeast in to make it rise by fermentation. The first kind, called Matzoth, "unleaven," was alone used at the Passover and in all the sacrifices of the Temple.[4] The latter was named Chometz, " fermented "

The cakes were round, from ten to twelve inches in diameter, the unfermented breads being as thin as a knife and the fermented about half an inch thick. They never cut bread with a knife, but broke it with their fingers.[5] At Passover and feasts the master of the house always broke the bread and handed it to his guests. The master of the house on Sion during the Passover broke the bread and handed a piece to the writer.

In the Church the celebrant breaks the Host before partaking, and if necessary he breaks the smaller Hosts when giving Communion. In the Latin Rite this Jewish

[1] Gen xviii. 6 , Levit. xxvi. 26; II Kings xiii 6-8; Jer vii 18   [2] I Kings viii 8-13.   [3] Osee vii 4-7 ; Jer. xxxvii 20 ; Migne, Cursus Comp S Scripturæ, iii 1135, etc   [4] Gen xviii 6, xix 3; Judg vi 11; III Kings xvii 12, Exod xii 15, 35, xiii 3, xvi 3, 4, 8, 12 , Levit ii. 4, vii 12-13, viii. 26, 31, 32; Deut xvi 3, Amos iv. 6.   [5] Isaias lviii. 7, Lam. iv. 4; Matt. xiv. 19, xv. 36, xxvi. 26.

custom of breaking the bread or Hosts is always followed, and the unfermented bread of the Jewish Passover and the patriarchs only is used. In the Greek and sister Rites, with a long ceremony at the credence table during Mass, the celebrant with a little lance cuts from a loaf of fermented bread a large piece for the sacrifice, one for the Virgin, one for John the Baptist, and one each for the Apostles. Let us see the bread in Hebrew homes and Temple.

Outside the house, they dug a hole like a well, two or three feet wide, and from three to six deep,[1] walled it up with stones, then plastered it with wet clay on the inside, leaving little holes for the flames to pass up into the oven. When the oven became red-hot, they removed the fire and put in the dough, covering the whole outside of the oven with earth.[2] When the cakes were baked on one side, they turned them over.[3] This was the smoking furnace shown Abraham in which to bake Passover cakes,[4] when the Lord, with an angel each side of him, visited the patriarch's tent. In this kind of an oven Lot prepared unleaven bread for the angels who warned him to flee from the wicked doomed Sodom and Gomorrah.

Later they used a movable oven called *tannur*, about three feet high, made of earthenware, glazed within and without with white potter's clay, resting on a movable base forming the furnace. After heating it with a fire inside, they removed the coals and pasted the dough to the sides.[5] In this oven they baked the proposition or "showbreads," of the Temple, type of the Eucharist.[6] It was the bread the raven brought Elias each day. Some writers say the raven was not a bird, but a member of the Raven tribe of Bedouin wanderers. The angel gave the great prophet this unleaven bread, which gave him strength to fast for forty days and nights, till he came to Horeb, foretelling the graces of Communion.[7]

Vessels of the same shape and materials were used to hold liquids. They also used an iron basket with three feet like a tripod, or rested it on three stones, built a fire under it and in it the dough was baked.[8] In this they

---

[1] Levit. xi 35   [2] Levit vii 9, 12, 3, etc   [3] Osee vii 8   [4] Gen xv 17   [5] Levit ii 4; Eccl x 30; Jer. lii 18   [6] See Edersheim Temple, 152   [7] Ill. Kings xix 6-8.   [8] Levit. ii. 5, vi. 14-15; Exod. xxix 2-3.

baked not only the unleaven bread for the Passover, the leaven bread for daily use, but also other kinds of cakes and bread made of different grains.

Unleaven bread, made before history opened, of only flour and water, is called in Hebrew Matzoth, in Greek Azymous, both meaning "unleaven," to distinguish it from Chometz, "leaven," which was made with yeast, was used at the Passover, offered in the Temple and eaten at all their religious feasts. Thirty-eight times this bread is found in the Old Testament, and hundreds of times in later Jewish writings.

Jews of our day prepare this bread, carefully following the customs of their fathers. The flour is ground of chosen wheat, it must not be musty, or mixed with other flour, and it is carefully kept. Mixed with purest water. they make a dough, roll very thin cakes about a foot in diameter and bake at once, lest the dough ferment. When baked they keep them in a clean box or chest. They then mix the remaining dough with honey, eggs and sugar, etc., but not with yeast. These, called *haschira*, "rich cakes," they send to friends, the sick, and to Christians. But strict Jews do not send the regular Passover bread to Gentiles.

To the Hebrew this unleaven bread was the "staff of life," no meal was held without it; it reminded them of the bread Melchisedech offered when he blessed their father Abraham; it recalled the proposition bread of the Temple, the desert manna, and it was handed down that when the Messiah came he would in bread renew the miraculous manna. For these reasons the blessings at the table were always said over the bread [1] and wine, and these blessings sufficed for all the other foods.

Each Sabbath eve with a ceremonial we will later give, the priests laid twelve thin cakes of unfermented bread of the patriarchal Passover, and between and mingled in mystic meaning with them twelve gold flasks of wine mixed with water.[2] These of purest gold were made like golden bottles.[3] The lamb sacrificed morning and evening every day foretold the crucifixion, and the bread and wine pointed to the Last Supper and the Mass. What was the Temple ceremony of the bread and wine?

---

[1] See Edersheim, Life of Christ, ii p 206, etc.   [2] Exod. xxv. 29, 30.
[3] Exod. xxxvii. 10 16; xl 4; Numb. iv. 7; xxviii. 9-10.

Early Friday afternoon the "new course" of priests chosen for the function representing all the priests, and Levites typical of the tribe of Levi, with the "stationary men" emblematic of all Israel, came to the Temple to take their places for the following week. The men chosen by "lot" take their places for the ceremonial of the proposition bread and wine.

When the sacrifice of the lamb begun at three P. M. had nearly ended, three blasts were blown from the silver trumpets to tell all in Temple and sacred city that the Sabbath was drawing near, for it began at sundown. Jacob, their last great patriarch, had established this hour of prayer, for it was the time when, later, Jesus died. The Roman emperor Augustus had issued a decree, that during this hour the Jews were exempt from attending the law courts, that they might attend the Sabbath worship.

Lamps and candles are lighted to foretell the Messiah. Priests robed in rich vestments, wash the sacrificial altar from stains of blood, "lots" are drawn to see who was to perform the varied functions of priest and Levite. Those so chosen first began the preparation of the proposition, "show," or "Face bread" in one of the Temple chambers. The Rabbis call it the "Bread of the Face of God Almighty," the "Angel of the Face" the "Perpetual Bread," the "Bread of laying out" the "Angel of his Presence" etc. They held it in great honor. Its renewal each Sabbath was an important Temple service, for it imaged the altar bread of the Last Supper and of the Mass.

In the Holies, with walls covered with plates of purest gold, at the northern or most sacred side, stood the credence table, three feet long, one and a half wide and high, made of purest solid gold, its feet, like those of animals, turned out, and connected in the middle with a magnificent gold crown. The table of the tabernacle was made of sitim wood, the acacia tree of the Arabian deserts, and all the wood was covered with plates of pure gold. At the time of Christ, the Temple table was of solid gold, which had been given by the Machabees to replace the one Antiochus Epiphanes took away. Josephus writes of a larger table which Ptolemy Philadelphus gave.[1]

[1] Antiq XII. ii. 8.

From purest wheat grown in Judea, ground with great ceremony, the flour was passed through eleven sieves, each with meshes one finer than the other. Mixed with the "water of precept," twelve cakes of unleaven bread were made, representing the twelve tribes of Israel. Each cake was made of two and a half quarts of flour and it was anointed with olive oil in the form of a cross.[1]

"The House of Garmo," a family of the Kohathites, descendants of Levi's second son,[2] had a monopoly of making these cakes, which they deposited on a marble table in the porch of the sanctuary, where they remained till the Sabbath service began. The Talmud tells us the ceremony of placing them on the gold table in the Holies the image of our sanctuary.

" Four priests enter the Holies, two carrying each one of the piles of six breads, the others the two vases of incense Four priests went before them—two to take off the two rows of old breads, and two the old vases of incense. Those who brought in the bread and incense stood at the north side, facing southwards, they who were at the south side facing north, these lifted off, and those replaced the hands of those, being right over against the hands of those, as it is written, " Thou shalt set upon the table bread of the Presence before Me always." [3]

Thus placing and removing the breads, the priests formed with their arms a cross, the sign of redemption found in all the Temple ceremonies to foretell the Redeemer's sacrifice.

" On a golden table in the porch of the sanctuary, the old breads were placed by two priests. Other priests then brought twenty-eight gold tubes, long like bottles, filled with wine. These they placed on the gold table in the Holies beside the new breads."

Then they removed the twelve golden flasks of wine, emptied them with mystic ceremony, filled them with new wine mixed with water, placed them on the credence table with the twelve breads before the Lord in his holy sanctuary, where they rested till the next Sabbath. This wine and water are mentioned many times in the Old

---

[1] Edersheim, Temple, p 155   [2] Gen. xlvi 11 ; I Par. ix 32, Talmud, Shekalim, v. 1   [3] Talmud, Men xi 7

Testament under the name of "drink offerings." The
priests drank this wine while eating the cakes.[1]

This bread and wine, the latter mixed with water, thus
placed before the Lord in the Holies, foretold the bread
and wine of the Last Supper and of the Mass. This is
the reason the wine is mixed with water, the latter foretelling the water flowing from the pierced side of the
dead Christ.

Now the ministering priests of that "course" gather
round the golden table in the Priests' Court, whereon the
bread and wine are placed and each receives his portion.

"Three times a year all the twenty-four orders of
priests were alike entitled to share the pieces of offerings
of the festival, and in the proposition bread, and on the
feast of Pentecost, the distributers say to each priest:
"Here is leavened bread for thee," and "here is unleavened
bread for thee." "If the festival falls before, or after
Sabbath, all the twenty-four orders share alike in the
proposition bread. But if a day intervenes between the
Sabbath and the festival, the order, whose regular turn it
was, received ten of the proposition breads, and the loiter-
ers receive two breads. At other times of the year the
order in which they entered on their duty received six."[2]

The high priest passes by, and each priest hands to
him a part of his bread, and they give him some of the
wine in honor of his pontifical office. Then they stand
by the table of gold and eat the bread and drink the wine
held most sacred because for a week they had reposed
before the Lord the Shekina in his Holies. No one but a
priest could eat this bread, he must be free from all
blemish[3] he must not have cohabited with his wife.[4] Thus
they foretold our unmarried clergy and the weekly renewal
of the Eucharist in our churches.[5]

Now let us see the wine of Temple, Last Supper and
Mass. Writers say the vine was cultivated before the flood,
that then they ate the grape like other fruits. The early
Church fathers write that Noe was the first to press the
grape and make wine, and that he did not know its intoxicating effects when he took too much.[6]

[1] See Edersheim, Temple, 158, 241, 242, 243; Talmud, etc.   [2] Succah, 88 to 91.
[3] See Heb. x. 1   [4] Kings.   [5] See S. Augustine, Contra Faustum, L. vi ix, L.
xxxii x xi.   [6] Gen. ix. 21; Migne, Cursus Completus, S. Scripturæ, Hl. 1254-
1256, etc.

Wine, in Hebrew *yagin*, "pressed out," "grape juice," typified excessive sorrow and physical pains which make men stagger. Thus the Saviour speaking to his Father of his sufferings and death said: "Let this chalice pass from me." The Holy Ghost drew back the curtain hiding the future and revealed the Crucified when Noe blessed and cursed the nations—the races—in his three sons. The mighty movements of mankind then begun have continued till our day.

Noe, the second Adam, father of mankind, high priest and image of Jesus Christ, planted a vineyard, pressed the grapes and made wine. Not knowing its effect he took too much, lay naked in his tent, an image of our High Priest stripped of his garments, crucified, dead on the cross. Ham, Noe's second son mocked his father as the Jews mocked the dying Christ. His two other sons, Sem and Japheth with a cloak, covered their father's nakedness.[2]

Rising from his sacrifice, Noe blessed and cursed, as Christ was to rise from the tomb after his sacrifice and bless his followers with the gift of the Holy Ghost, while the curse of his blood rested on the Jewish nation.

"Cursed be Canaan, a servant of servants shall he be unto his brethren."[3] He could not curse Ham, for God had blessed the three sons and the curse rested on Canaan's children. Ham's sons settled Palestine, which they cursed with the sin of Sodom and Gomorrah. But Ham's tribes settled Africa, and find their vocation as slaves and servants waiting on the white men. Cursed in the passion their father mocked in Noe, the African race love to serve as servants to the other races. Living since in deepest degradation, among them never rose religion, literature, invention, genius, or progress. The other races will not receive on an equality one in whose veins flows their tainted blood.

Prophetic words the Holy Ghost pronounced through Noe on the sons who covered him. "Blessed be the Lord God of Sem, let Canaan be his servant." Thus he determined that the "Lord God," Jesus Christ would be born of Sem's race, the Jews. Christ's genealogy shows him as son of Sem.[4] He is the glory of the Jewish

[1] Gen. ix 21.   [2] Gen. ix   [3] Gen. ix 25   [4] Luke iii.

Semites The other Semitic nations settled Asia, where they have remained stagnant, conservative, unprogressive, hardly improving since the patriarchs, for they were not blessed with the grace of change.

To Japheth: " The enlarging " or " The white man," Noe said " May God enlarge Japheth, and may he dwell in the tents of Sem, and Canaan be his servant." [1] The Hebrew has here for " God " the word " Shekina," the Holy Ghost, who spoke through Noe and gave Japhet's sons, the white races, that colonizing instinct, civilization, progress, advancement, invention, superiority—the unrest of bright minds which down the ages lifted them to the highest prosperity, culture and refinement. This is the reason the white men are so superior to the other races. God foresaw the Jews would reject Christ, that the white men would receive him, and thus he prepared them for their mission to receive the Gospel and carry on the Church.

Before this blessing Moses always mentioned these three brothers according to their age, Sem first and Japhet last; after the benediction the last is given first as the leader of the others. God later blessed the Jews through Abraham, Isaac, Jacob and the patriarchs, gave them the instinct of money-making that they might use the power of wealth in missionary labors. They rejected the call to Christianity when they killed Christ. But God works without repentance, the blessing still rests on them while the white races receive and administer the Church they refused.

This is the first lesson we read in wine Noe was the first to make. His son Sem, called Melchisedech, added bread and sacrificed the bread and wine of the Last Supper and the Mass on Sion. Now let us see that wine of patriarch, tabernacle, Temple and the Eucharistic Sacrifice.

Palestine, stretching from the high Lebanon mountains in the north, their tops nearly always crowned with snow, to the deep valleys of the Dead Sea, 1,300 feet below the ocean, rejoices in varied climates, and produces dry wines of temperate climates, as well as the sweet wines of torrid zones. Hundreds of times the vine or the wine is mentioned in the Bible as flourishing in Palestine.

[1] Gen. ix 27.

Moses' law has special rules The Hebrew farmer was forbidden to plant any other crop in his vineyard, he could not use the grapes, or make wine, before the vineyard was five years old ; but the widow, the orphan, and the stranger passing could eat all they wanted, but it was against the law to take any away. Priests while serving in the Temple, Nazarites while their vow lasted, judges while on the bench, Essenes and Rechabites were forbidden wine. Let us see the grape and the wine.

The grape is a native of the Orient, where it grows as a shrub like a dwarf tree It was cultivated from the days of Noe and wine spread among all ancient nations. It was in the beginning a desert plant, where it produces, when carefully cultivated, great crops, the fruit being in California more numerous than the leaves. It grows wood and leaves in cold climates, where it must be sustained with trellis and stake. But in its native climate it grows like a little tree.

In Palestine, especially in the north, the vineyards were on the north side of the hills facing south. In the fall all the members of the family gathered the grapes with song Psalm and canticle, and carried them to the press, generally in the center of the vineyard.

On steep hillside, of stone and cement, they built the press and receptacles for the grapes, so the "must" might flow down into the lower receptacle, both being about six feet in diameter and four deep. Into the upper they threw the grapes mixed with the stems and barefooted men, sometimes naked, danced on them till all were crushed. When the grapes were of the red variety, of which the clarets are made, they looked as though they were covered with blood.

Six centuries before he came, the prophet Isaias saw a vision of Jesus Christ in his agony in Gethsemane "The Winepress," when as the Scape-Goat of mankind, the world's sins were placed on him as though he himself had committed them. And ten thousand times deeper than we do he blushed with shame till his blood flowed out every pore, covering him with crimson gore, and the prophet thought he had treaded the red grape of the Winepress, Gethsemane.[1]

[1] Isaias lxiii 1--6, etc.

7

When the upper vat was filled with grapes and stems, thus the men, with psalm, and song, and jest, trampled them with their feet till every berry was broken, and the whole became a mass of grape-juice hulls and seeds. Then for about ten days it is left to ferment. It must be frequently mixed so all parts may come in contact with skins and stems, which bear the fermenting fungus yeast plant which floats in the air.

In warm climates the grapes are very sweet, in cold regions the grape does not develop so much grape sugar, —the first produce the sweet and the latter the "dry" wine. The fermentation of the sweet wines ceases before all the sugar ferments and that is the reason they taste so sweet. In the "dry" wine all the sugar changes into alcohol—hence these two great classes of wines, which divide into various families bearing different names according to climate, places where they are grown, age, care, etc.

Let us go a little deeper, for wine is one of the elements of the Mass and few understand how it is made. The yeast plant we mentioned feeds on the grape sugar and changes it into ethel "noble" alcohol, formed of carbon, 2, oxygen, 2, and hydrogen 2, and which when distilled becomes brandy. Grape-wine, is the oldest, finest and most harmless of all fermented beverages. Wine never forms a habit; no matter how much a person drinks of it he will not crave it. It is soothing to tired nerves, it induces sleep. Hence it has been celebrated in all ages.

Sugar of fruits, grains, etc, when fermented produce another kind of alcohol found in liquors, beers, etc., which acts on the nerves, cooks the albumen white so they cannot function, and develops into a mania for drink. It is a poison, slow but deadly In modern days were discovered these fermented drinks which seem to ruin more people than wars or famine. Among the wine-drinking nations you will hardly ever see an intoxicated person. The Mass wine must not be taken as composed of its varied chemical elements, but as one single fluid, as a human being is one person, although composed of soul and body, composed of many materials—the one living soul uniting the materials of the body, giving them its life. Thus the form of the wine united in one all the materials and fluids of which it is composed till it was changed into the Blood of Christ at the Last Supper as it is now in the Mass.

Let us return to the ancient world. When the Hebrews had fermented their wine in the upper vat, they drew it into a lower vat, leaving skins, seeds, etc., in the higher fermenting receptacle. Here the wine was left for a time carefully covered till it was still more purified by depositing in the bottom the rough matters, which made it taste harsh and crude. Then it was put in large earthen or stone vessels. Spring and fall it worked again, throwing down deposits of muddy matters. After a year or more, the wine had purified itself and was ready for use. Wine poisoned with drugs never shows a deposit, never changes. A sign of good wholesome wine is a dark deposit on the bottom of the vessel.

Great vessels, called amphoræ, were kept in wine cellars, but small farmers, dealers, and the poor, kept their wine in bottles made of goatskin taken whole from the body, cutting only around the feet and neck, which, after tanning, they tied with strings. Wine and water bottles made that way may be seen to-day in Mexico, Palestine and in the Orient. Wine working or fementing throws off carbonic acid gas which would burst such bottles, and that was why Christ said new wine should be put in new bottles but old wine in old bottles.[1]

Sweet grapes, when dried are called raisins.[2] The latter soaked in water make "new wine."[3] Frequently in our day Jews make wine for the Passover from raisins, especially when they are not sure of the purity of wine on the market. Strict Jews do not like to use Passover wine bought from or made by Gentiles.

Ancient receptacles for wine made of skins are almost as old as wine itself, and are frequently mentioned in Scripture. The Iliad tells us servants bore wine in bottles of sheepskin on their shoulders to banquets, from which the guests' goblets were filled. Herodotus writes that wine in pig or goat skins was carried from place to place. The Romans used leathern bottles large enough to hold a man, and Pompeii shows a mural picture of an

[1] Job xxxii. 19; Matt. ix. 17; Mark ii. 22
[2] II. Kings xvi. 1; I. Par. xii. 40.   [3] Acts ii. 13.

enormous leather bag like a boat on a wine cart, while
two men draw off the wine into amphoræ. Roman poli-
ticians used to deal out wine wholesale to their clients.

Leather bottles are still used in Spain, Portugal,
Greece, Mexico, etc., linking modern wine-making with
the dim past. The road from Athens to Petros winds for
miles through great Grecian vineyards stretching along
the gulf which ends in Corinth where the canal begins,
and to whose people St. Paul sent his famous Epistles.

Famous feasts, where wine flowed as water, are given
in history. The coronation of Ptolemy Philadelphus ex-
celled in pomp and pageantry every procession recorded
in history. Ptolemy wanted to dazzle his subjects that
they might forget the domestic crimes with which he ascended the throne. For that reason the feast cost over
$500,000, opening with the figure of the morning star,
and closing with that of Hesperus—the evening star.

The beautiful Egyptian climate furnished abundance
of grapes and wine. Eighty thousand troops—infantry
and cavalry—clad in gorgeous uniforms, marched to
sound of flute and song, while sixty satyrs, under Silenus,
bore the symbolic chalice, the great cantharus, in which
men treaded out the grapes flooding the streets with
must A car, thirty-seven by twenty-one feet, bore a
gigantic uter of leopard skins, holding 24,000 gallons,
filled with wine, the hides strengthened with bronze rods.
From this colossal receptacle the populace filled their vessels and drank as the car passed.

The scholastic name of the wine uter was butis, and a
small one the diminutive buticula, from which came our
word bottle. A black leathern bottle called a "black-jack"
was used in England, sometimes being lined with silver,
the origin of covering flasks with leather. Some of them
were formed like a boot, and French prisoners said "the
English drank out of their boots."

As arts advanced, bottles were made of clay, glass, etc.
In Pompeii you will find great earthenware amphoræ,
large enough to hold more than a barrel used by the un-
fortunate people to hold wine, oil, etc. These great vessels
were coated within and without with pitch to prevent leaks,
and to keep the liquids sound. Large ones were made in pits
baked within with a fire, while the smaller ones were made

on a potter's wheel. The largest sometimes held as much as a hundred gallons. When wooden round barrels were made we know not. In wine countries great round vats hold the wine. In wineries of California you will see some holding nearly 100,000 gallons. One was formed of cement, in the side of a hill, holding 500,000 gallons, and when finished, they held a dance in it.

Grape juice called "must" was drunk in the vineyard by the workmen. The Hebrews sometimes became intoxicated.[1] The Passover service states that each guest must drink four chalices of wine to fulfil the law. Sometimes this was too much, and they mixed the wine with water—when this began we cannot find, but thus began the custom of mixing wine with water. Although Mohammed forbade his followers to drink intoxicating beverages, still when they do, they mix them with water, saying a prayer as did the Jews.

Vinegar, "sour" or "black wine," was also called wine.[2] and mixed with water it was drunk.[3] It was offered Christ on the cross, but he refused it because being a Nazarite, he was forbidden by the Law to take it.[4]

Wine, water, oil and fluids the Jews kept in large earthen vessels the Romans called ampulæ, sometimes holding a barrelful. When filled with wine, they were sealed with clay, a cloth was stretched over the mouth of those holding oil, but when filled with water some aromatic herbs were scattered over the surface to keep it sweet. Later the mouth of the ampula was made smaller, and became our jug. The water Christ changed into wine was poured into six large ampulæ.

The first drinking vessel was a simple cup, later a handle was added at the side. A large cup found in the ruins of Troy, now in the museum of Athens, once belonging to Agamemnon is of massive solid gold. Wine-cups, shaped like the calyx of a lily are seen on the monuments of Persepolis and other places, showing that the chalice was used in very olden times.[5] Arabs of our day use drinking vessels of red earthenware like a vase, four holes being in the bottom of the deep lip so the

---

[1] Deut. xxxii 42; Psalm lxiv 10; Isaias v. 11, 22; xxviii 1, xxix 9, xlix 26; Jer vii 14, xxv 27. [2] Ruth ii. 14 [3] Numb. vi. 3, 4. [4] Numb. vi. 3-20; Matt. xxvii 48 [5] III. Kings vii. 26

fluid will not flow faster than you can drink. The chalice now used at Mass is about the size and form of the vessel used at the Last Supper.

In Scripture the chalice is first found as the wine-cup into which Pharaoh's butler pressed grapes and handed to the king.[1] No doubt Noe used such a chalice, when he did not know the effects of fermented wine.

The chalice of Temple and Passover used in the former to catch the victim's blood, and at the latter to hold the wine, was called in Hebrew the cos. At Passover a large chalice, called the Gabia, was at the place of the master of the feast, while the guests used the cos. When each one had taken his three chalices of wine mixed with water, the master filled again his large chalice with wine. Then with a blessing over the vessel of water he said a prayer and mixed his wine with water. Whence the blessing and prayer are over the water at Mass and not over the wine.

Then the master drank from his large chalice, and handed it round to each guest who drank from it. This was the end of the Passover. After this fourth chalice of wine was partaken of there was no other ceremony, and the Talmud states that a dessert was forbidden. This was the chalice Christ consecrated into his Blood and gave to his Apostles the night of the Last Supper, as we will describe later.

Following the Last Supper, in the early Church, the consecrated chalice was passed to the clergy to drink from, and the deacon brought it to the laity. The custom is still seen in the Oriental churches. In Greek and Russian rites it is even given to infants. Because of abuses this was forbidden in the Latin Church and our present discipline obtained.

New let us see how honored was the water mixed with wine in the Temple ceremonial, foretelling the water mixed with Mass wine.

" There was not a court in Jerusalem that was not illuminated by the lights of the water-drawing. Pious and distinguished men danced before the people with lighted candles in their hands, and sang hymns and lauds before them, and the Levites accompanied them with harps, psalteries, cymbals and numberless musical instru-

[1] Gen xl 11.

ments.   On the fifteen steps, which led into the women's court, corresponding to the fifteen Psalms of Degrees, stood the Levites with their musical instruments and sang. At the upper gate, which leads down from the court of Israel to the women's court, stood two priests with trumpets.

" When the cock first crowed, they blew a blast, a long note, and a blast.   This they repeated when they reached the tenth step, and again the third time when they got into the court.   They went on blowing their trumpets as they went, until they reached the gate that leads out to the east, when they turned westward with their faces towards the Temple and said : ' Our ancestors, who were in this place, turned their backs on the Temple of the Lord, and their faces towards the east, for they worshiped the sun towards the east, but we lift our eyes to God. We belong to God and raise our eyes to God.' [1]

" A golden pitcher that held three logs was filled with water from the brook Siloh.   (It is now called Siloam, a little village at the south of Jerusalem).   When they came with it to the water-gate, they blew a blast, a long note, and again a blast.   The priest then ascended the stair of the altar, and turned to the left.   Two silver basins stood there.   R. Jehudah said they were of gipsum, but had a dark appearance from the wine.   Each was perforated with a small hole at the bottom like a nostril, the one for the wine somewhat wider, the one for water narrower, that both might be emptied at once.   The one to the west was used for water, the other to the east for the wine." [2]

" He who has not witnessed the rejoicings at the water-drawing has through his whole life witnessed no real rejoicing.   At the expiration of the first holiday of the festival, they descended into the women's court, where a great transformation was made.   Golden candelabra were placed there, with four basins at the top of each, and four ladders were put to each candelabra, on which stood four lads from the rising youth of the priesthood, holding jars of oil containing a hundred and twenty logs, with which they replenished each basin."

The Talmud says the Hebrew maidens used to give a

[1] Babyl, Talmud, Tract Succah. 77.   [2] Babyl, Talmud, Tract Succah, 72.

dance in the vineyards, and the young men went to see them and choose their future wives. "Never were there any more joyous festivals in Israel than the 15th of Abib (the day Christ was crucified) and the Day of Atonement, for on them the maidens of Jerusalem used to go out dressed in white garments—borrowed ones, however, in order not to cause shame to those who had none of their own. The king's daughter borrowed from the daughter of the high priest, the daughter of the latter would borrow from the daughter of the Segan, assistant high priest, the Segan's daughter borrowed from the daughter of the priest who was anointed for war,[1] and she in turn would borrow from the daughter of an ordinary priest. The daughter of the ordinary Israelites would borrow one from another, in order not to put to shame those who had no clothes of their own[2]

"These clothes were to be previously washed, and thus the maidens went out and danced in the vineyards, saying: ' Young men, look and observe well whom you are about to choose as a spouse, regard not beauty alone but rather look to a virtuous family, 'for false is grace, and vain is beauty, a woman that feareth the Lord shall be praised.'[3]

" The pretty ones among the maidens would say : ' Regard but beauty alone, because a woman is made for beauty alone.' Those who were of good family would say : ' Rather look to a good family, for women are made but to bear children, and those of good family produce good children.' The homely ones would say : ' Make your selections only for the glory of heaven, but provide liberally for us.' "[4]

The Talmud says that to this dance in the vineyards, when the wine finished fermenting, made by men treading the grapes red with must or grape juice, relate the words of Solomon foretelling Christ in his scourging all covered with blood and crowned with thorns: " Go forth ye daughters of Sion, and see the King, ' The Peaceful '[5] in the diadem wherewith his mother[6] crowned him in the day of his espousals."[7]

The Mosaic law forbade members of different tribes to

[1] Deut xxi. 2   [2] See Babylonian Talmud, Taanith, iv. 80-81.   [3] Prov. xxxi 30
[4] Babylonian Talmud, Tract Taanith, Feasting, near end.   [5] Solomon in Hebrew is " The Peaceful "   [6] The Jewish people.   [7] Cant. of Cant. iii 11.

intermarry, but on this day of the dance the prohibition was removed, says the Talmud.[1] At a dance the 15th of Abib, in the vineyard, one of Christ's ancestors, Joachim, married into Aaron's family, for he who was to be sacrificed this 15th day of Abib was not only a Prince of David's royal race, but also a Temple priest. He therefore combined in his personality royalty, priesthood, and united the glories of the Temple with the dynasty of Hebrew kings.

Rabbi Simeon, son of that Gamaliel, who was St. Paul's teacher, in a Mishna of the Talmud, gives the following as a fragment of the maidens' song:[2]

> " Around in circle gay, the Hebrew maidens see
> From them our happy youths their partners choose.
> Remember, beauty soon its charms must loose
> And seek to win a maid of fair degree.
>
> When fading grace and beauty low are laid,
> Then praise shall her who fears the Lord await.
> God doth bless her handiwork—and in the gate
> Her works do follow her, it shall be said."

Now let us see the origin and history of the holy oil with which Christ anointed the apostles at the Last Supper, and which is used in the administration of the Sacraments.

From remotest times came down the custom of anointing with oil persons, objects and religious articles. When Jacob saw the ladder like a cross, reaching from earth to heaven, God resting at the top—a vision of the Crucified he set up the stone pillow as a monument " pouring oil on it."[3]

When God blessed him, foretelling that from him would be born races and kings, Jacob " set up a monument of stone, in the place where God spoke to him pouring drink-offerings upon it, wine and water, and pouring oil thereon, and called the place Bethel " House of God."[4]

God told Moses to anoint the tabernacle with all its utensils. With a special holy oil Aaron, his sons and priests of his family were ordained to the priesthood. With oil Samuel anointed Saul and David to be rulers

---

[1] See Babyl Talmud, Taanith iv 91   [2] See Migne, Cursus Comp. S. Scripturæ, iii. 1163, on Hebrew poetry.   [3] Gen xxviii 18   [4] Gen. xxxv. 14-15.

over Israel. Every official of church or state—priest, Levite, rabbi, or judge was inducted into his office with laying on of hands and anointed with oil, in Christ's day.

These officials foretold the Messiah; Christ "the Anointed," Jesus "Jehovah will Save," the "Hope of Israel, the "Expectation of the nations," who was to come and built an empire of religion spreading over all the earth.

From far beyond historic times oils, unguents, pomades, or perfumed mixtures had been used to anoint the body,[1] beautify the complexion and cure blemishes. But these differed from the holy mixture Moses made by God's command.

The Temple sacred oil was composed of myrrh, cinnamon, cassia and olive oil mixed in mystic manner. With it priest, king, and all Temple furniture were anointed. In Greek this mixture was called chrism from the word chrio, "to anoint," foretelling the Saviour, in Greek the Christ, in Hebrew the Messiah, "The Anointed," not with oil but with the sevenfold gifts of the Holy Spirit.[2]

This holy mixture was so sacred, that they were forbidden to use it except as laid down in the law, and the one who would give it to the stranger would be killed.[3] A hundred and eighty times it is mentioned in the Old Testament. Let us see the materials of this chrism.[4]

Myrrh, in Hebrew mor, eleven times found in the Old Testament, was one of the gifts the Persian high priests offered Christ to foretell his death,[5] as its Greek name, smyrna, shows us. The prophecy was fulfilled when the soldiers offered him, on the cross wine mixed with myrrh,[6] and when it was used to embalm his body.[7] Herodotus writes the Egyptians when embalming used to fill the abdomen of the dead with myrrh.[8]

According to Herodotus,[9] the tree producing myrrh, both wild and cultivated, grows in Arabia. In Egypt it was called bal, in the Sanscrit bola, in India bol, in Arabia myrrh; showing how ancient was the use of myrrh.

Travellers in Arabia describe the gum exuding from

[1] Migne, Cursus Comp. iii 1131; Edersheim, Sketches, 47; Life of Christ. 1, 565, 566   [2] Isaias li 2.   [3] Exod. xxx 33.   [4] Migne, Cursus Comp. ii 1341 [5] Matt. ii. 11.   [6] Mark xv. 23.   [7] John xix. 39.   [8] Euterpe ii. 86   [9] III. 107; Dioscorides, I 77; Theophrastus, ix 4, Sec 1; Diodorus II 49, Strabo, Pliny, etc

the bark of the *Balsamodendron myrrha*, a low thorny ragged-looking tree, with bright trifoliated leaves like an acacia tree of the desert. The tree is related to the citrous family on one side, and to the spruces on the other.

The yellow soft gum exudes through the bark, especially when wounded, dries and becomes dark reddish, brittle or brown according to age. It has an aromatic scent, easily dissolves in alcohol, and may be triturated in water. From remotest times it was used internally as a medicine, and externally for skin diseases, sores and ulcers. Powdered and mixed with wine, it became a soporific, deadened pain, and was given criminals about to be executed to ease their pains. This was the reason the soldiers offered it to Christ, who refused it because he would not deaden his sufferings with any anæsthetic, and because he was a Nazarite, and forbidden wine.

Balm, or balsam, "medicinal gum," or according to the Hebrew *tsori*, "royal oil," was one of the articles the Ismaelite caravan was bringing to Egypt, when his brothers sold Joseph to them.[1] Jacob sent a present of balm, storax, myrrh, turpentine, etc., to Joseph prime minister of Egypt, not knowing he was his son.[2] This balm grew in Galaad, and was used as a medicine by the Hebrews. Jeremias, foretelling the calamities which will fall on the Jews, asks: "Is there no balm in Galaad, or is there no physician there? Why then is not the wound of my daughter closed?"[3]

This balm, used as a medicine, was imported into Egypt, Tyre and along the coasts of the Mediterranian Sea. Luther translated the word by "salve," "ointment," "mastic." The Jewish rabbis Junius and Tremellius use the words balm or balsam, and say its Hebrew word, *tsori*, means the mastic tree of which the botanic name is *Pistacia lentiscus*. Others hold it is the *Amyris opobalsamum*—the balsam of Mecca. Dr. Hooker identifies it with the Balanites, he saw growing at Jericho.[4]

When in the spring of 1903 the writer visited Jericho, now a little village, with its four hotels, he saw the shrub

---

[1] Gen xxxvii 25   [2] Gen xlii 11   [3] Jeremias viii 22   See xlvi. 11 ; Eccl. xxiv 20, Ezech. xxvii 17.   [4] See Edersheim, Life of Christ, vol ii., p. 350

growing in the gardens irrigated by the waters of the great spring higher up, to the west, bursting from the desert, under the Lenten Mountain, where Christ fasted forty days. You will also notice there the Rhamnus, a low shrub covered with long sharp thorns with which they made the thorny crown for Christ

In the desert round the Dead Sea, and down through Arabia grows the Balanites Egyptiaca, a low evergreen shrub with numerous branches and a few small leaves. These desert plants, in place of sap, have gum like the desert plants of western America. This plant was cultivated in Palestine at Jericho "Fragrant", at Engaddi "the Goat's-spring," in the ravines to the west of the Dead Sea, in the Arabian deserts, but especially around Mecca and Medina

Wood and leaves are filled with balm. The flowers have a sweet scent, the fruit is like a little unripe walnut covered with a dry skin, but filled with a fluid as thick as honey, with a sharp and bitter taste. The Arabs gather these nuts, pound them in a mortar, and put the pulp into boiling water. When the oil rises to the top, it is skimmed off, and used internally for disease, and externally for wounds and skin troubles. This is the best and purest Balm

During the summer season, they cut the bark with glass or flint, for steel knives kill the shrub. The white gum oozes out, soon turns green, then like amber, and finally becomes like solidified honey. It has a strong, but agreeable odor, and a bitter and astringent taste When burned its smell is strikingly sweet and penetrating, filling the whole place with its agreeable perfume It is the basis of the incense used in Church functions.

These "principal and chosen spices,"[1] as St. Jerome says the Chaldaic and Septuagint versions of the Bible mean, distilled with all the science then known, mixed with olive oil, formed the chrism, with which in Moses' day all the ministers, the tabernacle and its furniture were anointed.

The priesthood of the Temple of the time of Christ were looked on as inferior in honor among the people to the priests of the days of David and Solomon. The syna-

[1] Exod xxx 23.

gogue Rabbis were held in higher esteem by some than Temple priests. The second Temple had not the flask of holy chrism handed down from Aaron's day in Solomon's Temple, for Jeremias had hid the ark in a cave on Mount Nebo, where Moses died, which they could not find.[1] Priests were set apart for their ministry by vesting them in their sacerdotal robes and imposing hands on their heads—they claimed that the anointment of their fathers with the holy oil in the first Temple was sufficient for their sons in the priesthood[2]

Jewish physicians used to anoint the sick with olive oil mixed with wine. R. Simeon Ben Elieser says: "R. Meir permitted the mingling of wine and oil and to anoint the sick on the Sabbath. But when once he was sick and we would do the same to him he would not allow it."[3] They anointed the head for headache[4] and they still use oil in the East for boils, etc.[5] We see that when St. James[6] gave the doctrine of the sacrament of extreme-unction, anointing the sick was not unknown to the early Christians converted from Judaism.

After imposing their hands on the head of the high priest to be consecrated as we have described, they poured the holy chrism on his head which was to wear the Aaronic miter. The Machabee priest-kings had made the miter into the form of a tiara with triple crown from which came the Pope's tiara. They poured the holy oil on his head so the ointment might flow down on his beard, to honor that mark of manhood, they incensed at the Passover.[7] From that ceremonial comes down to us the rite of anointing the bishop on his head when he is consecrated.

The first blessing God gave mankind was on marriage.[8] Afterwards the patriarchs blessed with the laying on of hands. Later oil and chrism were added to the imposition of hands, to more clearly signify the Holy Spirit on Christ. Priest, Levite, king, prophet, Judge of the Sanhedrin, and rabbi were thus ordained, set apart, or inducted into office.

In his last sickness, Jacob laid his hands on the heads

---

[1] Mach. ii 4   [2] See Geikie, Life of Christ, i 81   [3] Talmud in Hor. Heb II 415.
[4] Pliny, xxiii 38.   [5] Russeger's Travels, I. 247   [6] v 13-15   [7] Psalm cxxxii. 2.
[8] Gen. i. 28.

of his two grandsons, his arms forming a cross.[1] Moses
extending his hands over Egypt, brought signs and
plagues, which forced proud Pharao to let the Hebrews
depart. The laying on of hands by which spiritual power
is given was carried out in the ordination of the Temple
priesthood.

In the days of David from Eleasar, Aaron's son, had
descended sixteen courses of priests,[2] and from his
brother Ithamar, eight families came. These David
divided into the twenty-four "courses" of the Temple.
From these families the priests were chosen with greatest
care lest the young man might have a blemish of body or
defect of mind.

The young candidate, chosen in his thirtieth year,
bathed, shaved and anointed with olive oil, brought his
two goats to the Temple, stood before the Holies, having
two cakes of unfermented bread in his hands. The high
priest sprinkled him with water. He prostrated himself
on the ground before the Shekina of his fathers, his face
to the earth. Three times he makes the prostration.
This was the reason Christ prostrated himself in the
garden before he offered his sacrifice of the cross. This
is why the clergy prostrate themselves during the ceremony of ordination in our churches.

The young priest rises to his knees, crosses his arms
on his breast and the Temple priests impose their hands
on him their arms crossed like Jacob blessing Joseph's
sons.[3] He puts his sins on the two goats, the priests
sacrifice them and splash their blood on the horns of the
altar to foretell the cross. They take the flesh to be
burned outside the walls, to foretell Christ sacrificed and
buried outside Jerusalem.[4]

They put the blood of the victims on the young priest's
right ear, thumb and great toe. They mix the blood to
show the two natures of Christ, and with it they sprinkle
him and his vestments.[5] They anoint him on the head
with the holy chrism, place in his hands the flesh of the
sacrifice dripping with blood, and cakes of unfermented
bread.[6]

---

[1] Gen. xlviii. 13.   [2] Numb 60.   [3] Gen. xlviii 13   [4] Exod xxix. 10-14; Levit.
viii. 2, 3, 11, 17.   [5] Levit. iv 3, 5, 16, vi 15; Psalm cxxxii. 2.   [6] Exod. xxix.
19-34, Levit. viii. 32-36, etc.

To the young Levite they gave the symbols of his ministry, the sacrificial vessels, and the keys of the Temple gates. The latter he placed over a stone flag in the Beth ha Mocked each night on which a priest slept. These are the reasons, the keys, chalice, etc, are handed to the candidates for minor orders and subdeaconship while receiving these orders.

The Lord was anointed in an invisible manner by the Holy Spirit with his sevenfold gifts.[1] But was he anointed with oil as were king, priest, rabbi and judge who foretold him in ceremonial and office? He was anointed in this very visible manner, and he anointed his apostles the same way at the Last Supper when he consecrated them bishops.

On the fertile western shores of the Sea of Galilee, so rich as to be called the " Udder of the Land," at a place where then rose an ancient watch-tower called Migdol-El, " God's Tower," around which spread fertile fields where they raised wheat for the proposition Temple bread, was born to a wealthy Jewish family, Lazarus, Martha, and Mary, the latter being called the Magdalen from Magdala, the Greek name of the tower.

She married a strict Pharisee, Paphus, who devorced her because of adultery with a soldier Pandira, and with the latter she took up her residence in the neighboring city Herod had built on the site of an ancient cemetery on the shores of that Lake, seven hundred feet below the ocean level, which he called Tiberias, after the then reigning Roman emperor. There she lived in sin with soldiers of the garrison, till as the woman taken in adultery, she was brought before Christ who drove seven demons out of her and told her to sin no more.[2]

Healed and repentant she went back to her home in Bethany, and lived with her brother and sister. When the Sabbath before the Passion ended with sunset, Simon gave a banquet in Christ's honor in his house, a few blocks west of Lazarus' house. With the other guests the Lord reclined at the table on the couch, his feet stretched out as was the custom at feasts. Mary Magdalen came to anoint him. What kind of anointment was it?

The spikenard of olive oil mixed with many rare per-

[1] Isaias xi 1, etc.   [2] See Talmud, John viii. 8, 4.

fumes was for sale in costly carved alabaster flasks in cities of the Roman empire, but at such a price that only members of royal families and wealthy people could buy it. Mary being of a rich noble family, some writers say she was of royal stock, bought a " box " holding about a pound of this ointment and came to Jesus' feet, which first she washed with bitter tears for her sins, and wiped with her hair hanging down, sign of the harlot among the Hebrews.

The strict Pharisees found fault for they knew her. Judas complained of the price.[1] Christ reproved them because they did not anoint his head as was the custom at formal feasts,[2] and Mary poured the precious ointment on his head,[3] and the whole house was filled with the odor of the ointment.[4]

Thus as priest and king, and rabbi, and judge in Israel were anointed,[5] so was the Lord anointed by the woman who was a great sinner. And Jesus said : " Let her alone that she may keep it against the day of my burial."[6] They prepared the Lord's body for the grave with spices, myrrh, aloes, balsamodendron, resin of aquilaria, agallochum and perfumes, and this preparation the Greeks called *migma*, the Jews *chanat*, or *chunetto*, meaning to become " red like tanned leather."

During the feasts of Israel, especially at the Passover, the chamber was perfumed with myrrh, aloes and cinnamon.[7] Precious unguents were poured on the heads of guests. Anointing guests at these banquets, became such an abuse in the days of the prophets, that Amos denounced them.[8] Twenty-seven times in the Old, and fourteen time in the New Testament, ointment will be found.

From apostolic times down the centuries in all the Liturgies the bishop blesses the holy oils at Mass on Holy Thursday. In the Greek and kindred Rites the oil is mixed with thirty-two perfumes. He is attended by the lower clergy or altar boys, seven subdeacons, seven deacons and twelve priests. From Jewish customs, Oriental Rites and the unchanging Roman Church, we are

[1] Luke vii. 36-46.   [2] Luke vii 46   [3] Mark xiv 3   [4] John xii 3   [5] Migne, Cursus Completus, S Scripturæ, iii, 923-924   [6] John xii. 7.   [7] Proverbs vii. 10-17.   [8] Amos vi 4, 5, 6, 7.

forced to conclude that Christ blessed the oils at the Last Supper. There is no other way of explaining that rite, so old and universal.

" And the Lord said to Moses. Take unto thee spices, stacte, and oncha, galbanum of sweet savor, and the clearest of frankincense, all shall be of equal weight,[1] and thou shall make incense compounded by the work of the perfumer." That was the way they made the incense mentioned seventy-three times in the Bible. Let us see the materials of which it was compounded.[2]

Stacte, or storax, is a liquid, resinous, fatty matter, very odoriferous, of the nature of liquid myrrh and of great value. It comes from the officinalis tree of the styraceous family of plants related to the Canadian, Peruvian and Mecca balsams. It belongs to the same family and looks like the balsam spruces of America. This tree grows in Arabia and Asia Minor. Quantities of this balsam are shipped from Triste and ports of the Orient. It has a vanilla odor, and is closely related to benzoin. It was one of the spices the Ismaelite caravan was carrying to Egypt when they bought Joseph[3] and is translated myrrh in the Bible.

Onycha is a product of India, as Dioscorus says. It[4] gives forth a strong sweet perfume, which when burned fills the whole building with beautiful fragrance.

The cassia, or stacta, " a drop," in Hebrew *kiddah*, " to cleave," " to tear lengthwise," is the product of a reed growing in shallow waters. Twice Herodotus uses the word, and says the Arabs gather it in shallow lakes.[5]

Dioscorus mentions several kinds of cassia, and writes that they are produced in " Spicy Arabia." One kind, known under the name of mosyletis, or mosylos, is so called from the ancient city of Mosyllon, on the coast of Africa, near the present Cape Guardafui, from which it originally came. Much has been written regarding the plant and its products, entailing considerable confusion.

The plant belongs to the family of the leguminosa, is related to senna, and resembles the flag called " cat-tail." It grows in wet places and resembles " sweet flag." The root is aromatic, with a pleasant taste and a beautiful

---

[1] Exod. xxx. 34. [2] Geikie, Life of Christ, i 91 ; Migne, ii 869. [3] Gen xxxvii. 25.   [4] Lib. ii ch. 8   [5] Herodotus II , 86, III. 110.

8

perfume.   From remote times it was used as a cathartic, but the species called fistula furnishes the medicine.

Cinnamon, mentioned five times in the Bible, comes from a native tree of Ceylon.   The bark yields an oil with a strong perfume and it was used as a medicine. This oil is very strong.   God told Moses to use only half as much as myrrh.   From beyond historic times caravans from India brought all kinds of perfumes and spices to the west of Asia, Egypt and Europe.[1]

The calamus *Acorus calamus* called " sweet-flag " in this country, mentioned eight times in the Old Testament, is " the bruised reed Christ was foretold not to break." [2]   It grows in marshy places, has aromatic roots, which bruised yields the calamus of commerce.   In the middle ages, they strewed the floors of the cathedrals and churches with the flags, and wove them into mats, rugs and carpets.   The calamus has a strong aromatic taste, is slightly acrid and from early time has been used as a stimulant and for indigestion.   It is still mixed with candy and perfumers use it.

Galbanum is a resin-gum of the Ferula tree, belonging to the umbellifera species of plants, growing in India and the Orient.   Its gum oozes out like yellowish brown, or blue tears, or white drops like tears.   In Moses' day it was used as a medicine, internally to stimulate, and externally as a plaster.   When burned it produces a pungent, agreeable odor.

Frankincense, called in medicine olibanum, is a resinous gum produced by the *Boswellia serrata* of India and the East.   It is shipped now from Calcutta in round lumps, or tears, of a pale yellowish color.   The grains are translucent, but covered with a whitish powder, caused by friction.   It has an acrid bitter taste, and softens when chewed.   It burns with a fragrant odor.   Maimonides says it was used in the Temple as incense to conceal the smell of the sacrificed flesh   These, mentioned thirty-four times in the Old Testament, when mixed formed the incense used in tabernacle and Temple.   They have been used in Christian churches from the time of the Apostles.

The smoke of incense ascending up before the Lord in

[1] Gen. xxxvii. 25.   [2] Isaias xlii. 3.

the Temple at Passover, and in the Church, typified the prayers of Christ, and of his saints, offered up unto the eternal Father "Incense ground to finest powder is, like our good works, ground in our hearts as in a mortar.[1]

"Incense we make of aromatics, which we offer at the altar, showing forth a multitude of works of virtue."[2]

"Incense is the body made holy through temperance, a bridle for reason, and in our body formed of four elements. Stacte referred to water. Oncha typified earth dried up in desert lands, that is, mankind without grace; galbanum burning with fire, the scorching sun drying up the desert."[3]

"And there was given him much incense that he should offer of the prayers of the saints upon the golden altar, which is before the throne of God." "And golden vials full of odors which are the prayers of the saints."[4]

The Temple incense was prepared of the four ingredients mentioned,[5] with which, the Rabbis say, seven other materials were added, and a smaller quantity of the herb "Ambra" to give out a dense smoke—368 pounds of this mixture being made at once, and half a pound was used at the morning and evening services. The formula of mixing this incense was a secret of the Abtinas family.

While the lamb was being slain, they played the Magrephah, and priests and Levites hastened to their places for their service of sacred song. The priest chosen to offer incense in the Holies, who could officiate only once in his life, with the gold censer hanging from its chains, mounts to great sacrificial altar, fills it with burning coals, takes more live coals in a gold dish, with an assistant on each side, like the deacon and subdeacon with the priest ascending to our altar; vested in magnificent vestments, they slowly mount the marble steps to the Holies, and enter behind the veil.

The priest chosen by "lot" for that function, most sacred Temple ceremony except that of the high priest the Day of Atonement, with his two ministers, one on either side, like the deacon and subdeacon at a high Mass, enter the Holies, reverently spread the live coals on the altar of

---

[1] St. Gregory, in fine, I Moral. [2] St. Gregory, Lib. Moral, 39. [3] St. Basil, in Isaias, C. I. [4] Apoc. v. 8. [5] Exod xxx. 34.

gold, sprinkle it on the censer, and the two ministers retire, leaving the priest alone in the sacred sanctuary of the Lord of hosts.[1]

The lone priest, image of the Priest of mankind, Jesus Christ, offering prayer while on earth to his heavenly Father before his death, swings the censer three times to the west, over the smoking altar, towards the Holy of Holies, dwelling-place of the Shekina, the Holy Spirit, and then over each side, and at the two ends of the altar, each movement with mystic meaning, saying:

> " Let my prayer be directed as incense in thy sight,
> The lifting up of my hands as evening sacrifice.
> Set watch, O Lord, before my mouth,
> And a door round about my lips,
> Incline not my heart to evil words
> To make excuses in sins." [2]

The Jewish priest thus prayed alone in the Holy of Holies, and no one for him prayed, for he figured Jesus Christ, who wants no prayers, for he had no sin,[3] as St. Augustine says, " He is the Lord Jesus Christ, the only Priest and the only Mediator between God and men." [4]

On that altar of gold within the gold-walled Holies, image of the sanctuary of our Church from which Christ through his priest offers the Eucharistic Sacrifice, only incense was offered, the animals were sacrificed without, in the Priests' Court, for Christ is not slain now in our Church in a painful and bloody manner, as he was that fatal Friday by the Jewish priesthood. But on the Day of Atonement, the high priest reddened the horns of that gold altar with the blood of the victims, to foretell that the sacrifice of Calvary and of the Mass are identical.

Let us now describe a scene which took place in the Holies when the Jewish Church was about to pass into the glories of the Catholic Church.

Early morning of the 24th of September, six months before Gabriel " God is mighty " appeared in the holy house of Nazareth to the Virgin espoused to Joseph, to announce the Incarnation, the " iot " drawn by the Temple superintendent fell on Zachary " Jehovah is re-

---

[1] See Edersheim, Life of Christ, vol i 137, 138 ; Geikie, Life of Christ, i 91, 92, 210, etc. [2] Psalm cxl. 2 to 4 [3] I. Kings, ii. 25. [4] St Augustine, Enar, ii. in Ps. xxxvi.. Ser. ii. n. xx.

nowned," son of that Barachias Christ said the Jews had
killed between the altar and the Temple [1] For the first
and last time he was to offer that sacred incense.   He
was of the course Abia, " the eighth " of the twenty-four
divisions of the priests.   He had married Elizabeth " God
of the covenant ; " his home was about four miles northwest of Jerusalem, down in the valley on the side hill
facing north, just beyond the little village now called St.
John's.

They were both old and childless, a great disgrace in
these days, when every mother hoped and prayed that
she might bring forth the long-looked for Saviour.
Zachary had just returned from a three months' retreat,
spent with the Essenes, at their house built under the
cliff on the north side of the ravine, about a mile up from
Jericho, in the side of the Lenten mountain, where later
Christ fasted.   There he had spent his days praying
for an heir.   He had returned to the city, for it was
the time his course of Abia was to go on duty in the
Temple

Early in the morning from the tower on Olivet's top,
the priests announced that the sun illumined the tombs
of the patriarchs at Hebron, then that the sun was rising
over Nebo, where Moses' body reposed   The high priest
ordered the lamb brought from the Beth-Moked chamber,
where they had kept it for four days ; others bring the gold
and silver vessels, ninety-three in number, they examine
the lamb again for blemishes, water it out of a gold cup—
all this to foretell there would be no stain of sin on Christ,
and also to foretell the vinegar and gall they gave to drink
to Him the Jewish court had condemned to death four
days before that fatal crucifixion Friday.   They fasten the
lamb to the second row of hooks on the pillar at the north
of the altar, his feet tied with a cord to make a cross, his
head to the south, its face to the west, for so faced Christ
when sacrificed   The sign is given to open the great
gates with three blasts on the silver trumpets which had
replaced the ram's horns of the tabernacle, and vast
crowds of people fill the Courts.   The lamb is slain, its
blood put on the horns of the outside altar in the form
of a cross, and the priest Zachary was about to offer the

[1] Matt. xxiii 35 ; Luke xi. 51.

daily incense in the Holies He represented the foretold Christ, who was once to offer himself for mankind's wickedness.

Zachary, clothed in magnificent vestments, went up the inclined passage on the south side to the great altar, holding in his right hand the censer with its three chains. He scraped up the burning coals in a gold vessel called the *teni*, put them in the censer and came down. While he did this his two assistants trimmed the lamps of the great golden candlestick, poured into each olive oil, fixed the wicks made from worn-out vestments and lighted them. But the central middle lamp which bent towards the Holy of Holies could be lighted only from the ever-burning fire on the sacrificial altar.

The great organ, the Magrephah, began the music, the priests and Levites took their places—the first on the steps leading up to the Holies, the second on the steps of the Nicanor Gate, as Zachary with his two assistants ascend the steps preceded by the two priests who had dressed the gold altar, and the candlestick, and who had removed the vessels of their ministry and returned. One of the assistants spread the live coals on the altar, the other arranged the incense, and all retired leaving Zachary alone within that sanctuary before the altar, imaging the priest standing before our altar offering the Mass with its prayers, ceremonies and incense.

As the high priest without gives the sign, deep silence fell on the vast throng of priests and Levites while people prostrated themselves, fell down on their faces and bent the body down to the pavement Zachary spread the incense on the burning coals, and the smoke ascended up before the Lord of hosts, prophesying the prayers and sacrifice of Jesus and his Saints.[1]

Thus Zachary offered the incense,[2] most holy and solemn Temple function.[3] "When therefore," says S. Augustine, the "father priest, trembling, stood at the divine altar, Gabriel the angel suddenly cleaving the air stood beside him, now trembling when he saw the vision standing at the right side of the altar of incense. And Zachary seeing him was troubled and fear fell upon him.

[1] See Apoc viii. 1 to 4   [2] Luke i 5 to 23.   [3] Edersheim, Temple, 188 to 139.

But the angel said to him : " Fear not, Zachary, for thy prayer is heard, and thy wife Elizabeth shall bear thee a son, and thou shalt call his name John. And thou shalt have joy and gladness and many shall rejoice at his birth." [1]   The angel called him John " The Pius."

St Augustine tells us that Zachary was a faded, withered up old man, and that was the reason he did not believe the words of Gabriel " God is mighty," who in all Jewish history was in God's ministry to comfort Hebrews with revelations of the Incarnation [2]

Thus in the Holies, the golden sanctuary with its massive gold altar foretelling the sanctuary of our churches, was revealed the birth of John the Baptist, last of the great men of the Old Testament and first Evangelist of the New Testament. He was, said Christ, the greatest man born of woman,[3] prophet, priest, preacher, rabbi and martyr, who like the great men of olden days prepared the way for Christ preached the forgiveness of sins, and baptized the Lord.

When Herod killed the Bethlehem infants, all Judea was in a ferment of fear for her children, and they hid John in a cave they show under the house where his parents lived. When John was in his twelfth year they brought him to the Temple, priests imposed their hands on him with the Taleth vestments and confirmed him, the ceremony admitting him into the ranks of the men. Then he retired to the desert west of his home where he lived on locusts and wild honey as a hermit in watchings, prayers and fastings, clothed in one garment of camel's hair.

When John was thirty he came forth from his solitude to preach. As was the custom of the Rabbis of that day he gathered twelve disciples round him—one being that Simon who wished to buy the Holy Ghost with money and who later opposed Peter in his travels and at Rome. To Jordan's banks he came in the form and spirit of Elias who centuries before had ascended to heaven on the fiery chariot of the Lord from that very spot.

Before beginning his public ministry at the age of thirty

[1] Luke i. 12, 13, 14, etc.   [2] St. Augustin, Serm. LX in Nat. Joan Bap., i , n. lx ; Dutripon, Con. S. Scripturæ ; Smith's Dict. Gabriel, John the Baptist, etc.   [3] Luke vii 28

Jesus came to John at Galgal, " the Circle," where the Hebrews crossed to take possession of the Promised Land, where Josue built the monument of twelve stones in memory of the miracle of the waters sweeping south toward the Dead Sea turning back to let them cross.

There where the river sweeps round in a half circle, amid the tamarisks lining its desert shores, Jesus passed through the throngs, went down into the waters John baptized him and told his disciples he was the " Lamb of God who would take away the sins of the world," [1] and John's disciples followed from that time the Lord and became the apostles

John still continued to preach.   One day Herod Agrippa, passing from his capital, Tiberias, nestling on the western shores of Galilee, going on his way to his winter home east of the Dead Sea, passed where John was preaching. He had seduced the wife of his half brother Philip, then living in retirement in Jerusalem, divorced his own wife, daughter of Aretis the Arabian king, and was then living with that base woman, Herodias, in adultery.

Before the multitude John said it was against the law of Moses to live with his brother's wife.   Stung to the quick before the people Herod had him arrested and carried to his fortress Macarius, Josephus so minutely describes as having been built in the desert where the sulphur springs burst forth from desert sands.

At Macarius Herod celebrated his birthday with a great feast for his nobles and officers,[2] and during the banquet his half-niece Salome, daughter of the woman he was living with and his half brother Philip, half clothed danced the immodest suggestive Egyptian dance, and Herod half drunk, charmed with her graces promised her, before his guests, whatever she would ask, even half his kingdom.   Prompted by her adulterous mother Herodias, she asked the head of John the Baptist on a salver.

Pretending to be saddened that the banquet should be the scene of such a bloody murder, but remembering his oath before his guests, he gave the sign to his guards standing round the banquet hall. They went down to the deep dungeon, cut off John's head, brought the ghastly

[1] John i 29. [2] Mark vi. 21, 22.

trophy to the wicked woman Salome and she gave it to her mother.

All orientals honored the beard, called in Hebrew *zaqan*, a word found seven times in the Old Testament. God forbade the Hebrews to shave. "Nor shall you cut your hair roundwise, nor shave your beard."[1] This law was for all the people, but a special rule was laid down for priests, "Neither shall they shave their head, nor their beard, nor make incisions in their flesh."[2]

All Hebrews wore long beards, which they might trim, but not shave all off, nor trim in peculiar shapes like the heathens of that time. Egyptian priests cut their hair round. Pagans, when dedicated to their gods, cut the hair in peculiar shapes, sometimes forming a circle, as Empedocles said: "God is a circle, his center is everywhere without a circumference." To express that idea they often built their temples round, like the Pantheon, the vestals' shrine Numa built, and many other temples of that time.

Heathens dedicated their hair to idols or demons, and Hebrews dedicated their hair and beard to God. Many ancient religious ceremonies we find among the heathens relating to the beard. To preserve the Hebrews from these superstitions God forbade them to shave head or beard.

The leper shaved his whole body,[3] as a sign of his disease, while the Hebrew wore a long beard as a mark of manhood, virtue, perfection, strength and wisdom.

The Nazarite "Separated" never cut his hair or beard, to show that he was dedicated to God. His hair and beard were trimmed at the door of the tabernacle, at the Nicanor Gate when his vow ended.[4] This was the origin of the tonsure, a ceremony which admits a man into the ranks of the clergy of our day. Christ was the Nazarite foretold by the prophets.[5] On Monday of Passion week, he came to the Temple and received the tonsure. From apostolic custom comes down the clerical tonsure. In the early Church all the clergy wore beards, as we learn in the fathers' writings.[6] The Fourth Coun-

---

[1] Levit xix 27 [2] Levit xxi 5 [3] Levit xiv 9 [4] Numb vi 18 [5] Gen xlix 26, Deut. xxxiii 46; Lament iv 7, etc [6] Clem Alex L III Pedag C 3 Cyprian, L 3 ad Quirin Epiph Haeres, 80

cil of Carthage [1] rules " A cleric will not foster his hair
nor shave his beard "

Among the Hebrews the beard was so honored that no
one ever dared to touch it except to kiss manhood's greatest ornament as a sign of honor. Joab took Amasa by
the beard to kiss it, when he stabbed him. Hamon
shaved the heads and beards of David's ambassadors sent
to comfort him at his father's death, and that disgrace
brought on a war.[2] Arabs in ancient days shaved their
beards, and cut their hair in round forms, when they dedicated themselves to Bacchus, god of drunkenness,[3] and on
all these people of the Orient, for their superstitions, God's
condemnation was foretold.[4]

Following the Mosaic law, the beard was sacred to the
Jew, and at the time of Christ all wore beards. The
Jerusalem Jews of our day wear long ringlets of hair
hanging down before their ears, even boys after their
confirmation at twelve conform to this custom. But as
a sign of sorrow they shave off the beard and cut their
hair.

Arabs, sons of Abraham through Ismael, have the
greatest respect for the beard, which they say God gave
to distinguish men from women. They never shave. The
greatest insult offered an Arabian is to cut off his beard.
The longer the beard the more learned and venerable the
man. Wives and children still kiss the beard as a sign
of respect. They swear and make contracts by the beard;
and when they ask a favor they say, " By your beard.
By the life of your beard grant me this." " May God
deign to guard your blessed beard." " May God pour
out his blessings on your beard."

An Arab having received a serious wound in the jaw,
said he would rather die than allow the doctor to shave
off his beard, so the wound could be better attended.
When Peter the Great of Russia ordered all his subjects
to shave, he roused much opposition, and many asked
their friends to bury their beard with them. Polish Jews
looked on one who cut off his beard as having renounced
Judaism, and the rabbis preached against shaving. Moors
of Africa kiss the beard when they meet.

---

[1] Caput IV   [2] I Par. xix 4; II Kings x 4.   [3] Herodotus, Thalia, III. n. 8.
[4] Jeremias ix. 26, xxv. 23, xlix 32.

In our day when ceremonial visits are made in the
East, a servant sprays scented water, like cologne, on the
beard of the visitor.[1] When the Hebrews attended banquets at the time of Christ, a servant holding a censer in
his right hand, went from one guest to another and incensed the beard of each guest, swinging the censer up
and down before him, so the smoke rose up through his
beard. When this custom first arose we cannot find, but it
was customary at all banquets and at the Passover in the
time of Christ. This was the origin of the ceremony of
of incensing the clergy at a High Mass.

[1] D'Arvieux, Mœurs des Arabes.

THE SECOND PART.

THE MASS FORETOLD IN THE PASSOVER.

IV.—THE HISTORY OF THE HEBREW PASS-OVER.

At the Last Supper, Christ celebrated the Passover according to the historic Hebrew rite coming down from patriarchal days, Moses and the prophets, and changed it into the Mass. Let us therefore see the history of the Passover.

The word in our translations of the Bible given as phase, pascha, means the Jewish Passover. The word comes from the Hebrew *pesach*, " to pass over," because the Lord " passed over " the Israelites' houses in Egypt signed with the blood of the paschal lambs, when he killed the first-born of every family and animal the night they were delivered from slavery [1] Sts. Augustine and Jerome held it means " to suffer," [2] and foretold Christ's Passion.

Our Bible says, " It is the victim of the passage of the Lord, when he passed over the houses of the children of Israel." [3] The Hebrew word means " he leaped over " or " did not tread on " [4] But it has another meaning : " to spare " or " to show mercy to," for the Divine Son that night " spared " and " showed mercy " to the Hebrews.[5] The word Passover is given forty-seven times in the Old Testament [1]

The Passover, still held by the Jews as their greatest religious feast—the anniversary of the delivery of their fathers from Egyptian bondage, falls each year on the evening of the 14th moon of the lunar month of Ab, or Nisan " sprouting." The Rabbis call it the Tecupha

---

[1] Exod xii, 29 St Augustine Enar I in Psal lxviii Ser. I n ii Enar in Psal cxx n v Enar in Psal cxxxvii n viii [2] In Joan T lv, n I etc. Sermo xxxi, De Pascha, xi n. I [3] Exod xii, 27. [4] St Augustine, ibidem. [5] St Augustine, Enar I in Psal lxviii, Sermo I n ii iii Sermo vii De Pascha, n i etc

[6] See Migne's Cursus Comp. S. Scripturæ, vol ii., p. 182 ; vol iii 1141, etc.

" Equinox ; " the month corresponds to the last of March and the first days of April.[1] It is their Easter, the key of their calendar, and regulates all their movable feasts and fasts, as our Easter, to which it gave rise, governs our feasts, fasts, and movable seasons of the Church year.

Far beyond history, in prehistoric times, the patriarchs with roasted lamb and bread and wine celebrated the Passover. But the night of the flight from Egypt, when the Hebrews became a nation, God gave more minute details typical of the Redeemer's Passion, the crucifixion and the Mass. The prophets and holy seers of the Old Testament, directed by the Holy Ghost in Shekina form, added to the Passover ceremonial, till at the time of Christ it had become an elaborate and strikingly symbolic rite.

We must keep before our minds, that in Biblical writings, three chief objects were seen at the feast: the first night paschal lamb, the bread, the wine, and at the feast of unleaven bread, which lasted for a week, only the bread and wine. This first feast fell on Thursday the day before the crucifixion, and is forever enshrined in Christian writings under the name of the Last Supper or the Lord's Supper, which he fulfilled and changed into the Mass.[2]

As the Last Supper was that Hebrew Passover with all its elaborate ceremonial, we will first see its history, trace it down the ages, and then describe how the Samaritans and Jerusalem Jews hold the solemnity in our day.

First the Bible gives a full account of the feast,[3] as it was held in Egypt. Then the unleavened bread is mentioned with the consecration of the first-born.[4] Under the name of feast of unleaven bread, it is united with the two other great feasts of Pentecost and the Sabbath, in which the lamb, in Hebrew *taleh*, is called " My Sacrifice."[5] The festival is brought into relation with the redemption of the first-born, and the words specifying the Easter lamb[6] are repeated.[7] The same is again given regarding the days of convocation, and laws regarding the offering of the first-fruits, the Biccurim, with the offerings accompanying it when the Hebrews passed into the Promised Land.[8] Again the Shekina " The Divine Presence "

[1] Zanolini, De Festis Judaeorum, C. 4.
[2] See S Thomas, Sum, iii , q 46, Art 9 ad 1 et q 74, Art 4 ad 1, etc , etc
[3] Exod. xii. 1-51.   [4] xiii 3-10   [5] xxiii 14-19.   [6] Exod xxiii 18
[7] xxxiv. 18-26.   [8] Levit xxiii. 4-14.

repeats the law regarding the Passover at the beginning of the second year after going out of Egypt,[1] and the second Passover, a month later, is ordered for those who could not hold the first. Rules are revealed regarding offerings made on each of the seven days of the festival.[2] The last divinely given direction states the place of sacrifice the Lord will later chose in the "Land of Promise," that is where the ark rested till placed in the Temple in Jerusalem where the Passover was celebrated in Christ's time.[3] Here more minute details of the festal ceremonial are given.

On the tenth day of the month of Nisan, the Hebrews were to select the lamb, for on this day Christ was condemned to death by the Sandhedrin at Jerusalem.[4] They were told to choose a little ram and keep it till the fourteenth day of the same month, in the evening, for at midnight, following that day, 1300 years later, Christ was arrested. The paschal festival lasted a week, because during Passion week, Christ was sacrificed, lay in the tomb and rose from the dead.[5]

They sacrificed it in the afternoon, the Hebrew text having "between the two vespers." The "first vespers" among the Jews meant from noon till three, and the "second vespers" from three till night. At three in the afternoon, they were told to sacrifice the lamb, for, ages afterwards, at three o'clock, Jesus Christ, whom the lamb represented, died on the cross.

We find these two vespers mentioned in the Gospel, by the word "evening."[6] According to Hebrew ways of counting days, at sunset the next day began, and not at midnight.[7] This was the law relating to the feasts.[8] "From evening to evening you shall celebrate your sabbaths."

By the sacrifice and blood of the paschal lamb of the patriarchs, the Hebrews were delivered from Egyptian slavery. God himself laid down the ceremony of that sacrifice. The kind of lamb, the time, the place, the rite, the person to kill it, and the persons who could eat it, are all given with minute details.[9]

[1] Numb. ix. 1-14.   [2] Numb. xxviii. 16-25.   [3] Deut. xvi. 1-8.
[4] Exod xii 3   [5] Exod. xii. 6.   [6] Matt. xiv 15-28.
[7] See Levit. xxiii 5, 6.   [8] Levit. xxiii. 32.   [9] Exod. xii

Three directions God gives regarding the victim. It must be a male, for Christ was of that sex; it must be a year old, to tell that the Lord was sacrificed in the flower of his manhood; it must be without spot, stain, or blemish, to foretell the sinless Christ.[1] During night they fled from Egypt; then they were delivered from Egyptian slavery, to tell how in the last age of the Hebrew nationality in Palestine the Lord was arrested at night to be sacrificed, to deliver the world from demoniac slavery.

It was spring, the tenth day after the full moon, after the vernal equinox, when the earth is between sun and moon, so all could see, that the darkening of the sun when the Lord was dying was not caused by an eclipse; and the darkness of that Egyptian night when the Hebrews became a nation foretold the darkness at the crucifixion.

Although a lamb was ordered immolated to foretell the sinless Christ, they were allowed to sacrifice a kid as a victim for sin to shadow forth the Lord bearing the sins of the world. He was thus typified by Jacob clothed in kidskin, emblem of sin, when his father blessed him. [2] But the kid must also be a year old and without blemish.[3] The first night of the Passover these animals only could be offered. But the solemnity lasted from the 14th to the 21st day of the month of Nisan and sheep and oxen might be eaten the remaining days.[4] Each evening of that week, they held the feast in their houses and synagogues. That was the reason they would not enter Pilate's hall lest they might be defiled, and could not celebrate the remaining days of the Passover. They had all celebrated the ceremony of the paschal lamb the night before, and each night that week they were to offer the victims of peace-offerings, with wine and the unfermented bread. This week was called the feast of unleaven bread.

" Seven days you shall eat unleaven bread... The first day shall be holy and solemn, and the seventh day shall be kept with the like solemnity, you shall do no work in them, except those things that belong to eating."[5] Thus was the great Easter, a week lasting from the 14th to the

---

[1] Exod xii. 3-5.   [2] Gen xxvii 16.   [3] Exod. xii. 5, Levit. xxii, 19, 20, 21, 22.
[4] Deut xvi. 2. Numb xxviii 16, etc.   [5] Exod. xii. 15, 16.

21st, kept by the Jews in all their generations, to prophesy our Christian Easter. The first and last days were
like our solemn Sundays of Eastertide holiest time of the
Church year.[1]

The law was so strict, that the one who would not
keep the Passover was to be put to death " Whosoever
shall eat anything leaven from the first day until the
seventh day, that soul shall perish out of Israel."[2] " He
that eat leaven bread his soul shall perish out of the assembly of Israel, whether he be a stranger or born in the
land."[3] In Christ's day the penalty was excommunication.

Circumcision was a type of baptism. Only the circumcised Hebrew could eat the lamb which pointed to
Christ, and only the baptized should receive Communion.[4]

If a Hebrew were unclean, he could not partake of the
feast. He went through the ceremony of being cleansed,
and on the tenth day of the following month he could eat
the lamb, for the Christian in mortal sin must not receive
till he has been cleansed from sin by the sacrament of
Penance

Four places the lamb was sacrificed. The night the
Hebrews went out of Egypt, the head of the family slew
the lamb at the house, for the Hebrew priesthood had
not yet been established, and, as in patriarchal days, the
father of the family was then the priest.[5]

They offered the next paschal lamb in the desert of
Sinai, the second year after leaving Egypt.[6] Again, they
offered it after passing the Jordan at Galgal " the Circuit,"
as they lay camped in the deep desert valley, with the
tamarisks lining the shores of the historical river where
Christ was baptized, to foretell Christians partaking of
Communion.

After they conquered Palestine, they were told to
sacrifice the lamb only in tabernacle and Temple.
" Thou mayest not immolate the phase in any one of thy
cities, which the Lord thy God will give thee, but in the
place which the Lord thy God (the word translated here
as God is the Shekina in the original Hebrew) shall
choose that his name may dwell there. Thou shalt im-

[1] Exod. xli 17.   [2] Exod. xii. 15   [3] Exod. xii. 19.   [4] Exod. xii. 43, 44, 48.
[5] Exod. xii. 3.   [6] Numb. ix.

molate the phase in the evening, at the going down of the sun, at which time thou camest out of Egypt."[1] This command was given because the real Lamb of God, ages later, was to be sacrificed in Jerusalem, where the Temple stood. Till David chose Mount Moriah, in Jerusalem, for the site of the Temple, the tabernacle and ark of the covenant at different epochs rested at Galgal, Silo, Nobe, and Gabaon.

The night they went out of Egypt, this was the ceremonial: They cut the lamb's throat, caught the blood, " and put it on both the side-posts, and on the upper doorposts of the houses, wherein they shall eat, and they shall eat the flesh that night roasted at the fire, and unleavened bread and wild lettuce. You shall not eat anything thereof raw, nor boiled in water, but only roasted at the fire ; you shall eat the head, with the feet, and the entrails thereof. Neither shall there remain anything of it until the morning. If there be anything left you shall burn it with fire, and thus shall you eat it, you shall gird your reins, and you shall have shoes on your feet, holding staves in your hands, and you shall eat it in haste, for it is the Phase, that is the Passover of the Lord. And I will pass through the land of Egypt that night, and will kill every first-born, both man and beast. I am the Lord, and against all the gods of Egypt I will execute judgment. I am the Lord.

" And the blood shall be unto you for a sign in the houses where you shall be, and I shall see the blood and shall pass over you, and the plague shall not be upon you, to destroy you, when I shall strike the land of Egypt. And this day shall be for a memorial to you, and you shall keep it a feast to the Lord in your generations, with an everlasting observance. Seven days you shall eat unleaven bread,"[2] etc.

When Moses delivered the divine message to the Hebrews, they bowed their heads and worshiped. They followed the instructions, killed, ate the lambs, and sprinkled the blood. At midnight, the hour Christ was arrested centuries later, when he began his Passion to deliver the human race, the first-born of every family, and of every animal in Egypt was killed, as a prophecy

---

[1] Deut. xvi 5, 6.   [2] Exod. xii. 7-15.

9

of the death of the Virgin's First-born on the cross. This is the reason that Christ is called the "first-born" seven times in the New Testament.

The general impression is that God sent an angel, called the "angel of death," to kill, that night. But this is not so. For the text reads: "I am the Lord . . . I shall see the blood, and shall pass over you, and the plague shall not be upon you, when I shall strike the land of Egypt."[1]

Jewish writers, as well as these words, show that God himself killed the first-born, And reading carefully their writings, we see that it was the Divine Son who passed through Egypt that night, when he delivered the Hebrews as a prophecy of the time when he, made flesh, by his death, delivered the whole human race from demoniac error, sin, and slavery.

The Hebrews celebrated the feast in Egypt on the fourteenth moon of Abib, or Nisan,[2] and the next day went out of Egypt. Then their slavery ended. "Now the children of Israel departed from Ramesses the first month, on the fifteenth day of the first month, the day after the Phase, with a mighty hand, in the sight of all the Egyptians."[3] Following, then, the history of his forefathers and customs coming down the ages, the Lord and his disciples held the Passover on the fourteenth day of the month, and he died on the fifteenth to deliver the human race from the slavery of the devil and of sin represented by the Egyptian bondage.

The Hebrews did not go out the night they held the Passover, for they were told to remain within their houses. "Let none of you go out of the door of this house till morning."[4] The next day they began the march. All this foretold how, centuries later, Jesus Christ would celebrate the Passover with his disciples; that he would be arrested at night, and the next day, as the first-born, he died to deliver mankind from the bonds of sin, and slavery of the devil.

During the Passover[5] God gave directions they could not carry out that night; they related to future Passovers. They could not keep the next day, the fifteenth,

---

[1] Exod. xii. 12, 13   [2] Exod. xii. 6.   [3] Numb. xxxii. 3.   [4] Exod. xii. 22.
[5] Exod. xii. and xiii.

as a feast, for they were then on their journey.[1] They could not offer the "first-fruits, the Omer,[2] for they were then traveling in the desert where nothing grows. They could not immolate the special sacrifices mentioned later,[3] nor sprinkle the blood on the altar in place of the door-posts.[4]

For these reasons Jewish writers carefully distinguish between the "Egyptian Passover," held the night of the flight from Egypt, and the "perpetual Passover," celebrated later in their history. Both clean and unclean celebrated the feast that night, but afterwards God gave them special regulations,[5] and restricted the feast to men alone.[6] Thus it came to pass that Christ with his apostles, no woman being present, held the feast in the Cenacle, and there he ordained only men, and from that came the doctrine that only men are valid subjects for the priesthood. The Psalms forming the Hallel were not sung that night, for only in David's day were they composed.

Birth and death, origin and end of life, were most unclean to the Jew. The first reminded them of the fall of man, that children are born in original sin; the latter that from the gates of Eden death with his icy hand strikes down every member of our race.[7] During the wilderness wandering, the second year after leaving Egypt some men touched a dead body, became defiled, and could not celebrate the Passover.[8] God told Moses to institute a second Passover on the fourteenth of the following month, giving a like ceremonial as for the first, and these men purified themselves and held the feast. As the first Passover foretold our Easter Communion, so the latter imaged the time to come, when Christians, who, because of sin, cannot make their "Easter duty," can confess and later receive the "Lamb of God."

Jewish writers name the first "the greater Passover," and the latter "the little Passover," this lasting but a day, the Hallel Psalms being sung while the lamb was being sacrificed, but not during the supper, nor was the leaven searched for.[9]

<hr/>

[1] Exod. xii. 16-51.   [2] Levit xxiii 10-14   [3] Numb xxviii. 16-25
[4] Deut. xvi 1-16.   [5] Numb. xviii 11   [6] Exod xxiii. 17; Deut. xvi. 16
[7] Gen iii 16-19.   [8] Numb ix   [9] Tal., Pesachim, ix 3: Lex Tal, col 1766.
See S. Augustine, Ques in Exod l. ii, Ques xlii, Ques. in Num l ix, Ques. xv

Down the Hebrew history, they followed the law God himself, laid down. "Thou shalt keep this thing as a law for thee and thy children forever." [1] "This is the observable night of the Lord when he brought them out of the land of Egypt, this night all the children of Israel must observe in their generations." [2] In the desert of Sinai, when God commanded them to hold the Easter feast, he said: "Let the children of Israel make the Phase in its due time, the fourteenth day of this month in the evening, according to all the ceremonies and justifications thereof." [3] For the third time the Lord repeated the rule relating to breaking a bone of the lamb, or leaving any part till morning, and ends with these words. "They shall observe all the ceremonies of the Phase." [4]

The Hebrews could not again celebrate the feast of the Passover till they camped round Sinai, the second year after leaving Egypt, because they could not be circumcised while on the march. After being circumcised and receiving the Law and the Ten Commandments from the fiery Shekina, [5] the Holy Spirit, covering Mount Sinai, God renewed the command regarding the Passover, [6] to foretell how Christ first preached his Gospel and then was sacrificed. They did not keep the Passover for the next thirty-three years in their march through the Arabian deserts, for the males could not be circumcised during their continual wanderings. But when they crossed the dry Jordan and camped at Galgal within the Promised Land, Josue ordered the rite of circumcision, and then they held the Passover. [7]

Under the Judges they seldom held the Passover, because they were continually at war with surrounding heathens. But when peace came they held the feast with great solemnity each Easter. As the ages passed new rites and ceremonies were added to the Passover, each being a revelation of the sacrifice of Calvary and the Mass. Let us describe the most striking.

When the good king Josias brought back the Jews from idolatry, begun under Solomon, he commanded the people saying: "Keep the Phase to the Lord your God, according as it is written in the book of this covenant." [8]

[1] Exod xii. 24.   [2] Exod xii 42   [3] Numb ix 3   [4] Numb. ix. 12.
[5] Exod xx.   [6] Numb. ix 9.   [7] Josue, v 2   [8] IV. Kings xxiii. 21.

At a later date, " King Ezechias sent to all Israel and Juda, and he wrote letters to Ephraim and Manasses, that they should come to the house of the Lord in Jerusalem and keep the Phase to the Lord, the God of Israel." [1] The account says the priests received the blood which was poured out from the hands of the Levites,[2] showing that only priests could sacrifice the lamb in the days of Jewish kings " And the Phase was immolated, and the priests sprinkled the blood with their hand, and the Levites flayed the holocausts." [3]

After the Captivity, king Darius of Persia gave orders to search in the library for the holy books, and decreed the renewal of the sacrifices. " And the children of Israel of the Captivity kept the Phase on the fourteenth day of the first month." [4]

Again the Lord renewed the command of the Passover through the prophet Ezechiel, after Herod's temple was shown him in vision.[5]

Hebrew writings show that during the Passover the chief event of the history of the Israelites happened like the morning light of Christianity rising over the world before the Incarnation of the Sun of justice. At midnight of Passover, Abraham divided his forces, and conquered his enemies;[6] Sodom with all the wicked people were destroyed, while Lot, who, in the city filled with sinners, baked the paschal unleaven cakes, only was saved.[7] To Abraham, during the feast, appeared the Son of God, with an angel each side of him.[8] During Passover, Jacob wrestled with and overcame an angel;[9] Prince Haroseth's army was destroyed;[10] Bel's idol was overthronw, and dreams revealed the future to Joseph.

Passover night, proud Belshasser, king of Babylon, celebrated his feast in the great palace on the banks of the Euphrates; within the city's impregnable walls, praised his idols, mocked the God of Israel, called for the sacred vessels of Solomon's Temple, and from them drank to the glory of his kingdom and the gods of Babylon.

On the wall of the great banquet hall appeared the hand of light, wrote the sentence of doom on him and on

[1] II. Par. xxx. 1-5 [2] II Par xxx 16 [3] II. Par. xxxv. 11
[4] I Esdras vi 19-22 [5] Ezechiel xlv 21. [6] Gen. xiv. 15. [7] Gen. xix. 8.
[8] Gen. xviii. [9] Gen. xxxii [10] Judg iv.

his kingdom, which only Daniel could read to the horror-stricken king, satraps, rulers and concubines, while Cyrus' armies marched into the doomed city along the dry bed of the river which they had turned out of its course. That Passover night, Babylon was captured, king and nobles slain. Later, Cyrus, seeing his very name foretold by Isaias, sent back the Jews to rebuild the destroyed city and Temple.[1]

At the Passover the lands of Moph and Noph were swept of idolatry, Esther directed the Hebrews to fast and Haman was crucified. All the miracles God performed for the Hebrews took place at the feast to foretell the delivery of mankind by Christ, who was to be crucified the second day of this feast.

This was the order of Passover at the time of Christ as laid down in Scripture. The tenth day[2] the lamb was selected, washed, and tied to a stake till the 14th day of the moon,[3] the day they searched the house for leaven.[4] During this their great Holy Week, they were to eat only unleaven bread, foretelling our Easter Week and the reception of the sacraments.[5]

Every male Hebrew, not laboring under a legal impurity, under pain of death was to appear at the national sanctuary, the holy Temple,[6] bringing an offering in proportion to his means, foretelling Easter offerings in our churches. An offering was brought to every feast, but this was the oldest and greatest festival, and numerous costly gifts were brought. Part of these offerings was spent for burnt offerings and the rest for the Chagigah as the Talmud says.[7] Special rules related to the first-born [8]

Women went up to Jerusalem with the men,[9] but they did not then eat the Passover with the men,[10] preach or take part as leaders in the synagogue. The feast was held in the evening of the fourteenth of the month to remind them that their fathers in Egypt celebrated it at night.

God commanded them to sacrifice a lamb, because from the days of Abel the patriarchs sacrificed it to foretell "the Lamb of God sacrificed from the foundations of the

[1] Daniel v.   [2] Exod. xii 3.   [3] Exod. xii 6.   [4] Exod. xii 15.
[5] Exod. xii. 15.   [6] Deut. xvi 16-17.   [7] Chagigah 1, 2 etc.
[8] Exod. xiii 15   [9] I. Kings i. 7; Luke ii 41-42.
[10] Exod. xxiii. 17; xxxiv 23, Deut. xvi. 16, etc.

world." The lamb was a type and emblem of Him who was to come and bear the sins of mankind, who was "Like a lamb led to the sacrifice."[1] The sacrifice of the lamb in patriarchal times degenerated into pagan rites when Adam's religion had become dim, and in Egypt and other places Jupiter was adored under the form of a ram. The beasts first offered to God had become the gods of paganism.

A striking figure of Christ was that paschal lamb. Its immolation, by which the Hebrews were delivered, foretold the delivery of the whole human race by the sacrifice of Christ. Its blood, sprinkled on the door-posts, pointed to the Lord's blood sprinkled on the cross by which we are redeemed from sin and hell. The "Angel of death," God the Son striking the Egyptians, tells of the death of the soul by sin when not delivered by the Redeemer's blood. The lamb killed in the night typified the Lamb of God arrested at midnight, sacrificed in the darkness of infidelity at the end of the Hebrew nationality, typified by the darkness on Egypt and at the crucifixion.

As the lamb was sacrificed by the whole people, it pointed to that later time when the whole nation cried out: "Crucify him." "His blood be on us and on our children" The lamb was to be without spot or blemish to shadow forth the sinless Saviour. A kid might be sacrificed at the Passover in place of a lamb, for the goat represented Christ loaded with the world's sins as the scapegoat bore the sins of Israel. Jacob clothed in hairy kid-skins when his father blessed him foretold the Lord carrying our sins. The kid was prepared and roasted the same as the lamb.

The little lamb was to be not more than a year old, to foretell Christ sacrificed in the flower of his manhood, and without blemish, emblem of the sinless Christ. He was separated from the flock on the tenth day of Nisan, or Abib, because on this Monday the local Sanhedrin or Law Court of Jerusalem were to condemn the Lord to death, and that evening Christ hid in the Grotto on Olivet. These details we find in Moses' Law. Later the prophets and great Seers of Israel, following the Shekina's directions, added more details to the ceremonial. The leader

[1] See St. Augustin, Contra Littera Petil L ii n lxxxvii Isaias liii. 7.

of the band of Jews select the lamb; the women wash it, as Christ took a bath before the Passover. They sent it with perfume to shadow forth the odor of good works of the Lord's humanity. They tie it to a colored stake, as Christ was fastened to his cross. They called it after its selection the "Lamb of God," the name John the Baptist called the Saviour.[1] They anointed it with oil as the Lord was anointed by the Holy Spirit to be the Messiah. "The Anointed Jehovah," in Greek: "The Christ." For high priest, king, judge, and ruler of Israel were anointed and hands of ordination imposed on him.[2]

The lamb was the most striking image of Christ among all the various Temple sacrifices. Therefore morning and evening with an elaborate ceremonial like a pontifical High Mass, the high priest presiding, a lamb was sacrificed in the Temple. The daily immolation of the lamb in the Temple and the eating of its flesh, then took the place of what is now the Consecration and Communion during Mass. But the sacrifice of the paschal lamb was a still more strikingly typical of Christ.

The lamb was killed by the priests in the Temple to foretell how the Jewish priesthood would later demand of Pilate the execution of the Saviour. The blood was sprinkled on the great sacrificial altar, as the blood of Christ was sprinkled on his cross. The lamb was skinned as Christ was scourged. Then the dead lamb was brought to the house of the Jewish family.

There they drove a pomegranate stick down through its body, and out into the tendons of its hind feet. They were forbidden to use a metal spit, for the Lord was to be crucified on a wooden cross. They carefully opened out its body, and drove a pomegranate stick through the tendons of its fore-feet, as butchers do to-day. They called this operation "The crucifying of the lamb," to foretell Christ with his hands and feet nailed to the cross. The victim they now named the "Body of the Lamb" to which Christ alluded at the Last Supper when he said "This is my Body." This was the way the lamb was prepared centuries before Christ.

Roasting was the original way of cooking meat, and the shepherd patriarchs stuck the flesh on the ends of

<hr />

[1] John i 29.   [2] See Migne, Cursus Comp, S. Scripturæ, vol. ii, 863, 873.

sticks, drove the other ends into the ground so the meat would roast over the fire before their tent. Thus they used to roast whole lambs, chickens and animals. In Arabia, Egypt and in the Orient, you will see the Bedouin roasting meat in this way.

The crucified lamb was then placed in the oven resting on his cross, the flesh not being allowed to touch the oven, to foretell how Christ completely hung from the cross. Thus the lamb was roasted that its body might be penetrated by the fire, as the fire of the Shekina, the Holy Spirit, filled Christ with the love of mankind, moving him to die for our salvation. When cooked, the lamb was placed on the table, still resting on his cross, and was a striking prophetic portrait of the body of the dead Christ on the cross, his skin all torn off in the flagellation, the yellow serum oozing out and dried, made him look as though he had been roasted.

The flesh could be eaten only in the house, no part could be carried out,[1] for Communion is received only in the Catholic Church, and not in sects which have not holy orders—an ordained priesthood. Not less than ten, or more than twenty members, formed a "band" to eat the lamb, to image the congregation assembled for the celebration of the Eucharist. The tenth day of Nisan,[2] when the Hebrews celebrated their first Passover, they sacrificed the lamb on the Sabbath to foretell that on Sunday, the Christian Sabbath, the real Lamb of God would be sacrificed in our churches.

The waters of the Nile were turned into blood; in the ceremonial of tabernacle and Temple, the victims' blood was poured out on the altar; they were forbidden to eat meat with the blood. Even in our days, Jews complain that the "kosher" meat, completely drained of blood, tastes insipid. What did these rites of the Jewish religion mean? They were to bring before their minds the value of human life. They forgot all these that fatal Friday, when the whole nation cried out, "Crucify him!" "His blood be on us and our children!"[3]

The blood of the paschal lamb was sprinkled on the door-posts of their houses, as a type, a prophecy, of the blood of Christ sprinkled on his cross. The first-born of

---

[1] Exod, xii. 46.   [2] Exod. xii 3.   [3] Luke xxiii. 21, Matt. xxvii. 25.

the families living in the houses marked with the blood were saved that night. And Moses with the lamb's blood sprinkled Aaron, his sons, and all the utensils of the tabernacle. "What did you say, Moses? Can the blood of a lamb deliver a man? It is true, he said, not because it is blood, but because it was an example of the Lord's blood."[1] Beautifully, in his eloquent words, the Archbishop of Constantinople explains the great mystery of the blood.

The Hebrews were forbidden to eat any raw part of the Lamb, for the fire of the Holy Ghost completely filled the whole body of Christ. If they broke a bone in the lamb in the preparation, they were punished at the time of Christ with thirty-nine stripes on bare back and shoulders. This was to foretell that the soldiers would not break Christ's limbs when they came to remove the bodies of the crucified that day within the Passover.[2] Only circumcised Hebrews could eat the paschal lamb, as only baptized Christians should receive communion. Only in Jerusalem was the lamb sacrificed, so in the Church is the Lamb of God sacrificed and eaten. The lamb was eaten with unleaven bread, like the altar breads used to show forth the sinless Christ, on whom was no sin, prefigured by fermenting yeast. It was eaten with wild lettuce dipped in vinegar, to remind us of the bitterness of sin, and with what sorrow for our sins we should approach the table of the Lord.

The whole lamb was eaten, with its head, feet, entrails, etc., to tell us that under the appearance of bread and wine we partake in the whole Christ, receiving both his Divinity and human nature. What remained after the feast must not be taken out of the house, but was to be burned that night,[3] to foretell how the Lord's body was removed that afternoon he died.

The lamb was eaten by the Jews with loins bound up, shoes on their feet, staffs in their hands, clothed as for a journey, for as priests we partake of Communion clothed in vestments on a journey to our home, not in Palestine, like Jews, but in heaven, the Christian's real home.

On the fifteenth, the next day, in the time of Christ, the Hebrews gathered in the Temple to assist in the

[1] St. Chrystom, Hom. 48, in Joan. C 19 [2] John xix. 33 [3] Exod xii. 8 9, 10.

great celebration, held holy meetings in their synagogues, kept the day like a Sabbath, and did no work
except what was required for preparing food.[1] This day
and the six following days, two young bullocks, a ram, and
seven lambs, a year old, were offered in the Temple.[2]
With flour seasoned with oil, they made cakes of unleaven
bread, and offered them in the Temple to foretell the
Mass. On the sixteenth took place the ceremony of the
Omer, a striking figure of Christ's arrest the night he
was betrayed.

In the history of Abraham and his " Seed," the " Seed
of the woman who was to crush the serpent's head,"
God bound up in prophetic history the future of the
nations. Nature, history, blessings, symbols, ceremonies
and graces combine to give a special meaning to the feast.
The New Testament is filled with allusions to the going
out from Egypt, the feast appearing under the names of
pascha, phase, the paschal lamb, the bread and wine, the
Last Supper, the Eucharistic Sacrifice.

In countries bordering deserts, like Palestine, they plant
crops in the fall and harvest in the spring-time, as God
gathered Israel to himself from slavery in the Nile Land,
and to foretell when Christ would rescue mankind from
perdition, so Passover fell in the middle of the month
Abib, later called Nisan, both words meaning "sprouting," "green ears."[3] It was the "beginning of months,
the seventh month—the sacred month, reminding us of
the seven gifts of the Holy Spirit,[4] the seven sacraments.
All through the Bible runs the sacred symbol seven, and
in sevens the Gospels were written in the original Greek.
In the most astonishing way they are interwoven as
though the first Evangelist wrote last, and the last first,
and altogether run in and out, one with the other under
the same divine inspiring Spirit. From the days of the
Apostles, the Gospels have proven impervious to attacks
of infidels.

From Adam down, in Bible Books the spring feast of
Passover was celebrated by the patriarchs with the lamb,
the bread and wine. When God established the Hebrew
ceremonial, he enlarged the Passover rite into the grand
ceremonial of the tabernacle and of Solomon's Temple.

---

[1] Exod. xii. 16.   [2] Numb xxviii. 16-21.   [3] Esther iii. 7   [4] Isaias ii. 2, 3

The stately Liturgy and service of the Temple of Christ's day were but an extension of the patriarchs' Passover.

The patriarchal Passover with the roasted lamb foretelling the crucifixion, and the unleaven bread of the Last Supper and the Mass, had come down from prehistoric times to the Hebrews living in Egyptian bondage. But the night of their delivery God ordered bitter herbs to be added to the rite to remind them of the bitter slavery the race had suffered in the Nile-land. Later God revealed to them his laws, established the tabernacle ceremonial built on the simpler ceremonial of their fathers, the patriarchs. But as ages passed over the world, inspired prophets added new rites, new objects, and a wealth of details to the Passover and the Temple worship, each filled with types, figures and emblems of the crucifixion and the Mass.

The unleaven bread developed into the feast of unleaven bread celebrated for a week. But to show that the crucifixion and the Mass are one and the same sacrifice, this series of festivals was interwoven into the Passover held the first night. Thus Passover and feast of unleaven bread, often called by the same name, were never separated, always intermingled one with another.[1] Now let us see the other foods eaten at Passover and their mystic meaning, remarking that history is silent regarding the epoch when they were introduced.

The behemoth " a large beast "[2] represented during the Passover by a dish of meat, meant either the hippopotomus, " river horse," or the elephant, " chief animal." The former is a large species of the cow family like the buffalo, and the Fathers say it foretold the demon conquered, not by Job with his skin-disease, but by Christ in his Passion and death.

Jewish writers, the Talmud and other works give most exaggerated descriptions and stories relating to this beast. According to them, he was the greatest of the fourfooted animals which God made in the beginning, male and female. He killed the female, preserved her flesh for the elect at the coming of the Messiah; the male still lives and will be slaughtered for the Hebrew race, when they rise from the dead at the end of the world. They

[1] Edersheim, Temple, p. 178.   [2] Job xl. 10.

have many wild dreams of that kind regarding this animal.

The Lord spoke to Job of the leviathan [1] called in Hebrew lvyathan "great water animal," the whale or other marine animal, which Job could not catch with a hook.[2]

The flesh meat and the fishes on the Passover table figured the elephant and whale, signifying to the Hebrews one Assyria, the other Egypt, both ancient enemies of their fathers. But a careful reading of Job [3] shows that not only are these countries meant, but the demons, enemies of the human race. Job with his terrible skin disease, and his patience in sufferings, did not conquer the demons, who brought on him in his innocence all these sufferings, but he points to Christ, his skin torn off in his flagellation, dead for mankind, for he was to conquer the demons represented by these great Scripture beasts. In this sense Isaias foretells that "The Lord with his hard and great sword shall visit Leviathan, the bar-serpent, and Leviathan, the crooked serpent, and shall slay the whale which is in the sea " [4] showing that even with his strength and wicked wiles with which he deceived mankind in the Eden-serpent, he would be overthrown by the Redeemer, that is, his power broken.

At the time of Christ every act, every rite, every object and each ceremony brighter and clearer brought before them their Messiah foretold to come and die to atone for the world's wickedness, and bring back our race to innocence lost in Eden. But beyond the crucifixion, while lives our race, the story was to be continued in the Mass with its elaborate rite and ceremonial.

Christ's Last Supper and his death the next day were to fulfil, end, seal up Passover, Temple, Old Testament and all they foretold. But the last of the Hebrew inspired seers had revealed the rejection of the Jewish Temple and sacrifices because the Jewish priesthood would reject Christ, then he passed to the calling of the heathens, the offerings of the Christian priesthood, the Mass among the nations.

" I have no pleasure in you, saith the Lord of hosts, and I will not receive a gift from your hand. For from

[1] Job xl 41. [2] Job. xl 20 [3] Chap. xl [4] Isaias xxvii 1.

the rising of the sun even to the going down, my name is great among the Gentiles, and in every place there is sacrifice, and there is offered to my name a clean oblation, for my name is great among the Gentiles, saith the Lord of hosts." [1]

Now let us see what the celebrated Jewish historian says about the Passover.

Josephus writes as follows : " When God had signified, that with one more plague, he would compel the Egyptians to let the Hebrews go, he commanded Moses to tell the people that they should have a sacrifice ready, and that they should prepare themselves on the tenth day of the month Xanthus against the fourteenth, which month is called by the Egyptians Pharmuth, and Nisan by the Hebrews, but the Macedonians call it Xanthicus; and that he should carry away the Hebrews with all they had. Accordingly, having got the Hebrews ready for their departure, and having sorted the people into tribes, he kept them together in one place. But when the fourteenth was come, and all were ready to depart, they offered the sacrifice, and purified the houses with the blood, using bunches of hyssop for that purpose, and when they had supped they burnt the remainder of the flesh as just ready to depart. Whence it is that we still offer this sacrifice in like manner to this day, and call this festival Pascha, which signifies the feast of the Passover, because on that day God passed over us, and sent the plagues upon the Egyptians. For the destruction of the first-born came on the Egyptians that night, so that many of the Egyptians, who lived near the king's palace, persuaded Pharaoh to let the Hebrews go [2]

" In the month of Xanthus, which by us is called Nisan, and is the beginning of our year, on the fourteenth day of the lunar month, when the sun is in Aries, for it was in this month we were delivered from bondage under the Egyptians, the law ordained that we should every year slay that sacrifice, which I before told you we slew, when we came out of Egypt, and which was called the Passover. And so we celebrate this Passover in companies, leaving nothing of what we sacrifice till the day following. The feast of unleaven bread succeeds

---

[1] Malachias i 10-11.   [2] Josephus, Antiq., B ii., chapter xiv. n. 6.

that of the Passover, and falls on the fifteenth of the month, and continues seven days, wherein they feed on unleaven bread, on every one of which days two bulls are killed, and one ram and seven lambs," etc.[1]

"So these high priests, upon the coming of their feast, which is called the Passover, when they slay their sacrifices from the ninth hour to the eleventh, but that the company be not less than ten belong to every sacrifice, for it is not lawful for them to feast singly by themselves, and many of us are twenty in a company, found the number of sacrifices was two hundred and fifty-six thousand, five hundred, which upon the allowance of no more than ten that feast together, amounts to two millions, seven hundred thousand and two hundred persons, that were pure and holy. For as to those who have leprosy, or the gonorrhea, or women that have their monthly courses, or such as are otherwise polluted, it is not lawful for them to be partakers of this sacrifice, nor indeed for any foreigners neither, who come hither to worship."[2]

Now we will see how the Hebrew, of our day celebrate the Passover.

Rebelling against the threatened tyranny of Solomon's son, Roboam, more than a thousand years before Christ, the Samaritans separated from the Jews and worshiped in a temple of their own they built on Mt. Gerizim, in Samaria. It rivaled the holy Temple at Jerusalem. Separated in creed and religious matters from the Jews, looked on by the latter as "lower than pigs," a mutual hostility existed between the two religions all down the centuries to the time of Christ, and even down to our day. Last year (in 1903) the last family of pure Samaritan blood died out, about 250 members of mixed blood remain. This is the way the Samaritans held the Passover in modern times. Visiting Nablous in 1861, George Grove writes:

"The lambs, they require six now for the community, are roasted all together by stuffing them vertically, head downwards into an oven, which is like a small well about three feet in diameter and four or five feet deep, roughly

---

[1] Josephus Antiq., B. iii., chapter x. n. 5., B. xiv., chapter ii. n. 2, etc.
[2] Josephus, Wars, B. vi., chapter ix. n. 3.

scamed, in which a fire has been kept up for several hours. After the lambs are thrust in, the top of the hole is covered with bushes and earth to continue the heat till they are done Each lamb has a stake or spit run through him to draw him up by. To prevent the spit from tearing away through the roasted flesh, a cross-piece is put through the lower end of it."[1] The writer did not observe that the two sticks formed a cross. The cross-stick opened out the ribs as seen to-day in butcher-shops all over the world

With King Edward VII., then Prince of Wales, in 1862, at the Passover, Dean Stanley came to Samaria. On the top of Gerizim had assembled 152 persons, last of the Samaritans The women were shut up in tents, the men assembled near the summit of the rocky heights of their sacred mountain. Fifteen men and six youths, priests and Levites, were clothed in sacred vestments, the other men were dressed in holiday attire

" Half an hour before sunset they all gathered about a long trench, assumed the oriental posture of prayer, and led by a priest began the devotions, reciting in loud voices the Passover service and the account of the Passover given in the Bible.

" The six young men mentioned before came driving six sheep into the assembly. When the sun had nearly set, the recitation became more violent, and the history of the Hebrews going out of Egypt, the slaying of the lamb as given in Exodus, were sung more rapidly, and in a higher key. As soon as the sun had touched the western hills, the youths paused, threw the sheep on their backs, and with sacrificial knives cut their throats. They dipped their fingers in the blood, put it on their own noses and foreheads, and on all the others, including the children. The wool was then taken off and the bodies of the lambs washed in boiling water, the recitation continuing all the time.

" They wrapped bitter herbs in strips of unleaven bread, and passed the morsels to each in the meeting. After a short prayer, the young men skinned the lambs, they took off the right fore legs, and with the entrails burned them. They put back the liver into the carcase.

---

[1] Smith Dic. of Bible, Vol. III, p 2344, note.

Then down along the backbone they ran a stake, and with another stick opened out the ribs forming a cross. They carried the victims to an oven-like hole in the ground, in which a fire had been kindled, thrust the bodies of the lambs into this, sealed up the mouth with hurdles, sticks and wet earth, and left them for five hours to roast.

"Sometime before midnight, they assembled again for the feast. The hole being suddenly opened, a cloud of steam and smoke burst out, and they took out the roasted lambs each still impaled, each one on his cross. Rolling them in mats, they carried them to the first trench, between the two lines of Samaritans.

"The fifteen priests and youths clothed in vestments, now provided themselves with shoes, gird their waists with ropes for girdles, and hold staffs in their hands. Then all began the prayers. Suddenly they sat on the ground beside the trench, the roasted lambs between them. They tore away the flesh with their fingers, and rapidly and silently they consumed it, sending portions to the absent. In ten minutes the flesh was all eaten. Then they gathered the remains, all the bones and leavings, into the mats and burned them, searching carefully for every morsel. Then they returned to their dwellings."

Three thousand years ago Samaritans separated from Hebrew monarchy and religion and founded their own schismatic synagogue. Down these ages, mutual hatred between Jerusalem and Samaria was so deep they would hardly speak to each other. The woman at the well was surprised when Christ asked her for a drink of water.[1] From the Samaritan Passover we have described, although it seems grotesque and peculiar, we can judge how they celebrated it in the days of David and Solomon.

The place is chosen outside the gates.[2] Many were the sacrifices they offered outside the camp to foretell Christ crucified outside the walls of the city.

The men alone, the women excluded, offered the lambs,[3] for men only were to be ordained to the priesthood.[3] The time the lamb was killed was in the evening at the going down of the sun,[4] for at that time Christ died. The Passover was held at night, before the midnight hour,

---

[1] John iv. 9.   [2] Levit. ix. 11, etc.   [3] Deut. xvi. 16.   [4] Deut. xvi. 6.

10

then Christ celebrated the Last Supper, and just before midnight he was arrested.[1]

They ate it with unleaven bread and bitter herbs the Hebrews call wild lettuce [2] The way it was roasted,[3] the careful exclusion of foreigners and the women,[4] the haste with which the supper was eaten,[5] and the vestments, heads covered, staffs in their hands, the care to consume all, the burning of the leavings and bones that night,[6] the return to their dwellings before morning [7] show us how it was celebrated in days of Hebrew kings.

The Levites, the young men, sacrificed the lamb and gave the blood to the priests.[8] They skinned the animal,[9] the crucifixion of the lambs, the recitation of the Passover history in Exodus, prayers and liturgy—all show they come down from times before the separation of the Samaritans from the Hebrews.

In the square before the Church of the Holy Sepulchre, on Holy Saturday in 1903, the writer sat, talking with an Englishman and his guide about their journey down to Jericho and the Dead Sea. The guide remarked: "The Jews are going to celebrate their Passover to-night." "Yes, I will come for you at the Caza Nova about six." But he did not come. Engaging another "dragoman" we started for the store of an American born Jew, formerly an officer in our army, who had resigned and went to the land of his forefathers. "I know where he lives," said the guide. We started in a carriage out the Joppa Gate, down to the west, through new streets, where dwells nearly as large a population as that within the walls of Jerusalem; we found the American in the act of locking his house on his way to attend the feast.

"Yes, I will take you to see the Passover," he said after the introduction. "Why did I leave the States and come here? Well, there is something about this land that attracts me. The old associations. The history of my people is wonderful in my eyes. But I don't like the way they do things—the deep divisions, prejudices, religious hatred, which divide Jews and Gentiles. There is something I cannot understand. A man crucified nearly

[1] Deut. xii 26-27.   [2] Exod xii 8   [3] Exod. xii 8-9   [4] Exod xiii. 43.
[5] Exod xii 11   [6] Exod. xii 10   [7] Exod xii 22   [8] II Par xxx 16
[9] II. Par. xxxv. 11.

2,000 years ago has divided the religious world ever since. Here we find it in all its intensity. How one man could do that we cannot see. There is something mysterious in the whole thing. Come."

We hurried to the house of the chief Rabbi of Jerusalem. He did not live in a grand palace, as did Joseph Caiphas that fatal night when Jesus Christ was brought before him. His home was a hovel—it was a rookery in the Jewish quarters outside the walls. The Jews are poor and persecuted in the land of their fathers. All the glory of Israel has passed away as the prophets foretold.

But we forgot the surroundings, when we stood in the presence of this venerable personage. Tall, well-built, thin, of fine features, intellect written in every lineament, the blood of kings, prophets and seers of the chosen race flowing in his veins—he looked like another Abraham. With patriarchal welcome, he met us at the door clothed in flowing robes of light mauve, the exact cut and form of the Catholic priest's cassock. A kind and gentle dignity flowed from his form, lighted up by candles still burning on the table, as he told us in fine French that he had just finished the Passover. He would be pleased to let us see the feast, but it was now over, and all the guests had gone.

We went to another house. No, he would not let us see the Passover. He did not object himself, but his wife did. The table was all prepared, they were just going to sit down. We talked with his wife, offered any amount of money, used every argument. "No. The Christians of Port Said, Egypt, reported last year, that the Jews killed a Christian girl, and used her blood at the feast, and the story created a riot, in which Jews were killed, and she had made a vow that never would she allow a Christian at her table." We went to the Jerusalem Hotel kept by Jews and they refused.

It was getting late ; the American Jew would not ride in the carriage, but walked along beside, for they will not ride on the Sabbath. After it got dark when the Sabbath ended, he got in, and we hurried back to the city, drove up the long David Street, by David's Tower, and stopped at the street leading between two houses, where on one corner St. James lived while bishop of Jeru-

salem, the other corner being the site of the house of St.
Thomas the apostle. Here we dismissed the carriage and
went through the narrow street east about two blocks.
We were on the top of Sion, not far from the Cenacle.

Mounting outside stone steps like those leading up to
the Cenacle, we found ourselves in a large room about
twenty by fifteen feet, with a long table in the center
covered with a white table-cloth. The dish of roasted
lamb, bitter herbs, three cakes of unfermented bread, and
other things for the Passover were on the table.

"Yes," said the master in French after the introduction. "I like Americans. I have a brother in business on Broadway, New York. The Americans do not
persecute the Hebrews. You are welcome. Keep on
your hats. Come and sit at the table. You say you
cannot take part in a religious feast, but as a guest of the
house. You want to see the ceremonial Moses established
—all right, we are glad you came."

He was a young man of about thirty-three or thirty-
five years of age, and twelve Jews sat with him at the
table. The American-born Jew sat at the writer's right
hand instructing him while taking notes. The master of
the house sat at the head of the table. At his right sat
his wife next to him, then the writer with the ex-officer.
The other guests took their places at both sides of the
table. The men held the Liturgy of the Passover in
their hands. While the master sung the words they
followed him, repeating the words with him, as the priests
when being ordained do when the bishop says the Mass
of ordination.

On the table burned fifteen candles and lamps. Two
vases held flowers, a plate with the three unleaven cakes
was at the master's right hand, near by were two bottles
of Palestine wine, one having white and the other red.
At each guest's place was a glass-tumbler for the wine.
In the middle of the table, but in front of the master,
was a dish of roasted lamb and beef with little fishes.
Other dishes had bitter herbs, vinegar mixed with salt,
the chaggiah, cucumber, eggs and other dishes of the
Passover.

Sitting at the table, each rested the left elbow on a
little cushion in remembrance of the reclining position of

the time of Christ. While reading the Liturgy, they swayed their bodies back and forth, as customary with Jews during synagogue service. The feast began at 8 30 and lasted till 10 45, having three sections—that is, two intervals of rest, during which the conversation became general, the master smoking cigarettes and talking to the writer.

They first washed their hands, and then filled their glasses with wine, the women performing this function. The master sang the prayers of blessing over the wine while all held their glasses, after which they drank the first cup. Then the master blessed the lights. The master cuts the cucumber with blessing, dips the bitter herbs in the vinegar, and passes them to all the guests. Then they again wash their hands, and recite the prayer of blessing over the fruit of the earth.

Taking up the bread, the master says: "This is the bread of affliction our fathers ate in Egypt," etc. The words are shouted, as back and forth they sway, the words coming like an explosion, a sing-song of sounds, the last words of each sentence being prolonged.

"The Liturgy," said the Jew beside the writer, "comes down from the Second Temple, from the time of Zedekiah.[1] It is written in the old Hebrew of Esdras, as that of Moses was lost. But the ceremony goes back to the time of Moses."

At this part of the ceremony the master broke off a piece of the unfermented bread, rolled it around some bitter herbs, dipped the morsel in the vinegar, and handed it to the writer, saying, "Take this as a mark of friendship." This was always done when a stranger sat at the table, down from the time of Moses. This was the "sop" the Lord handed to Judas. When John asked, "Lord, who is it?" Jesus answered, "He it is to whom I shall reach bread dipped, and when he had dipped he gave it to Judas Iscariot."[2]

When they read that part relating to the ten plagues God sent on the Egyptians, each guest dips his finger in the wine, and lets a drop fall on the floor. Then they drank the second cup of wine, the first section ends, and the conversation becomes general.

[1] Jeremy xxxviii.   [2] John xiii 25, 26.

The first part of the second section begins by washing the hands, using the water from a flagon on the table. They bring on the dish of fishes. The master takes the cake from the plate before him, and breaks it into two equal parts, as the celebrant of the Mass breaks the Host, while the Jew says to the writer: "These cakes must be made of purest flour, ground of wheat sowed for that purpose, gathered during day-time, thrashed and ground by Jews with great care, and made into unleaven cakes."

Soup, with unleaven cakes broken into it, is now passed around, each guest having a plate of it placed before him, while from the Liturgy forming the Hallel they sing the Psalms[1] The master then covered the cakes with a napkin, as the celebrant covers the patin with the purificator during Mass. He placed a prayer-shawl on the shoulders of the youngest guest, handed him the plate holding the broken half cake, and this young man held the plate with the bread covered with the end of the shawl till towards the end of the feast, when he brought it to the master as the subdeacon holds the paten covered with the benediction veil during a High Mass. This ended the second section.

The third section opened with the prayers of thanks. All begin the chant together, the master leading, the twelve Jews becoming more vociferous, all united in the one mighty thanksgiving unto God. At the end of this prayer, they all drank the third cup of wine. One went and opened the closed door, which remained opened the rest of the service. A Jew took a filled glass of wine and placed it on the threshold for Elias, the forerunner of the Messiah,[2] while the prayer for the coming of the Redeemer was recited. This cup of wine remained on the doorstep till the end. They did not know that John the Baptist, filled with the spirit of the foretold Elias, had already come as the forerunner of the Christ.

The swaying of the bodies, the singing of the prayers, the shouting of the words, become still more vehement as they together say the thanksgiving prayers of the Liturgy. Back and forth, from side to side, they move in a kind of movement imparted to the whole body, as they said, so that even their "bones might praise the

---

[1] Psalms cxiii., cxiv., cxv., cxvii   [2] Malach. iv. 5.

Lord." They sing, " We beseech Thee, O Lord, to save us, ' like Hosanna, and " Bless Jerusalem," which word they pronounced as though spelled Barushlaym.

The master made a motion, took the cake hidden by the prayer-shawl on the shoulders of the young man, broke off and ate a part, and gave a portion to each guest. He drank some wine, handed his cup of wine to each at the table, "and they all drank from it." Then they sang the hymn mentioned in the Gospel sung by Christ and his Apostles.[1] This hymn, which will be found in the Passover Service, was more regular and musical than the other prayers. They seemed to throw their whole soul into it. The Hebrew, in which it is written, is as regular as a mathematical table. The master first intoned the hymn, following more regular musical notes, and the company responded in the nasal intonation peculiar to the Oriental, with rising and falling intonation. This closed the feast.

We rose, thanked them all, shook hands, and passed out into the night. Thoughts went back to that Last Supper in the upper chamber of the Cenacle, but a little distance from where we were then in this upper chamber of Sion, when the Lord and his Apostles celebrated the Passover according to this ceremonial, and changed this Jewish rite into the Mass. " And when they had sung a hymn, they went forth to the Mount of Olives."[2] We have given the ceremonial of the Passover as followed to-day in Samaria and Jerusalem, let us now see what that peculiar work, the Talmud, says of the feast at the time of Christ.

[1] Matt. xxvi. 30; Mark xiv. 26.   [2] Mark xiv. 26.

V.—THE TALMUD ON THE LAST SUPPER OR PASSOVER.

Many a time in his young days St. Paul, a strict Pharisee, had sat at Passover. When converted he saw in the Hebrew house-cleaning, the search for the unleaven bread, the preparations for the feast, the confession of sins and the symbolic ceremonies, the types and images of Christianity and of the Eucharistic Sacrifice.

Therefore he wrote: " Now these things were done in a figure of us . . . and they were written for our correction." [1] "To rouse us from dead works to serve the living God." [2] "Know ye not that a little leaven corrupteth the whole mass? Purge out the old leaven, that you may be a new mass, as you are unleaven. For Christ our Passover is sacrificed. Therefore let us feast, not with the old leaven of malice and wickedness, but with the unleaven bread of sincerity and truth." [3]

The reader will see a deeper meaning in these words when he reads the following pages. For here we will open the Tract of the Talmud called the Pesachim: "Passover," forming a volume of 264 pages in quarto, giving minute details of the feast we call the Last Supper. We will take the texts relating to our subject, and give explanations as we go along. These details, rites and ceremonies, the Jews claim, came down from the days of the Hebrew kings. They were written about the year 150 after Christ: They show the Jewish Passover at least in the time they were written.

The Jews are a Semitic race, and have the conservatism of all Asiatic peoples. The orthodox Jew has preserved pure his religion since the Temple stood. The synagogue in belief and practice has hardly changed since the days of Christ. The love of Moses and of his Books, the first five Books of the Old Testament, made the Hebrew cling

[1] I. Cor. x 11   [2] Heb ix 14   [3] I. Cor. 5, 6, 7, 8.

with a death-grasp to the most minute details of his religion, preserved them as a peculiar people among the nations and prevented their conversion, in spite of poverty, persecution, and wretchedness

When the Romans destroyed their city and Temple their misfortunes bound them closer to their traditions till they wrote them in the Talmud. We look therefore in this work for the details of the Passover as celebrated in the days of Christ. This work, little known among the Gentiles, is now, perhaps for the first time, laid before Christian readers. The descriptions, rites and ceremonies in the following pages seem like revelations from a vanished world now brought forth into the light to show how wonderfully the Mass with its elaborate ceremonial was foretold in the Passover of Moses, patriarch, prophet and Hebrew seers.

"At Or, 'light,' 'twilight,' 'daybreak,' on the fourteenth of Nisan, search should be made for leavened bread by the light of a candle, but it is not necessary to search all places in which it is not usual to put leaven."[1]

"Or," the Hebrew word for "light," was the name of the city where Abraham lived in Babylonia, before God called him into Palestine.[2] The Babylonians called it Ur, "light," of the moon, which they worshiped. The ruined city near the mouth of the Euphrates is now named Mughier, "The Betumined."

Thus at daybreak, to foretell that the twilight of his redemption from sins he has committed and which darken his mind, the sinner rises from sleep roused by the light of the Holy Spirit in qualms of conscience, to prepare and search his memory for his sins, and get rid of them by confession, when he is to receive the Lamb of God in Communion. It signified the light of the Holy Spirit in the sinner's soul, which shows him the way to forgiveness in the darkness of mind soiled by sin.

Thus with a candle the Jew searched his house for leaven. The Liturgy of the Passover has the following Rubric.[3]

"On the evening preceding the fourteenth day of the month Nisan, it is requisite for the master of every

---

[1] See Babyl. Talmud, whole Tract Pesachim, "Passover"   [2] Gen. ii. 28–31; xv. 7.   [3] See Zanolini, De Festis Judæorum, chapter 4.

family to search after leavened bread, in every place where it is kept, gathering all leaven lying in his way. The following is said previous to the search.

"Blessed art thou, O Lord, our God, King of the Universe, who hast sanctified us with thy commandments, and commanded us to reserve the leaven."

It is not enough to confess our sins and be sorry for them. We must hate and detest all sin, even those we have overlooked or forgotten. We must have no attachment to mortal sin, even for those we have forgotten, which are forgiven with the others we have told.[1] To foretell that the Jewish Liturgy continues.[2]

"After the leaven is all gathered, the following is said: 'All manner of leaven that I have in my possession, which I have not seen nor removed, shall be null, and accounted as the dust of the earth.'"

Sin is burned up in our souls with the fire of the Holy Spirit, who came on the Apostles in fiery tongues burning with the warmth of charity, the love of God above all. To foretell this the Jew burned the leaven in the early morning, saying:

"All manner of leaven—that is in my possession, which I have seen, and which I have not seen, which I removed, and which I have not removed, shall be null and accounted as the dust of the earth."[3]

Then follow long explanations, opinions and discussions of rules relating to the search for leaven bread, called in Hebrew Chometz, while the unleaven is Matzoth.

"One who leaves his house to go to sea, or to go with a caravan prior to thirty days before the Passover, need not search for leaven bread, but if he go away within the thirty days preceding the Passover, he must burn the leaven bread in his house. Said Abayi: 'A man who leaves his house within thirty days preceding the Passover, must burn the leaven bread, if his intention is to return on the Passover, but if such is not his intention, he need not do this.'[4]

"Why are thirty days particularly specified? It is as we have learned in the Boraitha,[5] viz., One may inquire

---

[1] See I. Cor. v. 7; John i. 17.   [2] See Pesachim, cap. i. p. 8, etc.   [3] Form of Service for the Two First Nights of the Feast of Passover, p. 3.   [4] Ibidem, p. 7.
[5] A Boraitha means in Hebrew "The Teachings of the Sages."

and preach concerning the laws of the Passover thirty
days before that festival, R. Simeon ben Gamaliel.[1]   (This
Gamaliel was St. Paul's teacher, a famous Pharisee who
presided over a school in Jerusalem[2]) said "two weeks
before."   Because Moses at the time of the first Passover
already made the regulations concerning the second
Passover, as it is written.[3]

"Let the man then renounce the use of the bread at
the fourth or fifth hour, as that is not the time either of
searching or for burning; there is fear lest a man forget
to do this at that time.   Let him renounce its use at the
sixth hour, when he is about to burn it."

The sixth hour is noon, six hours after sunrise, that
was the way they counted the hours of the day.   They
searched for the leaven at break of day, gathered and
burned it at noon, usually beginning at eleven, and finishing before the Temple prayers at noon.   It was done
with blessings and prayers given in the Ritual.

"All agree, however, that the benediction must precede
the act.   Whence do we adduce this?   Because R. Jehudah
(he was the famous president of the college at Tiberias
we have mentioned who wrote the Mishna) said in the
name of Samuel: 'Benedictions must be performed prior
to the performance of every religious duty.'   And the
disciple of Rabh (Rabbi Hisda) said: "In all cases, with
the exception of bathing, in this instance the benediction
should be pronounced after the act.'"

"The Rabbis taught search for leavened bread must
not be made by the light of the sun, of the moon, or of a
flame of fire, but only by the light of a candle, because
the light of a candle is efficient for search, and although
we have no foundation for this regulation, still we are
given a hint to that effect in the passage:[4] 'And it shall
come to pass at that time, that I will search Jerusalem
with lights.'[5] 'The spirit of man is the lamp of the
Lord, which searcheth all the hidden things of the
bowels.'"[6]

Why does the Jew search his house with the light of a
candle and why was he forbidden to make the search

---

[1] These Hebrew words in English are as follows. Rabbi (My Teacher),
Simeon (Hearing), ben (son). Gamaliel (God is Rewarder).   [2] Acts v. 34 and
xxii. 3   [3] Numb. ix. 2, 10, 11.   [4] Exod. xii. 9. Gen. xxxiv. 12   [5] Candles,
Sophonias i 12.   [6] Prov. xx. 27.

with any other light? In a former chapter the reader
will see that in the symbolism of Scripture and Catholic
Church the candle signifies Christ enlightening the mind
with his teachings. From him, the Son, proceeds the
Holy Spirit who enlightens the sinner's mind, dispels the
darkness of sin, shows the state of wickedness in which
he lives in spiritual laziness, and rouses him to burn up
his sins with the fire of love of God and hatred of wickedness The Spirit of God therefore enlightens the sinner,
spurs him on to go to confession and Communion.

" When was this search for fermented bread made? R.
Jehudah said search for Chometz (leaven bread) should
be made in the evening. "Or " (light), before the 14th, or
during early morning of that day. But the sages said:
'If the search had not been made on that day; if neglected
on that day, it may be made on the festival, and if omitted
then, it must be done after the festival, and whatever
Chometz is left over must be kept in a well-guarded
place, in order that no further search may become
necessary.'

"No guilt is incurred unless the man slaughtering the
lamb, or the one sprinkling the blood, or one of those
who are to partake thereof have leaven in his possession.
'Thou shalt not offer the blood of my sacrifice with
leaven.'[1] If any man slaughter the paschal lamb with
leaven, he thereby transgresses a negative command,
provided he himself, or the one who sprinkles the blood,
or one of the congregation, which is to partake of the
lamb, have leaven in their possession

" R. Jehudah also taught: 'Formerly during the existence of the Temple, two cakes of thanksgiving-offerings,
(these were cakes of the unleaven proposition bread, of
which twelve cakes were placed each Sabbath in the
Holies of the Temple, with the metal flasks of wine, to
foretell the bread and wine of the Mass,) which had
been desecrated, were exposed on a bench of the Temple.
As long as the two cakes remained, all the people still
ate the leavened bread. When one of them was removed
they abstained from eating it, but did not yet burn it,
when both were removed, all the people began burning
the Chometz.' Rabbon Gamaliel says: 'Ordinary Cho-

[1] Exod. xxxiv. 25.

metz may eaten during the first four hours, but heave-offerings may still be eaten during the fifth hour, both however must be burned at the commencement of the sixth hour.'[1]

"If the fourteenth of Nisan fall on a Sabbath, all leaven must be removed before the Sabbath.   On the mount of the Temple there was a double arched seat. It was called Istavanith "Columns," because a roof surmounted the seat, and the seat was composed of two arches, one within the other.   Because the cakes were such as had been brought with the thanksgiving offerings, and there being so many of them, they could not be consumed within the statutory time, hence they became desecrated by being left over.   When both were on the benches, all the people ate leaven bread, when one was removed, eating was abstained from, when both were removed the leaven was burned.   There was another sign: Two cows were plowing on the Mount of Olives.   While both cows were seen all the people ate leaven bread, when one of them was taken away, the people abstained from eating, and as soon as the other was taken away, they began to burn the leaven.[2]

"Gemara: We see thus, that at the commencement of the sixth hour all agree Chometz must be burned. 'Seven days no leaven shall be found in your houses.'[3] But on the first day you shall put away leaven out of your houses'[4]   In the morning leaven may be eaten, while in the afternoon it must not   And by the first day, is meant the day preceding the festival.   'Thou shalt not offer the blood of my sacrifice with leaven, neither shall there remain in the morning anything of the victim of the solemnity of the Passover.' "[5]

The first foretold the regulation which forbids the celebrant of the Mass to offer the victim of the Passover, Christ the Lord, at our altars in a state of mortal sin, as St. Paul says: 'Whosoever shall eat this bread or drink the chalice of the Lord unworthily shall be guilty of the Body and of the Blood of the Lord '[6]

"As long as it is lawful to eat leaven bread, one may also give it to domestics, wild animals, or fowls   He may

---

[1] Passover, cap 1, p 19-25   [2] Pesachim, p. 25.   [3] Exod xii 19.   [4] Exod xii. 15.
[5] Exod. xxxiv. 25.   [6] I Cor ii 27

also sell it to strangers, or derive benefit therefrom in any other way. When that time is passed, however, it is unlawful to derive any benefit from it whatever, not even use it for fuel, or to light therewith an oven or stove.' R. Jehudah said: 'The removal of the leaven cannot be affected except by burning.' From the verse just quoted, R. Simeon decrees in another Boraitha.

"A Boraitha is a section of the teaching of the Sages [1] that all things of sanctity [2] that which become desecrated, i. e. flesh of sacrifices, which had been left over must be burned. 'And if there remain of the consecrated flesh, or of the bread till the morning. Thou shalt burn the remainder with fire. They shalt not be eaten because they are sanctified.'" [3]

Thus pieces of the sacrificed bread left over from one Sabbath to another, when they were removed as well as the leavings of the Passover feast, if not eaten by the priests, were burned to foretell how Christ's body, the real 'Lamb of God,' was buried the day he died. If they did not burn them, they were punished with thirty-nine stipes. The Text gives many positive and negative commands, which if any one broke he was punished with "stripes." Severe laws were enforced by the pain of Kareth "Cut off" from Israel, excommunication, which St. Paul mentions to have been enforced in the early Church, and which comes down to us in the laws relating to excommunication.

"Rabh said: 'Earthenware pots, which had been used during the year must be destroyed before Passover.' For what reason? Let them be left over until after the Passover, and then used for other kinds of food, as formerly. This is a precautionary measure, in order to prevent the possibility of their being used for the same kinds of food as formerly. Samuel holds to his individual theory, for he said to the venders of earthenware pots for the Passover: 'Lower the price of your pots for the Passover, otherwise, I shall decree that the law prevails according to R. Simeon.'

"An oven was greased with fat immediately after it had been heated. Rabha bar Ahilayi forbade the eating

---

[1] See Edersheim, Life of Christ, i 103-105   [2] Things of sanctity were things offered to God in the Temple.   [3] Exod xxix 34 Babyl. Talmud, cap. i p. 30, etc.

of the bread baked therein, even with salt, lest it be eaten with Kutach." [1]

Long discussions follow as to how kettles, pots, dishes, plates, etc., must be cleaned by being heated with fire. Two days before the feast they began the preparations in the houses. They first cleaned all the cooking utensils, so the smell of Chomatz, " fermented bread," could not be perceived. Metal vessels they held over the fire till red hot and woodenware they scalded in boiling water. Some destroyed the earthenware vessels called *circenth*. The upper stone of the flour-mill, called *pelach*, and the under stone named *receb*, they dressed with iron tools till they looked like new. The shelves of the pantry, the box wherein the cakes were kept, all the kitchen utensils, they carefully cleaned, shadowing forth the cleansing of our hearts by confession before our Easter Communion.

"What should be done on Passover with knives?" And he answered. 'I buy new knives for the Passover.' And Rabhina rejoined, 'In the master's case it is proper, for thou art rich and can afford it, but what should a poor man do?' 'I do not mean exactly new knives, but renovated knives; knives, the blades of which are covered with clay and placed in the fire, and after being thoroughly burned are taken out, and together with the hilts are soaked in boiling water, when they become equal to new ones '

"A wooden ladle should be placed in boiling water, which had not been removed from the fire." 'What is the law concerning glazed pottery?' If the color of the coating was green, there is no question, they must not be used, but we refer to such as were glazed in black or in white. If the coating was cracked, there is no question, they must not be used. I notice that the fat cooked in such pots oozes out on the other side, and it is obvious that they absorb it, and the Scriptures say that an earthen pot never yields again what it once absorbs." [2]

Scribes and Pharisees carried things to extremes, and we see that dish-cleaning was observed in Christ's day. "Thou blind Pharisee," said Christ, "first make clean the inside of the cup and of the dish, that the outside

[1] A dish made with flour and milk which rendered unclean and prohibited the use of the oven for all time to come.   [2] Levit. vi 21.

may become clean."³ "For leaving the commandment of God, you hold the traditions of men, the washing of pots and many other things you do like to these."¹ The Jews see only the literal meaning of Scripture and religious ceremonial. They seem to be entirely blind regarding the symbolic or typical sense. They did not understand that under these figures, the purifying of the heart was hidden. They taught that sin was not in the mind but in the act, that as long as a person did not commit an action seen by others, he did not sin, no matter how corrupt was his heart. This they claimed was the teachings of their traditions. Whence Christ said to them. "Well do you make void the commandment of God, that you keep your own tradition."² Now let us see the way the Jews of our day prepare for the Passover.

In New York City, at present writing, dwell nearly 800,000 Jews. The housewife of the East side, in addition to her ordinary cares, has two dish cupboards, the contents of which must never be mingled, two sets of dishes, two dishpans, two dishcloths. These must never get mixed, or trouble will arise for the orthodox family. One set of dishes most kosher "clean" is to be used only for Passover, while the other set they use during the year. Milk foods must not come in contact with meat foods No oyster, clam, crab, eel, shell-fish, lobster, or other kind of sea food ever enters her kitchen, for only fish with scales are clean to the Hebrew. Even these fish must not be fried in lard, or butter, but in vegetable oils. They seem to prefer freshwater fish, newly caught, or taken from freshwater ponds, where they are kept for the Jewish market.

The day before the Passover, a frenzy of housecleaning seizes on all Jewesses, and they proceed to make the whole house from garret to foundation and all within it kosher for the great festival. Then the fury of a score of New England housewives takes possession of each Hebrew heart. All the accumulated rubbish of the year is gathered—old clothes, cooking utensils, broken shoes, battered hats, torn matrasses, dented tinware, useless coal scuttles, etc., are projected through doors and windows into the streets, to the eminent danger of all passing

¹ Matt. xxiii. 26.   ³ Mark vii. 9.

by, where they are gathered up to be carried to the dumps.

The slap of mop, broom and brush are heard on all sides, while mother, daughter, and older children are pressed in, kept from school to "make all things kosher." Every dish on Passover table, every utensil with which the feast is cooked must be new, or at least never used except for Passover. Out of box, trunk and hiding-place, come pots, pans, plates, and table ware, where they were laid away the spring before, after having been carefully cleaned and wrapped. But many new things must be bought, even by the poor; families save up their money for the feast, and there is a Passover relief association, founded to help the very poor, who otherwise could not keep the feast according to the law.

At sundown the Jews flock to their synagogues where they hold special services, and spend some time in silent prayer before beginning the Passover which reformed Jews hold for seven and the orthodox for eight days. Afterwards comes the feasts of Succoth when they build in their back yards huts of boughs, leaves and mud, wherein they live, sleep, and receive their friends on their knees, for the custom is to make calls from house to house, although it is forbidden to take food or drink during these visits. These booths out in the open air are in memory of the time their fathers dwelled in tents for forty years after they had fled from Egypt at the first Passover.

Dark-eyed Hebraic-featured push-cart pedlers go from door to door selling matzoths, unfermented cakes, bitter herbs and edibles for the feast of the first night and for the banquets of the remaining evenings. Gladness, joy and mirth light up every Hebrew face, and if there is sadness it is concealed as they recall their fathers' delivery from slavery.

There is a very strict school of Jews of our day, calling themselves Chasidim, "Godly men," "the Saints," a word derived from the Hebrew Perushim, "The Separated," from which came the word Pharisees—the Chasidim, mentioned in the Book of Machabees under the name of the Assideans [1]—they have held to the change-

[1] I Mach ii 42.

II

less customs and traditions of the Pharisees all down the ages till our day. They are found in this country and in the Old World, the most orthodox of the orthodox Jews.

With long prayers they plant the wheat, while growing carefully guard it from contact with an unclean person or a Gentile. With prescribed prayers they reap, thrash, and grind the flour which they place in three bags, one within the other. These bags they tie to the roof of a secret chamber and keep carefully under lock and key, where no one enters till the Passover eve, when they keep a strict fast.

In the dead of the night, with solemn ceremony, they go to a running river, lake, or spring, and with prayer draw the "Water of Precept" in special vessels, which filled, they carry on a long pole on their shoulders so the vessels will not touch any one who might be legally unclean and defile the water. Then with the prescribed prayers they make and bake the cakes for the Passover. These strict Jews claim they celebrate the feast according to the strict rules of the Talmud.

"All vessels in which leaven food had been kept while cold, may be used for unleaven food, with the exception of such vessels as contained actual leaven, for it is very pungent. Such vessels, in which leaven bread and vinegar were generally mixed, must also not be used, because it is equal to leaven." [1]

In Christ's days they made the unleaven cakes of wheat grown especially for the Passover. Pious people raised this wheat, and Lazarus' father had wheatfields at Magdala on the shores of the Sea of Galilee.

Such land was plowed with prayer and prepared with great care. When harvest time came, the reapers were told: "When you bind the sheaves, bear in mind that they are intended for the preparation of the Matzoth," whence we see that he holds that the unleaven bread must be observed from beginning to end.

"Thick loaves must not be baked on the Passover.[2] Such is the decree of the school of Shammai, but the school of Hillel permits this to be done. How thick should they be? Said R. Huna, 'One span, because that was

---

[1] See Talmud, Babyl, cap. ii   [2] Talmud ii. p 57.

the thickness of the showbreads." The "showbreads" were the twelve loaves of proposition bread, placed each Sabbath in the Holies of the Temple with the wine to foretell the bread and wine of the Mass. . . . "In the case of the showbreads, there were priests who were thoroughly competent for their work, but the Passover loaves are prepared by ordinary people."

The Garmo family from remote ages made the showbreads or proposition bread, and were very expert, having a secret way of making very fine thin breads, similar to our altar breads. Because they would not reveal the process they were blamed in the Temple prayers.

" The showbreads were prepared with the utmost skill, and how can they be compared to ordinary loaves? For the former dry wood only was used, while for the latter damp wood may be used. The former were baked in a hot oven, while the latter are often baked in a cooler oven. For the baking of showbreads an iron stove was used, while for the Passover cakes an earthen oven was considered sufficient. If such cakes are made, they should be made as thin as wafers, not as thick as loaves, because in the latter event they might become leaven "

The custom of making the altar breads as thin as possible in the Latin Church follows the ancient Jewish custom. To signify the Holy Ghost dwelling in the humanity of Christ hidden under the species of bread on our altars, the Jews mixed olive oil with the flour of which they made the wafers.

" The quantity of oil mixed with the dough is so insignificant, that it is not counted, for a quarter of a log of oil is used for a great many cakes. A woman should not knead dough for the Passover except with Shelanu water,—" Our " water,[1] that is, not water left over night, but drawn that day especially for the Passover bread."[2]

This was the water the man was bringing into the city when the apostles Peter and John met him, as Christ foretold, " Behold as you go into the city, there shall meet you a man carrying a pitcher of water, follow him into the house which he entereth."[3]

" A woman should not knead her dough in the glare of

[1] Passover, p. 66, 67.   [2] See Zanolini, De Festis Judæorum, c. 4, note.
[3] Luke xxii. 10-11.

the sun, nor with water that had been heated by the
sun. Also not with water that had been left over in a
muliar, "kettle," and should not remove her hands in
general, until her bread is baked. She also requires two
vessels filled with water. One to cool off her hands
while kneading, the other to moisten her dough before
putting it in the oven."

When she had rolled the wafers as thin as possible, she
made the imprint of her five fingers in each, as she supposed, to make them bake better, not knowing they foretold the five wounds in Christ's dead body. The Jewish
cakes for the Passover and the Temple, of unleaven bread
come down to us in the altar breads with figures of the
cross, etc., in crackers of commerce, the "hard tack" of
soldiers and sailors with their figures copied from the im-
prints of the fingers in the Passover cakes. Before baking they anointed each cake with oil in the form of a cross,
or Greek X[1] "The continual daily Temple sacrifice[2]
was slaughtered half an hour after the eighth hour and
sacrificed half an hour after the ninth hour."

They began to count the hours at six in the morning.
This relates to the afternoon service at three o'clock,
the morning sacrifice being offered at nine. For Christ
was condemned to death by Pilate at nine, nailed to the
cross at noon and died at three. The time given here is
from half-past two to half-past three P.M. for during that
and hour the Temple Liturgy was sung, the lamb slaughtered, the prayers sung.

"But the day before Passover, whether that day happened to be a week day or a Sabbath, it was slaughtered
half an hour after the seventh hour, and sacrificed half
an hour after the eighth hour. The statement refers to
the paschal lamb.

"The daily evening offering precedes the Passover-
sacrifice, and the Passover-sacrifice precedes the burning
of incense, and the incense precedes the lighting of the
candles.[3] There is nothing which may be offered up
before the daily morning sacrifice, except incense, which
is burned before the daily sacrifice.[4]

"Mishna: If the Passover-sacrifice had not been

---

[1] Edersheim, Temple, p 155 etc.   [2] Numb. xxviii. 3.   [3] Exod. xii. 6, Deut.
xvi. 6.   [4] Exod xxx 7

slaughtered for the purpose of sacrificing it as a Passover sacrifice, or its blood had not been received for that purpose, or if the blood had not been brought to the altar, and sprinkled for that purpose, or if one act had been accomplished in order to make it a Passover-sacrifice, and another not for that purpose, or if the reverse had taken place—it is not valid." One of the cakes was sent to the priests of the Temple as a "first-fruit offering." The three remaining were for the Passover. The dough remaining after the cakes now called Kiccar "circle" had been baked, they burned as an offering to the Lord.

"Have we not learned in a Mishna, however, that a trifle over five quarts of flour, equal to five logs in Sepphoris, and to seven logs and a trifle over as used in the desert, which in turn equal an omer, are subject to the first of the dough? Our wives bake in small quantities on the Passover, not over three logs of flour at a time.

"Three women may occupy themselves with their dough, but in the following manner, one should knead the dough, another form it, and the third bake it. The same woman who kneads should also moisten the dough, and the one next to her should then take up the kneading; while the former is baking, the latter should moisten the dough, and the third woman should take up the kneading. Thus the first woman will commence the kneading, while the last is moistening the dough and so on in rotation."[1]

This was the unfermented bread the Greeks called azymus mentioned forty one times in the Old Testament. St. Matthew called it "the azymes."[2] The Jews of our day at Passover bake a bread called "rich azymos" made with eggs, milk, sugar etc., which they give to the sick and Gentiles, while some give away the ordinary Passover bread[3]

"Formerly the hides of the sacrificed animals were left in the chamber of Parvah (one of the Temple chambers mentioned in the Tract Midath). At night the priests ministering during that week, would divide those hides among themselves. The more powerful among the priests would appropriate more than their share. So it was ordered that the division should be made every eve of Sabbath in the presence of all the men composing the

[1] Passover Cap. 111-77. [2] Mat. xxvi. 17 [3] See Zanolini, De Festis, c. 4.

twenty-four "courses" watches of the Temple. Still the
more powerful priests would appropriate more than was
due them. In consequence, persons bringing sacrifices
decided to consecrate the hides for the use of the Temple.
It was said that it did not take very long before it was
possible to cover the entire Temple with disks of gold,
one ell square and of the thickness of a golden Dinar.
At the time of the festivals, the disks were placed on the
mound of the Temple, in order that the pilgrims coming
up to Jerusalem might see them, for they were beautifully worked and were not counterfeited.

"There were sycamore-trees in Jericho, which the
priests forcibly appropriated for their own use, in consequence of which the owners consecrated them for the
use of the Temple. Concerning such outrages and such
priests, Abba Saul ben Batnith in the name of Abba
Joseph ben Hanin said :

"Woe is me on account of the house of Baithos.
"Woe is me on account of their rods.
"Woe is me through the house of Hanin and through their
      calumnies.
"Woe is me through the house of Kathros[1] and through their
      pens.
"Woe is me on account of the house of Ismael ben Piakhi and
      of their fists.
" For they were all high priests.
" Their sons were the treasurers.
" Their sons-in-law were the chamberlains,
" And their servants would beat us with rods."

The Temple was famed all over the world because it
was covered with these plates of solid pure gold, each
about a yard square and as thick as a twenty-five cent
piece. From another part of the Talmud we learn that
they first filled every crack between the white marble
stones with beeswax, and attached the plates with gold
nails. The great building inclosing the Holies and the
Holy of Holies was therefore called in Hebrew writings
"The Gold House." It was 150 feet square—all its walls
and roof within and without covered with gold.[2]

The reader may judge from this statement the avarice
of the priests. Another account says that at first the

[1] Kathros means the quarrelsome.   [2] See Passover, p 108.

priests were chosen for the weekly ministry as they came into the Temple. But once as they were rushing up the marble steps of the Nicanor Gate, one priest pushed another down and broke his leg Another time while they were running in, one stabbed the other to death and the Beth Din "The Judges of the House of Law," established the custom of choosing them to minister the following week by counting fingers.

In the poem we have given on their degradation, the "house of Hanin" was the family of Annas, father-in law of Joseph Caiphas, who sentenced Christ to death. This Annas had five sons and five daughters and his sons-in-law, one after the other, became high priests. But like himself they were deposed from the office by the Roman procurators for their crimes.

" Mishna. The inhabitants of Jericho were wont to do six things; three of these were done contrary to the wishes of the sages, and three were done with their sanction. They would graft palm-trees the whole day of the 14th, they would read the Shema with the additional versicles, and they would heap up new grain into sheaves, before acquitting the Omer, "first offering" thereof.[1]

" Six things were done by King Hezekiah,[2] three of which met with approval, and three with disapproval. He caused the bones of his father (the wicked Achaz) to be transported on a litter of ropes (the Talmud has here in a note, "As a mark of disrespect") and this was approved of ; he caused the brazen serpent to be broken to pieces (this was the brazen serpent Moses made in the desert,[3] which the Jews adored as an idol) and it was also approved ; he secreted the book of medicine, and this was also approved. He cut off the gold from the gates of the Temple, and sent it to the King of Assyria ; he stopped up the upper mouth of the waters of Gihon, and made the month of Nisan intercalary, all of which were not approved.[4]

" From the time of Min'hah," etc. The schoolmen asked : Does this refer to the long Min'hah, the time for which commences at the half of the eighth hour (that is

---

[1] Passover, p 99, 102, etc.   [2] Ezechias I , was the 16th king of Juda, born in the year 3 309, nine years after the founding of Rome, 743 before Christ His history will be found in IV Kings, chapters xv, xvi , and II Par. xxvii, 28
[3] Numb xxi, 9.   [4] Passover p 99-102

at 1.30 P. M.,) or to the short Min'hah, the time for which
commences at the half of the tenth hour ? (That is at 3.30
in the afternoon.)   Is it not lawful to eat from the time
of the long Min'hah, because thereby the time in which
the paschal offering must be brought will be taken up ?

"We have learned : Even King Agrippa [1] whose wont it
was to eat at the ninth hour of the day, (three P.M.) should
not eat on the eve of the Passover until it becomes dark.
Now if the short Min'hah is meant, after which it is not
lawful to eat, then the case of King Agrippa is worthy of
note.   But if the long Min'hah is meant, what proof does
this case exhibit then, that it was only because the meal
would interfere with the paschal offering, and why is
Agrippa's case specially mentioned ?   Hence we may infer that the short Min'hah is meant.

"Mishna : On the eve of any Passover, it is not lawful
for a person to eat from the time of Min'hah until after
dark.   Even the meanest in Israel shall not eat until they
have arranged themselves in proper order, at ease round
the table, nor shall a person have less than four cups of
wine, even if they must be given him from funds devoted
to the charitable support of the very poor.   A person
must not eat aught on the eve of the Sabbath, or of a
festival, from the time of the Min'hah on, in order that
the entry of the Sabbath, or the festival, may find him in
a condition to relish a meal.

"A table must not be brought for each guest separately,
unless the Kiddush had already been recited by the head
of the household, but if a table had been set before him
before the Kiddush had been recited, then the guest
should cover the table set before him with a cloth, and
himself pronounce that benediction."

The Kiddush, "Prayer," was the prayer said before
meals.   The table was always covered with linen table-
cloths at the Passover.   In rich houses they used three
cloths, one over the other.   This was the origin of the
three linen altar cloths covering our altars in churches of
the Latin Rite.   The Greeks use altar cloths of silk.

---

[1] This Herod Agrippa, Acts ii., was the grandson of Herod the Great,
through Mariamne descendant of the Machabees, his father being Alexander,
whom the first Herod strangulated to death.   Claudius, the Roman emperor,
made him king over Judea.   He was the last king of the Herod family   See
Acts xxv. 26

On the ninth day of Ab, God ordered the Hebrews, because of their sins, to wander forty years in the desert, living on manna, figure of the Eucharist. On the ninth of Ab, five hundred and ninety-eight years before Christ, the Babylonians destroyed Solomon's magnificent Temple. More than six hundred years later, on the ninth of Ab, in the year A. D. 70, the Romans under Titus destroyed the great Temple Herod built, and which Christ had visited so many times. On the ninth of Ab, Bethar fell, and vast numbers of Jews were slaughtered. On the ninth of Ab a year later, Hadrian drew the plow over the ruins of the holy city. Jerusalem became a Roman colony called Aelia Capitolina, and Jews were forbidden, under pain of death, to enter within its walls. Down the centuries since, the Jews fast on the ninth of Ab, in memory of these five great calamities which fell on their nation.

They also observe three other fast days in connection with the fall of Jerusalem,—the tenth day of Tebet, when the siege began, the seventeenth of Tamuz, when the first breach was made in the wall, the third day of Tishri, when Gedaliah, their leader, was assassinated,— the last day being known as the Fast of Gedaliah.

During these days, beginning with the first of Ab, no meat is eaten, no wine drunk, no pleasure permitted. The " Nine days," so-called, are days of mourning in all Israel, and the synagogues are filled with weeping, mourning and fasting Jews. The homes are all darkened, shutters closed, blinds drawn and home lighted only by candles.

Barefooted, ashes on their heads, strict Hebrews of our day clothe themselves in sackcloth, recline on the floor, or on low seats and boxes, and they tell their children the story of the sieges and calamities of Jerusalem. They read the Lamentations of Jeremias to their families, and in the synagogues sermons are delivered on the sorrows of Israel. The Hassan and Rabbi in mournful cadence sing the plaintive songs called Kinoth, with the congregation chanting the woes of Israel, especially the Ode to Sion, by Judah ha Levi. In the synagogue of Jerusalem, the Scrolls of the Law, as well as the holy shrine, the Aaron where it rests, are draped in black.

Clothed in black, they go to the western wall of Solomon's
Temple, the great foundations still standing in the
Tyropœon valley, within the city, and, turning their
faces to the ancient walls called the " Wall of Wailing,"
they chant the prayers for the restoration of Zion.
From this mourning service, with its black garments,
the Church copied the black vestments and the dark
mourning decorations of our funeral services.

It is sad to see them there in Jerusalem, with faces
turned to the wall, swaying back and forth, and from
side to side, wailing, weeping, lamenting the destruction
of their city, the scattering of Israel, the ruin of the
Temple. But it seems God hears them not, for they
pray, not for spiritual, but for temporal things,—the
coming of their Messiah to make them rulers over all
the earth. Christians, with Mohammedans, look on, and
many mocked them.

" The sages, however, said it was customary in Judea
to work until noon on the day preceding Passover, but in
Galilee no work was performed on that day. The night
preceding that day the school of Shamai prohibits work
to be done, while the school of Hillel permits it till sunrise. Said R. Meir: ' Every occupation which had been
commenced prior to the fourteenth of Nisan, may be
finished on that day, but no new work may be commenced, even if it can be finished on that day.' The
sages, however, are of the opinion that the three following crafts, tailors, barbers, and clothes-washers, may
pursue their calling until noon that day.

" Tailors may pursue their occupation, because any man
may of necessity mend his garments on the days intervening between the first and last days of the festival.
Barbers and clothes-washers may pursue their calling,
because those that arrive from a sea-voyage, or those
that are released from imprisonment, may trim their
hair, and wash their clothes on the days intervening between the first and last days of the festival. R. Jose ben
Jehudah says that shoemakers may pursue their calling,
because pilgrims, who journey to Jerusalem for the
festival, mend their shoes in the intervening days."

When the Passover fell on the eve of, or on a Sabbath,
lest they might break the Sabbath by any kind of labor,

they stuck the sacrificial knife in the sheep's wool, or tied it between the goat's horns, as they led the animal to the altar.

"Mishna : Under what circumstances is it allowed to bring a festal offering in addition to the paschal sacrifice? When the paschal sacrifice is sacrificed on week days, when those offering it are legally clean, and if it is insufficient for those appointed to partake thereof, the festal offering may be brought as a flock of cattle, lambs, or goats, and may be either male or female. The festal offering, brought on the fourteenth with the paschal sacrifice, only fulfils the duty of enjoying the festival, but the injunction, not to come empty into the Temple, is not satisfied thereby. It should be consumed in the course of one day and night, and must not be eaten except it be roasted, and not by any one except those appointed to eat the paschal sacrifice." [1]

Thus were foretold the offerings the laity must make for the support of religion. The collections in our churches go back to apostolic times, and beyond to the days of Hebrew kings. The following relates to the joy with which we celebrate Sundays and feasts.

"Peace-offerings brought on the eve of Passover fulfils the duty of rejoicing on the festival, as it need not be brought at the time when rejoicing is already a duty, but may be brought previously ; but it does not fulfil the duty of bringing the festal offering, because it is consecrated, and the festal offering must be brought."

Under priests' directions the laity slaughtered the lambs, foretelling that the Swiss Guards of Pilate's palace crucified Christ, and the Roman procurator urged on by the priests who cried "Crucify him," etc., condemned the Lord to death.

"The priests removed the blood, the priest nearest the altar squirted the blood on the altar, etc., as it is written : 'Their blood only thou shalt pour on the altar, and their fat thou shalt burn for a most sweet odor to the Lord.'" [2]   "It does not say its blood or its fat, but in the plural, their blood and their fat, which signifies that the blood of the firstlings, and of the first tithes, and of

[1] Deut. xvi. 2.   [2] Numb. xxviii. 17.

the Passover-sacrifice, must be sprinkled, and the pieces which must be offered should be offered on the altar.

" ' And he shall immolate it at the side of the altar that looketh to the north before the Lord, but the sons of Aaron shall pour the blood thereof upon the altar round about.'[1] And he shall put of the same blood on the horns of the altar, that is before the Lord, in the tabernacle of the testimony, and the rest of the blood he shall pour at the foot of the altar of holocaust.'[2]

" The Passover-sacrifice was slaughtered for three successive divisions of men, because it was written.[3] ' The whole *assembly*, of the *congregation*, of *Israel* shall slaughter it.' These three divisions were necessary according to the expressions " *assembly*," " *congregation*," and " *Israel*." The first division entered until the court of the Temple was filled, when the doors of the court were closed, and the cornet horn sounded Tekiah, one blast, Teruah a succession of quick blasts, and Tekiah another blast. The priests then placed themselves in double rows each priest holding a chalice of silver or a chalice of gold in his hands, but one row of priests had to hold all silver chalices and the other all gold—they were not allow to be mixed. These goblets had no stands underneath, so that the priests might not put them down and allow the blood to coagulate.

" The Israelite slaughtered, and the priest received the blood, and gave it to another priest, who in turn passed it to another, each receiving a full chalice, at the same time returning an empty one. The priest nearest the altar squirted it out in one stream at the base of the altar. The first division went out, and the second entered ; when that went out, the third entered in the same way as the first, so did also the second and third division proceed.

" The Hallel prayer of praise was read by each division. If they had finished before completing their duties, they began it over again, and might even say it for a third time, although it never happened that there was occasion to say it thrice.[4]

" The same things that were done on week-days were also done on the Sabbath, except that the priests would

---

[1] Levit. i. 11.   [2] Levit iv 18   [3] Exod xii 6   [4] The Hallel prayer consists of the recital of the Psalms from cxiii. to cxviii. inclusive.

that day wash the court, contrary to the wishes of the sages.' R. Jehudah says : 'A cup was filled with the mixed blood of all the sacrifices and was squirted in one stream on the altar.'"

This chalice of mixed blood from all the sacrifices pointed to the one sacrifice of Calvary. The skin of the lamb was taken off while the victim was tied up to the pillar, to foretell how Christ was scourged when he was tied to iron hooks in the granite pillar in Pilate's Forum.

" In what manner was the paschal sacrifice suspended and its skin removed? Iron hooks were fixed to the walls and pillars on which the sacrifice was suspended and its skin removed. Those who could not find a place to do it in that manner, used thin smooth sticks of wood provided there for that purpose, on which they suspended the paschal sacrifice, resting the sticks between the shoulders of two persons to remove the skin. If the 14th of Nisan occurred on a Sabbath, one person would place his left hand on the right shoulder of another, and the latter would place his right hand on the left shoulder of the former, and thus suspending the sacrifice on the arms they would remove the skin with their right hands.

" When the sacrifice had been opened, the pieces which were to be sacrificed on the altar were removed, placed on a large dish and offered up with incense on the altar. When the first division had gone out, they would remain on the Temple mound, the second would remain in the open space between the walls of the Temple, and the third division would remain in its place. As soon as it became dark, they all went out to roast their sacrifices.

" The paschal sacrifice was not slaughtered unless there were three divisions of thirty men each. Why? Because it is written : " The whole *assembly* of the *congregation* of *Israel*—thus "assembly" means ten men, "congregation" ten men, and "Israel" also ten men. It was doubtful however whether the thirty men had to be taken together, or whether ten men only at a time had to be present. So it was ordered that thirty men should enter, and as soon as ten were ready, they went out, and ten others took their place; the next ten then left, and another ten entered; finally the last thirty went out together—thus each division numbered fifty men, or all three divisions one hundred and fifty men.[1]

" Agrippa the king once wanted to know how many male Israelites there were. So he told the high priest to keep an account of the paschal lambs. The high priest then ordered that one kidney of each paschal lamb be preserved, and it was found that six hundred thousand pairs of kidneys were preserved, and this was twice the number of the Israelites who went out of Egypt. Naturally this was exclusive of all Israelites who were unclean, and could not offer the sacrifice, and all those who lived at a great distance from Jerusalem and were not in duty bound to be present. There was not a paschal lamb that did not represent at least more than ten persons." [1]

Josephus[2] tells the same story of the kidneys counted, and we learn that 12,000,000 persons offered the Passover sacrifice that year, which was known as the "large Passover." We can then imagine the vast crowds, who clamored for the death of Christ and what a multitude saw him die. The strangers used to camp around Jerusalem, filling the country for miles in all directions. They followed the rules Moses laid down to regulate their desert encampments. Olivet was covered with the tents of Juda and Benjamin ; to the south, toward Bethlehem, rose the tents of Issachar and Zebulon mingling with sons of Simon, Gad and Ruben ; to the west were Ephraim, Manasses, while in the level plain to the north camped Dan, Asher and Nephthalim.

The Talmud says the gold chalices were worth 200 and the silver 100 denars; the denars equalling about 17 cents, each chalice was worth respectfully $34 and $17. The denar, in Latin denarius, was so called from the letter x, meaning ten.

" Mishna : How should the paschal lamb be roasted ? A spit, made of wood of the pomegranate tree, should be taken, put in at the mouth and brought out at the vent thereof. The paschal sacrifice must not be roasted on an iron roasting spit or on a gridiron.[3]

" Mishna : If any part of the roasted lamb touched the earthenware oven on which it was roasted, that part must

[1] Passover, 121.   [2] Antiq xvii 9, 3 ; Wars, v 9, 3   [3] Passover, cap, vii ; First. Mishna. p. 148.

be pared off If the fat dripping from the lamb had fallen on the oven, and then again had fallen on the lamb, that part of the lamb must be cut out. If the dripping however fell on fine flour, a handful of that flour must be taken and burned. If the paschal lamb had been anointed, or basted with the consecrated oil of the heave-offering, and the company appointed to partake thereof consists of priests, they are allowed to eat it. But if the company consists of Israelites, they must wash it off if the lamb be yet raw." [1]

The pomegranate, "grained apple," called in Hebrew rimmon, was extensively grown in the Jordan valley and around Jerusalem at the time of Christ. The stick was extended so that its lower end passed through the tendons of the hind feet, and the cross-piece of the same kind of wood passed through the tendons of the fore feet The operation was called "crucifying the lamb." The lamb rested entirely on and was roasted on its cross, and foretold the dead Christ hanging from his cross. Seeing this crucified paschal lamb, a striking image of the Crucified, the Rabbis of the Talmud left out the details of the sticks passing through the tendons of the feet. But other writers (Justin Martyr and the early Fathers) describe the lamb thus roasted on his cross, emblem of the crucifixion coming down from the days of the Hebrew kings.

"Mishna: Five kinds of sacrifices may be brought, even if those who offer them should be in a state of ritual uncleanness, but they should not be eaten by them while in that condition They are the Omer "Sheaf offering," the two loaves of Pentecost, the showbreads of the Sabbath, the peace-offerings of the congregation, and the he-goats offered on the feast of the New Moon. The teaching may be in accord with the sages, but in that event, it treats of the whole community, and not of an individual, and we have learned that a community may sacrifice the paschal offering, even if all the members thereof were defiled." [2]

The whole community of the Jews sacrificed the real Lamb of God foretold by the paschal sacrifice when they cried out "Crucify him," "Let him be crucified," etc., in

[1] Passover, cap. vii 146.   [2] Passover, 148.

Pilate's hall, and this was foretold by the passage we have quoted.

"Mishna : If the whole, or the greater part of the congregation had become defiled, or the priests were in a state of defilement, but the congregation was undefiled, the sacrifice may be brought in this state of defilement, But if the minority only of the congregation had become defiled, the majority that are clean, shall sacrifice the paschal offering at its proper time, and the unclean shall sacrifice a second paschal offering on the 14th of the following month." [1]

The Apostles, disciples, Joseph of Arimathea, Nicodemus the holy women, Christ's followers, did not demand his death, and these were represented by those called undefiled in the Mishna we have given. To foretell how the Lord was crucified at Jerusalem, the following was the revealed law:

"Thou mayest not immolate the phase in any of thy cities, which the Lord thy God shall give thee. But in the place which the Lord thy God shall choose." [2] "Even if one tribe were unclean, and the remaining eleven tribes of Israel were clean, the members of the unclean tribe must bring a separate sacrifice, because he holds that each tribe constitutes a congregation." [3]

"Mishna : The bones, sinews, and other remaining parts must be burned on the sixteenth, and should that day fall on the Sabbath, they must be burned on the seventeenth, because the burning of these does not supersede the laws of the Sabbath, or those of the festival. The bones of a paschal offering, however, which remain whole, could have been broken and the marrow extracted from them only after becoming "a remainder," and for that reason they must be burnt. "Neither shall there remain anything of it till morning. If there be anything left you shall burn it with fire." [4]

This disposal of the remains of the lamb, was a prophecy in Moses' day, that the body of Christ would be buried the day he died. But the following prophesied that while they broke the legs of the two thieves, they did not break Christ's limbs.

---

[1] Passover, vii p. 154.   [2] Deut. xvi. 5   [3] Passover, vii. 155   [4] Exod. xii. 10 ; Passover, vii. p. 162.

"Mishna: Whosoever breaks any bones of the clean paschal lamb incurs the penalty of forty stripes. 'Neither shall you break a bone thereof'[1] 'In one house shall it be eaten, neither shall you carry forth of the flesh thereof out of the house, neither shall you break a bone thereof,'[1] and hence we must say that only if a bone was broken of a lamb, which must be eaten, but not of a lamb which must not be eaten, is the penalty of stripes incurred. They differ, however, concerning a man who breaks the tail of the lamb, which must not be eaten but offered up on the altar[2]

"The attic of the Holy of Holies was even more holy than the Holy of Holies itself, for while the latter was entered once every year, the former was entered only once in seven years, according to others twice in seven years, and according to others only once in fifty years, and then only to see whether any repairs were necessary.[3]

"Concerning the Temple it is written: 'Then gave David to Solomon his son, a description of the porch and of the temple and of the treasures, and of the upper floor, and of the inner chambers and of the house for the mercy-seat, etc . . All these things he said came to me written by the hand of the Lord,' etc.[4]

"When two companies eat their paschal sacrifice in the same house, or room, each turning their faces in a different direction while eating thereof, and the warming pot containing the water to be mixed with the wine is in the center, the waiter, or servant, must close his mouth, that is not eat, while he waits on the other company to, pour out the wine for them. Then he must turn his face towards the company he eats with, and he must not eat till he joins his own company."[5]

Was it because the servants thus came between the tables and poured out the wine that the acolytes, deacon, sub-deacon or altar-boys pour the water and wine into the chalice during Mass? The Greek and Oriental Rites prescribe warm water mixed with the wine at Mass.

"Mishna: If her husband slaughtered for his wife a paschal sacrifice, and her father also slaughtered one, she must eat that of her husband. If she came to pass the

---

[1] Exod. xii 46 [2] Passover, vii, 165, 167, etc [3] Passover, vii, p. 169. [4] I. Paralip., xxviii. 11-20. [5] Passover, vii, p. 170.

12

first festival after her marriage at her father's house, and her father and husband have each slaughtered a paschal sacrifice for her, she may eat it at whatever place she prefers. If several guardians of an orphan have slaughtered paschal sacrifices for him, the orphan may go and eat it at the house he prefers.[1]

"Mishna: If a man say to his sons: 'I slaughter the paschal sacrifice for whichever one of you shall first arrive in Jerusalem,' then the first of them, whose head and greater part of whose body first appears in the city gate, thereby acquires a right to his own share, and acquires the same for his brothers."

The following pages explain and define rules relating to the benefits or graces acquired by those for whom the lamb was sacrificed. This shows that they offered sacrifices for particular persons and families. Thus we have a custom, coming down from the Apostles, of offering Masses for persons, families or particular intentions.

"Mishna: If a person, having a running issue, had observed such issue twice on the same day, and the seventh day after his disease had subsided fall on the fourteenth of Nisan, when he is no longer defiled, he may have the paschal sacrifice slaughtered for him that day. But if he observed the issue three times in one day, it may be slaughtered for him only if the eighth day, when he again becomes clean, should fall on the fourteenth of Nisan.[2]

"Mishna: For a mourner, who has lost a relative for whom he is obliged to mourn on the fourteenth of Nisan, for a person digging out of a heap of fallen ruins persons buried among them, for a prisoner who has assurance of a release in time to eat the paschal sacrifice, and for the aged and sick persons, it is lawful to slaughter the paschal sacrifice, while they are able to partake thereof a quantity at least the size of an olive."[3]

The reader will here see the origin of the custom of giving Communion to those who cannot come to church. The following shows that only Christ and his Apostles formed the "band" to eat the Passover Only men could sit at the table when free from defilement, and all were

---

[1] Passover, viii , First Mishna, p. 173   [2] Passover, viii., p. 185.   [3] Passover xiii., p. 187.

circumcised to foretell the baptized. The unbaptized are incapable of the other sacraments. For these reasons Christ ordained only men

"But we have learned in our Mishna, that a company must not be formed of women, slaves or minors, that is of any of three. And Rabha replied, 'Nay, it means that a company must not be formed of the three together.'

"Mishna: A mourner may eat of the paschal sacrifice at eve, after having taken his legal bath, but he must not eat of other holy sacrifices."

This shows that all who celebrated the Passover were obliged to take "a legal bath," similar to that of the priests who went on service in the Temple. Washing the body was a type of baptism, and Christ raised it to the dignity of this sacrament, which wipes out all sins and gives the three virtues of faith, hope, and charity.

The Talmud here gives many rules and regulations relating to the "second Passover," held on the fourteenth of the following month, which all observed if they could not celebrate the first. If a Jew did not celebrate either one or the other, he became guilty of Kareth "Excommunication." He was driven from the synagogue and excluded from communications with all Israel, as the Law of Moses says: " But if any one is clean, and was not on a journey, and did not make the Phase, that soul shall be cut off from among his people."[1] " He that shall eat leaven bread, his soul shall perish out of the assembly of Israel, whether he be a stranger, or born in the land."[2]

"The following persons were obliged to observe a second Passover: Men and women afflicted with a running issue, with running sores, women suffering from their menstruation, and such as had sexual intercourse with them during that time, women lying in (women in childbirth), those that neglected the observance of the first Passover, either through error or compulsion, those that neglected it intentionally, and those who were on a distant journey And the Lord spoke to Moses saying: 'Say to the children of Israel. The man that shall be unclean by occasion of one that is dead, or shall

---

[1] Numb. ix 13.   [2] Exod. xii. 19.

be on a journey afar off in your nation, let him make the Phase to the Lord in the second month, on the fourteenth day of the month, in the evening they shall eat it, with unleavened bread and wild lettuce.'[1]

"Kareth is the penalty for the non-observance of the first, as well as of the second. Thus the conclusion is as follows. If a man had intentionally neglected the first and second Passover, all agree that he incurs the penalty of Kareth. If he had inadvertenly neglected both, all agree that he is not guilty.

"But the person that eateth of the flesh of the sacrifice of peace-offering that pertaineth to the Lord, having his uncleanness on him, even that person shall be cut off from his people. Whence we infer that if an unclean person eat of the flesh, which may be eaten only by clean persons, he incurs the penalty of Kareth, but if he ate the flesh, which was not fit for a clean person, i. e. unclean flesh, he is not guilty. We might assume that if persons having a running issue had intruded into the sanctuary, in a state of defilement, while the sacrifice was being offered, they thereby incur the penalty of Kareth, to that end it is written, 'Command the children of Israel that they cast out of the camp every leper, and whosoever hath an issue of seed, or is defiled by the dead. Whether it be a man or a woman, cast ye them out of the camp, lest they defile it, when I shall dwell with you.' "[2] This Kareth, " cutting off" or excommunication from the Jewish church, is in Hebrew, Anathema, Maranatha, " Get behind when the Lord cometh. "[3] This Christ said to Peter.[4]

If a person cannot make his Easter duty during holy week or at Easter, the Church extends the time within which the obligation can be satisfied till Saturday before Trinity, the end of the Paschal season. If a Christian does not make his Easter confession and Communion during that time, he is supposed to become a Kareth, " cut off," " excommunicated." The Church in making this law had the example and sanction of God himself, who laid down the same penalty for the Hebrews.

"What must be considered a 'distant' journey?

[1] Numb ix. 10-11.   [2] Numb. v. 2, 3   [3] See Edersheim Temple, 48; Jewish Cyclopedia, etc.   [4] Mark viii. 33

According to R. Aqiba it is from Moodayim and beyond, and from all places around Jerusalem situated at the same distance. Any distance beyond the threshold of the Temple-court should be considered as coming under that term." [1]

" Said Ula: 'From Moodayim to Jerusalem is a distance of fifteen miles.' What is the distance that a man can travel in one day? Ten Parsaoth."

Moodayim, translated Modin, [2] was the city and mount where was born Mathathias father of the Machabees.[3] It contained their family tombs, which Simon had built there [4] setting up seven pyramids of polished stone, one each for his father, mother, himself and his four brothers. " Parsaoth " is the plural of Parsah, "a measure of four miles " called in Hebrew " Milin."

" When eating the first paschal offering the 'Hallel' should be recited, but not while eating the second, from the, passage. 'You shall have a song as in the night of the sanctified solemnity, and joy of heart as when one goeth with a pipe to come into the mountain of the Lord to the mighty One of Israel. And the Lord shall make the glory of his voice to be heard." [5] Hence on the night which ushers in a festival 'Hallel' should be recited, but on the night of the second Passover, when no festival follows, the recital of the 'Hallel' is not necessary. Both the first and second Passover require that the man who offers up the paschal lamb remains in Jerusalem over night.[6]

" What is the difference between the Passover as celebrated by the Israelites in Egypt, and that observed by later generations? The Egyptian Passover-sacrifice was specially ordered to be purchased on the 10th of Nisan, and its blood sprinkled with a bunch of hyssop on the lintel, and on the two sideposts of the door, also that it be eaten with unleaven bread on the first night of Passover, in a hasty manner, while in later generations the law of the Passover applies to the whole seven days of the festival. Vows and voluntary offerings must not be sacrificed on a festival.

---

[1] Passover ix 194. [2] I. Mach xiii. 27 [3] I. Mach. ii 9, 13, 16. II. Mach xiii 14. [4] I. Mach xiii. 27-30 ; Smith's Dict., v 3, word " Modin." ; Josephus, Antiq , xiii 6, 6 [5] Isaias xxx 29. [6] Passover, ix, p. 200

"Those who heard the Kiddush pronounced in the synagogue, need not recite it at their homes, but should merely pronounce the customary benediction over the wine. Why should a man recite the Kiddush at home? In order to give the household an opportunity to hear it. Why should the Kiddush be recited in the synagogue? In order to afford the guests, who eat, drink and sleep in the synagogues, an opportunity to hear it. If a person hears the Kiddush recited in one house, he should not eat in another, but it makes no difference as to rooms in one house."

The Kiddush was the synagogue prayers said before they sat down at the passover table. They were said either in the synagogue or in the house. As the Cenacle was a synagogue, Christ and his Apostles began the synagogue services of Thursday at the Bema before the supper as we will explain later.

" R. Huna thinks that the Kiddush must be recited only in the place where the meal is taken. Abayi said: 'When I was at Master's house, while he recited the Kiddush, he would say to the guests, 'Partake of something before you go to your houses, for should you go home and find the candles gone out, ye will not be able to recite the Kiddush in your homes, and thus you will not acquit yourselves of the duty unless you eat something where the Kiddush was recited.' "

They were forbidden to eat the lamb except candles burned. No religious services were ever carried out in Israel without lighted candles. From this the Church derived the custom of lighting candles at every service.

" Two benedictions must not be made over one cup. When one enters his house at the close of Sabbath, he pronounces a benediction over wine, light, incense, and then the benediction of Habdalah. The Habdalah was the blessing pronounced at the close of the Sabbath services over one cup, and if he has not another of wine in his house, he may leave that cup until he has had his evening meal, and then recite the benediction after the meal over the same cup of wine. Rabh mentions all these benedictions, but omits that of the season, it must be presumed that he refers to the seventh day of Passover as the festival, because that day the benediction of the season is not said, and at that time it is possible that a man has only one cup of wine.

" When is this possible ? On the first day of a festival, when a man surely has more wine; still Abyı said over one cup the benediction of wine, the Kiddush of the season of light, and the Habdalah, and finally of the season, etc.

" When the time for the Habdalah prayer arrived, the servant of Rabha lit several candles, and joined them into one flame. R. Jacob said to him ' Why dost thou light so many candles ? ' and Rabha replied. ' The servant did this of his own accord.'

" We have learned in a Boraitha : That one who is accustomed to incorporate many benedictions in the Habdalah prayer he may embody as many as he chooses.

" How is the order of the Habdalah to be observed ? As follows. ' Who hath made a distinction between sanctified and ordinary, between light and darkness, between Israel and other nations, between the seventh day and working days, between clean and unclean, between sea and dry land, between waters above and beneath, between priests, Levites and Israelites,' and he concluded with : ' Blessed be He who hath arranged the order of creation.' "

The following relate to the seven benedictions and prayers which will be found later in the Passover Seder.[1]

" It is not lawful to begin eating before the prayers. No interruption is allowed during the service If the Sabbath, which began at sundown, was ushered in while they were at the Passover table, they stopped eating and said the Habdalah of the Sabbath, and after citing laws and customs the following eight things follow.

" First : One who included the Habdalah in his evening prayer, must recite it nevertheless again over a cup. Second: The benediction after a meal must be made over the cup of wine. Third : The cup used at the benediction must be of a prescribed capacity, i e a quarter of a log, for were this not so, it could not be divided, and part used for the Habdalah, and another part for the benediction. Fourth : One who pronounces the benediction over the cup of wine, must taste some. Fifth : As soon as

[1] In Chap XII of this work.

part of the wine is tasted after a benediction the cup of
wine is rendered unfit for any other benediction.   Sixth:
Even if a full meal is eaten at the close of Sabbath, and
the sanctification of the day had passed, it shall be the
duty to recite the Habdalah.   Seventh: Two degrees of
sanctification may be bestowed on one cup of wine,
Lastly: The entire Boraitha is in accord with the school
of Shammai and with the interruption of R. Jehudah."

We have given these because they relate to the fourth
chalice of wine, which each one at the table must drink.
This was the chalice Christ blessed and consecrated into
his Blood.   According to the rules we have given, this
must be a large chalice.   The one who pronounced "the
benediction over the chalice of wine, must taste some,"
says the Talmud.   Christ then partook of the consecrated
chalice before giving It to his Apostles, and this is the
reason the celebrant first receives Communion before
giving It to others, The benedictions over the chalice
gave rise to the blessings or crosses over the Elements
after the consecration.   Then follow many minute regulations for the order of procedure.

"Neither Kiddush nor any other benediction should
be made with anything except wine.   The teachings of
the Rabbis relative to other benedictions mean that the
chalice given for the benediction after meals should only
be of wine.

"When eating, the unleaven bread on Passover-night,
one should recline in an easy position, but this is not
required when the bitter herbs are eaten.   When wine
is drunk, it was taught in the name of R. Na'hman, that
a reclining position should be taken, and also that it need
not be taken.   Still this apparent contradiction presents
no difficulty.   The statement quoted of R. Na'hman that
a reclining position is necessary when drinking wine,
refers to the first two cups, and the statement that it is
not necessary, refers to the last two cups.   The first two
cups symbolize the beginning of liberty for the previously
enslaved Jews, while the last two cups have no such
significations.[1]

"Leaning backward is not considered reclining, nor is
leaning over on the right side considered reclining in an

[1] Talmud, Babyl., 225.

easy position. The woman who sits with her husband need not recline when eating, but if she is a woman of prominence she should do so. A son sitting with his father must recline

"Each cup must contain wine, which when mixed with three parts of water will be good wine If unmixed wine was drunk, the duty has nevertheless also been fulfilled If all the four cups were poured into one and drunk, the duty has also been fulfilled. If the wine was drunk un-mixed, the duty of drinking the wine has been acquitted, but the symbolic feature thereof has not been carried out. The cup must contain the color and taste of red wine The duty of drinking the four cups devolves upon all alike [1]

"It is the duty of every man to cause his household and his children to rejoice on the festival, as it is written: 'And thou shalt rejoice on thy feast'[2] The men with the thing they like best, and the women with what pleases them most. The thing men like best is of course wine. But what is most pleasing to women? In Babylonia multicolored dresses, and in Judea pressed linen garments. Small fishes should be eaten, as it is taught in the Mishna.[3]

"When the first cup is poured out, the blessing pertaining to the festival should be said, and then the benediction over the wine must be pronounced.

"Herbs, and vegetables are then brought, the lettuce is then to be immersed, parts thereof eaten, and the remainder left until after the meal arranged for the night is eaten, then the unleaven cakes are to be placed before him, as well as the lettuce, Charoseth (sauce), and two kinds of cooked food, although it is not strictly obligatory to use the same. During the existence of the holy Temple, the paschal sacrifice was placed before him. Two immersions are necessary, one when the lettuce is immersed, and the other when the bitter herbs are immersed. Fish, together with two eggs, may also serve for the two kinds of cooked food. A man should not place the bitter herbs between the unleaven cakes and eat them that way. Why not? Because the eating of unleaven cakes is a biblical command, while the eating

[1] Babyl. Talmud, x p 226   [2] Deut xvi. 14   [3] Talmud, x. p. 227.

of bitter herbs in this day is only a rabbinical ordinance. It was said of Hillel, (who lived in the second century before Christ,) that he would take a piece of the paschal offering, an unleaven cake, and some bitter herbs, and eat them together, as it is written, 'They shall eat it with unleaven bread and wild lettuce.'[1] The mode of procedure should be said over the unleaven bread, a piece thereof eaten; then another blessing should be said over the bitter herbs and a piece tasted, and finally the unleaven bread, and the bitter herbs should be put together and eaten at the same time, saying, 'This is in remembrance of Hillel's actions when the Temple was still in existence'[2]

" When anything is dipped in sauce, the hands should be perfectly clean, that is, previously washed. Thence we infer that the lettuce must be entirely immersed in the Charoseth sauce, for otherwise what need would there be of washing the hands, they would touch the sauce. If a man washed his hands prior to dipping the lettuce the first time, he should nevertheless wash his hands again when dipping the second time. Unleaven bread, bitter herbs, and Charoseth must be dealt out to each man separately, but immediately before the Haggada is read."

The Haggada is the Seder or Liturgy of the Passover. Sometimes they placed a separate table at the head of the couch for each person. But at the Last Supper there were many tables arranged in the form of a U. The father of the family, or master of the band, recited the service, the others holding the scroll of the Liturgy in their hands, and all recited it with him as the newly ordained priests recite the Liturgy with the bishop during their ordination. The sauce called the Charoseth was a kind of salad made of apples, nuts, almonds, spices, etc., mixed with vinegar.

"What religious purposes serves the Charoseth? It serves as a remembrance of the apple trees. It serves as a remembrance of the mortar which the Israelites were compelled to make in Egypt. Therefore the Charoseth should be made to have an acid taste in memory of the apple-trees, also thick in memory of the mortar. The

[1] Numb. ix. 11.   [2] Babyl. Talmud, x. p. 237.

spices used in the preparation of the Charoseth were in memory of the straw used in the preparation of the mortar. The sellers of spices in Jerusalem used to cry out in the streets, "Come and buy spices for religious purposes."

"A second cup is poured out, and the son should then inquire of the father the reason for the ceremony. Where a band, and not a family, celebrated the Passover, the youngest at the table took the place of the son and asked the question. "What is the reason of these ceremonies?"

"Rabbon Gamaliel, (St. Paul's teacher,) used to say: 'Whosoever does not mention the following three things on the Passover, has not fulfilled his duty. They are the paschal sacrifice, the unleaven cakes and the bitter herbs. The paschal sacrifice is offered because the Lord passed over the houses of our ancestors in Egypt, as it is written, 'You shall say to them, It is the victim of the passage of the Lord, when he passed over the houses of the children of Israel in Egypt, striking the Egyptian and saving our houses.'[1] The unleaven bread is eaten, because our ancestors were redeemed from Egypt as it is written · 'The people therefore took the dough before it was leaven, and tying it in their cloaks put it on their shoulders.'[2] And the bitter herbs are eaten because the Egyptians embittered the lives of our ancestors in Egypt, as it is written: 'And they made their lives bitter with hard work, in clay, and brick, and with all manner of service, wherewith they were overcharged in the works of the earth.'[3]

"It is therefore incumbent on every person in all ages, that he should consider as though he had personally gone forth from Egypt, as it is written: 'And thou shall tell thy son that day saying, This is what the Lord did to me when I came forth out of Egypt.'[4] We are therefore in duty bound to thank, praise, adore, glorify, extol, honor, bless, exalt and reverence Him, who wrought all these miracles for our ancestors and for us. For He brought us forth from bondage to freedom, He changed our sorrow into joy, our mourning into a feast. He led us from darkness into light, and from slavery into re-

[1] Exod. xii-27. [2] Exod. xii 34. [3] Exod i 14. [4] Exod. xiii 8.

demption.   Let us therefore say in his presence Hallelujah,
sing the Hallel Prayer."

Hallelujah is in the Hebrew: " Praise Jah " (Jehovah,)
" Praise Jehovah." In Church services it is Alleluia.

"The unleaven bread and bitter herbs must be lifted
up when about to be eaten, but the meat need not be
lifted up, and moreover, if the meat were lifted up, it
would appear as if consecrated things were eaten outside
the Temple."

This lifting up called in Jewish writings, " waving "
was done in this way. First the bread, and then the
wine were each in their turn raised up and offered to the
Lord, then lowered and " waved " to the north, south,
east and west, making a cross. This was done with
every sacrifice in the Temple, and this gave rise to the
ceremony of raising up and offering the bread and wine,
then lowering and making a cross at the offertory of the
Mass. This was also probably the origin of lifting up the
Host when saying: " Behold the Lamb of God, Behold
Him who taketh away the sins of the world!" before
giving Communion. The " meat" or the roast paschal
lamb was not lifted up during the Passover supper, because it had been lifted up, and " waved " while being
sacrificed in the Temple as we will describe later.

"The canticle in the Scriptures[1] was sung by Moses
with Israel, when coming up out of the sea. Who recited
the Hallel? The prophets ordained that at all times,
when they are delivered out of affliction they should say
it on account of their redemption.

" All the praises uttered in the Book of Psalms were
uttered by David, as it is written: 'Here ended the
prayers of David the son of Jesse.'[2] My son Eleazar says
that Moses, together with Israel, said it when coming out
of the sea, but his colleagues differ with him, maintaining that David said it, but to me, my son's opinion
seems more reasonable, for how can it be that the Israelites
should slaughter their paschal offerings and take their
palm branches and not sing a song of praise?

" All the canticles and hymns in the Book of Psalms
according to the dictum of R. Eleazar were sung by David
for his own sake. But R. Joshua says that he did so for

[1] Exod xv,   [2] Psalm lxxi 20

the congregation at large, and the sages say that some were uttered by him for the congregation at large, while others only for his sake, namely, those he uttered in the singular were for his own sake, and those uttered in the plural were for the community at large. The Psalms containing the terms Nitzua'ch and Nigon, were intended for the future, those containing the term Maskil were proclaimed through an interpreter. Where the Psalm commences "Le-David Mizmor" the Shekina rested on David, and then he sang the Psalm, but when it commences "Mizmor Le-David," he first sang the Psalm, and then the Shekina rested on him. Whence it may be concluded that the Shekina does not rest on one who is in a state of idleness, or sorrow, or laughter, or thoughtlessness, or on him who indulges in vain words, but only on one who rejoices in the fulfilment of a duty, as it is written: "But now bring me hither a minstrel (a musician). And when the minstrel played, the jand (inspiration) of the Lord came upon him.

"They said 'Not for our sake,[1] O Lord, not for our sake, but unto thy name give glory.' And the Holy Spirit replied[2] 'For my own sake, for my own sake, will I do it.' 'Josue and Israel said it when they did battle with the kings of the Canaanites.' Israel said: 'Not for our sake,' etc., and the Holy Spirit said 'For my sake,' etc. Deborah and Barak said it, when Sisara waged war on them, they said 'Not for our sake,' etc., and the Holy Spirit replied, 'For my own sake,' etc. King Hezekiah and his companions said it when Sennacherib waged war upon them They said 'Not for our sake,' etc., and the Holy Spirit replied, 'For my sake,' etc., Hananiah, Mishael and Azariah said it, when Nebuchadnezzar was about to throw them in the fiery furnace. They said, 'Not for our sake,' etc., and the Holy Spirit replied, 'For my sake,' etc., Mordechai and Esther said it, when Haman the wicked rose up against them. They said, 'Not for our sake,' etc., and the Holy Spirit replied, 'For my sake,' etc."[3]

We have given this quotation from the Talmud, to show that they had a knowledge of the Holy Spirit. These words with others found hundreds of times in the

---

[1] Psalm cxiii. 1.   [2] Isaias, xlviii. 11   [3] Babyl. Talmud, x. pp 744 to 246.

Old Testament and Jewish writings show us, that they had a vague knowledge of the Three Persons of the Trinity.

"How far is the Hallel to be said? According to Beth Shammai till, 'The joyful mother of children,'[1] according to Beth Hillel till 'Who changeth a rock into a pool of water,'[2] according to another till, 'When Israel went out of Egypt.'"[3]

Beth Shammai "House of Shammai" and Beth Hillel "House of Hillel," were two schools of thought founded by these famous leaders of Israel who lived in the second century before Christ. Hillel in Hebrew means "Rich in praise" and Shammai is "Desolated."

"In reading the Shema" (we will give the prayer later) "and the Hallel, the redemption of Israel should be referred to in the past tense, namely: 'Who hath redeemed,' etc., while in the prayer embracing the Eighteen Benedictions, it should be referred to in the future tense, 'Who wilt redeem,' etc., should refer to the future, not to the past. In the prayer for redemption, the sentence 'He causeth to sprout the foundation of help,' should be said and the benediction pronounced after the recital of the Haphtorah (the Prophets) which should be concluded after the blessing for the redemption with the 'Shield of David.'

"A third cup is then poured out, and the benediction after meals is said. After pouring out the fourth cup, the Hallel should be concluded over it, and the blessings on the songs of praise be said. A person may drink as much as he chooses between the second and third cup, but not between the third and fourth. On the fourth cup the Hallel is concluded, and the great Hallel should also be recited thereon.

"If it is necessary to recite the great Hallel why must the small Hallel be recited at the Passover-meal? Because the small Hallel contains the following five things; the exodus from Egypt, the dividing of the Red Sea, the giving of the Law to the Israelites, the resurrection of the dead, and the sufferings of the Messiah. The small Hallel is recited for another reason, namely because it contains prayers for the transporting of the souls of the

[1] Psalm cxii. 9.   [2] Psalm cxii. 5.   [3] Psalm cxiv. 1.

just from Gehenna (purgatory, not hell of the damned) to heaven as it is written; "O Lord, deliver my soul." [1]

"After the meal and the beverages will have been consumed, the Lord will hand the chalice used for the benediction after meals to Abraham, and Abraham will say: 'I am not worthy, for from me issued Ishmael "God is hearing"; Isaac "Laughter," will then be asked to pronounce the benediction, but he will refuse on the ground that from him issued Esau, "hirsute, hairy"; Jacob, "The Supplanter" will then be offered the chalice, but he will refuse on the ground that he married two sisters, which was afterwards prohibited by law. Moses "Drawer out" will then be requested to say the benediction, but he will refuse on the ground that he was not destined to enter the Promised Land, neither before nor after his death; Josue (in Greek Jesus, "Jehovah will save") will then be asked to accept the chalice, and he will also refuse saying: "I am not worthy, for I died childless." David, "Beloved," will finally be offered the chalice, and he will accept it saying, 'I am indeed worthy and shall recite the benediction,' as it is written,[2] 'I will take the chalice of salvation, and I will call upon the name of the Lord.'"

The Talmud has "The cup of salvation will I lift up." The David given here is not King David, who seduced Uriah's wife, killed her husband, a man of blood and battle all his life, whom God would not let build the Temple, that honor being reserved for his son Solomon. The David, innocent according to God's own heart, was the Messiah, who at the Passover or Last Supper took his fourth chalice in his holy and venerable hands with these words, and consecrated it into his own Blood.[3]

"It is unlawful to conclude the eating of the paschal sacrifice with a dessert. The paschal offering after the hour of midnight renders the hands unclean. Sacrifices which are rejected, or that have remained beyond their prescribed time also render the hands unclean:"

(See the book Pesachem, Passover of the Babylonian Talmud, which then closes with a few unimportant explanations.)

The Tract, Yomah, "Day of Atonement," has as an Ap-

---

[1] Psalm cxiv. 4   [2] Psalm cxv 13   [3] Babyl. Talmud, x. p 256

pendix the following letter written by Marcus Ambivius, third Roman consul of Syria, whose headquarters were at Cæsarea. The fourth consul of Judea was Annius, the fifth Valerius Gratus, the sixth was Pontius Pilate, who was appointed in the year B. C. 25; the first important act of his administration being to move his head-quarters from from Cæsarea to Jerusalem.[1] The scenes thereforefore here described took place about the time Christ was born,

"A WRITTEN REPORT SENT BY MARCUS, CONSUL OF JERU-
SALEM, TO ROME.

(Appendix to Tract Yomah, " Day of Atonement.")

"Concerning the service at the Temple, these Jews were reluctant to inform me about it, as they declared it was against their law to inform a Gentile about their manner of serving God. They enlightened me about two subjects only, part of which I saw with my own eyes, and was greatly rejoiced thereat. One was the sacrifice, which they brought on the feast they call Passover; and the second is the entrance of the high priest, whom we call sacerdos major, into the Temple, on the day which to them, in regard to holiness, purity and strengthening of the soul, is the most important of all the days in the year

"The Passover sacrifice which I have partly witnessed as also I was told, the entire ceremony takes place in the following manner. When the beginning of the month, which they call Nisan approached, by the command of the king and the judges, swift messengers visited every one in the vicinity of Jerusalem, who owned flocks of sheep and herds of cattle, and ordered him to hasten to Jerusalem with them, in order that the pilgrims might have sufficient animals for sacrifice and food; for the people were then very numerous, and whoever did not present himself at the appointed time, his possessions were confiscated for the benefit of the Temple. Consequently all owners of flocks and droves came hastily on, and brought them to a creek near Jerusalem, and washed

---

[1] See Josephus, Antiq. xiv. xi.; 1. Wars, 4 x etc.

and cleaned them of all dirt. They believe that in regard to that Solomon said: "As flocks of sheep that are shorn, which come up from the washing, all with twins."[1]

"When they arrived at the mountains which surround Jerusalem, the multitude was so great that the grass was not seen any longer, as everything was turned white by reason of the white color of the wool. When the tenth day approached—as on the fourteenth day of the month the sacrifice was brought, every one went out to buy his paschal lamb. And the Jews made an ordinance that when going forth on that mission, nobody should say to his neighbor: 'Step aside,' or: 'Let me pass,' even, if the one behind was king Solomon or David. When I remarked to the priests that this was not seemly or polite, they made answer that it was so ordered to show that before the eyes of God, not even at the time of preparing to serve Him, more especially at the service itself—at that time all were equal in receiving His goodness.

"When the fourteenth day of the month arrived, they all went to the highest tower of the Temple, which the Hebrews call Lul, and the stairway of which was made like those in our temple towers, and held three silver trumpets in their hands, with which they blew. After the blowing they proclaimed the following:

"'People of God, listen: The time for sacrificing the paschal lamb has arrived. In the name of Him who rests in the great and holy house.'

"As the people heard the proclamation, they donned their holiday attire, for since midday it was a holiday for the Jews, being the time for sacrifice.

"At the entrance of the great hall on the outside stood twelve Levites with silver staves in their hands, and within twelve with gold staves in their hands. The duties of those on the outside were to direct and warn the incoming people not to injure one another in their great haste, and not to press forward in the crowd, to prevent quarrels; as it previously happened on one of the feasts of Passover, that an old man with his sacrifice was crushed in consequence of the great rush. Those on the inside had to preserve order among the outgoing people, that they should not crush each other. They were also

[1] Cant. of Cant., iv. 2.

13

to close the gates of the court, when they saw that it was already full to its capacity.

"When they reached the slaughtering place, rows of priests stood with gold and silver chalices in their hands: one row had all gold chalices, and another row had silver chalices. This was done to display the glory and splendor of the place. Every priest who stood at the head of the row received a chalice full of the sprinkling blood. He passed it to his neighbor, and he to his until the altar was reached. And the priest who stood next the altar returned the chalice empty, and it went back in the same manner, so that every priest received a full chalice and returned an empty one.

"And there occurred no manner of disturbance, as they were used so to the service, that the bowls seemed to fly back and forth as arrows in the hand of a hero For thirty days previous they practised that service, and therefore found out the place where there was a possibility that a mistake or a mishap might occur. There were also two tall pillars on which stood two priests with silver trumpets in their hands, who blew when each division began the sacrifice, in order to give warning to the priests, who stood on their eminence to begin the Hallel, amid jubilee and thanksgiving, and accompanied by all their musical instruments. The sacrificer also prayed the Hallel. If the sacrifice was not ended the Hallel was repeated.

"After the sacrifices, they went into the halls, where the pillars were full of iron hooks and forks, the sacrifices were hung upon them and skinned There were also many bundles and sticks. For when there were no more empty hooks, they put a stick on the shoulders of two of their number, hung the sacrifice upon it, skinned it, and went away rejoicing, as one who went to war and returned victorious.

"The one that did not bring the paschal lamb at the appointed time, was eternally disgraced During the service the priests were dressed in scarlet, that the blood, which might accidentally be spilled on them, should not be noticed. The garment was short, reaching only to the ankle. The priests stood barefooted, and the sleeves reached only the arms, so they should not be disturbed during the service. On their heads they had a miter, around which was tied a three-ell-long band, but the high priest, as they told me, had a band which he could tie around his miter forty times. His was white.

"The ovens, in which they roasted the paschal lambs, were before their doors, in order, as they told me, to publish their religious ceremonies, as also on account of the festival joys. After the roast, they ate amid jubilee. songs and thanksgiving, so that their voices were heard afar. No gate of Jerusalem was closed during Passover night, because of those who were constantly coming and going, who were considerable in number. The Jews also told me that on the Feast of the Passover the number of those present was double that which went out of Egypt, for they wished to acquaint the king with the number.

"The second service was the entrance of the high priest into the sanctuary. Of the service itself they did not tell me, but of the procession to and from the Temple. Some of it I have also seen with my own eyes, and it surprised me greatly so that I exclaimed, ' Blessed be He who imparts His glory to His nation.'

"Seven days before that day, which they call Atonement Day, and which is the most important in the entire year, they prepare at the house of the high priest a place, and chairs for the chief of the courts, the Nassi (in Hebrew, "the Prince "), the high priest, or his substitute (the Sagan), and for the king, and besides these, also seventy silver chairs for the seventy members of the Sanhedrin. The oldest of the priests got up and delivered an oration before the high priest, full of earnest entreaty. He said :

"' Bethink thyself before whom thou enterest, and know that if thou wilt lose the devotion of thy mind, thou wilt at once drop down dead, and the forgiveness of the Israelites will come to naught. Behold, the eyes of all Israelites are turned upon thee. Investigate thy deeds. Perchance thou hast committed some slight sin. For there are sins which equal in weight many good deeds, and only Almighty God knows the weight thereof. Investigate also the deeds of the priests, thy brothers in office, and have them repent. Take it to heart that thou art to appear before the King of all kings, who sits upon the throne of judgment, who sees everything. How darest thou appear when thou hast the enemy within thee?'

"The high priest then makes answer, that he has already investigated himself, and has repented all that seemed to him sinful, that he has also already assembled all the priests, his brother officers in the Temple. and by Him whose name rests there, conjured them that each one should confess the transgressions of his brother officers, as well as his own, and that he prescribed for each transgression a corresponding penance. The king also spoke to him kindly, and promised to shower on him honors, when he should safely come out of the sanctuary. After that, it was publicly proclaimed that the high priest was about to take possession of his room in the Temple.

"Whereupon the people made ready to accompany him and march before him in the following order, which I witnessed myself. First went those who traced their ancestry to the kings of Israel, then those who were nearer in the priesthood, then followed those who were of the kingly house of David, and, indeed, in the most perfect order, one after the other, and before them was exclaimed: 'Give honor to the family of David.' Then followed the Levites, before whom it was exclaimed, 'Give honor to the family of Levi.' Their number amounted to 36,000. At this time the substitute Levites donned violet silk garments, but the priests, 24,000 strong, vested in white silk garments.

"Then followed the singers, the musicians, the trumpeters, then the closers of the gates, the preparers of the incense, the preparers of the holy veils, the watchers, the masters of the treasury, and then a band, which was called Chartophylax, then all who were employed at the Temple, then the seventy members of the Sanhedrin, then a hundred priests with silver staves in their hands to make room, then the high priest, and behind him the older priests in pairs.

"At the corner of every street stood the heads of colleges, who spoke to him thus: 'High priest, enter in peace. Pray to our Creator for our preservation, so that we may occupy ourselves with the study of his Law.'

"When the procession reached the mount of the Temple, they halted, and prayed for the preservation of the members of the house of David, then for the priests, and the Temple, whereat the Amen exclamation, because of the great crowd, was so loud that the birds overhead fluttered to the ground.

"After that the high priest bowed before the entire people very respectfully, and, weeping, separated himself from them all, and two substitute priests led him into his room, where he took leave of all the priests, his brothers in office.

"All that took place at the procession to the Temple. But at the procession from the Temple (after the whole ceremony was finished seven days later), his honor was double, for the entire population of Jerusalem marched before him, and most of them with burning candles of white wax, and all attired in white. All windows were draped in varicolored kerchiefs, and were lighted dazzingly, and, as the priests told me, the high priest during many years, because of the great crowds and rush, could not reach his house before midnight, for although they all fasted, nevertheless they did not go home before they convinced themselves whether they could kiss his hand.

"On the following day he prepared a great feast, to which he invited his friends and relatives, and made that day a holiday, because of his safe return from the sanctuary. After that he caused a goldsmith to make a gold tablet, with the following inscription engraved on it. 'I, so and so, the high priest, son of so and so, and in the great and holy Temple, in the service of Him who rests his name there, in the year of creation so and so. May He who favored me with the performance of that service, favor also my son after me to perform the service before the Lord.'"

VI.—THE FEAST OF UNLEAVEN BREAD AT THE PASSOVER.

THE Passover and feast of unleaven bread were intermingled, woven one into the other to foretell that the crucifixion and the Last Supper—Christ's Passion and the Mass, were to be not two but one and the same identical Sacrifice.[1] The first day of the feast they held the Passover Supper, the feast of unleaven bread lasted for a week, from the evening of the fourteenth moon to the evening of the twenty-first. The last day was the octave of the Passover and closed the series of feasts with a great banquet. This gave rise to the octaves of our Church feasts.

The whole week was called the Passover. Each night they held a feast called the Chagigah. This was the reason they would not enter Pilate's hall: "that they might not be defiled, but that they might eat the pasch"[2]

The Jews, divided into bands of not less than ten nor more than twenty men, held these feasts during this week; each evening they ended the day with a great banquet, the most celebrated being held in the Cenacle. "The Banquet Chamber." They called these banquets, mishteh, or shatha, "to drink," because wine was the chief beverage. In former times it was named "yayin," "wine" or "grape juice."[3]

The feasts of this week were celebrated from the days of Moses. Jesus son of Sirach in his advice to a ruler, writing more than two hundred years before Christ, mentions, "the crown" the presiding elder wore at the table, "the concert of music in a banquet of wine," "the signet ring of gold worn on the finger," "the melody of music and moderate wine," "in the company of great men," "when the ancients are present."[4] Now let us see

---

[1] See Luke xxii 1, Mark xiv 12   [2] John xviii 28; Levit xxii 5-6   [3] Cant. of Cant. ii. 4; Eccle 32, etc   [5] Eccle 32, etc

198

these banquets, for the details tell us how the Last Supper was held.

In memory of their father's delivery from Egyptian slavery at the Passover, they used to demand the liberation of a prisoner condemned to death.[1] The Talmud alludes to this ancient custom, which even prevailed among the Romans.[2] The Gospel history enshrined forever in human hearts the incident when the Jews asked Pilate to deliver to them a criminal in place of the Lord that fatal Friday of the crucifixion the second day of the Passover. Many ancient MSS of the Gospel,[3] supported by the Armenian version, cited by Origen,[4] held by Tischendorf in his second edition, but rejected later, states that this robber's name was Jesus Barabbas. Therefore this was the question Pilate asked: "Whom will you that I release to you, Jesus Barabbas or Jesus who is called Christ?"[5]

The Passover celebrated the first night and the feast of unleaven bread held each night after during the week,[5] were emblematic of the Church, the Messiah's kingdom, and the Eucharist.[6] In Christ's time the Rabbis promised their followers, that they would pass entire eternity eating at "the Lord's table," thus they understood the prophecies of the Eucharist.

During the nights of this week synagogues and houses where they celebrate the feasts were illuminated with terra cotta lamps and torches; and had beeswax candles on the table. The Temple Courts were brilliantly lighted up, the seven-branched candlestick, quenched during other nights, burned all night in the Holies, and the Temple gates were left opened.

At that epoch the streets had no lamps and outside the houses there was exterior darkness and gnashing of teeth, image of hell, for those under kareth, "cut off"—because of sin or uncleanness.[7]

The second evening took place the ceremony of the Omer, the sheaf of barley foretelling Christ's arrest.[8] In Palestine, Arabia, California, and desert regions, grain is

[1] Matt. xxvii 15, Luke xxiii 17; John xviii 39　[2] Livy, v 13. Pesachim, viii 6　[3] Matt xxvii 17　[4] On Matt v 35　[5] Geikie, Life of Christ, i. 190, 204, and ii 434, etc　[6] Luke vii 32-39; xiii 25, 26-29　[7] Prov ix 2, Amos vi. 4; Isaias v 12, Matt xxvi 20, 26, Luke vii 46-49, John xii 2.　[8] Geikie, Life of Christ, i. 201; Edersheim, Life of Christ, ii ; 205-210, etc.

sowed in the fall, grows during the winter rains and is reaped in the spring. Therefore God commanded them to offer the barley sheaf, the Omer, in the Temple before they began the harvest. The Omer was the "first-fruit," of the harvest.

"And the Lord spoke to Moses saying ... When you shall have entered into the land which I will give you and shall reap your corn, you shall bring sheaves of ears, the first fruits of your harvest to the priests."[1] Down, their history from Moses, additions were made to that yearly Passover ceremony, so that in Christ's time it had become an elaborate rite,[2] for it foretold first-fruit of mankind, Jesus Christ, offered to his Eternal Father.

The "morrow after the Sabbath,"[3] the day of the crucifixion, all the Temple priests were so engaged in that ceremony they did not oppose Joseph's request for Pilate to give him Jesus' dead body hanging on the cross.

Josephus[4] and other Jewish writers show the rite took place after sundown on the evening of the fifteenth of Nisan, the day Christ died. The evening of the fourteenth, the day Christ was arrested, delegates from the Temple went down into the Cedron valley, just to the north of Gethsemane, to the very spot where Christ was arrested, carrying money from the Temple treasury, the Corban, as they took money from the same Corban which they gave to Judas. To the owner of the field they gave the thirty pieces of silver for the standing barley, which they tied still standing in the very place where they tied Jesus' hands.

The time for cutting the sheaf was next day, the fifteenth day of Abib, while Jesus' body hung in death. Even if the day fell on the Sabbath, the ceremony was carried out. As the westering sun was setting a noisy band of Temple guards and Levites led by priests and Pharisees—the very men who the day before had arrested the Lord, went out the Sheep Gate, and down into the Cedron valley just east of the Temple walls. The rabble of the town and loafers followed them each year as they did that fatal night of Christ's arrest.

Only after sunset could they cut the barley, for at

---

[1] Levit, xxiii. 10.   [2] Levit. xxiii 14   [3] Levit. xxiii 11.   [4] Antiq. iii. 10, 5, 6; Philo. Op. ii. 294.

night they arrested the Saviour Not wheat, but barley, could they cut, for the inferior grain foretold the Lord that night with the sins of mankind on him in his Passion They gathered round the tied standing sheaf as they had surrounded Christ. No Psalm was sung, no prayer was said, while they waited for the setting sun, for it foretold that covenant with hell they made with Judas,[1] for the betrayal of the Master on the very same spot.

Three times the leader asked the bystanders, " Has the sun set yet?" Thrice they replied, " Yes, it has set." Three times he repeated " Shall I reap with this sickle?" to which they answered thrice, "Yes." Three times he says : " Into this basket?" and to each they reply " Yes." Again three times he asks, "On this Sabbath " or " Day of the Passover?" and to each question they shout " Yes." Lastly he inquires, "Shall I reap?" and they yell " Yes."

Then they cut the tied sheaves of standing barley, enough to fill an ephah, three seahs, ten omers nearly half a bushel. Across the bridge spanning the Cedron, over which they used to lead each animal for sacrifice, across which they led Christ tied the night they arrested Him, they brought the tied sheaves of barley, which they delivered to the priests in the Temple, as they delivered up Christ to the priests that historic night.

The priests stretched their hands over the barley with prayer, putting their sins on it as they used to do over the victims, then they offered it to the Lord by " waving." That is, they raised it on high, and moved it to the four points of the compass making a cross, for it foretold the Victim of the cross bearing mankind's sins.

The Temple servants thrash the grain with rods as the Lord was scourged, till the grain separates from the chaff as the Saviour was stripped of his garments.

In a pan perforated with many holes, they parch the grain, as the Redeemer was filled with the fire of the Holy Spirit. They ground the grain as the body of Christ was broken, they pass the flour through thirteen sieves, each finer than the other, one of the Cizbarim " Treasurers," plunging in his hands during the sifting as long any flour adhered[2] Of the ten omers only one now

---

[1] Isaias xxviii 18   [2] Men. vi. 6, 7.

remained, a little more than two quarts of fine barley flour.

This they mix with about a pint of olive oil, and a handful of incense, foretelling the Messiah anointed by the Holy Ghost, praying for mankind during his life and Passion, and his body prepared for the grave with incense, a handful of the flour thus prepared they burned on the great sacrificial altar, to show that the Omer was united with all the victims there sacrificed.

This yearly ceremonial of their fathers they called "the presentation of the first wave-sheaf." The harvest could not be begun before this ceremony. From it they counted all their movable feasts and fasts as now in the Church we count the movable feasts from Easter. The Jews of our day still follow the practice. The Jewish Prayer Book counts each day from the Omer till Pentecost. But since the destruction of Jerusalem they do not hold the ceremony of the presentation of the Omer.[1]

" On the same day that the sheaf is consecrated, a lamb, without blemish shall be killed for a holocaust of the Lord, and the libations shall be offered with it, two tenths of flour tempered with oil, for a burnt offering to the Lord, and a most sweet odor; libations also of wine, the fourth part of a hin."[2]   Thus the Omer foretelling Christ's death, the sacrificed lamb, the bread and wine of the Last Supper were offered, and linked together tabernacle, Temple, Crucifixion, Passover and the Mass.

The last days of the feast of unleaven bread were called Moed Katon, "Minor Festivals," and the Talmud lays down many regulations relating to them.[3]   In the time of Christ they were also called the Chagigah " Festival," from the Hebrew Chag, " to dance," because of the ceremonies ; not realizing the sacredness of the feast, sometimes dancing girls exhibited before the guests, as did Herodias before Herod and his guests when she asked the head of John the Baptist.[4]

Many Scripture texts mention these banquets, over which they were to sound the trumpet;[5] the eatables were to be bought with money received for tithes sold ;[6]

---

[1] See Zanolini, De Festis, Judæorum, c. 4 , Jewish Prayer Book, etc.   [2] Levit. xxiii. 12, 13.   [3] Talmud, Mishna, Moed Katon.   [4] Matt. xiv. 8.   See Migne, iii 850-855 , xxiii. 1024, 928, etc   [5] Numb x. 10.   [6] Deut. xiv. 25, 26.

they were to be eaten before the Shekina dwelling in the Temple.[1] The word translated " Lord " in the text is Shekina in the original Hebrew.

Under the pious king Ezechias, the Levites banqueted during the seven days of Passover ;[2] "immolating victims of peace offerings, and praising the Lord, the God of their fathers " with sacrifices mentioned in the law.[3] Onkelos understands here the paschal lamb.[4] The good Ezechias and his princes gave the people at this great Passover 2,000 bullocks, 17,000 sheep. At another Passover Josias gave, besides the lamb " for the Passover offerings, 3.000 oxen," foretelling rulers, princes and wealthy families supporting the Church in Christian times

These passages tell us that the Chagigah, or last days of the Passover, were celebrated with great and holy solemnity If the fifteenth day fell on the Sabbath the lamb might be sacrificed, but not the other victims, for they were killed on the day before so as not to break the Sabbath's solemn rest.[5]

These victims for the Chagigah might be roasted or boiled.[6] The lamb, foretelling Christ crucified, was always roasted, the Law forbade it to be boiled.[7] " And they roasted the phase with fire, according to that which is written in the law, but the victims of peace-offerings they boiled in chaldrons, and kettles, and pots, and they distributed them speedily among all the people."[6]

The remaining days of Passover week they celebrated as solemn feasts Each day they sacrificed special offerings.[8] After the morning sacrifices had been offered in the Temple,[9] private individuals, heads of families or chiefs of tribes brought victims, male or female, without spot or blemish, laid their hands on their heads, putting on them their sins, and the sins of the family or tribe. Then the offerer killed the victim and gave the blood to the priests to be splashed on the altar. Such private offerings might be sacrificed any day in the Temple for private devotions on any day of the year, but during this Easter week, victims with bread and wine were offered with greater devotion. They foretold the stipends and offerings now

[1] Deut. xiv 23 24. [2] II Par. xxx 22 [3] Deut xvi 2 [4] II Par xxxv 6, 7, 8 [5] Pesach, iv. 4, x 3 [6] II Par. xxxv. 13. [7] Exod. xii. [8] Numb xviii 16 to end; Levit, xxiii. 8. [9] Numb, xviii. 17 to end.

given the clergy for Masses for the living and the dead, a custom coming down from apostolic times.

The victim's blood was sprinkled on the horns of the altar, but the tail, fat, and kidneys, were burned on the altar. The breast was given the priest who "waved" it, offering it to God in the form of a cross, with the right shoulder as a heave-offering.[1] What remained of the victim was given the offerer, who with his guests formed a feast and they ate them that day or the day following. If any part remained till the third day it was burned.[2]

Hebrews filled with devotion for their religion and Temple, copied from Moses' ceremonial, and their banquets were always saturated with religion. To the south of the great Temple altar was the great bronze laver resting on twelve brazen oxen. In it priests bathed the whole body before taking part in the services. They had besides many bathrooms in the Temple. Before they celebrated the Passover, each one bathed the whole body, as he plunged into the water, saying:

"Let it be thy will, O God, my Lord, that thou causest me to come in and go out in peace, that thou causest me to return to my place in peace, and save me from this and from like danger in this world and in the world to come."[3]

Priest, Levite and people coming into the Temple to take part in its grand ceremonial, must bathe and be clean as becomes one in the presence of their King. It was a figure of baptism, which was to come and wash men's souls from sin. This was the origin of the holy water at the doors of our churches. At every Moslem mosque you will find people bathing their feet before entering the edifice, a custom coming from the Temple.

The Jews at the time of Christ were noted for their feasts.[4] They used to invite their relatives and friends and divide into bands of not less than ten or more than twenty persons, for this was the number in the bands at Passover. Men and women did not feast together. The lady of the house invited her female friends, and with them held a feast, but the men did not take part with them. The separation of the sexes is still carried out in

---

[1] Levit. iii 1-5; vii 29-34.   [2] Levit vii 17, 18; Pesach., vi. 4.   [3] Talmud, Day of Atonement.   [4] Migne, Cursus Comp, S Theologiæ v 2, p. 117.

the Orient. A wealthy Christian of Bethlehem gave a dinner in honor of the writer which lasted more than two hours, but not a female of the household was seen.

The father of the family, or the master of the house, in the time of Christ received each invited guest at the door with the word Salama : " Peace," or " Peace be with this house," to which the guest replied : " May your heart be enlarged." This was the Marahaba of the Hebrews, the Alaic of the Talmud, the Oriental greeting of friends It is still seen in the Roman Ritual.

Laying their shoes, or sandals, at the door, the guests went barefoot in the house. Before they reclined at the table, servants or the master of the house washed their feet. The custom came down from the patriarchs.

Abraham washed the feet of the three angels who visited him in his tent[1] Laban prepared water to wash Eleazar's feet, when he came into Mesopotamia seeking a wife for Isaac.[2] Joseph's steward brought water to wash the feet of Jacob's eleven sons, when they came back to his house after finding the money in their sacks.[3] Abigal asked of David only the privilege of washing his servants' feet.[4] David told Urias to go into his house and wash his feet as a preparation for supper and bed.[5] When Tobias went to wash his feet, a fish came to devour him.[6] Job washed his feet with butter.[7] The Spouse, speaking to the Church, says of the night of the Last Supper. " I have put off my garment. How shall I put it on? I have washed my feet, how shall I defile them ? "[8]

In rich families servants performed this service, among the middle classes sons and daughters did it, but if he wished to show special honors to his visitors, the father washed their feet. Being a servant's work, we understand how Christ took a towel, girded himself with it, and went from one to another washing the disciples' feet with water in a basin. Peter could not understand why the Master would do a servant's work, protested and was told to obey, or his refusal would lose for him his call to the apostolate. All had taken a bath, as was the custom before celebrating the Passover, their feet were soiled walking over the floor, and Christ said: "He that is

[1] Gen. xviii 4 [2] Gen. xxiv 32 [3] Gen xliii 24 [4] I Kings xxv 41 [5] II. Kings xi. 8. [6] Tobias vi 2 [7] Job xxix 6 [8] Cant. of Cant. v. 3.

washed needeth but to wash his feet but is clean
wholly."

Cleanness of body signified the soul washed from sin.
All were innocent but Judas, Caiphas' nephew, who had
all along acted as a spy for Temple priests, secretly received money from them for his promise of betrayal, and
Jesus said: "And you are clean, but not all." For he
knew who he was that would betray him, therefore he
said: "You are not all clean."[1] Before sitting at the
table, they washed their hands, for they dipped them
into the dishes to grasp the morsels of food.

The master with a large knife carved the meat, handing
to each his portion, a custom still followed till our day.
The knife was often like a lance, and gave rise to our
carving knife. There was no other knife on the table.
Table knives were introduced in the tenth century, and
the fork later. Stools were introduced in Charlemagne's
day, in the middle ages backs were added so they became
chairs. At ordinary meals the people sat on the floor
around the table, their limbs curled under them. But at
formal feasts they reclined on couches.[2]

Many waiters served guests in rich houses, but among
the poor, wives and daughters cooked the food and waited
on the table. Sarah and her servants prepared the meal
and waited on the angels who visited Abraham. Samuel
warned the Hebrews that if they insisted on having a
king, in place of God who was then their Ruler, he would
take their daughters to make his ointments, and serve as
cooks in his kitchen[3] as servants served in Pharaoh's
palace as eunuchs, butlers and bakers.[4]

The master of the feast, called the architriclinus,
"master of three beds," on which they reclined, served
the guests like the carver of our day. When there were
many tables, each had a master or carver who presided.
When Joseph gave a dinner in honor of his brothers,[5] he
sat at a separate table, because he was Pharao's prime
minister, and had to uphold his dignity. The food was
placed first before Joseph, who served it to his brothers.
When Elcana with his two wives went up to the Lord's
tabernacle to adore, and following the custom, he held a

---

[1] John xiii. 11.   [2] See Migne, Cursus Com., S Scripturæ ii, 1170.   [3] I. Kings
viii 13.   [4] Gen. xl. 1.   [5] Gen. xliii. 82.

family feast, he waited on the table, giving to the members of his family their portions, but that of his wife Anna he gave with sorrow, for she was childless.[1] Later she brought forth Samuel the great prophet.

Homer tells us the Greeks had each a table and the master served the guests. Banquets of Persian kings were elaborate ; tables were placed along the sides of the great court, around which the palace was built, or in the "Hall of a Hundred Columns," of which the ruins still stand on the great platform of Persepolis.

Sweetest of the meats was the flesh of the kid, and this was why Rebecca told Jacob to kill a kid, when he received his dying father's blessing. Jacob's words were not a lie, but a mystery, as St Augustine explains. Covered with the kid-skin he typified the scapegoat with the sins of Israel, and foretold Christ with the sins of mankind on him in his Passion. Jacob did not lie to his dying father Isaac, for he had bought the right of the firstborn from his brother Esau, and beautifully the great Fathers explain the whole action relating to the Church and to Christ—they were prophecies in each action.

Solomon's feasts were famous. Each day saw laid on his table thirty measures of fine flour, sixty measures of meal, thirty fat cattle, a hundred rams, besides harts, roes, fowls, etc., with products of the hunt.[2] David gave to the Israelites each a cake, and a piece of roasted meat when they came up to Jerusalem, while the ark remained in his house before the Temple was built.[3]

When Isaac blessed Jacob, when man and wife were reconciled, when David ate with Saul, and when the prophet dined with Jeroboam they sat on the ground, at a low table, their limbs curled up under them in Oriental fashion, and this was the way the common people ate in Christ's time. In days of the kings the master at the table sat on a little stool[4] as a mark of honor. This was the primitive way of eating among all nations. During the heroic age in Greece, they sat at the table.[5] Ruined walls of Korsabad, Nineve, Calne, etc., show kings sitting on high chairs at table.

In course of time, kings and nobles introduced the

---

[1] I. Kings i 4-5. [2] III. Kings iv 22, 23 [3] II. Kings vi. 19 [4] IV. Kings, iv 10.
[5] Homer, Il., x. 578; Od i. 145.

couch, on which they reclined when eating. It is first found in the prophet's words; "You that sleep on beds of ivory, and are wanton on your couches"[1] "Thou satest on a very fine bed, and a table was decked before thee, whereupon thou didst set my incense and my ointment."[2]

The table was placed in "the parlor,"[3] or in a room called the "bed-chamber."[4] In Persia it was called "the king's chamber."[5] The Romans called it the triclinium "three couches," because the couches occupied three sides of the room with the table in the middle.

This was the arrangement of table and couches in the Cenacle at the Last Supper.

At the feasts of unleavened bread, guests were placed according to rank and dignity, the place of honor being at the head or at the cross-table, where the master of the feast, or architriclinus, reclined. Thus Samuel placed Saul at the head of the table when he invited the thirty men to meet the future king of Israel.[6] The place was generally next the wall, where Saul sat on his chair of state, when he tried to kill his rival David.[7] In the days of the kings they sat, but later they learned from Greeks or Romans to recline at the table.[8] The custom of reclining was introduced in the days of the prophets.[9] where for the first time couches are mentioned in Holy Writ. Scribes and Pharisees, filled with pride, sought the first places at feasts [10] and wanted to be leaders in all public places.[11]

King Assuerus with his queen Esther, and his prime minister Aman, reclined on couches at the banquet, and when Aman pleaded for his life, he fell on the queen's couch to entreat her, and the king thought he wished to commit a rape on the queen and ordered him crucified.[12]

The couches or divans were placed with their heads next the table and Christ and his Apostles reclined on their left elbows on a little cushion, and took the food with their right hands. The divans were so large that more than one could recline on each. Dear friends reclined on a couch together, often laying the head on his friend's breast. Thus reclining, confidences were ex-

---

[1] Amos vi. 4 [2] Ezechias xxiii 41 [3] I. King ix. 22 [4] IV Kings ii. 2 [5] Esther ii. 13 [6] I Kings ix. 22 [7] I Kings xx 25 [8] Prov. xxiii 1. [9] Amos vi. 4-6; Tobias, ii 3; Ezech. xxiii 41 [10] Josephus, Antiq. civ., n. 9 [11] Luke, ii. 43. [12] Esther, vii. 8.

changed.[1] John laid his head on Jesus' breast, and the Lord told him in confidence that Judas was about to betray him.[2]

The tables formed a ∪, so the servants could enter between, one side being open. The Lord reclined at the head as Master of the "band" celebrating the Passover. Down the outer sides of the other tables reclined the Apostles—six opposite to and facing the other six. The cross-table at which Christ was, formed the altar on which he offered the Eucharistic sacrifice; called "the table of the Lord," it gave rise to the altar in the church in all Christian rites. This table was at the toe of the horse-shoe, and the Apostles at his right and left in the positions, gave rise to that custom in the early Church in which the celebrant faced the people when saying Mass. That may be seen in the position of the main altar of St. Peter's, Rome, standing over the body of the apostle. The six apostles thus at the sides of the shoe facing each other gave rise to the stalls of our churches and the arrangement of the clergy in our chancel or sanctuary.

Washing the hands, because they were dipped into the dishes, became an act of religion among the Pharisees. "He who washes not his hands before eating is guilty of as great a crime as to eat pork." "He who neglects handwashing deserves to be punished here and here-after."[3] "He is to be destroyed out of the world, for in handwashing is contained the Ten Commandments." "He is guilty of death." "Three things bring poverty, and to slight handwashing is one of them."[4] "He who eats bread without handwashing is as if he went into a harlot."[5] "It is better to go four miles to water than to incur guilt by neglecting handwashing."[6] "He who does not wash his hands after eating is as bad as a murderer."[7] "The devil Schulchan sits with unwashed hands and on the bread."[8]

Numerous such quotations might be given to show the importance they placed on washing hands before meals. Christ and his disciples did not follow all these senseless rules, and the Pharisees rebuked them. "Then came to

[1] Pliny, Epist. iv. 22.   [2] John, xiii 23-25   [3] Book of Sohar, Gen F lx 2.
[4] Mishna, Shabbath, 62, 1   [5] Rabbi Jose.   [6] Talmud, Calla F. lviii. 3.   [7] Talmud, Tanchuma F, lxxiii. 2   [8] Joma F, lxxvii. 2, Glos.

him from Jerusalem Scribes and Pharisees saying.
'Why do thy disciples transgress the traditions of the
ancients? For they wash not their hands when they eat
bread.'"[1]

Before sitting at the table they washed their hands, a
custom which survived the centuries. For before beginning Mass, the celebrant washes his hands in the
vestry. As the feast progressed, they washed again at
different times; the celebrant washes after putting wine
and water in the chalice and again at the postcommunion.
As food would soil the hands after the feast, they washed
their hands at the end as the celebrant does after Mass.

After washing hands, feet, and finishing other preparations, they took their places at the table, each standing
at his place. Every meal began and ended with prayers.
The Passover opened with the synagogue prayers we will
give later. During prayer all stood, for the Jew stood in
Temple and synagogue when praying, the custom of kneeling coming from the example of Christ who in his agony
knelt in the grotto.[2] This is the reason Christians pray
before and after meals standing at the table, and why the
clergy stand at the altar while saying Mass. When they
had taken their places at the table, the master or leader
began thus:

The leader. "Let us say grace.

The others. "Blessed be the name of the Lord from
this time forth and forever.

The leader. "With the sanction of those present.

The others. "Blessed be our God, he of whose bounty
we are about to partake, and through whose goodness we
live.

The others. "Blessed be his name, yea, continually to
be blessed forever and forever."

The leader repeats the same prayer and then says different prayers for different feasts

Before beginning to eat each dish, the master took the
dish and offered it to the Lord, as the sacrifices were offered in the Temple He raised it up as high as his eyes,
then "waved" it to the four points of the compass, making
with it a cross saying: "Blessed art thou, O Lord our
God, King of the Universe, who bringeth forth," here he

[1] Matt xv 1, 2   [2] Luke xxii. 41.

mentioned the kind of food in the dish "from the earth." It was the way Melchisedech offered bread and wine, a Temple ceremony they were careful to observe, especially at the Passover. The celebrant does the same when he offers the bread and wine at Mass.

The Egyptians always shaved, as the mummies of their dead show. When Joseph was released from prison before he could appear before Pharao he shaved.[1] Herodotus says they let the beard grow while mourning, but shaved at all other times.[2] They sometimes wore a false beard. Shaving became a religious rite among them and the Hebrews wore a beard as a protest against Egyptian and heathen superstitions, for pagan priests cut their hair and shaved in peculiar ways in honor of their gods, whence the Lord's command about "the corners of the beard "[3]

By the lapse of ages the beard became highly honored among the Hebrews, and at the time of Christ all wore beards, a custom still seen in the Orient. S. Augustine says " The beard is a sign of perfection "[4] " Christ's beard was a sign of his divine power "[5] " it is a sign of manhood "[6] Jews of our day in the old countries wear long beards, like Arabian chiefs, as a sign of age and authority.

Clothed in rich white robes, sometimes of cloth of gold, beautifully embroidered[7] they carried out these feasts with pomp and ceremony, and wealthy families displayed their riches in the decorated rooms, costly clothing,[8] quantity of food and variety of dishes.[9] Candles and vases of flowers were on the table which was loaded with eatables.

From the Greeks and Romans they copied the custom of wearing crowns of flowers, which the prophet condemns.[10] They anointed the head and feet of the most honored guest with costly perfume, as Mary Magdalen did during the feast Simon the leper gave in Christ's honor that Sabbath evening in Bethany.[11]

Poems were recited, music entertained, bands of dancing girls exhibited, while speeches, riddles, jests, puns,

---

[1] Gen xli 14   [2] Herodotus I. 36.   [3] Levit. xix 27, xxi 5 See Migne, S Scripturæ, ii 1157   [4] Enar. in Ps cxxxii , in xii   [5] Enar in Ps xxxiii , Ser ii in iv   [6] De Civit Dei , L xxii , cap xxiv in iv   [7] Eccl ix. 8 ; Matt xxii 11, 12   [8] Gen xviii 6 ; xxvii 8-9, 43-44 ; Job xxxvi 16   [9] Amos vi 4-5 ; Esther i 5-8, 7-9 II. Esdras v. 18-21   [10] Isaias xxviii 1 ; Wisdom ii 7.   [11] Luke vii 38-46 , John ix 11.

and all kinds of amusement prevailed.[1] The great prophet speaks of ornaments of "shoes," "little moons,"
"chains," "necklaces," "bracelets," "bonnets," "bodkins,"
"ornaments of the legs," "tablets," "sweet balls," "ear-
rings," "rings," "jewels hanging on the forehead,"
"changes of apparel," "short cloaks," "fine linen," "crisp-
ing pins," "looking-glasses," "headbands," "fine veils,"
"sweet smell," "girdle," "curled hair," "stomacher," etc,[2]
used at these feasts.

Feasts lasted sometimes for a whole week, even two
weeks.[3] Weddings of virgins lasted for days and gave
rise to wedding celebrations of our time. The engagement was very solemn, took place in the Temple, where
the priest blessed the couple, as when Joseph and Mary
were espoused.[4]

Honey, salt, oil and butter were always used at these
feasts. We find no record of spices, these having come
later into the western world from India.[5] Wine flowed
in abundance. Sugar not being known, honey was used
in its place. The mother presided over the cooking,[6] the
chief dish being beef.[7] In that hot climate wine was
much diluted with water, and it was drank towards the
end of the feast. Often it was mixed with aromatics, the
fragrance of which filled the banquet chamber.[8] Wines
made of palm fruits called sekar, was much used, especially among the poor, but forbidden the priests during
their ministry.[9]

Towards the end of the banquet, a servant put live
coals in a censer, spread incense on them, entered in between the tables, and going from one guest to another, he
swung the incense before their faces to honor the beard
of each, a sign of his manhood All stood during this incensing in memory of the Temple incense and prayers
offered there to Jehovah of their fathers, for all stood
when praying in the Temple. This rite comes down to
us in the ceremony of incensing clergy and people during
a High Mass.

[1] S. Augustine mentions the abuses of Roman banquets, De Civit. L III cxxI.
Wisdom ii 6, 8; II Kings xix 35, Isaias v. 12 25-6; Judges xiv. 12; II.
Esdras viii 10; Ecclesiastes x 19; Matt xxii 11; Amos vi 5, 6; Luke xv 25
[2] Isaias iii. 18-24 [3] Gen. xxix 27; Judges xiv 12, Tobias xi 21 [4] Luke i 27.
[5] Cant vi 5, 13 [6] Proverbs ix 2, 5, etc [7] Matt. xxii 4. [8] Esther v. 6. Cant
viii 2. [9] Levit x 9; Numb. vi 3, Deut xiv. 26, etc.

Modesty and temperance ruled according to the Lord's words : "And thou shalt eat before the Lord thy God, in the place which he shall choose, that his name may be called upon therein."[1] The word here given as "Lord" in the original Hebrew is Shekina: "the Holy Presence."

They sent from the table food for the poor, following the Lord's directions. "There will not be wanting poor in the land of thy habitation, therefore, I command thee to open thy hand to thy needy and poor brother."[2]

Filled with religious feeling, governed by strict rules, these feasts were types or figures of the great Passover feast. Talmudic writers tell us no other food placed on the table was honored as the bread. This bread was not mixed with any other food, nor thrown into a dish, nor given to a dog, for it was like the bread placed before the Lord each Sabbath in the Temple. Baked for the Passover it was received with highest religious feelings. It foretold the bread used at the Mass. Following the Passover custom a cup of wine was poured out for Elias, John the Baptist foretold by the prophets, to come and prepare the way for the Messiah.

Elias, prophetic type of Christ, was supposed to be at every feast; unseen angels surrounded the table, portions were set aside for them, and at the end the fragments were carefully gathered up. After feeding five thousand with five loaves, Christ followed this custom, when he said to his disciples : "Gather up the fragments that remain lest they be lost."[3]

The banquet over, carefully they laid aside the carving knife, and dishes, and folded the napkins, laying each at his plate, and all together, following the Passover custom, they recited Psalm lxvi., "May God have mercy on us, and bless us," etc. The master purified his glass, or chalice of precious metal, with water, fills it with wine, pouring in a little water, takes the unfermented bread in his hands, breaks off a little piece, and hands it to each Taking the chalice of wine, he drinks from it and hands it to every guest to drink, saying:

The master. "Friends, let us bless Him of whose goodness we have eaten."

[1] Deut. xiv. 23. [2] Deut. xv. 11. [3] John vi. 12.

The others.   " Blessed be He who hath filled us with his gifts and in whose goodness we live."

After all have partaken of it the master drinks what remains in his chalice and says a long prayer which differed for each feast.   Then rising from the table, they wash their hands, giving thanks to God who feeds all animals and men, who brought their fathers from Egypt into Palestine and made the covenant with them to be his people.   St. Jerome says they asked the Lord to send Elias to prepare the way for the long-looked for Messiah, to restore David's dynasty and receive them all at the heavenly banquet in the skies, etc.

After the feast, what was left was given to the children, servants, and the poor.   These leavings were called " crumbs which fell from the table."   Thus Adonibezec gloried that " seventy kings with fingers and toes cut off gathered up the leavings of his table." [1]   Christ and the Canaanite woman talked about the crumbs which fell from the table and which were given to children and dogs.[2]   Lazarus received them from Dives' table, the priests of Bel took them from the idol's table when they came by night into his temple.[3]   From these examples we learn that the table at the time of Christ was raised from the floor almost as high as tables in our day.

Hebrews held certain feasts in the Temple, where they gathered in worship before the Lord.   " And thou shall eat before the Lord thy God in the place which he shall choose, that his name may be called upon therein, the tithes of thy corn and thy wine, and thy oil, and the first-born of thy herds, and thy sheep, that thou mayest fear the Lord thy God at all times." [4]   " Thou shalt take the first of all thy fruits, and put them in a basket, and shall go the place, which the Lord thy God shalt chose, that his name may be invoked there " etc.[5]   The Hebrew word translated here as Lord is the Shekina

The Jews called these " feasts of devotion."   They held in the Temple a holy feast in the spring after the first fruits of farming were gathered and the tithes paid the priests.

Families also held feasts in the Temple to which relatives, friends, priests, Levites and the poor were invited.

[1] Judges i, 7   [2] Matt. xv. 20   [3] Daniel xxiv.   [4] Deut. xiv. 23   [5] Deut. xxvi. 2

Following this custom the early Christians held feasts they called the Agapæ, from the Greek "to love," which were known as "love feasts" or "feasts of friendship," in memory of the Lord's Last Supper.[1] They held these feasts in the churches, after evening prayers[2] and sermon. They first celebrated Mass, received Communion, and then held the feast. In that apostolic age, before churches were built, following Christ's example, they offered the Eucharistic Sacrifice in private houses, in the evening, fasting the whole day before receiving Communion. But some came drunk, attracted by the feast, and abuses rose among the people of Corinth, to whom St. Paul wrote:

"When you come together, therefore, into one place, it is not now to eat the Lord's Supper. For every one taketh before his own supper to eat, and indeed, one is hungry, and another is drunk. What, have you not houses to eat and drink in? Or despise the Church of God, and put them to shame that have not? What shall I say to you? Do I praise you? In this I praise you not.

"For I have received of the Lord, that which I also deliver to you, that the Lord Jesus the night in which he was betrayed, took bread and giving thanks broke and said:

"This is my body, which shall be delivered for you. Do this for a commemoration of me.

"In like manner also the chalice after he had supped saying,"

"This chalice is the new Testament in my blood. This do ye as often as you shall drink it for a commemoration of me.

"For as often as you shall eat this bread, or drink this chalice, you shall show forth the death of the Lord until he come. Wherefore, whosoever shall eat this bread, or drink this chalice unworthy, shall be guilty of the body and blood of the Lord. But let a man prove himself, and so let him eat of that bread and drink of the chalice. For he that eateth and drinketh unworthily, eateth and drinketh judgment to himself, not discerning the body of the Lord."[3]

---

[1] See Die Arch. et Philos. de Bible, Calmet. [2] Migne, Cursus Com. S. Scripture, iii. 800. [3] I. Cor. xi. 20 to 29

Nothing could be clearer than this doctrine of the real presence of Christ in the Eucharist. These "Love Feasts" continued to be held in the churches for centuries. But they became such a source of scandal and disorders, that in A. D. 397 the council of Carthage forbade them, and they fell into disuse. But the French with their changeless ways, and other European peoples, continue a shadow of them in the "Blessed Bread," they distribute in the church Sundays, and at some of the great feasts.

EXPLANATION OF PICTURES FACING PAGES 217 AND 317.

These pictures show the outside and inside of the Cenacle as it stands in our day, with hardly a change since the time of Christ.

The stone steps leading to the roof are on your right, but were not taken in the photograph. You walk over the stone roof and enter the historic "Upper Chamber" lighted by the windows shown.

The picture of the interior shows the Bema or Sanctuary closed by an iron grill. At the end of the room, to your right, is the stone stairway leading to the Catafalque over the relics of David, Solomon and the Kings. The table of the Last Supper stood in the middle of this room between the two large pillars shown.

THE THIRD PART.

HOW THE MASS WAS FORETOLD IN THE CENACLE.

VII.—THE HISTORY OF MELCHISEDECH, SION, AND THE CENACLE.

CHRIST chose the Cenacle in which to celebrate the Passover, because there lived, died, and were buried Melchisedech, David, Solomon and all the kings of David's family till the Babylonian Captivity.

Melchisedech comes into history under this name in the account of the four Mesopotamian kings, who went into Palestine, captured Lot, Abraham's nephew, and started for home. Abraham roused his servants, fell on them at night, rescued Lot, took their spoils, and returning passed by Salem, as Jerusalem then was named.

"But Melchisedech, the king of Salem, bringing forth bread and wine, for he was a priest of the most high God, blessed him and said : ' Blessed be the most high God by whose protection thy enemies are in thy hand.' And he gave him tithes of all." [1]

Here for the first time in Holy Writ we find a priest "of the most high God " offering the " bread and wine " of the Passover and Mass. Eight centuries of silence pass, and 1,100 years before Christ David wrote of Christ's priesthood: " Thou are a priest forever according to the order of Melchisedech." [2] Then this great pontiff-king appears no more, in Holy Writ, till St. Paul in his Epistle to the Hebrews mentions him eight times as a type of Christ. [3]

In patriarchal days, the chief of the tribe, or the king,

---

[1] Gen xiv 18-20. [2] Psalm cix 4. [3] Hebrews v. 6-10, vi. 20, vii 1 10, 11, 15-17

united in his person the two offices of priest and ruler
Abraham was a priest, and sacrificed suffering animals, for
of his race the priests of Aaron's family were born—the
Hebrew priests who demanded the death of Christ—as
they had in tabernacle and Temple immolated the victims
which foretold the crucifixion.

But here for the first time in history, comes forth
another order of priests, this mysterious Melchisedech
offering bread and wine of the Last Supper and Mass.
To him Abraham offered tithes—the tenth part of the
fruits of his victory. Therefore Melchisedech's priesthood was higher than that of Abraham; it was to be
eternal; it pointed to Christ's priesthood of the Last
Supper and of the Catholic Church. The whole prophetic
scene in that vale beside the sacred city was emblematic
of the future.

First dimly the bread and wine appear in patriarchal
sacrifices, but brighter in the Temple ceremonial, and still
clearer in the Passover. Beautifully S. Augustine explains prophetic Noe naked in his tent after taking the
wine, an image of Christ crucified nearly naked. Ham,
his son, reviling him, foretold the Jewish people mocking
the dying Lord.[1] To the wine his son Melchisedech added
bread, and from that time the bread and wine were always
offered with the bloody sacrifices of the Hebrew Temple.

Who was Melchisedech? Early heretics hold he was
the Holy Spirit himself, who in human form appeared as
the "Just King." But this is wrong. Origen, Didymus
and others of that age say he was an angel, but this we
cannot hold.[2]

It is certain he was a man. He was the king of Salem,
as Jerusalem was then named, who offered bread and
wine in sacrifice.[3] Others think him one of the Canaanite
kings, who lived a holy life amid the awful corruptions
of that age.[4]

Coming into history to bless Abraham, to receive the
tenth part of all he had, nothing given of whence he
came, his history, his parents, his origin and end, of him
St. Paul says : " Without father, without mother, without

---

[1] S. Augustine, De Civitate Dei, L XVI C i and ii   [2] S Augustine, Quest.
in Gen. Quest lxxii.   [3] Epiphanius, Heres, 56, St. Cyril, etc.   [4] Theodorus,
Eusebius, etc

genealogy, having neither beginning of days, nor end of life, but likened unto the Son of God, continueth a priest forever." [1]

Not according to Aaron's priesthood killing countless animals foretelling the Redeemer's awful death, but according to this great high priest's order, Jesus Christ offered bread and wine at the Last Supper.

Melchisedech, "King of Peace," in that Palestine where kings were then called Abimelech, as in Egypt they were named Pharaoh, and later the Ptolomies, in his innocence and justice he was a striking figure of Christ, spiritual King and High Priest of mankind. Ignatius of Antioch [2] and other fathers say he was a virgin, without father or mother, foretelling the Redeemer without mother in heaven, father on earth or posterity. [3]

Many learned works on this subject give various solutions. But Oriental traditions, Jewish and Samaritan writers clear up the difficulty. The Targums of Pseudo-Jonathan and Jerusalem, [4] Jewish Cabalistic works, [5] Rabbinical writers, [6] Samaritans [7] of ancient time, with Luther, Melanchthon, Lightfoot, Selden, etc., say Melchisedech was the patriarch Sem, sole survivor of the flood, eldest son and heir of Noe, king and high priest of the world. [8]

Noe established the right of primogeniture, that the eldest son should succeed the father in his property, kingship and priesthood, a custom coming down to our day. In monarchies, the eldest son sits on his father's throne, or becomes owner of the family estates. Of this Virgil sang "King Anius was indeed the king of men and the priest of Phebe." [9] Sem was therefore heir of Noe.

What is the meaning of the word Melchisedech? The Hebrew word for king is *melek*, and for justice *tsaddiq*, the latter coming from the Babylonian *sadyk*, " the just one," Therefore the name of this Pontiff-Founder of Jerusalem is " My King is Just." In our day, at Tel-el-Amarna in Egypt, terra-cotta tablets were discovered inscribed in the Babylonian tongue, the diplomatic language of the nations a hundred years before Moses led the Hebrews from the Nile land. When Melchisedech died

[1] Hebrews vii. 3   [2] Epist ad Philadel.   [3] St Augustine, De Doct Christ, L IV, XLV, Epist clxxxii. v   [4] Rashi, in Gen xiv   [5] Apud Bochart, Phaleg, Pt. I, b ii, sec. 69   [6] Schotgen, Hor Heb II. 645   [7] Quoted by St. Epiphanius, Her. LV, 6.   [8] See Bereshith Rabbah. S. 9, etc.   [9] Eneid, III, V. 80.

Adoni-Zedek, his successor as king of Jerusalem, sent
these tablets to the Egyptian king, telling of the great
king Melchisedech his predecessor, who had founded the
city, stating he had five sons. A wealth of Jewish and
Arabian lore is found relating to this personage. Smith
in his Dictionary says under the name Shem:

"Assuming that the years ascribed to the patriarchs in
the present copies of the Hebrew Bible are correct, it appears that Methuselah, who in his first 243 years was
contemporary with Adam, had still nearly 100 years of his
long life to run after Shem was born. And when Shem
died, Abraham was 148 years old, and Isaac had been nine
years married. There are therefore but two links—
Methuselah and Shem—between Adam and Isaac. So
that the early records of the Creation, and the Fall of man,
which came down to Isaac, would challenge, apart from
their inspiration, the same confidence, which is readily
yielded to a tale that reaches the reader through two
well-known persons, between himself and the original
chief actor in the events related. There is no chronologi-
cal improbability in that ancient Jewish tradition, which
brings Sem and Abraham into personal conference."

Sem or Shem, " Name," " Renown," or " Yellow," father
of the yellow Asiatics, was born before the flood, when
Noe was 500 years old.[1] " He (Sem) begot Arphaxad
two years after the flood, and Sem lived after he begat
Arphaxad five hundred years."[2] When the latter was in
his thirty-fifth year, he begat Sale. And when Sale was
thirty years old his son Heber was born.[3] Heber became the father of Pheleg in his thirty-fourth year. The
latter had a son in his thirtieth year named Reu, who in
his thirty-second year had a son born to him called Sarug.
This Sarug in his thirtieth year begat Nachor, and the
latter in his twenty-ninth year had a son Thare, who in
his seventieth year became Abraham's father.[4]

According to this statement, Abraham was born 352
years after the flood, when Sem was 450 years old. " Sem
lived after he begot Arphaxad five hundred years."[5]
Born 92 years before the flood, Sem lived till Abraham
attained his forty-sixth year. Josephus has the following " Abraham, who accordingly was the tenth from Noe,

[1] Gen. v 31, [2] Gen xi 10, 11. [3] Gen. xi. 12-15. [4] Gen. xi. 12-26. [5] Gen. xi. 11.

was born in the two hundred and ninety-second year after the flood."[1] Following this Sem died when Abraham was ninety-two, and eighty years before Isaac's birth.

Sem therefore died when Abraham was either forty-six, ninety-two or one hundred and forty-eight years of age, and he could have been that great pontiff of mankind, high priest of the nations, whom the Canaanites called Melchisedech. Oriental and Hebrew traditions have the following, we think the best, solution of the difficulty. But we do not say that the following statements are all true. Let the reader judge for himself.

Dying Adam said to his son Seth: "Now I die for my sin, but bury me not till God shows you the place where I will sleep till the 'Seed of the woman,' who will crush the serpent's head will come."[2] They embalmed the body, patriarchs passed it down, Noe had the skull in the ark, and before he died, 350 years after the flood, he gave it to Sem his eldest son telling him the tradition.

There was born of Ham's family, his grandson Nemrod, "Valiant," or "The Rebel," who comes down among the Heathen nations as Baal, Bel, the god Jupiter, Hercules, Thor, etc. "He was the grandson of Ham, a bold man of great strength of hand. He persuaded them not to ascribe it to God, as it were through his means they were happy, but to believe it was their own courage, which procured them that happiness. He also changed the government into a tyranny, seeing no other way of turning men from the fear of God, and to bring them into a constant dependence on his power. He also said he would be revenged on God, if he should have a mind to drown the world again For that he would build a tower too high for the waters to reach, and he would be revenged on God for destroying their forefathers."[3]

This Nemrod turned mankind from Adam's religion; taught that the sky was a crystal ceiling; that their forefathers, the patriarchs, went to heaven and became the planets; that the natural forces were gods, and thus he founded paganism. Guided by him, the seventy-two families, born of Noe's grandsons, built the Tower they called Bab Il, "Gate of God," in the Babylonian tongue, which the Hebrews later changed to Babel, "Confusion,"

[1] Antiq B I, c vi. n 5.   [2] Gen iii. 15.   [3] Josephus, Antiq. B. I. c. iv. n. 2.

whence they called the nearby city Babylon, "City of the Gate of God." [1]

Infidelity, the worship of their father-patriarchs, the degradation of woman, immorality, irreligion were spreading through the people tyrannized over by this wicked Nemrod. But before the Tower of Babel was finished, God changed their language so each family spoke a different tongue and they could not understand the other families so they had to separate. Japheth's children migrated to the southern shores of the Caspian Sea; Sem's sons remained in his father's house, Asia, because he was the eldest; Ham's dark tribes went to Africa, except the tribes which had rebelled against Sem over the division of the continents. They remained in the rich plains between the Tigris and Euphrates, where they founded the Babylonian empire, of which Nemrod was the first king. From these seventy-two families or tribes came the great nations of antiquity.

Sem, father of numerous tribes, eldest son and heir of Noe's civil and priestly power, was stripped of all authority in this revolt. Left alone in his old age, his children gone, an angel told him to come and he would show him where to bury Adam's skull. For full many a day they went west, till they came to a little hill, whereon he entombed our first father's relic, and called it Golgotha, a Babylonian word meaning "The Place of the Skull" Greeks later rendered it Cranion, and Romans Calvaria—Calvary. There the angel told him to guard the relic of the first man.

The Revelations of Moses, an ancient book the Jews honored, gives a long account of how the angels embalmed Adam's body. "And God said to Adam: "I will set thee in thy kingdom, on the throne of him that deceived thee, and he shall be cast down in this place (Calvary) that thou mayest sit upon him" Beside him they buried Abel's body, and there they laid Eve, when she died six days after Adam. Thus the thirty children of Adam laid to sleep our first parents with the priest Abel beside them. And the archangel Michael said to Seth: "Thus bury every man that dies until the day of the resurrection."

[1] Dutripon, Concord S Scripturæ, Babel.

We give this as a specimen of numerous doubtful
Oriental traditions. On the way to Damascus, not far
from the vast ruins of Baalbec, amid the Libanon mountains, they show you the tombs of Noe and the patriarchs.
Perhaps Adam was buried there and later his skull taken
up and guarded as the relic of the first sinner and saint.
The Church in honoring the relics of the saints, follows
the customs of ancient races, especially the Hebrews. In
the Church of the Holy Sepulchre they point out Melchisedech's tomb

Half a mile south rose rugged rocky heights surrounded
on three sides by deep valleys, which Sem fortified and
called Sion, "the Projecting." There he reared his palace,
round which rose a little city he named Salem, "Peace,"
from the Oriental salute. Salama, "Peace," a word still
used in these countries, as we say "How do you do?"

In the migrations of the tribes, Caanan's cursed sons,[1]
Jebusites, Hittites, whom the Greeks called Phenicians,
had colonized the land, where thay had built many a city
and town. Not knowing Sem, who he was, or whence
he came, they called him "The Just King," the King of
Salem, in their language Melchisedech

Last of the great patriarchal fathers of the nations,
heir of Noe's fatherhood, royalty and priesthood going
back beyond the flood to Abel and to Adam, in his palace
on Sion, on the very spot where Jesus Christ celebrated
the Last Supper, this great high-priest king first offered
the bread and wine of the Mass.

He was then the last link of the world before the flood.
No writing, record, or monument of the ages before God
wiped out the world's wickedness with waters of his
wrath survived, but Sem, who had preserved them according to the patriarchal customs of that epoch, when
the eldest son was sole depositary and heir of all his
father's learning, property and priesthood.

In Chaldea, at Ur, "Light of the Moon," where she was
worshiped, now the ruined Mughier, "The Betumined,"
lived Abraham. His father made a living manufacturing
and selling idols, says the Talmud. But his son did not
believe in them, and God gave him supernatural faith,
and told him to go into Palestine, where he would meet

[1] Gen. x 16.

this great pontiff-king from whom he would learn Adam's religion, the story of creation, the fall of man, the prophecy of the Redeemer, the story of the world before the flood. According to patriarchal custom, these truths passed down to Isaac, Jacob, to the Hebrews as traditions, till Moses gathered them up in the Book of Genesis.

Jewish rabbis say Sem called the little city Salem, "Peace";[1] that after offering Isaac on Moriah, Abraham named the city Jireh, "Possession"; that the two great patriarchs disputed about the city's name; but then agreed to unite the two words making Jerusalem, "The city of Peace,"[2] a word found six hundred times in the Old Testament, and seventy times in the New.

Hebrews called it Ariel, "Lion," or "Hearth of God";[3] Grecian Jews said it was Agia Polis "The Holy City";[4] when Hadrian destroyed it the Romans named it Ælia after his first name.[5] It was the holiest of all the cities of earth, because of Him foretold to come and there redeem our race.

When Omar, Mohammed's cousin, captured it, Moslems called it El-Kuds, "The Holy," Beit-el-Makdis, "The House of the Holy Sanctuary"; Esh-Sherif, "The Venerable" or "The Noble." To them Jerusalem is a most sacred place, where lived the prophets they hold inspired, and in their eyes Jerusalem in sanctity is second only to Mecca where Mohammed was born, and Medina where he lived.

Sem, bearing the name of Melchisedech, lived on Sion, his palace being built on the very spot where Herod built the Cenacle in which Jesus Christ said the first Mass.[6] This great prophet-king priest of the most high God,"[7] "bringing forth bread and wine,"[8] offered this sacrifice of thanksgiving for the victory God gave Abraham; he offered this bread and wine to God as an image of the Mass, and not for food for Abraham's troops as Calvin wrote.

And Abraham "gave him tithes of all.[9] Why did he do this? To show that there was to come a priesthood,

[1] S Augustine, Enar in Ps xxxii Ser 1, V [2] Young's Concord of the Bible, Edersheim, Temple, 3; Smith's Dic of Bible, Jerusalem, etc [3] Isaias xxix 1, 2, 7. Ezech 43-15 [4] Matt iv. 5, xxvii 53 [5] Ælius Hadrianus [6] See Josephus, Antiq. vii. c ili n 2 [7] In Hebrew, vehu cohen. [8] Hotseti mincha. [9] See Migne, Cursus Comp S. Scripturæ, v. 47; Gen. xiv. 20.

offering the Mass in bread and wine, superior to the Aaronic priesthood offering bloody sacrifices, suffering animals immolated in the Temple by the priesthood to be be born of Abraham's race.

Abraham gave tithes to Melchisedech because that was the custom in those days. Pagans gave tithes, that is the tenth part of the spoils of their victories to their priests.[1] Zenophon[2] says: "For of this money collected from the captives, the tenth part consecrated to Apollo or to Diana of Ephesus the pretors received." Agesilao writes: "Offerings, that is fruits of the earth, every two hundred years a hundred talents or more, the Ephesians dedicate the tenth part of that to God."

Christ was therefore a priest according to the order of Melchisedech when he offered bread and wine at the Last Supper, and a priest according to the order of Aaron when he brought the lamb of Passover to the Temple to be sacrificed.[3]

Sem and Abraham slept with their fathers, and were buried one on Sion, the other at Hebron, sixty years of silent history passed, and Jebusites, sons of the third son of wicked Canaan, captured Sion, fortified its ramparts, and their dwellings rose round Melchisedech's fortress. They called the city Jebus, "Trodden down," in memory of their father.

It was a place of extraordinary strength. Recent excavations in Jerusalem laid bare the ancient ramparts running from near the Joppa gate, down deep into the Tyropœon valley, separating Sion from Moriah, and continued along the southern slopes and to the west bordering the Hinnom vale to the place of beginning They show Sion must have been in that day an acropolis, "A Citadel." They then called it "The Dry Rock." The Tyropœon valley was then twenty-six, thirty-three and and eighty feet lower than now, while to the south and west the ramparts rose hundreds of feet over the Hinnom and Cedron vales. At one spot a fragment of the ancient wall of Sion on the north was built close against the cliff, and though only rising to the top of the rock behind it, it was yet thirty-nine feet high towards the ravine

[1] Livy, L 6   [2] Cyro, L. 6.   [3] See Migne, Cursus Comp. S. Scripturæ xxv. 319 to 325, v. 47, etc.

in front."[1] This was at the north side of Sion towards
the present city. There the land was more level, where
to-day the long David Street gently rises from the modern
city up to Sion.[2]

In the imagery of the Old Testament Sion was a prototype of the Church with its Eucharistic Sacrifice, while
Jerusalem was emblematic of heaven, and these meanings will be found in hundreds of texts.[3]

When the victorious Hebrews under Josue were sweeping over Palestine, Gibeonites, "Dwellers on a hill,"
possessed four cities a little north of Jerusalem—one of
them being "The city on the hill which cannot be hid,"[4]
which you can still see about five miles north of Jerusalem.
They deceived Josue[5] and were condemned to be
"hewers of wood and drawers of water." Their descendants lived in Ophel and boarded the Jewish priests
while serving in the Temple. The Hebrews could not
take Jerusalem because of its strong fortifications. The
Hinnom vale then divided the tribes of Juda and Benjamin, and later the division line was run through the
center of the Temple.

For 824 years Jebusite sons of Canaan held Jerusalem
till David " The Beloved " was firmly fixed on his throne
in Hebron. The city was on the high spur of the central
mountain range running through the center of the Hebrew
kingdom, and was a place of extraordinary strength.
After reigning seven years in Hebron all the chiefs of the
twelve tribes swore fealty to David, firmly fixing his
dynasty.

Leaving Hebron, twenty miles to the south, over these
Judean hills David marched his troops, invested Jerusalem, and promised to make general over his armies the
first who would scale the walls. In spite of the blind
and crippled defenders placed on the walls in mockery of
David's soldiers, Joab, "Jehovah is Father," son of
Zeruiah, " Balm," David's nephew, scaled the ramparts.[6]
" And David took the castle of Sion the same is the city
of David "[7]

" When David had cast the Jebusites out of the citadel,

[1] Recent researches in Jerusalem   [2] See Migne, Cursus Comp S Scripturæ,
iii 1474, etc   [3] S Augustine, Enar. in Ps. xcviii n iv Epist clxxxvi n viii
[4] Matt. v. 14   [5] Josue ix.   [6] Josephus, Antiq. B. VII., c. iii, A. I.   [7] II Kings, v.7.

he rebuilt Jerusalem, named it the City of David, and abode there all the time of his reign . . . Now when he had chosen Jerusalem to be his royal city, his affairs more and more prospered by the providence of God, who took care that they should improve and be augmented. Hiram, " The noble born," the King of the Tyrians, sent ambassadors to him, and made a league of friendship and assistance with him. He also sent him presents, cedar-trees and mechanics, and men skilled in building and architecture, that they might build him a royal palace at Jerusalem. Now David made buildings round about the lower city. He also joined the lower city to it, and made it in one body. And when he had encompassed all with walls, he appointed Joab to take care of them. It was David therefore who first cast the Jebusites out of Jerusalem and called it by its one name, the City of David, for under our forefather Abraham it was called Solyma or Salem." [1]

David's palace was celebrated. It was built on the very site of Melchisedech's palace. There David prepared a place for the ark; there the great Mosaic ceremonies were carried out, till Solomon built his famous Temple on Moriah, another hill a little to the north of east. From that time Sion became a sacred place in Hebrew story, there they celebrated solemn feasts in David's day, and called Sion " The Holy Mountain."

On the walls of the palace, David's notices of administration, laws, etc., were posted. The fortress was called Mello, " Multitude," and handsome houses and palaces rose round the summit of the City of David, Sion and Melchisedech.

Down deep in the soft limestone rock, where Melchisedech was buried, David excavated passages, rooms and tombs. There he hid vast treasures for the building of the Temple which God told him his son Solomon would erect—the gold and silver amounting to $19,849,260, with bronze and brass and other treasures of far more priceless value. His tomb interests us for reasons given later.

" He was buried by his son Solomon in Jerusalem, with great magnificence, and with all other funeral pomp which kings used to be buried with. Moreover he had

[1] Josephus, Antiq. B. VII, c. iii, n. 2.

great and immense wealth buried with him, the vastness of which may be easily conjectured by what I shall now say. For a thousand and three hundred years afterwards, Hyrcanus the high priest, when he was besieged by Antiochus, that was called the Pious, opened one room of David's sepulchre, and took out three thousand talents, and gave part of that sum to Antiochus, and by this means caused the siege to be raised, as we have informed the reader elsewhere. After him, and that after many years, Herod, the king, opened another room, and took away a great deal of money, and yet neither of them came at the coffins of the kings themselves, for their bodies were buried under the earth so artfully, that they did not appear even to those who entered into their monuments." [1]

Solomon, "The Peaceful," stretched a stone bridge across the deep Tyropœon vale separating Sion from Moriah, under which ran what was called in Christ's time the Cheesemongers' Street. Herod, with his mania for building, enlarged that bridge so that it was fifty-one feet wide and 350 long, its entrance being at the southwest of the Temple area. It was across that bridge that Christ and his apostles went when carrying the lamb for the Passover or Last Supper. Part of the eastern abutment is now called Robinson's Arch.

Solomon enlarged and fortified the old fort built by Melchisedech and David. There abode the ark of the covenant from the time David placed it in his palace, till Solomon had finished his famous Temple on Moriah [2] Now on the site of Melchisedech's and of David's palace rose Solomon's great palace, which took thirteen years to build.[3] It was celebrated for its magnificence and extent. Court rooms, prisons, halls—all were of fine Judean marble and cedar of Lebanon. It was burned and totally destroyed by the Babylonians, when they captured Jerusalem.[4]

In the deep soft, yellowish-white Judean rock, beneath that palace, beside David's tomb, other vault rooms and galleries were dug, and there Solomon and all the kings

---

[1] Josephus, Antiq B. VII, c. xv, n. 3. See Migne, Cursus Comp. S. Scripturæ, 11, 783, etc. [2] II Kings vi ; III Kings vili. [3] III Kings vii [4] IV. Kings xxv

Note.—The reader will find the different opinions regarding this vast sum David had accumulated in Migne, Cursus Completus, Sacræ Scripturæ, Vol. II, pp. 637 to 650.

of Judea were buried with the prophetess Huldah "the cat."[1]   When Jerusalem was rebuilt, after the Babylonian Captivity, Sion was again fortified as the city's citadel. The Machabees enlarged the Sion fortress and there they lived as warrior high priests.   They fortified the Baris rock to the northwest of the Temple area which Herod rebuilt and called the Antonia.   There Pilate lived, and there Christ was tried and sentenced to death.

Herod, the Edumean, born of Judah's tribe, last of Hebrew kings foretold to reign till the Messiah came,[2] hearing of David's vast treasures hidden in his tomb, before beginning to build his famous Temple twenty years before Christ was born, sought for the treasures David had hid under his palace.

"As for Herod, he had spent vast sums about the cities, both within and without his own kingdom.   And as he had heard that Hyrcanus, who had been king before him, had opened David's sepulchre, and taken out of it three thousand talents of silver, and that there was a much greater number left behind, and indeed enough to suffice for all his wants, and he had a great while an intention to make the attempt.   And at this time he opened that sepulchre by night and went into it, and endeavored that it should not be known in the city, but took only his faithful friends with him.   As for any money, he found none, as Hyrcanus had done, but that furniture of gold, and those precious goods that were left there, all these he took away.   However he had a great desire to make a more diligent search, and to go farther in, even as far as the bodies of David and Solomon, when two of his guards were slain by a flame that burst out upon those that went in, as the report goes.   So he was terribly frightened and went out and built a propitiatory monument of that fright he had been in, and this of white stone at the mouth of the sepulchre, and that also at great expense."[3]

Thus over the tombs of the great kings rose the pile of buildings called the Cenacle,[4] "Banquet Hall," by the Romans, for there public banquets were held.   The Greeks named it the Huperoon, "high," or Anageon, "Beautiful," and the Jews Aliyah, "chamber," because it was the high-

[1] Talmud Babyl , Ebel, 60.   [2] Gen. xlix. 10.   [3] Josephus, Antiq., B XVI c. vii. n I.   [4] See Migne, Cursus S Scripturæ iii , 909

est, largest, finest and holiest room, except the Temple, of all places in the sacred city at the time of Christ. It was beautifully furnished with carpets, rugs, tapestries— its walls were decorated, its furniture most costly as became that building, over the tombs of the sleeping kings resting in the rock rooms beneath. There synagogue services were held, and it was the largest and finest of the 480 synagogues in Jerusalem at the time of Christ.

We mentioned the dead sleeping beneath Sion. Kings' and prophets' relics rested there the night Christ celebrated over them the first Mass, and said "Do this for a commemoration of me." [1] Every incident of that night— the room, the surroundings, the services impressed themselves on the apostles' minds.

When they went forth to establish the Church, among the nations, they said Mass over the remains of saints and martyrs. Persecuted in Rome they offered the sacrifice in the catacombs. They later placed the relics in altar stones, and thus down the ages, that custom has obtained till our day in all the Rites and Liturgies of Christendom.

The clergy of the Latin Rite use a stone on which to rest Chalice and Host, and in this stone, as in a little tomb, the relics of the saints are placed and ceiled up, as were relics of prophet and kings under the Cenacle. The Oriental Christians, who use only silk for altar cloths, place the relics of saints in the double silk folds forming the altar covering, on which the Eucharistic Elements rest.

All Oriental Christians follow the same custom. We trace it back to apostolic times, beyond Roman persecutions, and earlier than the catacombs. Some writers say it came from the catacombs, but going deeper they will find it comes from the Last Supper.

When the apostles went forth to found churches in many lands they found customs of entombing the honored dead in pyramids, "flamed-shaped," in tombs, "mounds," but the Greeks called their burial-place the necropolis "city of the dead" The Christians followed the lessons of Sion and the Last Supper. In vaults beneath churches the early Christians buried their dead. The custom was

---

[1] Luke xxii. 19.

followed till modern times in Europe where historic personages still sleep in churches. In this country they entomb the bishops under the cathedrals. These customs are traced to Sion and the Cenacle.

Sion is a hill higher than that of Moriah to the northeast, where rose the "Gold House" of the great Temple, flashing the sunlight over the city. Sion is 2,700 feet over the sea and 4,000 over the Dead Sea. The Temple with its priesthood and sacrifices was to pass away. The Church with its priesthood and Eucharistic Sacrifice was to be eternal. Therefore, down the Old Testament 177 times the prophets, in burning words pour forth the glories of Sion, image of the Church, while condemning Moriah with its wicked Jewish priesthood.

In the time of Christ, round the Cenacle rose the homes of richest Jews, wealthy Pharisees, learned Scribes, Judges of the Sanhedrin. Joseph Caiphas and his father-in-law Annas there had palaces worthy of princes. Sion was the aristocratic residence quarter of Jerusalem. Therefore when we select the richest and most wealthy quarters of our cities as sites for our cathedrals and churches, we follow, perhaps without thinking, the example of Christ when he celebrated the first Mass on Sion.

The Cenacle belonged to David's family. The Lord's Mother was the Princess of the royal family and David's heir. Therefore Christ, Prince of the House of David, had a right to the building. Joseph of Arimathea and Nicodemus were leaders of the synagogue congregation worshiping in the Cenacle. There gathered the apostles, disciples and Christ's followers for the synagogue services on that historic Thursday night, and on that Sabbath eve while the Lord's body lay in the tomb. There they remained during these forty hours till he rose from the dead. From that spot 500 persons followed him down the Tyropœon vale, across the Cedron, up the slopes of Olivet, the day of the ascension. Ascending the Mount of Olives, the Arabs now call Gebel et Tur, the Lord before he ascended told James to take care of the disciples at Jerusalem.

Day by day they there assembled for the synagogue services, preparing for the feast of Pentecost, waiting for the promised Paraclete. They were in the Cenacle that day, when at nine in the morning the Holy Ghost, the fiery cloud of the Shekina of the burning bush, Sinai, tabernacle, Temple and Thabor filled the room of the Last Supper and rained down tongues of fire, giving each apostle a knowledge of the language of the nation to which he was to preach.

"On Wednesday," says an ancient writer.[1] "St. James first said Mass according to his Liturgy, which he said he received from the Lord, changing not a word." The apostles used the Cenacle as a church while they remained in Jerusalem. While the Roman army under Titus was marching down from the north to invest the holy city in the year A. D 70, Simeon, who had been elected bishop after James was thrown down from the roof of the Temple, and killed with a fuller's stone, preached on the Lord's words foretelling the terrible siege, the destruction of the city, and warned them to flee. In a ravine to the east of the Sea of Galilee, nestled then the little city of Pella, and there they found a home while the war lasted, after which they returned to find Jerusalem a heap of ruins.

Round the Antonia tower and the Temple had raged the fierce fighting, Josephus so graphically describes.[2] The Romans knew nothing about the little band of Christians worshiping in the Cenacle, and the building was little damaged. After the war St. James's Liturgy of the Mass was again followed. The Cenacle was called "The Church of the Apostles" or the "Church of Sion." Pilgrims in the early ages mentioned it.

Again the Jews rebelled and Hadrian leveled the city and walls, drew the plow over it, and forbade a Jew under pain of death to enter, except once a year to celebrate the Passover. The holy building of the Last Supper had survived the calamities of the two wars. Syrian clergymen now called the Maronites then served the people. Eusebius, the famed historian, gives a list of fifteen bishops of Hebrew birth, and twenty-four of Gentile parentage who governed the See of Jerusalem.

A century and a half passed, and Silvester sat on the high Apostolic See Peter had established at Rome, of whose bishops Eusebius mentions twenty-nine names,

[1] Dion. Barsilibus, Hist. S. James' Liturgy.   [2] Jewish Wars.

beginning with Peter and bringing them down to the Council of Nice in 325. The empress Helena, mother of Constantine, after her son's conversion came to Jerusalem.

It was easy to find where slept the famous kings, and the building where the Lord said the first Mass still stood. Jerusalem, then as now, was built of stones, all rooms and ceilings arched. You could not burn the buildings, for wood is only in doors and windows. Only man or an earthquake could ruin Jerusalem.

Under Helena's directions the Cenacle was purified, consecrated, and in it Mass was again said. It became the seat of an archbishop—a patriarchal See second to Rome and Alexandria. In the Cenacle they said Mass according to St. James's Liturgy, and the Mass St. Peter composed at Antioch. The first is written in Greek, the latter in Syro-Chaldaic the language of the people of Judea at the time of Christ. The Church of Jerusalem with the Cenacle as its cathedral flourished till A. D. 636, when with fire and sword came the fanatic followers of the false prophet of Arabia. Omar, Mohammed's cousin came and negotiated with the patriarch Sophronius for the surrender of the holy city. He treated the Christians with kindness, gave them the Church of the Holy Sepulchre and the Cenacle, retaining for the Mohammedans the site of the Temple.

Maronite priests served the Christians till the crusaders came, after which at the request of their founder St. Francis who went to Jerusalem, the Cenacle fell into the hands of the Franciscan Fathers who held if for more than 200 years. Then some Mohammedans, claiming direct decent from David's family, drove out the monks, and they still serve as the guardians of the Cenacle, calling it Bab Neby Daud "The House of the Prophet David."

Bright was the April day in 1903 when we started up David Street, leading south up the holy hill. On the right we passed the dark battlemented Tower of David, a little South of the Joppa Gate, now used as Turkish barracks. The great stones look old and black enough to have been placed there by the Royal Prophet. On the opposite side are Cook's office, a Protestant school, and higher up is the site of the house of Thomas the apostle. Farther

on your left you come to the Armenian church, built on
the spot where they say St James, first bishop of Jerusalem, lived. By the bishop's throne in the sanctuary they
show you his tomb Outside the wall east of the Temple area cut from the living rock his tomb still stands.
Why they buried him within the city we do not know,
as Jewish laws forbade burials within the sacred walls.
Perhaps they brought his relics to the church on Sion.

The land is now level, and continuing south you come
to the site of Caiphas' house or palace, where Christ was
twice tried and condemned to death. A little church occupies the site. It is twenty-one by twenty-seven feet,
built of the gray limestone of Judea. Six square pillars,
three on each side, support the stone arched roof. Inscriptions tell you six bishops were buried under the
building. In the eastern part is the sanctuary, its altar
stone being the round rolling flat stone with which they
closed the door of the tomb of the dead Christ. To the
right, or south of the altar, within the chancel is a little
stone room over the cell in the basement, in which they
imprisoned Christ that night, till they could hold court in
the morning to legally sentence him, for night sessions
of the court were forbidden by the Jewish law.

The church occupies but a small part of the high priest's
palace. In the yard behind the church, they had dug
away some of the debris of centuries, exposing a large
beautiful mosaic pavement, made of little colored square
marbles done with art, forming flowers and beautiful
tracery—perhaps the floor of Caiphas' house. Half a
day's work would have uncovered most of the yard, and
the rest of the figures. But the Turks forbade further
search, lest Christians might discover David's tomb and
treasury.

Now south slope Sion's summit and suburbs. Debris
of walls and houses destroyed centuries ago cover fields
and gardens. You will see men plowing sites of rich
abodes of Scribes, Pharisees, priests and judges, who sentenced the God-Man to death, fulfilling the prophet's
words, Jeremy quotes: "You that build up Sion with
blood, and Jerusalem with iniquity. Her princes have
judges for bribes . . . Therefore because of you, Sion
shall be plowed as a field, and Jerusalem shall be a heap

of stones, and the mountain of the Temple as the places of the forest.[1]

You come through the walls, pass out what was once called the Sion Gate, which now Moslems name Bab en Neby Daud, "Gate of the Prophet David." On your right, inclosed by a wall, is the Armenian cemetery, and farther on the Protestant burying-ground. Walk over a little to the west where Melchisedech's palace once rose, and you look down into the deep Hinnom valley, 170 feet below, where you see the Gihon pool partly filled with water. At your left, to the east, is the Tyropœon vale, then comes the hill where Ophel stood, below the Temple area, then the Cedron and Gethsemane—around on all sides rise tombs, and east is Olivet—all inspiring memories of historic incidents.

As you run your eyes along over the land below, spread like a map before you, wonderful stories of the past rise in your mind. There Solomon was crowned. There opposite is the hill with its steep eastern side toward you, on which Judas hanged himself that fatal Friday morning of the crucifixion, when his body fell down seventy-five feet onto the road below and his bowels gushed out. It is the very spot where wicked Achab and Manasses burned little children to the fire-god Moloch in that cursed Topheth, where emptied the city sewers, where ever-burning fires were kept for consuming garbage, animal carcases and criminals. Well was it named Topheth and Gehenna. It was an image of that hell down to which went the soul of the Master's faithless apostle.

South about half a mile the two vales of Hinnom and Cedron unite forming the ravine leading their waters in winter and spring down 4,000 feet to the Dead Sea. Almost hanging from the western cliffs of the Hill of Evil Council, where Solomon reared temples to the gods of his pagan wives, you see the empty tombs and homes of Moslems, wretched in ignorance, poverty and filth—many being afflicted with leprosy. That is Siloam "Fleece-Pool," for in that pool before you they washed the lambs for Temple and Passover. There Christ told the man to anoint his blind eyes with its clay when he received his sight.

---

[1] Jeremy xxvi 18 , Micheas iii 10-12.

Sion, image of the Church Universal, whose glories prophets sang, now outside the walls, has become a waste. Who cultivates these fields? Come with me, gentle reader, and see a specimen of her inhabitants. We are coming up the Cedron ravine from the place, down below, where Judas hanged himself. On our right, wretched stone houses, and tombs of Siloam, cling to the steep hill. On our left is the Virgin's Spring, now called Ed Derez, "Spring with steps," still flowing from underground cisterns Solomon excavated under Temple and city.

Above us, about ten feet away almost above us, there like an apparition, suddenly appears a woman of about twenty-five, her bare feet nearly on a level with our heads. On a matted shock of black hair, making a cushion on her head, rests a round earthen water vessel, shaped like those of the days of Juda's kings. She had just drawn that water from the Virgin's Spring. Her only garment, of camel's hair, rough and thick as a carpet, is so covered and permeated with dirt, for she has worn it day and night for years, that you could scrape off the crusts of filth with a hoe. It comes not quite to her knees and the frayed edges hang in dirty ringlets. Her breast is bare, and great holes are worn in the garment under her arms. If she washed the garment it would fall to pieces, for the dried dirt keeps it together.

Her skin is the color of old copper. Fanaticsm, dirt, degradation, debased womanhood are written in every lineament and move, as there she stands like a bronze statue, and through dark decayed teeth she yells in Arabic to someone in the village of Siloam across the Cedron vale. She is the wife or daughter of a farmer who cultivates the fields of Sion now desolate and uninhabited.

A little south of Sion's summit, but outside the city walls Moslems built in the seventh century, about 400 feet south from site of Joseph Caiphas' palace, rises the ancient pile of the Cenacle buildings, black with age and looking as though the storms of twenty centuries had passed over them. It is composed of various buildings, gables, and sides, some one, others two stories high. There, guarded by Moslems, you find the upper chamber in which Christ said the First Mass.

On the outside, a stone stairway about twelve feet

high leads to the roof of the adjoining building; mounting and passing to the left, you walk over the cemented stones forming the roof covering the vaulted rooms below, and through a door you enter the " Upper Chamber " of Gospel and history. Four windows on the south side light the room.

The room is fifty by thirty feet, and two square stone pillars in the center sustain the vaulted ceilings. The floor is of irregular flat stones cemented together. To the east is an alcove like the chancel or sanctuary of a church, closed by an iron railing. In the time of Christ this formed the Bema or sanctuary, and gave rise to the sanctuary of our churches. Attached to the wall on your right is a flight of high stone steps leading up to another chamber about ten feet higher than the floor of the Cenacle. You ascend, enter, and at your left through an iron grill closing the door, you see a catafalque covered with a faded canopy of silk, reminding you of the catafalque used in our churches at Masses for the dead when the body is not present. Down deep in Sion's rocks, under these rooms, rest the bodies of Melchisedech, David, Solomon, and the kings of David's dynasty.

The walls of all the rooms are blackened with age. Decorations of synagogue, Last Supper, and Masses of apostolic days appear no more. The vaulted ceilings, the ornamented capitals of the two pillars, the great stones of walls and ceilings, the carved groins of the Bema where the synagogue "ark" rested—all show great antiquity. They point out to you the marked place where Jesus Christ reclined with his disciples that historic night.

At your left as you come into the Cenacle, in the corner, a flight of stone steps leads down to the lower apartments. The door below was open and the writer started to go down. The Moslem ran before him, shut the door and forbade him. They will not allow a stranger to enter their female apartments. The writer was in negotiations with them to enter David's tomb before he left the city; difficulties rose, a great price was asked before hand, a firman from the Sultan was required, which was almost impossible to get lest David's treasury might be found, the excavations would take weeks and might be stopped at any moment, and the project was abandoned.

The custom of artfully hiding the bodies of the dead the Hebrews brought with them from Egypt. You will find that Cheops in his pyramid near Cairo, used remarkable means of concealing his body in the stone coffer in the " king's chamber," and different means were used to conceal the mummies, remains of nobles in their desert tombs along the Nile valley.

In 1839, some Jews were allowed to see the tombs of their kings on Sion. Later, Miss Barclay went down to what she thought was the tomb of David, and says:

" The room is insignificant in its dimensions, but is furnished very gorgeously. The tomb is apparently an immense sarcophagus of rough stone, and is covered with a green tapestry richly embroidered with gold. A satin canopy of red, blue, green and yellow stripes hangs over the tomb, and another piece of black velvet tapestry, embroidered in silver, covers the door in one end of the room, which they say leads to a cave underneath. Two silver candlesticks stand before this door, and a little lamp hangs in the window near it which is kept constantly burning." [1]

The catafalque the writer saw was not as ornate as the one she describes, and the coverings were faded.

[1] City of the Great King p 212.

VIII.—THE SYNAGOGUE SERVICES IN THE CENACLE.

WRITERS say in the time of Christ synagogue services were held in 480 schoolhouses and public buildings of Jerusalem.[1] The finest of these public buildings, except the Temple, was the Cenacle over the tombs of David and the kings. There, on Sabbath, Passover and feast, they gathered for morning worship, in the afternoon for the Micha: "vespers" and night prayers. The Rabbis hold that these hours of prayer came down from Abraham, Isaac and Jacob, which Moses and the prophets had developed into the Temple and synagogue ceremonials of the days of Christ.

Moses led the Hebrews in sight of the Promised Land, but did not himself enter Josue, or as he was called in Greek Jesus, brought them into Palestine after Moses' death. A mystery is written in this. For a greater than Moses, Jesus Christ, was foretold to lead the world into the mysteries of the Canon of the Last Supper, the Mass with the Consecration, the Eucharistic Sacrifice and Communion. The synagogue services carried the Mass as far as the end of the Preface. There the worship of the Jewish Church stopped. But Christ and the Apostles brought the Last Supper to the end of the Mass. The first part of the Mass is founded on the worship of the Jewish Temple and synagogue little modified. But supernatural Christian faith enables us to see the heavenly wonders of the Real Presence. Let us therefore see the synagogue and its worship at the time of Christ. Then we will better understand the rites, ceremonies and prayers of that historic night.

When the Hebrews were carried into Babylonia, in every place where ten men, called batlanim, formed a band, named kehillah, lived, they worshiped God according to the ceremonial of the ruined Temple, sacrifice

[1] Jerusalem Talmud, Megilla, iii 73, Edersheim, Life of Christ, i 119, 432.

excepted, which was forbidden except at Jerusalem.[1]
Then they built edifices facing the sanctuary toward the
sacred city, to remind them of Palestine, the splendors of
Solomon's ruined Temple, and the foretold Messiah to be
born of their race, and, as they thought, to found for them
a kingdom of matchless splendor extending over all the
earth.[2]

In these buildings they worshiped the God of their
fathers who had punished their race for the sins of idolatry.   They then began to better study their sacred
books, and the traditions coming down from immemorial
times   Since that epoch the Jews never again fell into
idolatry, the synagogue having kept them in Jewish faith.[3]

A tradition came down and crystalized into the Talmud,
that Moses ascended Sinai on Thursday, where he remained forty days and received the Law, and that he returned on Monday, when he found them worshiping the
golden calf,[4] and they set apart Mondays and Thursdays
in addition to the Sabbath as days of fasting and prayer.
Of this the Pharisee gloried: "I fast twice a week." [5]
These days called Sabbaths farmers came into the cities to
sell their produce, the Sanhedrin or Court sat, and special
services were held in the synagogues.[6]

During the Captivity Daniel, Ezechiel and other prophets consoled them with God's oracles foretelling they
would return to Palestine, that the Temple would be rebuilt and that the Messiah would come.   Seeing his very
name in Isaias' prophecy, learning that they worshiped
the same Almighty God he adored under the name of
Ahura Madza, that Zoroastriansm taught by Persian Magi
priests was similar to the Hebrew worship of Jehovah,
Cyrus sent them back to rebuild city and Temple.[7]

When under Esdras the exiled Jews returned, in every
town and hamlet of the Holy Land they built a place of
worship they called in Hebrew *haccenseth* " house of meeting," in Syro-Chaldaic *beth cnishta*" " or beth-hath-tiphil-
lah, "house of prayer," in Greek, synagogue, " gathered together," and in Hebrew, Asaph, "a congregation." [8]   Their

[1] Deut. xvi 5, 6, etc.   [2] See Geikie, Life of Christ, I , 81, 174 to 187 ; II , 614.
[3] See Edersheim, Life of Christ, I 19 to 30, 433 to 456 [4] Exod xxxii 19 [5] Luke
xviii. 12.   [6] Mark i 21, iii 2, vi 2 ; Luke iv. 16, xiii. 10 , Acts xiii 14, xv 21, xvi.
13, xvii 2, xviii 4, etc   [7] Isaias xliv 26, 28, 45 ; Daniel x.   [8] St Augustine,
Enar in Psal. lxxvi. n 11.

ruins are still seen scattered all over Palestine. Captain Wilson examined the remains of seven synagogues in Galilee, the largest being ninety by forty-four feet six inches, and the smallest forty-eight feet six inches by thirty-five feet six inches. At Rome, Alexandria, Athens, Antioch and in every place into which the Jews scattered to engage in trade before the time of Christ, they had synagogues for the members of each trade, profession and guild of workmen, where the service was in Hebrew, and the sermons in the language of the people. There the Hebrews worshiped Jehovah of their fathers in the midst of the awful debasement of paganism, hoping for the coming of the Messiah, who they thought would gather them again into Judea and make them rulers over all the earth. Thus they understood the prophecies relating to Christ and the Church.

God gave his revelation to mankind through the Jewish race, Christ was a Jew and followed every religious rite and custom of his people.[1] The Church is the daughter of Judaism. We find no Church ceremony which was copied from paganism, as some writers hold. For twenty centuries Church and synagogue have come down side by side, entirely separated, but having much in common. Let us see the synagogue that we may understand the Last Supper and the origin of the Mass ceremonial. The word synagogue is found once in Exodus, four times in Numbers, the same in Psalms, once in Proverbs, six times in Ecclesiasticus in the Latin Vulgate Bible. Few writers treat of the synagogue in an exhaustive manner, perhaps prejudice has been an obstacle or the persecuted Jew would not give the information. Eighty times the word will be found in the Bible as a meeting. When they saw Moses' face " horned," they returned, both Aaron and the rulers of the congregation,[2] the word here translated "congregation" being synagogue. But in other places the word synagogue is retained in translations of the Bible.

Let us first see the name. Synagogue is the Greek of the Hebrew Moed, " Appointed place of meeting." In later times it was named Beth-ha Cennesth, " House of Gathering." Classic writers, like Thucydides[3] and Plato[4]

[1] St. Augustine Enar. in Psal. xliv n. xii.   [2] Exod. xxxiv 31.   [3] ii 18   [4] Repub. 526.

16

use the word synagogue. The Septuagint Bible trans-
lates twenty-one Hebrew words by the term synagogue,
implying a gathering. It is used 130 times for an appointed meeting, twenty-five times for a meeting "called
together," and Church and congregation appear in the
same verse.[1]

In the New Testament, the word is often applied to the
tribunal on which the judges sat,[2] or to the court.[3] But
as a house of worship it was named, Beth Hakkene-
seth, "house of assembly." During week-days the building was used as a schoolhouse for the children, and
named beth hamidrash, "house of study."

The New Testament gives the word twenty-four times,
often as the meeting places of the apostolic converts.
St. Ignatius of Antioch uses the word for Church,[4] as
does Clement of Alexandria.[5] Later, when the division
between Jews and Christians became more marked, the
latter used exclusively the word Church.

Jewish writers claim a high antiquity for the synagogue,
holding that every place where the Hebrews, "appeared
before the Lord," or "prayed together" was a synagogue.
The Targum of Onkelos, and that of Jonathan, think they
find it in Jacob dwelling in tents,[6] and in the calling of
assemblies.[7] Where did the Hebrews living in places far
from the Temple, many miles from the sacred city
worship? Where did they observe the feasts, fasts, and
new moons, when they could not go up to Jerusalem?
The Jewish writers say in the synagogues built in every
town in times remote far beyond the Captivity.[8]

When in addition to the Temple priests and Levites
rose the prophets to instruct the people and foretell the
Messiah, they established schools of prophets to sing God's
praises. In different parts of Palestine were purified houses
or synagogues where the phylacteries or teraphim, called
"Frontlets," were almost worshiped. The ancients of
Israel sitting before Ezechiel[9] to learn of the prophet God's
oracles show that during the Exile the synagogue was revived. The great Seer told them God was in Babylonia as

[1] Prov. v 14. See S. Augustine, Ques. in Evang. l. ii viii.; Enar in Psalm
lxxxiv; in Psalm lxxiii., 1, Enar in Psalm lxxx 11; Enar in Psalm lxxxii. 1.
[2] Matt x. 17. [3] Matt xxiii. 34; Mark xiii 9; Luke xii. 11, xxii. 11. [4] Epist ad
Trall. c 5   [5] Stroma, VI. 633   [6] Gen xxv. 27   [7] Judg. v. 9; Isaias i. 13, etc.
[8] See Migne, Cursus Comp. S. Scripturæ, in. 1233, etc.   [9] Ezech. viii 1, xiv. 1,
xx. 1, xxxiii. 31

well as in Judea, and would gather them together—back again into Palestine.[1]

The whole history of Esdras' time supposes synagogues, if not existing before at least in his day, and many writers give him as their founder.[2] At that epoch the synagogue was either instituted or revived. The words of St James the apostle : "For Moses from ancient times hath in every city them that preach him in the synagogues, where he is read every Sabbath,"[3] seem to date the synagogue from Moses. But the Machabees mention only Maspha as a place of prayer,[4] perhaps because Jerusalem was then in ruins.

Jewish writers say the synagogue of the time of Christ existed from Moses' day, was developed during the Captivity, fostered by Esdras, still more developed under the high priest John Hyrcanus, and that in the days of Christ every town and hamlet in Judea, where 120 families lived, had a synagogue, and that the surrounding country was divided into districts, each having its own synagogue. The apostles copied the Jewish Church, and divided districts into dioceses, placing over each a bishop with his twelve priests or presbyters

During the Captivity, the synagogue exerted a deep influence on the Hebrews, united them to struggle under the Machabees, trained them in the faith of Israel, and established schools for the children, so that they never afterwards abandoned Judaism. When the bloody sacrifices were re-established in the rebuilt Temple, the synagogue services, with their deep devotion, edifying worship and stately liturgy of the Temple united the people, attracted converts from paganism, and satisfied the human heart's cravings for pure religion.

The prophets had ceased to teach, and beside the Temple ministers flourished another order of religious teachers—the Scribe and Rabbi, not necessarily born of the tribe of Levi and the house of Aaron. Schools and colleges flourished in which these men were educated, after which they were ordained with the imposition of hands. The synagogue and Rabbi have come down to our days substantially as in the time of Christ.

[1] Ezech. ii 14 to end [2] I. Esdras viii 15 ; II. Esdras viii 2, ix. 1 ; Zach vii. 5. [3] Acts xv. 21. [4] I. Mach iii, 46

While the plan of the tabernacle and Temple came from heaven, no fixed size was laid down for the synagogue building; it varied with the size and wealth of the congregation. But the building was always in a prominent part of the city, on a hill near by, or a tall pole rose from its roof to tell the passer by the site. The building was erected by levying a tax on the people of the surrounding district, by free offerings of wealthy Jews,[1] or by a friendly convert. Often it was by the tomb of a celebrated Rabbi or prominent Jew.

When finished it was dedicated with great ceremony, like Solomon's Temple—forever consecrated to God; like our consecrated churches, it could not be used for any other purpose, and common acts of life, like eating, drinking, sleeping, etc., were forbidden. There was only one exception to this rule. The Passover, being a religious feast, could be, and was usually held in the synagogue. No one was allowed to pass through it as a short-cut; if it ceased to be a synagogue, it could not be turned into any other use, as a bath, laundry, tannery, etc. At the door stood a scraper, on which they cleaned their feet; there they left their sandals or shoes, but they wore their turbans in the building all the time.[2]

The synagogue building was modeled after the Temple. Entering the latter you first came to the Chol: "The Profane," where the Heathens could worship, beyond which they were forbidden to pass under pain of death. The Chol represented the Gentiles without faith. It surrounded the whole building. The next was called the Chel, "the Sacred." Then came the women's Court, beyond which no female could penetrate, to remind them of Eve's sin. Farther in was the Court of Israel where the men adored. It was separated from the priests' Court by a low marble railing, beyond which was the priests' Court, in the middle of which rose the great sacrificial altar. To the west was the Holies. Within the "Gold House" was the Holy of Holies. Each of these spaces and Courts was higher than the outside spaces we have described, and were approached by magnificent stone staircases.

The divisions of the synagogue were three—the porch,

[1] Luke vii 5   [2] Babyl. Talmud, Megalla, Chap iv , Gemara, p 77.

nave, and sanctuary. Church buildings, having been copied after the synagogue, have always these three divisions—the porch represents the infidels, the nave, the Christians, and the sanctuary heaven, copied after the Holies of the Temple or the sanctuary of the Cenacle. Let us see the synagogue in detail.

In the synagogue porch were money-boxes like the money-chests of the Temple—the latter being called the Corban. In one they put money for the expenses of the synagogue, in another offerings for the poor of the congregation, in another alms for the poor of Jerusalem, and in others gifts for local charities, of which St Paul writes [1] Whence rose the custom of having poor-boxes in our churches. On the walls were posted notices of feasts, fasts, and the names of those under Kareth, "cut off," excommunicated, and the names of the dead for which their friends asked prayers. Near by was a box in which were kept the musical instruments used by the choir.

On the right door-post hung a little box, the Mezuzeh, having a parchment with a prayer written on it, which they said while entering. It reminded them of the blood of the paschal lamb on the doorposts when their fathers left Egypt On the left of the staircase leading up to the Temple Holies was a great bronze " sea " in which priests bathed before entering on their ministry.[2] This and the box gave rise to the holy water fonts in the porch of our churches, and to the custom of taking the holy water and praying when entering, to remind Christians of baptism through which they enter the Church.

The synagogue nave has galleries on three sides, the side opposite the door being occupied by the sanctuary. A synagogue of our day is so like a Catholic church, that hardly a change, except to place an altar in it, would be required to turn it into a church. Thus church and synagogue buildings have not changed for twenty centuries.

In the days of Christ, all synagogues did not have these galleries, the nave was divided into equal divisions, men occupying the part to your right, women the other, a partition about six feet high running down the middle A still stricter separation of the sexes now prevails among

[1] I. Cor. 16, etc.   [2] See Edersheim Life of Christ, i. 273, etc.

Oriental and orthodox Jews, the galleries being screened off by lattice work. Orientals looked on women as being deeper defiled by Eve's sin,—this especially prevails among Moslems. The Jew of our day prays : " " O Lord, I thank thee that thou didst not make me a woman," and the woman says : " O Lord, I thank thee that thou didst make me as I am." [1]

They planned the synagogue so the sanctuary would face towards Jerusalem; in the latter city it faced the Temple, the direction being called in Hebrew Kedem, " The Front." The sanctuary of the Cenacle faced the east, from that rose the ancient custom of facing the sanctuary of our churches towards the east.

In the time of Christ the sanctuary was named by the Grecian Jews the Bema, while the Roman Hebrews called it the rostrum "stage"[2] as of theaters and public buildings. Only men could occupy the sanctuary during divine services; and women were never allowed to take part during public worship.[3] Whence St. Paul says: " Let women keep silent in the churches . . . . For it is a shame for a woman to speak in the church." [4] As a sign of subjection, they always wore a head covering when praying " Doth it become a woman to pray to God uncovered ?" says St. Paul;[5] whence women even in our day never uncover their heads during church or synagogue services.

At your right, but within the sanctuary, was a rostrum or pulpit called the darshan, from which the preacher delivered the midrash "sermon, " on the part of the Law or Prophets read. From this came the custom of preaching on the Epistle or Gospel, and the pulpit in our churches. As the men read the lessons from the Bible one stood by, called the meturgeman,[6] and translated the words into the language of the people,who in the days of Christ did not understand the ancient Hebrew.

Before the Babylonian Captivity the people of Palestine spoke the pure Hebrew called Leshon Hakkodesh, " Holy Language, or Leshon Chakamim," " Language, of the Learned." But during the seventy years of exile

---

[1] Jewish Prayer Book [2] In St Chrysostom's Liturgy the sanctuary is called the Bema [3] See Migne, Cursus Comp. S. Scripturæ, iii. 1432, etc. [4] I. Cor. xiv. 34 [5] I Cor xi 13. [6] Edersheim, Life of Christ, i 10, 11, 436, 444, 445

they mixed Hebrew with Babylonian words, and when they returned, the common people spoke the Syro-Chaldaic, which some writers call the Aramean language.[1] After the Greek conquest, many Greek words were adopted. When the Romans came they introduced numerous Latin terms, so that at the time of Christ a mixture of languages prevailed, especially in Galilee, meaning "The Circle of the Gentiles," from Gelil, "Circle," and Haggoyin, "Gentiles." This part of Palestine was so rich that it was called "the udder of the land," and many Gentile families who had settled there broke down the isolation of the Jew. Hence Christ converted many Galileans and chose his apostles from them, Judas, Caiphas' nephew, being the only strict Jew among them.[2]

The sermons of these ancient preachers come down to us under the name of the Targums and Midrashes. But they made no change in the ancient Hebrew of Moses and Temple, and synagogue services even to our day remain in the pure Hebrew, which only the learned Jews now understand. People who find fault because Mass is said in Latin, Greek, and tongues the people do not understand, do not realize that Christ worshiped in the synagogues where the services were in a dead language.[3]

Within the sanctuary, before the ark containing the holy Scrolls, hung an ever-burning lamp, fed with olive oil, reminding them of the Shekina, "a cloud by day and a fire by night," in the tabernacle and first Temple. This lamp is now seen in our sanctuary lamp before the Blessed Sacrament. Along the two sides of the sanctuary were seats for the officers who carried out the services for the kneseth, "the congregation." These seats are seen in the seats and stalls of our churches. In wealthy synagogues these seats were very finely carved and ornamented, as are the stalls of cathedrals, and the large churches of Europe. Let us give the following from the Babylonian Talmud:

"Who has not seen the diplostoa, 'double portico,' of Alexandria in Egypt, has not seen the glory of Israel. It was said it was a great Basilica, 'palace with colon-

---

[1] Migne, Cursus Comp. ii 1346; Edersheim, Life of Christ, i. 10, 130. [2] Edersheim, Sketches, 40 [3] See Migne, Cursus Comp S Scripturæ, i. 529 to 600, etc

nades,' and the palace could contain twice the number of men who went out from Egypt. There were seventy-one cathedras, 'armchairs with footstools,' for the seventy-one sages of the Great Sanhedrin, and each cathedra was made of no less than twenty-one myriads of talents of gold. And a wooden Bema was in the middle of the palace, were the hassan or sexton of the congregation stood with a flag in his hand, and when the time came in the prayer to respond 'Amen,' he raised the flag, and the whole people said 'Amen.' And they did not sit promiscuously, but separately. The golden chairs were separate, and silver chairs were separate, smiths sat separately, carpenters separately, and all of the different trades sat separately, and when a poor man went in, he recognized who his fellow-tradesmen were and went to them, and thus got work for the support of himself and his family.[1] The account says that Alexander of Macedon killed all of them, because they broke the command,[2] which forbade the Israelites to return to Egypt.

"The court of the women was formerly without a balcony, but they surrounded it with a balcony, and ordained that the women should sit above, and the men below. Formerly the women sat in inward chambers, and the men in outer ones, but thereby was produced much levity, and it was ordained that the men should sit inwardly, and the women outwardly. But still levity arose, and therefore it ordained that the women should sit above and the men below."[3]

The account then treats of the two Messiahs they thought the prophets foretold, one to be born of Joseph's tribe, who would be the suffering Messiah, quoting prophecies of his sufferings and death relating to Christ, and the other the glorious Messiah, born of David's family, who was to come in triumph and establish his kingdom over all the earth, ending with these words "And the Lord showed me four carpenters.[4] Who are the four carpenters? The Messiah son of David, and the Messiah son of Joseph, Elias, and the Priest Zedec."[5]

The word "carpenters" in the original Hebrew in the Douay version is "smiths," but in the King James

[1] Babyl. Talmud, Tract Succah, c. v   [2] Deut. xvii 16   [3] Talmud Babyl. Succah, 78. See Edersheim, Life of Christ, i 58 to 64   [4] Zach. i 20   [5] Succah, 79 to 82

version it is "carpenters." Thus it was handed down in these Jewish traditions that the Messiah would be a carpenter. The Gospels and writings of that time tell us that Christ worked as a carpenter before he began his public life

A railing, copied from the golden lamps forming a balustrade between the priests' Court and Holies of the Temple, separated the sanctuary of the synagogue from the nave occupied by the people. This was the origin of the altar railing in our churches.

On your right within the sanctuary, was a great candlestick with seven lamps, modeled after the famous one of gold in the Temple, called the Tsemath, "The Branch." It reminded them of the "Branch" of David's family, the Messiah, "The Anointed," "The Christ," foretold to come filled with the sevenfold gifts of the Holy Ghost,[1] and fill the world with heavenly truth, effulgent rays, the teachings of his Gospel. They thought he was to found a matchless kingdom extending over all the earth. The Scribes, Pharisees and Rabbis thought that only the Jews would be rulers in this kingdom.

From the days of Moses, they kept in the Temple the Yachas, "genealogies," birth and marriage records of Aaron's family, which they consulted when electing the high priest and inferior clergy.[2] Following this in each synagogue they kept careful records of births, marriages, deaths and confirmations of boys. The local Sanhedrin or court, found wherever 120 families lived, kept these records. Sts. Matthew and Luke could have therefore found Christ's genealogy, recorded in their Gospels, in the synagogues of Bethlehem and Nazareth. Whence come down in parish churches, records of births, deaths, confirmations, funerals, etc.

The synagogue teacher, the Darshan, was called Rabbi, Rabban, or Rabboni. The word *rab* in the Babylonian language means "lord" or "master." Thus Nabuzardan is called *rab tabachim*, "master of the army."[3] Assuerus placed a *rab* or "master" to preside over each table at his great feast.[4] Asphenez was *rab*[5] of the eunuchs. A *rab* of the *saganim*, "satrap," was the ruler of each

---

[1] Isaias ii 1, 2, 3, Zach. iii 8, 9, vi 12.   [2] See Edersheim, Life of Christ, i 9; Geikie, Life of Christ, i 51.   [3] IV Kings xxv 8.   [4] Esther i. 3.   [5] Dan. i. 3.

province, and a *rab* of the *chartunim* was "chief of those who interpreted dreams." [1] The first to be called Rabbi was a son of that Hillel who was so famous as the founder of the Beth Hillel, "School of Hillel." This son was, according to some, that holy Simeon, who took the Child Jesus in his hands when presented in the Temple. The title Rabbi was not generally used before Herod the Great. [2]

The president of a school or college was a *cacham*, "sage" or "doctor." When he became famous as a teacher he was a *cabar rabbin* "companion of masters," who decided disputes about the Law, [3] married people, granted divorces, lectured, presided over large synagogues, punished the wicked and could excommunicate. [4]

These learned Rabbis went around the country preaching and gathering disciples to the number of twelve, as the high priest was served by twelve priests in his Temple ministry, in memory of the twelve sons of Jacob, fathers of the twelve tribes of Israel. This custom Christ followed when he traveled over Judea with his twelve apostles.

John the Baptist from the day he was confirmed at twelve till he was thirty, lived in the desert. Then following the customs of the Rabbis, he gathered disciples round him—many of them followed Christ after John had pointed him out to them as the "Lamb of God" who was to take away the sins of the world. [5]

Besides the twelve immediate followers, these Rabbis had seventy-two followers, images of Noe's grandsons, fathers and founders of the nations. [6] Often wealthy ladies followed these Rabbis to learn the Law and wait on them. [7] Bands of Jews, each led by a Rabbi, used to come up to Jerusalem for the feast of Passover, thus great crowds followed Jesus to the Temple on Palm Sunday.

Christ was known by names applied to these Rabbis. The Greek of the Gospels shows us the names they called him. He or calls himself—

didaskalos : "teacher," Matt. x. 24, xxvi. 18 ;

[1] Dan i 2   [2] Geikie, Life Christ, i 6, 26, 77, 169, 170, 215 to 248, etc   [3] Migne, Cursus Comp S Scripturæ, iii. 1189   [4] Geikie, Life of Christ, ii., p 178   See Edersheim, Life of Christ, i. 11   [5] John i 29   [6] Gen 10. See Edersheim, Life of Christ, ii 135 to 142.   [7] Luke xxiii 27

kathegetes : " leader," " guide," in the sense of Rabbi, Matt. xxiii. 8–10;

grammateus, " scribe," " learned," " a lawyer," Matt. xiii. 52.

He is called—

didaskalos : " master-teacher," Matt. viii. 19, ix. 11, xii. 38, xvii. 23, xxii. 24;

rabbi : " great man," " teacher," Matt. xxvi. 25–49; Mark xiv. 45, ix. 4, xi. 21 ; John i. 38–49. iii. 2, 26, iv. 31, vi. 25–92 ;

rabboni : " my rabbi," " my lord," Mark x. 51 ; John xx. 16.

Rabbi, " my Master," or " my Lord," was first given to religious teachers in the time of Herod the Great,[1] when Rabbis got the most extravagant ideas of their importance.[2]

In his Gospel St. Luke uses the Greek Didaskalos as the equivalent of Rab or Rabbi, " My Lord," applied many times to Christ. The lowest order of the Rabbis was the Rab, then the Rabbi, and the highest the Rabboni, titles coming down in the Church as Rev., Very Rev., and Rt. Rev., applied to spiritual rulers. The English is " My Lord," the French Monseigneur, the Italian Monsignor, etc., a title applied to bishops in Europe. It is the equivalent of the title they addressed to Christ in these days, when it was not respectful to call a teacher by his own name.[3]

· The Pharisees, Scribes and Rabbis liked to be called " Father " as priests are addressed to-day. But they had so exaggerated their own importance, and abused the title, that Christ told his apostles to call " God their Father in heaven, and Christ their Father on earth."[4] The custom of calling a priest or bishop " Father " comes down from this title our Lord applied to himself.

No one would listen to a Rabbi before he was ordained with the laying on of the hands of the Rabbis in his thirtieth year. If he began to preach before that time all would laugh at him. That is the reason Jesus lived in private, working as a carpenter at Nazareth after Joseph's death, supporting his widowed Mother till he was in his thirtieth

[1] See Palestine in the Time of Christ, 305   [2] Geikie, Life of Christ, i 69-70; ii 19, 20, 161 ; ii 585, etc ; Migne, Cursus Comp. S Scripturæ iii 1189   [3] Nork 192.   [4] Matt xxiii 9, 10.

year. Then he called members of the band of John the Baptist and fishermen of Galilee to be his followers, selecting from these his twelve apostles. For more than three years they wandered over Judea like many bands led by the Rabbis of that time.

On the hillsides and valleys, in the streets of villages, where night overtook them they said the Temple and synagogue prayers, after which they spread the two blankets and straw each carried in a basket, and with a stone for a pillow like Jacob [1] they slept beside the sacred form of Jesus Christ.

Why did the Lord spend his public life wandering from place to place? He wanted to train his apostles like soldiers, accustom them to hardships, drill them by a severe novitiate, harden their muscles, strengthen their wills, that they might be prepared later to travel through the nations while preaching his Gospel, and to enable them to stand all kinds of trials and hardships, even martyrdom destined for them all, except St. John.[2]

Judea was then densely populated, and the Rabbis with their bands used to pass through country and city followed by crowds of people. When they entered a town the whole population turned out. In country districts the Rabbi often sat on a high rock, or on the top of a hill or mountain, as Christ did when he delivered the sermon on the mount. The Rabbi placed his most advanced scholars at his feet, surrounding him like the apostles around Christ, the hearers less advanced below them, like the seventy-two disciples below the apostles and the people lower down sitting on mats or on the ground.

Great honor the children offered the teacher Rabbi of the Beth-ham-Midrasch, "School House." He whispered his words, which an advanced scholar spoke so that all the scholars could hear.[3] The Jews of that time told their children, "Rub yourselves in the dust of the feet of your teachers." Children used to wash the feet of their teachers as a mark of love and veneration. To show them his love, Christ reversed the custom when he washed the apostles' feet at the Last Supper.

The Jews claim thirteen classes of Rabbis—teachers,— Moses, Josue, Eleazar, the Seventy men Moses chose to aid

---

[1] Gen. xxviii. 18. [2] John xxi. 22. [3] See Geikie, Life of Christ, i. 231 to 235.

him in the government, the Judges, the members of the
Sanhedrin of that epoch, the Prophets, the twenty-six
great teachers after the Captivity, the Thanaim mentioned
in the Talmudic Mishna, the Amoraims who commented
on the Mishna, the Giours "Excellent Doctors," the
Seboreens, "Doubters," and lastly the Gaons, teachers
of our day.

The Rabbis, called Maggid, went through the country
teaching in the synagogues, each followed by his band of
disciples. "Jesus went about all Galilee teaching in their
synagogues, and preaching the gospel of the kingdom, and
healing all diseases and infirmities among the people."[1]

"And when he was departed from thence, he came into
the synagogue."[2] "And coming into his own country,
he taught them in their synagogues."[3] "And on the Sabbath day going into the synagogue he taught them."[4]
Eight other texts of the Gospels say he went into the
synagogues, taught and performed miracles before the
assembled Jews. His sermon relating to eating his Body
and drinking his Blood was preached in a synagogue of
Capharnaum,[5] "village of the prophet Nahum," the word
meaning "the comforter."

One Rabbi presided over a small synagogue. But
large flourishing congregations were ruled by a college of
twelve Rabbis,[6] called in Hebrew *parnasim* and in Greek
presbyteri: "aged men." The presbyters, first mentioned
in Esdras,[7] are found twenty-four times in the Bible,
translated as "elders" in the King James Bible and as
"ancients" in the Douay version. The ruler or chairman
of this senate the Greeks called the *archisynagogos*
"ruler of the synagogue." He governed the congregation, took care of the building and property, and could
punish unruly members with the pain of Kareth "cut
off," "excommunication." This senate was an image of
the high priest with his twelve priests, who carried out
the Temple ceremonial.

Christ acted as a Rabbi during his public life, twelve
times this name is applied to him in the Gospel, and when
he chose his twelve apostles, he followed Temple and
synagogue custom. The apostles founded dioceses, "resi-

[1] Matt. ix 35   [2] Matt. xii 9   [3] Matt. xiii 54   [4] Mark i. 21.   [5] John vi. 60.
[6] See Geikie, Life of Christ, ii. 595   [7] I. Esdras vi 8.

dence" or "administration," among the nations, as Judea
was divided into districts with a synagogue in each, with
these twelve rulers at its head. In every city they
ordained twelve priests, called presbyters, over whom
they placed a bishop, "superintendent," to rule the church
with its senate of twelve priests, similar to the constitution of the Jewish Church In the early Church we find
only the diocese. The parish took its rise in Rome,
when the city was divided into districts in the days of
Peter. Alexandria soon followed, the other cities copied,
but the country parishes with a priest as pastor over each
were not founded till the twelfth century.

In the days of Christ the archisynagogos was always
an ordained Rabbi, as were the members of the senate, or
parnasim. But in later times a layman might occupy the
position and now he is called the "president of the congregation," or the *rich-hac-ceneseth,* "ruler-of-the-meet-
ing-house." He called the members to meet, presided at
all meetings, sat in the Bema during the services, invited
preachers, called up the seven men to read the Law, and
looked after business matters. The Rabbi had little to
say in the finances, but looked after the doctrines of
Judaism.[1]

An important official of the synagogue was the *sheliach*
in Hebrew, or *apostolos* in Greek, meaning "to be sent."
The apostle carried the collections taken up in Babylonia
and Jewish colonies of the Roman empire to Jerusalem
for the support of the Temple, with the half shekels each
Jew was obliged to give every year for the expenses of
religion—the Temple and its sacrifices.[2]

The Temple priests also sent each year apostles from
Jerusalem to the different synagogues of the world to
bring greetings from their brethren in Judea, and to see
that the synagogue worship was rightly observed in these
distant lands.[3] When therefore Christ's followers went
forth from Jerusalem into the nations to preach the
Gospel to the heathens they were called apostles, both
name and mission being well known in Judaism long before Christ.

---

[1] Mark v. 22, 35, 36, 38 ; Luke viii 41, xiii 14, Acts xviii. 8-17, Edersheim, L
C , i 63   [2] Migne, Cursus Comp S Scripturæ, h. 1328.   [3] Migne, Cursus Comp
S. Scripturæ, iii. 828, 829.

Each synagogue had a committee of seven "standing men," who used to fast sometimes four times a week, from Monday till Thursday inclusive. On Sabbath the standing men read the Bible sections commencing: "In the beginning God created," etc;[1] on Monday they read, " Let there be a; firmament," etc. ; on Tuesday, "Let the waters," etc.[2]; on Wednesday, "Let there be lights," etc.[3]; on Thursday, "Let the earth bring forth, etc.,[4] and on Friday, "Thus were finished," etc.[5]

" The long section was read by two persons, and the short by one, this was done however during the morning, and during the additional prayers, but in the afternoon they entered the synagogue, and recited the sections by heart, as the Shema is recited. On Friday they did not go to the synagogue at all in honor of the Sabbath."[6]

These men were called up into the Bema or sanctuary of the synagogue to read the sections of the Scripture. It is called reading the Scrolls of the Law. In synagogues of our day, on Passover and holidays they read five, on Passover before feast and on Sabbath seven lessons from the Law, and one from the Prophets. The Rabbi and Hassan also each read one section making nine lessons." This was the origin of the nine lessons of the Matins. The lessons of Holy Week like those of the Jews have no " Command, Lord bless," etc., as the lessons of the ordinary offices.[7]

The seven men who read the Law were the leading members of the congregation, and sometimes they looked after widows, orphans and the poor. When the apostles selected and ordained the seven deacons, they followed the ancient custom of the synagogue.[8] The reader was called the Maphtir[9] and was classed with Moses, the patriarchs and prophets.

Temple priests and Levites were born of Aaron's and Levi's family, but any one could become a Rabbi. Therefore Christ chose his apostles and disciples not from among the Temple priests but among the Galileans without doing violence to custom. The Rabbi when a boy

[1] Gen i 1 to 5   [2] Gen i 6   [3] i 14   [4] i 24   [5] ii 1 to 4   [6] Talmud, Taanith, cap iv 79-81, 62, 63, etc   [7] See Babylonian Talmud, Cap iv for regulations regarding "Standing men" The Babylonian Talmud, Megilla, "Book of Esther," gives minute directions regarding the ceremonies of reading the sacred Books   [8] Acts 6   [9] See Migne, Cursus Comp S. Scripturæ iii 967.

attended the school of his native place, and went up to
Jerusalem to finish his studies. The conditions and
talents were the same as St. Paul lays down for the
selection of a bishop.[1] Before they ordained him he had
to be learned, active, father of a family, apt to teach, a
good singer, and not engaged in business. These are still
required for Rabbis of our day.

The next personage was the *chazzan*,[2] called to-day by
Jews *hassan*, "minister," in Greek *diakonos*, "worker," in
Hebrew *shemash*. The word is mentioned in the account
of Christ in the synagogue. "And when he had folded
the book he restored it to the minister,"[3]—the hassan.
He thus fulfilled the duties of the deacon and sub-deacon
when waiting on the Rabbi.[4] The same rules were followed in his selection as for the Rabbi. He opened the
synagogue doors, prepared things for the service, often
acted as the school-teacher, sang the services and responded to the Rabbi during divine worship. Good
singers and active hassans of our day receive large sala-
ries, sometimes $2,000 to $3,000 a year. With the Rabbi
he was ordained in the time of Christ with a long ceremony, and the laying on of the hands of the Rabbis and
hassans on his head. This gave rise to the custom of
imposing the hands of the clergy with the bishop on the
head of the clergyman the day of his ordination.

Besides these officials, in every congregation were ten
men, called batlanim "men of leisure." They were not
obliged to labor for their living, and could therefore attend, not only the Sabbath, but the Monday and Thursday services. No congregation was complete, nor could
any service be held without them. At one synagogue
the writer attended, they had to wait before beginning
the service till ten men were present, the women not
being considered, as they cannot take part in any religious
function. Seven of these men, called *Stationarii*, or *viri
Stationis* in the synagogue of the Roman empire, collected
the synagogue alms for the poor, read the Law during
the services, and gave rise to the church clergy in minor
orders. They are sometimes called shepherds, in Hebrew
hassans, in Greek *hiepeus* "priest" while the Rabbi was

---

[1] I. Tim. iii. 1-7; Tit. i. 6-9   [2] Geikie, Life of Christ, i. 178   [3] Luke iv. 20.
[4] Edersheim, Life of Christ, i. 231, 438, 443.

sometimes named *apostolos* " sent," " legate " of the congregation. These words are found in decrees of later Roman emperors regarding the Jews after the destruction of the Temple.

Each synagogue had either five or seven Gabai Zedakah. " Charity Collectors," who took up the collection during the service. The people offered either money or victuals. This took place after reading the Law and Prophets. The custom was continued in the early Church when the people brought their offerings and placed them on a table in the sanctuary and that part of the Mass is called the Offertory.

Two Jews took up the collection, and four or five distributed them. They were the leading men of the congregation and took care of the widows and orphans. We trace the collectors in the Church back to the synagogue. Some writers think the apostles had these seven men in mind when they ordained the seven deacons.[1]

The Jews of the time of Christ had an order of exorcists : " Who went about and attempted to invoke over them that had evil spirits."[2] When Christ gave power over unclean spirits he followed the synagogue regulations.

The reader will see in these four officials of the synagogue the minor orders of the Church coming down from the apostolic days. They are mentioned in the most ancient records and are found in all the apostolic Liturgies. The priests who prepared the bread and wine in the Temple imaged the acolytes, the men who read the Scriptures the readers, the chassans who opened doors of Temple and synagogue the porters, and the men who drove out demons, the exorcists.

The synagogue service was always sung in the days of Christ. From the time Jubal invented musical instruments,[3] song, timbrel and harp[4] were used at weddings, religious gatherings, and feasts of joy. Music and poetry went hand in hand. Poets composed and sang their songs accompanying themselves on musical instruments. This custom obtained among all primitive peoples.[5]

---

[1] Acts vi. ; Edersheim, Sketches, p. 283. [2] Acts xix 13 ; Matt. xii. 27 ; Mark iii. 15–30 ; Luke vi 18, viii 29, xi 24 [3] Gen. iv. 21. [4] Gen. xxxi. 27. [5] Migne, Cursus Comp. S Scripturæ iii 1029

Moses sang his hymn of glory to the Lord.[1]   All Israel, forming a mighty choir, voiced their joy in Jehovah's praise when they found water in the desert.[2]   Before his death God told Moses to write a glorious canticle of praise and prophecy.[3]

Down the history of the Hebrews we find the hymn, " sacred song" and canticle of " praise" during religious worship.   Seventy-four times the canticle is found in the Old Testament.   When Moses built the tabernacle, parts of the services were sung by priest and Levite choirs, and that was the order of exercises till Temple replaced tabernacle.[4]

David, Jesse's seventh son, keeping his father's flocks on Bethlehem's hills, moved by the spirit of poetry, composed songs of praises to the God of his fathers.   Chosen king in place of Saul, when he had brought the ark to Jerusalem, David formed priests and levites into twenty-four courses for the better service of the Temple his son Solomon was to build.   Then began the composition of the Book of Psalms, the Temple Hymn-book.   Later other prophet-poets added psalms " songs of praise," till the Hebrew Hymn-book, the Book of Psalms was formed as it comes down to us.

Written in pure Hebrew, in verse sometimes in faultless meter, in striking figures, filled with history of the nation, uniting past, present and future, telling the story of David the king, and David the Christ, the Hebrew Church and the Catholic Church, David's sorrows and Christ's sufferings, the Babylonian Captivity, and the glories of Christianity, the preaching of the Apostles, and the conversion of the Heathens, the glories of the Redeemer's reign, and the triumph of the Saints,—the Psalms come down from the reigns of David and of Solomon as the most remarkable compositions of any age or people.

Used ever after as Temple Hymn-book, sung twice a day by two choirs of priests and Levites, each formed of more than 500 members, the Psalms were sung in the synagogues after the destruction of the Temple.   To this day in their synagogues, scattered over the world wherever they have wandered, the Jews still sing these wonderful

---

[1] Exod xv. 1.   [2] Numb xxi. 17.   [3] Deut. xxxi. 19, etc.   [4] See Migne, S. Scripturæ, ii. 1129, 1131, 1132, 1155, etc.

devotional prophetic hymns and religious canticles. They look on David as their holiest and greatest king. But why they should now hold that these hymns relate to a king, an adulterer and a murderer 3,000 years dead, especially when in hundreds of places the long-looked-for Messiah is mentioned, is surprising.

The flute, in Hebrew *mashroqitha,* " to blow," under different forms was used in Egypt 2,000 years before Christ. It was a favorite instrument of Greek and Roman shepherds, and was used in military bands, and at festivals and funerals. Its Latin name comes from *fluta,* an eel of Sicilian waters, with seven spots on each side like flute holes.[1]

The piccolo is an octave higher, and many flutes, tuned in unison, became the organ used before the flood.[2] David introduced the organ into the Temple services[3] translated "musical instruments."

Musicians sometimes played two flutes at the same time, one an octave higher than the other, as we see in sculptures and pictures of shepherds and satyrs. The pagans played the flute at feast and funeral. The Rabbis taught that not less than two flutes must be played at a funeral, Jews having learned that custom from Greeks and Romans.

Many flutes formed into one instrument became the organ run by water invented by Ctesbius of Alexandria in the second century before Christ. In the Temple was a large organ they called the magrephah, the bellows being of elephant hide.[4] It sustained the singing. The Rabbis write it could be heard down to Jericho, but this is incredible for the distance is fifteen miles. When it gave forth a peculiar note, the priest behind the veil in the Holies spread the incense on the gold altar. From the beginning the organ has been used in our churches.

In David's day 4.000 singers formed choirs of Levites under the leadership of Asaph, Heman and Idithun, and they sang the Temple service. Asaph had four sons, Idithun six, and Heman fourteen, each son being placed over a choir or band, and thus David divided the Levites into twenty-four bands or "courses." Each son of these

[1] See Migne, Cursus Com. S Scripturæ, iii. 1002. [2] Gen. iv. 21. [3] I Par. xv. 16.
[4] Edersheim, Temple, 137 ; Geikie, Life of Christ, i. 338.

great music teachers, had under him eleven teachers of
vocal and instrumental music. They taught the priests
and Levites to sing the glories of Jehovah. Families became famous for musical abilities. These sons of Caath,
at the time of Christ, stood in the center, with the sons
of Merai on the left, and the descendants of Gerson on the
right. While Idithun's family in David's day played the
cithern called the cinnor, Asaph's family drew music
from the psaltery, called in Hebrew *nabat*, and Heman's
struck the Mizlothaim, " the timbrels," with them beating
time. These were the three chief musical instruments
used in the temple from David's day, and are called by
Jewish writers the viol, psaltery and cymbal.

" And now David, being freed from wars and dangers,
and enjoying for the future a profound peace, composed
songs and hymns to God of several sorts of meter, some
of which he made were trimeters and some were pen-
tameters. He also made instruments of music, and
taught the Levites to sing hymns to God, both on that
called the Sabbath-day, and on other festivals. Now the
construction of the instruments was thus. The viol was
an instrument of ten strings, it was played on with a
bow. The psaltery had twelve musical notes, and was
played by the fingers The cymbals were broad and
large instruments, and were made of brass." [1]

According to Josephus, David composed the Book of
Psalms, not at different times as is generally supposed,
but towards the end of his life, and he alone is their
author. He says Moses composed his Canticle at the Red
Sea and his other Canticle in hexameter meter. But the
Psalms were of various meters.

The Hebrews carried their music, instruments and the
liturgy of the destroyed Temple to Babylon, and used
them in the synagogues. When they returned and rebuilt the Temple, they continued the Temple service in
the synagogues they built in all the towns of Judea, and
in cities and towns of the world into which they had
scattered at the time of Christ. Synagogue services were
always sung by priests Levites and members of the congregation. [2]

---

[1] Josephus Antiq , B vii C. xii. n 3.　　[2] See Migne, S. Scripturæ, iii. 915-2,
1345.

The choirs of Levites in Solomon's Temple were clothed in white tunics of byssus and fine linen, to distinguish them from the priests vested in cloth of gold; on solemn feasts they put on vestments of magnificent embroidery. Some time after the death of Christ, Herod Agrippa gave the Levites permission to vest in robes like those worn by the priests in their ministry, which Josephus says was contrary to the law.

Priests and Levites formed two choirs, one responding to the other, using as hymn-books, Psalms, Job, Proverbs, Ecclesiasticus and Canticle of Canticles—the Book of Psalms being the one most used. Following the example of Moses' sister Mary and the women with her who sang and danced,[1] women sang in the synagogues. We do not find that women ever formed a choir in the Temple, perhaps they sang in congregational singing in the Women's Court.

The priests' choir began the Psalm, sang as far as the star in our breviaries, and the Levites sang the rest of the verse like a response. This is the reason that the latter part, in thought is like an echo of the former, for the Psalms were written for the Temple service. The two choirs of Temple and synagogue passed into the two choirs of the Church or into the priests' choir in the sanctuary, and the lay-choir in the organ gallery. From the Jewish church came the versicles and responses, and parts taken by the celebrant of the Mass, and they are seen in missals, Breviaries, rituals, liturgical books, and are found not only in the Latin, but in all Oriental Churches.

Temple service of sacred song and hymn were introduced into the synagogue long before the time of Christ, and continue down to our day among both Jews and Christians. The Passover services was always sung in imitation of the Temple worship. Many reasons force us to conclude that the services of the Last Supper were sung The Gospel states they sang a hymn before they left the Cenacle.[2]

The Passover the writer attended in Jerusalem was sung by the thirteen Jews in their own peculiar tone and melody. The Oriental Christians sing Mass in their crude

---

[1] Exod. xv. 20, 21 [2] Matt xxvi 30; Mark xiv. 26.

nasal tone, reminding you of Jewish vocal music.   Roman
Catholics sing the offices of Holy Week round Christ's
tomb in Jerusalem, and it is so strikingly superior to
Oriental music that great crowds gather.   The prophecies relating to the Saviour's Passion and death are
then read in the spot where they were fulfilled.

The next week the Oriental Christians, Armenians,
Copts, Greeks, Nestorians, Jacobites, etc., gather in the
Church of the Holy Sepulchre, each band being led by
their clergy and bishop, the laity going first, then the
clergy and last the bishop.   One band follows another
to the number of six or eight, and each band, having a
different language, rite, and method of singing—all together make the most awful discord heard on earth.

Pope Gregory I. reformed the crude Jewish and oriental
music, and he is the author of what is now called the
Gregorian or plain chant—the official music of the Church.
St. Augustine says St. Athanasius condemned certain ways
of modulating the voice in singing the Psalms, which he
himself does not condemn, which shows that our services
were sung in the early Church.[1]

In the Temple Holy of Holies, the ark with the Shekina
resting on its mercy-seat, having the tables of the Law,
was most holy to the Hebrew.   The synagogue ark, containing the Torah "the Law" and the Haphtorah, the
"Prophetic Books" was the most sacred object.   It was
a box about three feet square and high, and covered by a
vail, it rested next the farther wall in the middle of the
sanctuary and was approached by steps.   In the early
Church the altar was made the same size and shape as
the Jewish ark.   The Greek and Oriental Christians have
altars of the same kind rising in the middle of the veiled
sanctuary, the bishop's throne being behind, where he
sits facing the people.   The Orientals cover the altar
with silk altar cloths and allow on it nothing but the
liturgical books—the Book of the Liturgy in the center,
that of the Gospels on your left and that of the Epistles
on your right, resting on the silk-covered altar table.
Even the candles must be on a little shelf in the Slavonic
Rite.   The Jews allow nothing but the Scrolls of the
Law in the ark.

[1] S. Augustine, Confes. l. xc., xxxiii.

Jews in this country form the ark as an ornamental recess curtained off, having two doors opening out, behind which they keep the Scrolls, the place being approached by steps. The synagogue ark came down from the Temple, for God told Moses to place the Law, that is the first five Books of the Old Testament in the ark.[1] At the time of Christ another box received the Haphtorah "The Prophets," for they were not written till after Moses' time.

The writer examined different synagogue Scrolls which Jews claim are now written the same as in the days of Moses. They are in the peculiar angular Hebrew letters written with a reed pen. The last line of a paragraph has the letters spread out, so that all lines will be of an equal length. These Scrolls come from Europe, where they are produced by learned Scribes—generally old men learned in Biblical and Talmudic lore. The Torah used in the synagogues was never printed with type, but is always copied with the extreme care and labor as in the ancient days of Christ and the prophets.

The Jews say it is hard to read these Scrolls, as they must remember the vowels and put them in as they go along during the reading of the Law in the synagogue. Many centuries ago the vowels were put into some writings In other Hebrew writings the vowels were put in, and they appear as little dots and signs. But no change was ever made in the Scrolls of Moses' Five Books, still copied, in the purest Hebrew.[2] The Jerusalem Talmud was written in the Hebrew of Moses and the Temple, while the Babylonian Talmud was written in the mixed Hebrew and Babylonian forming a language called the Syro-Chaldaic of the time of Christ. The Jews of our time publish works and newspapers in their vernacular language, such as German, Russian, etc., using the Hebrew letters in Scrolls, Talmuds and their modern publications.

The Jews call these five first Books of the Bible, "The Five Books of Moses," the Greeks named them the Pentateuch, "The Five Books" But their ancient Hebrew name is Torah, "The Law," a word found more than six hundred times in the Bible Sometimes the word law means these five Books Moses wrote, in other texts it

---

[1] Deut xxxi 25, 26.   [2] Geikie, Life of Christ, i. 553 , ii 607, 608, etc.

refers to the Law and the Temple ceremonial, while often it signifies the whole Hebrew religion with the Old Testament, Temple, synagogue and Jewish faith. But when the Jews of our day mention the Torah or Law, they mean these five books Moses wrote on the scrolls and placed in the Temple in a special ark, and which they claim come down in the synagogue to our day in the exact form as Moses wrote them on the vellum scrolls.

The Sheepskins are about two feet square, each cut from a whole skin, scraped nearly as thin as paper, and tanned white; they are called vellum, from *vel*, "skin," whence our word volume. They are then sowed together with sheep-gut, so as to form a band many feet in length. In the middle of each square piece of vellum are written two or three columns of the Hebrew writings, which read, not from left to right like our books, but from right to left like all Semitic writings. You begin at what would be the back of our books.

The long sheets of vellum are rolled on two sticks, the ends having rollers so the vellum does not touch the table. The ends of the sticks and rollers are ornamented with silver, gold, or other ornaments, decorated and richly finished according to the wealth of the congregation. The scroll of the Law, with its ornaments, is covered with a rich embroidered case when placed in the ark. During the synagogue service, officers vested like our inferior clergy, go up to the ark, draw aside the veil and take out the Law. Forming a procession, they go to the reading desk, where it is read in a loud singing tone. This gave rise to the ceremony of singing the Gospel. The deacon taking the missal places it on the altar and kneels in prayer. Taking the missal from the altar, he receives the celebrant's blessing, and goes with the other ministers to the place where the Gospel is sung. The reader will find in Zanolini [1] accurate descriptions of the synagogue worship at the time of Christ. Jewish and Protestant writers we have quoted treat the subject extensively.

The synagogue service [2] began with the Psalms, prayers, and doxology: "praise." Then they read the part of the Law or Torah of Moses relating to the feast. Dur-

[1] De Festis et Sectis Judæorum.   [2] See Palestine, 338-343.

ing this reading, all except the reader sat, and that is the reason that in the church to-day, all sit during the reading of the Epistle at Mass.

As the Scriptures were in the ancient Hebrew, which the people did not understand, one stood by the reader and translated the sentences into the language of the people, into Syro-Chaldaic in Palestine, or into the Babylonian, Greek, Latin, etc., according to the place where the synagogue was.[1] The reader, or Maphtir, covered his head with the prayer-shawl, called the tallith, to which St. Paul alludes.[2] As the Jews considered themselves a nation of priests, any one could rise in the synagogue and read the Scriptures.[3]

After reading the portion of the "Books of Moses" relating to the feast, they read a part of the prophecies. Generally they stood while the prophecies were read, and that gave rise to the custom of standing during the Gospel in our churches. After this they sat while the reader, Rabbi, or one of the congregation preached the sermon from the pulpit. The parts were marked so that the whole Torah, or Pentateuch was read in the course of three years. Later, but before Christ, it was arranged so that they read the whole Torah in one year. That gave rise in the early Church of reading a part of each of the Books of the Bible during the year.

In Scripture and Jewish writings, the word Sabbath, "rest," means not only Saturday, the Jewish day of worship, but any solemnity, festival, or feast.[4]

During Sabbath feasts, and Passover, the latter being the highest holiday, all work stopped, they could even walk only half a mile. They worshiped God with solemn synagogue and Temple worship at Passover. The Talmud Tract,[5] under thirty-nine heads, cites things forbidden on Sabbath. Three chief things were done on the Sabbath and feast—trumpets sounded, tables were prepared, lamps and candles lighted, synagogue services held, and Law and Prophets read But the preparations and services of Passover were most elaborate.

The Laws of Moses were first read in what the Greeks called Parasca "section," and its appendix, the prophecy,

---

[1] Acts xv 21; Luke iv. 16. [2] Rom. iv. 7. [3] Luke iv 16; Acts xiii. 15. [4] Zanolini, Disp de Fest Judæorum, Cap. Prim. [5] The Sabbath, Cap. vii, Sec. 2.

was also sung, as we read first the Epistle, and then the Gospel. The regular prayers were said, and two added for the Passover, the last being a prayer for the king whom they served.[1] St. Paul, asking Christians to pray for and obey their princes[2] followed the synagogue and Temple, where day by day sacrifices were offered for the Roman emperor. After these services they sat or reclined at the table to eat.[3] Some writers claim the custom of reading sections of the Scripture came from Moses, others from Esdras, but the council of Jerusalem defines in these words: " From the most ancient times, Moses had in each city men, who preached the Scripture in the synagogues where every Sabbath it was read."[4]

In Babylonia, at the time of Christ, they read the whole Law or Pentateuch once a year. This is still the practice of modern Jews, but in Judea they read the whole of Moses' Books in three years. They were divided into sections[5] not marked in scrolls, but each part was fixed by custom. As the reader read the Hebrew, one stood by with a pointer so the reader might not miss a word. Ordinary Sabbaths six men of the congregation were called up, and on feasts seven men, each reading a portion. Then two other men, called by the Hassan, read two lessons of the Prophets. This gave rise to the nine lessons of Holy Week, and of the Breviary. Holy Week services have remained almost unchanged since the beginning of the Church. In the Church of the Holy Sepulchre, Jerusalem, these lessons are read facing the door of the tomb, and the prophecies are striking when heard in the very place where they take place. People from all nations of the earth fill the ancient building St. Helena erected A. D. 312.

The Talmud tells us how they were read in Christ's day. " When the Sabbath of Shekalim (the time for collecting the half-shekel at Passover) falls due, the portion proper to this Sabbath is Thetzaveh. Six persons should read from verse 20 of xxvii. to verse 11 of xxx., and one from 11 of xxx. to verse 17." Said Abbyi: The people will think the portion is too long, and will not notice

---

[1] Zanolini, Cap I   [2] Titus, 3-1   [3] Zanolini, Ibidem   See his Note regarding the three sections of the session at the table.   [4] Syn. Jerusalem, C. 15, V 21
[5] See Geikie, Life of Christ, ii 584.

that they read the portion Shekalim, and therefore he says six should read from 20 in xxvii., to 17 in xxx., Thetzaveh, and then should come another and repeat from 11 in xxx. to 17. When the first of Adar falls on the eve of Sabbath, said Rahb, the portion Shekalim should be read on the preceding Sabbath, because the tables of money-changers are set up two weeks after the reading," etc. These were the money-changers Christ drove from the Temple. The Temple priests derived a discount of $45,000 from the traffic.

"Three men are called [1] to read the Holy Scrolls on Mondays and Thursdays, and on the afternoon of the Sabbath, neither more nor less than that number may be called, nor shall any section from the Prophets be then read. He who commences the reading of the Holy Scrolls shall pronounce the first benediction before reading it, and he who concludes the reading shall pronounce the last benediction after reading it. On all days when an additional offering is prescribed, which are not nevertheless festivals, four men are called, five on festivals, six on the Day of Atonement and seven on the Sabbath."

The synagogue service on the afternoon was mostly formed of Psalms, and this gave rise to our Vesper service, when the Gospel is not read. "It is not so with the reading of the Torah (the Law), which can be read only when the congregation sits.

"The scrolls of the Pentateuch one should read, and the other should interpret, but not one read and two translate, but the Prophets one should read and two interpret. One must not read less than ten verses in the house of prayer. To what do these ten correspond? To the ten unemployed men in the synagogue. The beginner shall pronounce the benediction before the reading, and the last reader after."

They kissed the sacred words of the Scrolls before and after reading. In our time they rub the corner of the prayer-shawl worn on their shoulders on the text and kiss that. The Jewish rite of kissing the Scrolls of the law we see when the celebrant of the Mass kisses the beginning of the Gospel after reading it, and pronounces

[1] Balyl. Talmud, Megilla, 57-89.

the blessing over the kneeling deacon. This rite comes
from the Jewish benediction before reading the law.[1]

The Temple service was more elaborate than that of
the synagogue. Twelve priests served the high priest,
six on either side, and the Segan at his right as assistant
priest. " The six men who read on the Day of Atonement,
to whom do they correspond? He said, 'To the six who
stood on the right and the six on the left of Esdras as is
written.[2] The names of the six men who stood on the
right and of the six that stood on the left.'"

The Mass, having come from the Passover or Last
Supper only indirectly from the Temple, follows the former
in the number of its ministers and ceremonies. Whence
the bishop, the high priest of the Church, is served not
by twelve priests as the pontiff in the Temple, but by
seven ministers as the Rabbi was served in the synagogue. "The Torah was read by seven men." We find repeated in many places of the Tract Megilla of the Talmud :

" Not less than three verses of the Holy Scrolls may be
read in the synagogue by each person. One verse only
of the Law may at one time be read to the interpreter.
From the Prophets however may be read three also, but
if each verse form a separate section, each must be read
separately. Passages may be skipped in the reading of
the Prophets, but not in that of the Holy Scrolls. Two
weeks before the Passover it shall be lectured about the
Passover. On the first day of Passover, the portion in
Leviticus relating to the festival must be read.[3] On
Passover should be read the portions referring to the
festival, and the portions from the Prophets should be
from Josue v. 9, about Gilgal (Galgal in our version), etc.,
and at present in exile, when we keep two days as festivals, the first day should be about Gilgal, the second
day, from IV. Kings, xxiii, about Josias, and the last day
of Passover should be selected small portions, in which
it is spoken about Passover."

At all Jewish feasts parts of the Bible relating to the
feasts were read in the Temple and synagogues, and from
this was derived the custom of reading in the church
portions of the Bible relating to the feasts.

---

[1] See Babylonian Talmud, Taanith, cap ii. 41, 75, etc., where the order of
benedictions is given.   [2] II. Esdras, viii, 4.   [3] Levit. xxii. 5-22.

"One shall open the Holy Scrolls and look on them, pronounce the benediction, then read. He who rolls together the Holy Scrolls, shall do it so that the sewn rolls should be in the middle, that it be done easily. They may be rolled together only from the outside, so that the letters should not be seen outside."

Then follow details of rolling and holding the scrolls. Books were first written on long scrolls rolled up, whence perhaps our word volume, "rolled." During the synagogue services the Rabbi and ministers always stood, as the celebrant and his ministers stand while carrying out Church functions. In Temple or synagogue the people prostrated themselves thirteen times on the floor at the name of Jehovah and during the most solemn parts of the services. We see the remains of this at the end of the Gospel, when the standing congregation bend the knee. The celebrant reads the Epistle and Gospel before they are sung. This was also the way in the early Church. St. Augustine tells us that "While Lazarus the deacon read the Acts relating to the coming of the Holy Ghost and gave the book to the bishop, Augustine, the bishop said, 'I wish to read, for the reading of these words gives me more pleasure than to preach.'"[1]

When did they begin to read the Prophets? When the Greek king Antiochus forbade all sacrifices and public and private reading of Scripture under pain of death, the Jews divided the prophetic books into sections and began to read them in the synagogues.[2] The Machabees restored and endowed the synagogue worship with greater splendors. The Acts says "After the reading of the Law and the prophets, the rulers of the synagogue sent to them Paul and Barnabas, asking them to preach to the people."[3] Christ himself read the prophet Isaias in the synagogue of Nazareth.[4]

It was the text of the prophet[5] relating to him that he read that day, towards the end of August. Christ read the Nitzauim "Section" of that day. But the Jews, seeing him foretold in it, later changed it for another section which they read in our time on that day lest the people might see the Redeemer it foretold. Reading the

[1] S Augustine, Sermo ccclvi de Vita Cler. [2] Zanolini, Opere citato; I Mach i 52. [3] Acts xiii 15 [4] Luke iv 16 [5] Isaias lxi 1 etc

Law and the Prophets in the church therefore comes down to us from the Jewish Church which from early times followed the synagogue custom.[1]

How did it happen that Christ was called up that day to read Isaias's words relating to himself? Any man in the congregation might be called up to read if he were over thirty years of age. After his fast of forty days on the Lenten mountain, Christ, in his thirtieth year began his public ministry "And he came to Nazareth where he was brought up, and he went into the synagogue according to his custom on the Sabbath day, and he rose up to read. And the book of Isaias the prophet was delivered to him. And as he unfolded the book, he found the place where it was written:

"'The Spirit of the Lord is upon me, wherefore he hath anointed me to preach the gospel to the poor, he hath sent me to heal the contrite of heart, to preach deliverance to the captives, and sight to the blind, to set at liberty them that are bruised, to preach the acceptable year of the Lord, and the day of reward.[2] And when he had folded the book, he restored it to the minister and sat down. And the eyes of all in the synagogue were fixed on him."[3]

As one of the men read the Scrolls in the original Hebrew which the Am-ha-Arets, "Country people" did not understand, one stood by and translated it into the Syro-Chaldaic they spoke. Then the preacher addressed them on the text. The man's name who translated the text of Isaias for Christ that day is not given. But Jesus then preached to the people in the synagogue his first sermon "And they wondered at the words of grace that proceeded from his mouth, and they said. Is not this the son of Joseph."[4]

If a Jew could not be present at the synagogue services because of sickness, etc., he clothed himself with the taleth, "prayer shawl," place his phylacteries on brow and left arm, stood by his bed, in a quiet corner of his house or in his place of business, and recited the prayers while they were being held morning, noon and afternoon in

[1] (See Apostolic Constitut. Book 8, Clementine Recognitions, etc For the synagogue worship, see Migne, ii 1346-1368. Babyl Talmud, Magilla, Whole Tract   [2] Isaias lxi 1, etc   [3] Luke iv. 16-20.   [4] Luke iv. 22.

synagogue or Temple.   This the Rabbis called "Stirring up in them the kingdom of God" or "of heaven."[1]   These services recalled to them the long-looked for kingdom of the Messiah, the Prince of David was to establish for them over all the earth.   From these customs came down to us morning and evening prayers.

During Temple and synagogue services the priests praying stretched out their hands, following the example of Moses praying for victory over the enemies of Israel when Aaron and Hur upheld his arms.[2] But during these prayers they were forbidden to hold their hands higher than the Phylacteries on their brows.[3] "Why," say the Talmud, "is it then the custom at present for the priests to raise their hands in the afternoon prayer of the fast day?   Because the afternoon prayer is said very near sunset, it is regarded the same as the closing prayer."[4]

Isaias in his prophetic description of the Last Supper [5] foretold the Lord during the first Mass on Sion, as we will later explain. He continues, "As he shall spread forth his hands in the midst of them, as he that swimmeth spreadeth forth his hand to swim," etc.

Following Temple, synagogue, and Last Supper, at the Mass the celebrant still stretches forth his hands, with his body forming a cross.   For the Jewish ceremony related to the Crucified who stretched forth his hands on the cross when he would redeem our race.   And the celebrant who now offers the Mass as a memorial of the crucifixion still stretches forth his hands during the prayers.   As he cannot hold his hands out all the time in the form of a cross he holds them near his body.

At every Mass we pray for the repose of the souls of the dead.   Did Christ pray for the dead at the Last Supper?   We find no record, but it was the custom of the Temple and synagogue in his day.

Prayers for the repose of the souls of the dead are found in the earliest records of the Temple and synagogue. Even Mohammed prayed for the dead as all Mohammedan sects still do   The writer was shown an ornamental

[1] Matt vi 5   [2] Exod xvii 12, Edersheim, Temple, 141   [3] Levit ix 22
[4] Tract Taanith, "Fasting," of the Babyl Talmud, 81   [5] Isaias xxv 6 to end of chapter.

table on which, each Friday, the Khedive of Egypt places the Coran and beside it kneels to pray for the repose of the souls of his two daughters, where their bodies rest within the mosque rising at your left as you go up to the citadel of Cairo. The Jews of New York called the attention of the writer at different times to the solemn prayers for the dead during the synagogue services. Their belief regarding purgatory, souls detained there and helped by fasting and prayer of their friends on earth, is the same as that of the Church.

Let us give the words of a learned Protestant writer, who investigated the question.[1] "Whatever account may be given of it, it is certain, that Prayers for the Dead appear in the Church's worship, as soon as we have any trace after the immediate records of the apostolic age. It has been described by a writer, whom no one can suspect of Romish tendencies as "an immemorial practice." Though "Scripture is silent, yet antiquity plainly speaks." The prayers "have found a place in every early liturgy of the world."[2] How indeed, we ask, could it have been otherwise? The strong feeling shown in the time of the Machabees, that it was "a holy and wholesome thought to pray for the dead,"[3] was sure, under the influence of the dominant Pharisaic Scribes, to show itself in the devotions of the synagogue. So far as we trace back these devotions, we may say that there also the practice is "immemorial," as old at least as the traditions of the Rabbinic fathers.[4] There is a probability, indefinitely great, that prayers for the departed, the Kiddish of later Judaism, were familiar to the synagogues of Palestine, and other countries, that the early Christian believers were not startled by them as an innovation, that they passed uncondemned by our Lord himself. The writer already quoted sees a probable reference to them in II. Tim. i. 18 St. Paul, remembering Onesiphorus, as one whose "house" had been bereaved of him, prays that he may find mercy of the Lord "in that day." Prayers for the dead can hardly therefore be looked on as anti-Scriptural.[5]

In all Apostolic Liturgies, in every one of the Oriental

[1] Rev E. H. Plumptre, M. A., Prof of Divinity in King's College, London, in Smith's Dic of Bible, Vol iv p, 3137. [2] Ellicott, Destiny of the Creature, Ser vi [3] II Mac xii 43 to 46 [4] Buxtorf, De Synagog p 709, 710 ; McCaul, Old Paths, C. 38 [5] Quoted from Smith's Dic of Bible, Art, Synagogue

Rites, we find prayer for the dead, offerings for prayers, stipends given by the laity for Masses for the repose of the souls of the departed. Along the walls of the Catacombs, on tombstones, on monuments of the apostolic age, on walls of church buildings now made into mosques, in Constantinople, etc, the writer has seen "Let them rest in peace," "Pray for the repose of the soul of such a one" etc. These inscriptions are in Greek, Latin and other ancient languages. The Jewish Prayer Book, used all over the world, copying Temple and synagogue services, has prayers for the repose of their dead relatives and friends, no synagogue service is complete without the Kaddish, called "Prayers for the Dead." The abuses of offerings for Masses for the dead, and of indulgences, rife before the Reformation, induced the reformers to go too far, and abolish these prayers and doctrine relating to purgatory.

The Jews of our day believe that their dead go to a place like purgatory, where they remain for a time and are aided by their friends' prayers. Children pray for their parents on the day of death, on the third, seventh, thirtieth day, and on the anniversary of their death. These customs coming down from the Temple and synagogue services gave rise to the burial of the dead on the third day, the "Month's Mind," the anniversary and Masses for the departed.[1]

The Jews observed peculiar burial custom, the third, seventh and thirtieth days being held as special mourning days, but when these days fell on feasts they had special regulations.[2] Cohabitation, wearing shoes, etc, were forbidden these days.[3] Only near relatives rent their garments and ate "the mourning meal."[4] "When a coffin is being removed from one place to another, those present must stand in a row and pronounce the mourning benediction and the words of consolation."[5] A learned scholar, or a Rabbi, pronounced the funeral oration sometimes in verse.[6] The "mourning women" wailed these days but did not clap their hands.[7]

In the time of Christ the Jews prayed [8] for the repose

---

[1] See Sketches of Jewish Life, 173, Geikie, Life of Christ ii 605. See whole Tract Ebel Rabbath, "Great Mourning," in Babyl. Talmud   [2] Tract Moed Katan, "Minor Festivals." Mishna p 36   [3] Ibid 39   [4] Ibid. 40.   [5] Ibid 41.   [6] Ibid 42, 43   [7] Ibid 45   [8] See Smith's Dic of Bible, art. Synagogue Worship, n. 4.

of the souls of the dead.   Jews of our day do not continue praying for them for a whole year, lest it might imply that they remained for a year in purgatory.[1]   The Jewish Prayer Book used to-day in the synagogue,[2] in the prayer for the dead has the following words.

"May God remember the soul of my revered father, (mother) who has gone to his (her) repose.   May his (her) soul be bound up in the bond of life.   May his (her) rest be glorious with the fulness of joy in thy presence, and pleasures for evermore, at thy right hand.   Father of mercy, in whose hand are the souls of the living and the dead, may thy consolation cheer us, as we remember (on this holy day) our beloved and honored kinsfolk, who have gone to their rest. . . And may their souls repose in the land of the living, beholding thy glory and delighting in thy goodness," etc.

They followed the example of their fathers, who offered sacrifices in the Temple for the repose of the dead, as the Machabees did.   "For it is a holy and a wholesome thought to pray for the dead, that they may be loosed from their sins."[3]

The Rabbis of the time of Christ made a distinction between the Onen, "The suffering," and the Avel, "The mourner."   The first applied to the day of the funeral, and the seven following days, the latter to the month following the funeral.   The prayers for the dead were said in the synagogue, or elsewhere.   A strict rule was laid down for the High Priest.[4]   It was customary to say "May we be thy expiation," or, "Let us suffer what ought to have fallen thee," to which he replied "Be ye blessed forever," or "Be ye blessed of heaven."   At the "wake," the friends partook of a "mourning meal," at which no more than ten cups of wine should be drunk.[5] The Mergillath Taanith, "Roll of Feasts," gives the day on which mourning was forbidden.

They also prayed to the Saints in heaven in the following words "May they in heaven show forth our merit for a peacable preservation, and may we receive a blessing from the Lord and justice from the God of our salvation, and good understanding in the sight of man."   Prayers

[1] Edersheim, Sketches of Jewish Life, p 174, 180   [2] Daily Prayer Book, p 326.   [3] II. Mach. xii. 46.   [4] Levit. xxi 10-12   [5] Ter. Ber. iii. 1.

to the Saints in Church services were copied from the Jewish Church at the time of Christ.

The New York Ghetto has many queer trades, one of them being the saying of the Kaddish for the repose of the souls of the dead. Sons or members of the family say them morning, afternoon and evening, every day for a year after the funeral, as long as a male member of the deceased lives. The Kaddish must be recited in a congregation of minyan " ten or more men " in synagogue, or house. If no male issue survives, a professional band of Kaddish prayers are paid to say the prayers

Often Jews on their deathbed make provision by leaving money for " a Kaddish of their own," as Christians leave bequests for Masses for their souls. Usually a friend of the sick is appointed to see that these prayers are said, and he is specially remembered in the will This provision for prayers for the repose of the soul is the pious wish of every Jew.

The professional Kaddish sayers, called " batlonim " are mostly beggar students of the Torah and Talmud, wishing to become Rabbis, law students or enter the learned professions, but who have not the money for their education, and take this means of continuing their studies of the Laws of Moses, their " dear bride."

There is no fixed stipend and they offer their services to the family not blessed with sons, during the time of mourning, and agree to pray the soul of the dead from purgatory into Paradise. These prayers have come down in Judaism from far beyond the days of Christ, and on them was founded the Masses, stipends and prayers for the repose of the dead.

Nov. 23, 1905, it seemed that almost the whole Jewish population of New York turned out in a vast procession through the streets of the east side, to mourn the massacres of their brethren in Russia. The streets for blocks around the headquarters in Grand Street were filled, fairly packed, with one mass of surging, pushing, gesticulating Hebrew humanity, as four men passed through bearing on their shoulders an empty coffin, covered with a black velvet silver embroidered pall, typifying the dead, as the catafalque does in our churches at a requiem Mass, when the body is not present. This is one of the

oldest of the Jewish ceremonials coming do wn from Moses
or the kings. These prayers lived side by side in both
the Christian and Jewish faiths whose members were
often hostile in the middle ages.

All branches of the Semitic race were well represented.
Jews from Germany, Poland, Russia, Turkey, Spain, and
countries of the Orient were there, crowding sidewalks,
massing in the middle of the streets, mounting steps of
business and private dwellings—all united in heart and
mind, as every tongue uttered the prayers for the repose
of the souls of their murdered Russian brethren.

Patriarchs with velvet skull-caps, waist-long white
beards, every hair of which was precious, shoved and
talked with younger generations, with women with wigs
and shawls showing their widowhood, with girls be-
plumed, products of the sweatshops, and with young
men born in freedom, who hardly showed the Jewish
features.

But the bearing of the vast crowds was different, from
that which usually turns out for a parade. There was no
laughter, no jokes were heard, no good-natured nudging as
they marched, headed by black flags, red union banners,
each wearing black badges on their arms, or draped in
deep mourning. They went four abreast, stretching
along five blocks, moving like a vast human flood, soon
swelling into a mighty stream, filling the streets as
though they would mount the high walls of buildings,
through which they passed as through a canyon.

In mournful music they sang the dirge of sorrow and
prayers for the souls of the dead, accompanied by bands
of music. As the sound of the band reached ahead, windows would go up, women with heads covered with black
mourning prayer shawls would appear, hold up their
hands with distorted faces, eyes filled with tears, and
mingle their cries with the vast crowds in the streets.
From the heart of every Israelite came the cry : El Male
Rachnin, " God have mercy on their souls," repeated over
and over again.

When they came to a synagogue, the whole procession
stopped before the crowded steps. In the place reserved,
the Rabbi, and leading men of the congregation, led in prayer
for eternal rest for the departed, part song, part chant,

part wail: "God have mercy on their souls:" "God have mercy on their souls:" "God have mercy on their souls." The band struck up the Kim Allel Eclun, "the mourning song of Solomon," and they began over again the touching prayers for the repose of the dead. They stopped for the longest time before the Beth Hamedrish, "The House of Prayer," the synagogue where the famous Rabbi Joseph used to preach, that leader in Israel most learned in the Talmud, whose funeral produced almost a riot against the Jews. There the men and women sang in separate ranks, for they do not think it seemly for the sexes to mingle in divine worship, even in our day. It was a weird chant the singing made. The differences in tone and pitch met in the middle, and made a half gruff, half shrill, wholly strange sound, that rose and fell, swelled and diminished in a cadence, as different from the Christian choir, as Arab singing. We have given this incident of our day, with customs of the ancient synagogue, to show that in all his history the Jew prayed for the repose of the souls of his dead, and that from him the Church fell heir to that doctrine, the human heart cry for the dead we loved in life, which has been, perhaps, the most attacked.

Now let us see the origin of our wedding customs and the nuptial Mass.

The Talmud forbade marriage in the case of a male under thirteen years and a day, and in the case of a girl under twelve years and a day. Wednesday was the day of the betrothal of a virgin, and Thursday of a widow.[1] Modern Jews appoint Wednesday and Friday for the former, and Thursday for the latter. The parents choose the wife for their son. Modern Jews often employ a matchmaker, a schachun who acts as a friend between the parties.[2]

Consent of bride and parents having been obtained, the betrothal followed. This was not like our "engagement," but a very solemn and formal agreement ratified by presents to the bride called mohar, the word occurring thrice in the Hebrew Bible.[3] Her father gave her a dowry, which after the Captivity was bestowed by a written

---

[1] Mishna Ketub. i. sec. 1. [2] Gen. xxiv. 12. [3] Gen. xxiv. 10-22; Exod. xxii. 17; I. Kings xviii. 25.

ketubah, "a writing," which dowry her husband controlled.

The betrothal, called by the Romans the espousal, was celebrated with a great feast, where the groom placed the wedding ring on her finger, as a token of fidelity and of adoption into his family. She was now regarded as a wife[1] If she was unfaithful, among the Hebrews before her father's house she was stoned to death,[2] but the man could put her away by quietly getting rid of her, if he did not want to have her killed. This is what Joseph thought of doing when he found the Virgin with child.[3]

The essence of marriage was in the removal of the bride to her future home. This was a great public ceremony. The bridegroom clothed himself in his festive dress and put on his head the handsome turban the prophet calls the peer[4] formed like a crown.[5] Myrrh and frankincense was offered before him, or he was incensed by a servant as the clergy are incensed at a high Mass. The bride prepared herself the day before with a bath,[6] robed herself in her bridal garments, and a little before the appointed time covered her whole person with the bridal veil called the *tsa'iph*; the Romans called it *nubere*, "to veil," whence covering not only her face, but her whole person[7] it was a sign of submission to her husband The Greeks called the bridal veil *exoysia*, "authority." She bound up her waist with a costly sash called the *kishshurim*, "the attire," which Romans named *zona*. On her head she placed the *callah*, "bride," a crown of pure gold, or gilded if the family was rich, but of orange blossoms if the family was poor. After the destruction of the Temple under Titus, in A. D. 70, this gold crown was forbidden as a token of humiliation

If the bride were a virgin, she wore her hair hanging down her back;[8] but a widow tied up her hair. The virgin's bridal robes were white, often embroidered with gold thread, a widow was dressed in colored garments and the ceremonial was short and simple.

When the hour fixed arrived, usually late in the evening, the bridegroom came to her house attended by his groomsmen, called in Hebrew *mere'im*, waited on by his

[1] Phil. De Spec. Leg, p 788 [2] Deut xxii. 23, 24 [3] Matt i 19 [4] Isaias lxi 10
[5] Cant. iii 11. [6] Picart i 240 [7] Gen xxiv 65, xxxviii 14, 15. [8] Ketub, ii Sec 1.

paranymph, we now call his "best man," and preceded by a procession, surrounded by a band of musicians and singers, with men bearing torches, they went to the bride's home, who with her virgins waited for them. Bride, parents and friends, with the bridegroom formed a great procession, and with music and song they marched back to the groom's house, near which a party of virgins, ten with lighted lamps, met them in the street and all marched to the house.[1] At the house they held a great feast, all the friends of both families attending, each guest having on a white wedding garment.[2] If she was a virgin, parched wheat and grain was distributed, the origin of rice at our weddings, as a sign of prosperity and happiness for the couple. The festivities lasted for seven days sometimes for a fortnight, but in the case of a widow for only one night.

From the Hebrew wedding we copy the bishop's ring, for he is wedded to his diocese, the orange blossoms, the bridal veil, the nuptial Mass, the blessing of the bride. But the widow is not blessed at her second marriage. Among the Oriental Christians the bride and groom wear metal crowns during the wedding ceremonies.

The wedding feast was very elaborate in wealthy families, the ceremonial and etiquette being the same as at the feast of unleaven bread.

Moses made a covenant, the Old Testament, between God and the Israelites, who broke that covenant when they fell into idolatry under their Kings. But the prophet foretold that, "the days shall come, saith the Lord, and I will make a new covenant with the house of Israel, and with the house of Juda. Not according to the covenant which I made with their fathers, the covenant which they made void," etc[3] Moses made the covenant with blood of animals, foretelling the New Testament, the covenant made with the blood of the Victim of Calvary,[4] " of the New and eternal Testament the mystery of faith." The Greek text says, diathekn, " in his blood " " And they shall not break bread to him that mourneth, to comfort him for the dead, neither shall they give them to drink of the cup to comfort them, for their father and mother."[5]

[1] Matt xxv. 6. [2] Matt. xxii. 11. [3] Jeremias, xxxi. 31, 32 [4] Exod. xxiv. 8.
[5] Jeremias, xvi. 7.

"Thus saith the Lord, Behold I will profane my sanctuary, the glory of your realm." [1]   At Christ's death the Old Testament passed away, the New had begun. The synagogue was rejected, the Church was established on Pentecost.

The Lord broke the Eucharistic bread to the doubting disciples at Emmaus and only then they knew him.[2] The apostles went forth from house to house, breaking the Eucharistic bread of the Mass with prayers ; [3] "continuing daily with one accord in the Temple and breaking bread from house to house, they took their meat with gladness and simplicity of heart." [4]   "On the first day of the week when we assembled to break bread," [5] "going up and breaking bread and fasting."   The Greek words of the original, "eulogia" and "eucharistia" show that the breaking of bread was the Eucharistic sacrifice of the Mass.   The first word, eulogia, "praise," shows that they began with the synagogue praise and prayers, following Christ's example at the Last Supper, and finished with the consecration and the distribution of the Eucharist.[6]

Following the example of the Last Supper, the meetings were held in the evening, in the synagogues, on the Sabbath, and the instructions took up the time till after midnight.[7] Psalms and Prayers of the synagogue were sung, the members of the infant Church saluted each other with a holy kiss.[8]   St. Paul mentions four times [9] the kiss of friendship and of love, a Hebrew custom continued in the Church, and was the origin of the ceremony of the "kiss of peace," the clergy give during Mass.[10]

The apostles following the Lord's example went into the synagogues in all the lands where Jews were found, and preached first to the Hebrews.   As the synagogue the Sabbath service on Saturday was the best attended, they preached that day, and in the evening said the Mass. The services were protracted into the night, and later Mass was said in the early morning hours of Sunday. Whence, in apostolic times, Sunday took the place of Saturday of the Jews.   When at last the Church

---

[1] Ezech, xxiv. 21. [2] Luke, xxiv. 30, 35   [3] Acts ii. 42   [4] Acts, ii. 46   [5] xx. 7 [6] I. Cor. ii 20, 21, etc ; St Ignatius, Epist ad Smyr, c. 4 ; Sozomen, Hist. Eccl. VII c. 19, Council of Carthage, Can XLI   [7] Acts xx. 7   [8] I. Cor. xvi. 20 ; II Cor. xiii. 12   [9] Rom xvi 16; I. Cor. xvi. 20; II. Cor. xiii. 12, I. Thes. v. 26 ; I. Peter v. 14   [10] Tertullian, De Orat. c. 14; Justin Martyr, M. Apol. 11 ; Migne, Cursus Comp. ii. 1348

broke with the synagogue, it was called the "Lord's day," in memory of the resurrection and of the coming of the Holy Ghost on Pentecost Sunday.[1]

Thousands of candles lighted the Temple courts, lights burned in synagogues during services, numerous lights you will find in the synagogue of to-day as candles illuminated the Cenacle during the Last Supper; "and there were a great number of lamps in the upper chamber where we were assembled," says the Acts.[2] Mass being said at night in the Apostles' day, candles burned on the altars. The candles burning on our altars came down, not from the catacombs, as some writers hold, but from Temple, synagogue and Last Supper.

This synagogue service—singing Psalms, reading the Law and the Prophecies before the Eucharistic Sacrifice, developed into the Matin-Lauds with their Psalms, Nocturns, "By night," prayers, versicles, responses, vespers and offices of our breviaries. The peculiar divisions and arrangements show they came down from the apostolic age. The Last Supper began with the synagogue services which were always said at night before beginning the Passover feast, and this is the reason of that ancient custom of saying the office, as far as Terce, before saying Mass.

Many were the disputes between Christians and Jews regarding the Crucified; at last the synagogue excluded the apostles, who then went to the homes of converts. They found that the synagogue service would not do for the Eucharistic sacrifice. New elements, the Divinity of Christ, the Real Presence, the sacramental system, and numerous other truths had been added to Judaism

On the Liturgy of the Last Supper they founded new Rites—Liturgies of the Mass which were handed down by word of mouth till they were later written down. These were in the languages of the people. Oriental Christians claim that their Liturgies have come down to us unchanged from the apostles. Numerous Hebrew terms they incorporate into these Liturgies, as, "Amen;" "Let it be so;" Alleluia, "Praise Jehovah;" Hosanna, "Save, I beseech thee;" Sabaoth, "Hosts;" "The Lord be with thee," "Peace be to thee," etc.

[1] Acts ii. [2] Acts xx. 8.

We have shown how the Holy Ghost wrote a religious truth in every object and movement of Temple and Passover worship. The Passover Liturgy and ceremonial were loaded with type image and symbol of the Messiah, his Passion and of the Eucharistic Sacrifice. When the apostles founded the Liturgies of the Mass, they followed the lesson God gave in the Jewish ceremonial and worship. Every object, movement and ceremony of the Mass teaches the people truths hidden in the service, so that the Mass is a book written by God himself through the apostles. These rites and ceremonies we have explained in a former work.[1]

The apostles carried out the synagogue services, read the Law and the Prophecies and then preached, exhorting the people to live good lives. The "Lord's Table" was prepared with candles, flowers, and ornaments.[2] The twelve priests with the apostle read the prayers of the Liturgy, and thus they celebrated the Eucharist. They took up a collection for the support of religion.[3] Sometimes these offerings were sent to the poor converts of Jerusalem.[4]

The apostle remained with them instructing, making converts till a congregation was formed. Then he ordained twelve of them priests, called in Greek presbyters. He laid hands on one of them and anointed him a bishop, consecrating him with the holy oils as was the custom at the ordination of Rabbis and judges of Israel long before the time of Christ. Many works of the early Church mention these facts.

Thus the Clementine Homilies[5] says Peter founded a church in Tyre and set over it as bishop one of the presbyters and then departed for Sidon[6] where he did the same,[7] as at Bayrout and Laodicea.[8] "And having baptized them in the fountains which are near the sea, and having celebrated the Eucharist, and having appointed Maroones as their bishop, and having set apart twelve presbyters, and having designated deacons and arranged matters relating to widows, and having preached on the common

---

[1] Teaching Truth by Signs and Ceremonies [2] Acts xx 7-11 [3] II. Cor ix 1-15, Justin Martyr, Aplogo I [4] Ibidem [5] This work is of doubtful authenticity, mentioned by Origen, Cap 22, Philocalia and other writers as existing in the beginning of the third century [6] Hom VII Cap v [7] Cap VIII. [8] Cap XXII

good what was profitable for the ordering of the Church, and having counseled them to obey the bishop Maroones, three months being now fulfilled, he (Peter the apostle) bade those in Tripolis of Phœnicia farewell, and took his journey to Antioch of Syria, all the people accompanying him with due honor." [1]

This curious work of antiquity states that they reclined at the table when eating,[2] and shows us that Peter vested like the bishops of our day. When Clement asked that he might go with him, Peter smilingly replied. "For who else shall take care of these many splendid tunics, with all my changes of rings and sandals." [3]

The Apostolic Constitution says : [4] "Now concerning those bishops who have been ordained in our lifetime, we let you know that they are these :—James the bishop of Jerusalem, the brother of our Lord ; [5] the second was Simeon the son of Cleophas,[6] after whom the third was Judas, the son of James. Of Cæsarea of Palestine, the first was Zaccheus,[7] after whom was Cornelius and the third Theophilus. Of Antioch Evodius ordained by me Peter, and Ignatius by Paul of Alexandria, Annianus was the first ordained by Mark, the evangelist. Of the Church of Rome, Linus the son of Claudia was the first,[8] and Clement after Linus' death, the second ordained by me Peter. Of Ephesus, Timothy ordained by Paul, and John by me John. Of Smyrna, Aristo the first,[9] after whom Strateas son of Lois.[10] Of Pergamus, Gaius. Of Philadelphia, Demetrius by me. Of Athens, Dionysius.

---

[1] Clementine Homilies Hom xi Cap. xxxvi See J Iahn Archæologia Biblica De Liturgia Apostolica, etc. [2] Ibidem Hom x Cap xxvi [3] Hom xii Cap vi [4] Some like, Whiston, Bunsen, etc , think that with a few corruptions these come from the apostolic age—others that they come from the second or third centuries Book VII. Sec. iv. [5] He was his cousin who according to the Jewish custom was called his brother.

[6] Cleophas was the brother of St Joseph, the Virgin's spouse He married Mary the Virgin's sister, by whom he had four sons and and two daughters. His eldest son was named Joseph, the second James called Alpheus, the third Judas Thaddeus, and the fourth Simon. His first daughter was called Mary after her mother ; the second, Salome married Zebedei, by whom she had James and John the apostles It was Cleophas who went with another disciple to Emmaus after the crucifixion, whom the Lord met on the way. See Dutripon, Concordantia S. Scripturæ, word Cleophas

[7] This was the rich publican of Jericho, a tax collector, "little of stature," Luke xix 2-6, who climbed the sycamore tree to see the Lord, when he was passing through the city on his way up to Jerusalem to die He entertained the Saviour that Thursday night, and to him Jesus said "This day is salvation come to this house " Luke xix 9 Rabbinical writings mention a Zaccheus who lived in Jericho at this time who was once a publican.

[8] Mentioned by St. Paul, II Tim iv 21 [9] This is a mistake, for Polycarp was the first bishop of Smyrna. [10] She was Timothy's grandmother, II. Tim. i. 5.

Of Tripoli, Marathones, etc.,——These are the bishops who are intrusted by us with the dioceses in the Lord." [1]

Saying, "Increase and multiply." [2] God blessed man and animals, that they might propagate their race. Fol lowing this example the patriarch blessed his eldest son, making him heir of his property and priesthood, and on his deathbed he blessed all the members of his family. At the end of the Temple ceremonial the high priest blessed the multitudes, and the Rabbi dismissed the congregation with his blessing.

According to these ceremonies of the Jewish Church, when ascending into heaven, Christ blessed his disciples. "And lifting up his hands he blessed them. And it came to pass that whilst he blessed them, he departed up into heaven." [3] Following these examples, the celebrant blesses the congregation at the end of Mass. This ended Mass in the early Church, and later St. John's Gospel was added. Therefore when the people ask priest or bishop to bless them they follow the old custom of the Hebrew church. This blessing finds it highest form in the Apostolic Benediction of the Pope, which comes down from the days of Apostles and Patriarchs.

Now let us see the vestments Christ and the Apostles used at the Last Supper, for in them we will find the origin of Church vestments.

[1] Apost Const. B. VII Sec. iv , xlvi. We give this as a specimen of this peculiar ancient work, not vouching for its authenticity   [2] Gen. i. 22, viii 17, ix. 1.   [3] Luke xxiv. 50.

IX.—THE VESTMENTS CHRIST AND THE APOSTLES USED IN THE CENACLE.

Why do clergymen wear vestments at our altars? Why does the Church clothe her ministers in such peculiar robes? Did Christ and the apostles wear a distinctive dress at the Last Supper? Can Church vestments in material, form and color be traced back to that night of the Last Supper? People often ask these questions, for few writers trace clerical robes and vestments to their origin in Temple and Passover. Let us see the reasons and the origin of the Church vestments.

Clothes show a person's position in the community, a ragged dirty tramp excites disgust, while a well-dressed person inspires respect. An individual's clothes, their form, color and material strike the eye and make the first impression. Hence woman is often honored more than man, not because she is his superior, but because she is better dressed.

In all ages dress showed the wearer's position in society, and from the beginning officials wore distinctive garments and insignia of their office. In the ancient world, the king dressed in stately robes. When in patriarchal days the priest-king offered sacrifice, he vested in priestly garments. Sculptured ruins of Assyria, Persia, Egypt, etc., show kings dressed as the high priest of the nation, vested in sandals, alb, chasuble, girdle, miter and vestments, offering sacrifices, while in Babylonian ruins a mysterious figure shows him the forbidden fruit, and near by stands the tree of life. It is startling to see the figure of pontiff-king of these empires dressed in vestments of the same kind and shape as those now used at our altars, showing that vestments have hardly changed since the days before Abraham.

Fashions change, the old costumes are abandoned new styles are taken up; it is hard to find two men or women dressed alike. But the Church never changes her vestments coming down from the Temple and the Last Supper. No Pope, Council or power on earth could forbid them because they are of divine origin.

When fanatic ignorant reformers of the sixteenth century swept over the north of Europe, not understanding the nature of the Eucharistic Sacrifice, they dismantled churches of religious signs, symbols and emblems, and their ministers preached in ordinary garments. But a reaction took place; ritualism revived, clerical robes again were seen in non-Catholic pulpits; disputes waxed warm; color, shape and number of ecclesiastical garments divided denominations, and high ritualistic churches introduced vestments. Let us see the origin of vestments

From the beginning of civilization, the want of a distinctive dress was felt, that a man's calling might be seen in his clothing. The officer, soldier, sailor, conductor, fireman, nurse, judge, ruler, king, wear a distinctive dress to picture to the eye the calling, position and office of the wearer.

When God called Aaron and his sons to the priesthood of the Hebrew religion, and the sons of Levi for his ministers, with a wealth of detail and a striking minuteness, he laid down material, color, shape and ornament of vestments worn in public worship, and forbade them at any other time. Down the ages in the Temple till its destruction by the Romans under Titus, priest and Levite wore these vestments while ministering before the Lord. A hundred and seventy-six times they are mentioned in the Old Testament, and fifty-nine texts of the New Testament refer to them.

They were always used in the Church It was a great sin to sacrifice without them. Popes forbade them used except in Church functions. Writers of apostolic age mention them. Pictures in catacombs show them. The great Fathers write of them. Pagans mocked them. All Oriental Churches still use them. A thousand proofs from the Fathers might be given to prove them used from the beginning of Christianity.

"What is there, I ask, offensive to God," writes St. Jerome, "if I wear a tunic more than ordinarily handsome, or, if bishop, priest, deacon and other ministers of the Church come forth in white garments in the administration of the sacrifice?"

"We ought not to go into the sanctuary just as we please, and in our ordinary clothes defiled by the usages of common life, but with a clear conscience, and in clean garments handle the sacraments of the Lord."

Church vestments, altar cloths, etc., are of linen and not of byssus, the word given in translations of the Bible. Temple vestments, table-cloths, napkins, etc. used at Passover in the time of Christ were of linen. From that time in the Latin Rite linen has always been used for altar cloths, purificators, albs, etc., in Church services. Why was linen and no other material used?

St. Augustine, explaining the work of the wise woman of Proverbs,[1] says flax, from which linen is made is emblematic of our bodies in which lives the soul. The flax is prepared by beating, and then woven into linen, as our flesh is purified by suffering. He says the people's clothing and the vestments were then of linen.[2]

During the Babylonian Captivity the Hebrews saw kings and nobles clothed in silk, and this material, which came from China, the Israelites brought back with them to Palestine. When Alexander conquered these countries he found the same silken clothing, his soldiers brought silk to Greece and silk garments spread over the Grecian world long before Christ. When the apostles spread the Church in the Greek empire they made the altar cloths of linen and vestments of this silken material, and that is the reason that silk is exclusively used in the Oriental Rites, and why our more costly vestments are of silk while altar cloths, albs, purificators, etc., are of linen.

God revealed to Moses the most minute details of material, form and color of the priestly vestments. They were to be made only of linen, formed of beaten flax, to signify that the perfection of the priest only comes with bearing patiently the trials of this life. The colors were white, red, violet and green, signifying innocence, suffering, penance and youth. Later, black, typifying sorrow, was added. Josephus writes that these colors of the vestments of his day were emblematic of the colors

[1] Prov. xxxi 13   [2] St. Augustine, Sermo xxxvii. in Prov. n v, vi., Contra Faust. L. vi., n 1.

of the sanctuary of the Lord of hosts, and that they were embellished with beautiful embroideries. They are now the five colors of Church vestments.

Gold wire was woven into the cloth. "And he cut thin plates of gold, and drew them into small threads that they might be twisted with the woof of the aforesaid colors." [1] Here for the first time in Holy Writ, we find the famous " cloth of gold," still found in vestments, regalia, etc. Gold cloth is rare in this country, gilt silver wire called " half fine " and brass, gilt or varnished, takes its place.

Linen, mentioned thirty times under the name of byssus, dyed in these different colors, was used for vestments, veils, etc., in the Temple. [2] Linen is made of flax, while byssus is formed of the long delicate silky fibers, with which the pina, a shell-fish of eastern Mediterranean waters, attaches itself to the rocks. A careful microscopical and chemical examination of ancient Biblical byssus, shows it to be linen, proving the Church right in making her altar cloths, albs, etc., of linen and not of byssus.

Around the rocky isle on which Canaan's sons built Tyre, "The Rock," which Alexander's army captured after uniting it with the mainland, in the blue waters of the Mediterranean Sea still grows the murex, a shell-fish of the gasteropod molusk, which bruised gives forth the beautiful crimson and purple colors, in which they dyed the garments of high priests, emperors, kings and rulers of antiquity To-day wild waters dash with loud roar against that rockbound shore, where Tyre rose in power of commerce and art. For her sins she has fallen as the prophet foretold. [3] No more Tyrian purple clothes kings, for the color is obtained from products of coal tar. [4]

It is surprising how certain colors distinguished families. In the middle ages heraldry showed forth in the colors of the champions. In the Orient green is the sacred color of the false Prophet; members of Mohammed's family are always clothed in green from head to foot, and you will find Muslems kissing their hands to show respect. Arab chiefs still wear colored turbans, each head of a tribe having his proper color.

The Levites in the Temple dressed in simple white

---

[1] Exod. xxxix. 1-3   [2] Exod xxxvi , xxxix., lx., etc.,   [3] Isaias xxiii.   [4] See Edersheim, Life of Christ, ii. 278.

linen,[1] till Herod Agrippa II. gave them permission to vest in priestly garments, which Josephus says "was contrary to the laws of our country."[2]

Temple priest and high priest wore four vestments of shape and color common to both. To-day priest and bishop saying Mass wear identical amice, alb, girdle, stole, manuple and chasuble. But the Hebrew pontiff wore four other vestments proper to his office, and the bishop in addition to the priest's vestments vests in tunic, dalmatic, cross, gloves, miter and ring. Let us see the story of the Temple vestments and of the Last Supper, whence came Church vestments.

Born of Aaron's family, bluest blood of glorious high priests flowing in his veins, learned in the Torah, the Books of Moses, versed in the prophets and in Israel's history, bright of mind, spotless of body,—such were the requirements of the candidate for the high priesthood of the days of Christ. Maimonides mentions a hundred and forty defects which would forever debar him, and twenty two, which he might in time overcome. St. Paul quotes qualities required in a bishop taken from the Temple rules relating to the high priest's office.[3]

If he passed the strict examination, his ordination lasted seven days, each day being devoted to a part of the ceremonial. The first day they poured the holy chrism in his head in the form of the Greek ✠ not knowing it foretold the cross, the oil flowing down on his beard.[4] In former times this was the holy oil with which Moses had consecrated his brother Aaron and his sons, and which had been preserved in the sanctuary.

With this oil they consecrated Saul, David, and the kings of David's line, when there was no dispute about the succession, as well as the ordinary priests. The cup containing this holy oil, preserved since Moses' day Jeremias hid with the ark in a cave on Nebo. From that time the Rabbis claimed the oil was not necessary, as the consecration of their fathers sufficed for the priests of the time of Christ. The oil was put on the pontiff's head and on the priest's hands. This is where bishop and priest are anointed with oil in our day.

[1] II Par. v. 12. [2] Josephus Antiq. xx. 9, 6. [3] I. Tim. iii; Titus i. [4] Edersheim, Temple, 71. Geikie, Life of Christ, i. 84 to 87, 523, 524.

19

Priest and pontiff, before sacrificing victims to the Lord of hosts, put on the linen drawers. Over this they wore a seamless white linen garment, having sleeves and falling down to the feet. In material, shape and color it was exactly like the alb of our day. Only descendants of Aaron's family could wear it. Christ's grandfather, Joachim, had married into Aaron's family [1] and his Mother made this seamless robe for her Son, because he was a Priest as well as Prince of David's line. Christ wore this white alb all his life and at the last Supper It was the robe on which the soldiers cast lots, for they could not cut and divide it among them without destroying it. This was the origin of the alb used at our altars.

Priest and pontiff bound up this seamless robe with a girdle when sacrificing in the Temple and celebrating the Passover. "Thus shall you eat it," said the Lord regarding the Passover, "you shall gird your reins," [2] and the Hebrew word given in this text is *chagar*: "to bind up." When man first bound a sash round his waist we do not find, for the sash or girdle comes down from earliest history and was found among all ancient peoples.

The people of Christ's day were long flat sashes wound round the body many times, the folds often serving as pockets. The bishop's girdle of our time is flat similar to that of the Temple priests, while the priests wear over the alb a round linen cord.

The miter of the Temple priest was called the *mygboath*, "hilt-shaped," that is opened, similar to the bishhop's miter in the Latin rite, and was formed like the inverted calyx of a flower. The high priest's miter was higher and more ornate, like our bishop's miter The people always wore their turbans in Temple, synagogue and at Passover, for to uncover the head would show disrespect during divine worship These customs of the Jewish Church are continued during the first part of the Mass, during which bishops and priests wear the miter and beretta. The drawers, alb, girdle and miter were the four vestments common to priests and pontiff in the Temple.

Now let us see the four vestments of the high priest, called by Jewish writers "the golden vestments," because

<hr>

[1] Luke ii.   [2] Exod. xii. 11.

gold, symbol of purity and authority, was woven through them.[1]

The ephod, "garment," called also the *meil*, entirely made of "woven work," of a dark purple color without sleeves covered him to his knees. At the hem it was adorned with alternate violet, purple and red pomegranate blossoms, having seventy-two gold bells between them, tinkling when he walked, in memory of the seventy-two families descending from Noe's grandsons, which had become the great nations of antiquity. This vestment in material and shape was like the bishop's rochet to which it gave rise.[2]

He wore on his breast the "rational," bearing twelve precious stones, each representing one of the twelve tribes of Israel. They were embedded in massive gold work, arranged in four rows, three in a row, each gem having engraved on it[3] one of the Hebrew letters. Before they fell into idolatry in the days of Solomon, Jewish writers say the stones glowed with a supernatural light one after the other enabling them to read Jehovah's decrees.[4] After the destruction of the first Temple the rational was lost, and the God of their fathers spoke no more through gems of the rational. Nine times the Old Testament mentions the rational.

On his shoulders he wore two great onyx stones, each engraved with six names of the twelve Hebrew tribes. They were called the Urim and Thummim: "Light and Perfection," "Knowledge and Virtue," dogmatic and moral theology, to foretell the faith and morals of the future priesthood of the Church.

Aaron's miter, called *miznepheth*, Moses made of finest white linen with lace and embroidered work, covering his head like a crown.[5]

God himself told the Hebrews to vest in sacred garments when celebrating the Passover. "And thus shall you eat it, you shall gird your reins, and you shall have shoes on your feet, holding staves in your hands, and you shall eat it in haste, for it is the phase, that is the Passage of the Lord."[6] In this account of the first Passover the Hebrews

---

[1] Exod. xxxix. 1-3; Migne, Cursus Comp. S. Scripturæ ii, 97, 98, vi 374, 9, 137, etc.   [2] St. Augustine, Ques. in Jud. L vii. Ques. lxi   [3] St. Augustine, Ques. in Exod., cxvi and cxxix.   [4] Edersheim, Temple, 112.   [5] See Migne, iii 924, 925. See Babyl. Talmud, Yomah, 105; 72 bells? Migne iii. 931.   [6] Exod. xii. 11.

celebrated as a nation, we find prescribed by God himself the bishop's shoes, girdle and crosier.

But as ages passed, the Hebrews copied the vestments of the Temple priests and vested in them for the Passover, so that at the time of Christ, they celebrated the feast vested in the elaborate robes Christ wore at the Last Supper.

But did Christ wear all the vestments of the bishop in our day? We must take into consideration the peculiar climate of Judea. Sion is 2,700 feet over the sea, while the deep Jordan valley and the Dead Sea are 1,300 feet below sea level. In April Jerusalem is quite cold, while the Jordan plains are excessively hot. The people of Judea must be prepared for these changes of climate when traveling from the stifling Jordan up to Jerusalem. For these reasons Christ and his apostles wore many garments while in Jerusalem, and when celebrating the Last Supper. This is the reason that the bishop robes in so many different vestments when pontificating.[1] Ten garments are mentioned as having been worn by Jews of that time. The first-born among the Hebrews always dressed in costly garments, and if he belonged to a royal family they were purple.[2]

In the days of Christ every Hebrew wore the phylacteries on brow and left arm.[3] They were capsules of rawhide calf-skins, inclosing four little square parchments, on which was written a part of the law of Moses they recited at night and morning prayers.

The first parchment had in Hebrew: "Sanctify unto me the first-born, etc."[4] The next had: "And when the Lord shall have brought you into the land of the Canaanite, etc."[5] The third had: "Hear, O Israel, the Lord our God is one Lord, etc."[6] The fourth had: "If then you obey my commandments,"[7] etc.

At the present time these four parchments are inclosed in little square boxes of rawhide making two square capsules ⅞ of an inch square, the one for the head being called the *tflin-schel-rosh*, "tflin-of-the-head," and they wear it on the top of the head while praying. Leather straps

---

[1] See Babyl. Talmud Tract Ebel, 38, 40, 41   [2] Migne, Cursus, S Script., 5, 942
[3] Migne, Cursus Comp S Scripturæ, i. 1347; iii. 1005, 1155   [4] Exod. xii. 2 to 10 inclusive.   [5] Exod. xiii. 11 to 16 inclusive.   [6] Deut. vi. 4 to 9 inclusive   [7] Deut. ii. 13 to 21 inclusive.   See Edersheim, Life of Christ. i 76, 228; ii. 408.

running through it bind it to the head, hang down behind, and the ends are brought forward to hang down on the breast. Each side of the capsule has the Hebrew letter S. The knot behind the head is tied in the form of four squares, making a cross, which they say represents the letter D.

The capsule of the other tflin is worn on the left arm, above the elbow next the heart, and a long strap is wound seven times round the arm, brought down, and wound three times round the two middle fingers of the left hand, the knot tying it to his arm also representing the letter D, but it is not in the form of a cross.

Taking the two Hebrew letters, Sh and D, and putting in vowels, we have the word Shadai, "Almighty God," or "The Greatest God," the word implying greatness, majesty, power, etc., to whom prayers are always offered in the synagogue in which Elohim represents God in strict justice and Adonai, God as Lord or Supreme Ruler.

When pontificating the high priest wore a gold band as a phylactery or tflin across his brow on which was engraved "Holiness unto Jehovah," and the straps with which it was tied hanging down, gave rise to the two bands hanging down behind from the bishop's miter. The Day of Atonement he did not wear a gold band across the brow when pontificating. The Pharisees very wore large phylacteries. Because of the ostentatious way they wore them Christ reproved their spirit of pride.[1]

There is a dispute regarding the origin of the phylacteries. Jewish writers say that in the days of Moses all kinds of ornaments, armlets, rings, etc, were worn as charms and spells, often having immodest pictures, engravings, sayings, etc., and that God ordered Moses to make the phylacteries for the Hebrews to wean them from the Egyptian superstitions, as the Law says: "And it shall be as a sign in thy hand, and as a thing hung between thy eyes for a remembrance."[2] The Hebrew writers before the Babylonian Captivity do not mention the phylacteries.

The Cairo museum, containing the richest collection in the world of ancient Egyptian relics and curios, shows that they followed all kinds of such superstitious practices.

[1] Matt. xxiii 5.　[2] Exod. xiii. 9-16; Deut. vi. 8, 9

Gods and goddesses are on all sides, and statues show kings and nobles holding forms of gods. Little scarabs, various gods, emblems, jewelry of gold and silver formed into charms, tokens and religious emblems filling many cases, prove they were very prone to superstitious practices. Jews of liberal tendencies of our time condemn the phylacteries and call the strict Jews who wear them " bridled asses."

But orthodox Jews hold that the phylacteries came from Moses. Eleazar, whom Ptolemy Philadelphus sent as ambassador to the king of Egypt, stated they came from Moses. St. Jerome and the Fathers of his day write that they were very common in their times. All Jews of Christ's day wore them in the Temple, synagogues and during their prayers especially at the Passover. Some think that Christ and the apostles wore them at the Last Supper. But we are not sure of this. Following these Jewish high priests, St John and some of the other apostles wore gold plates on their brows when saying Mass, similar to the gold phylactery worn by the high priest when pontificating in the Temple. The early Christians wore these phylacteries. But by lapse of time the custom degenerated into an abuse, for they were worn as charms, seals, pagan devices, and gave rise to superstitious practices. Popes Gelasius and Gregory I. condemned the abuse and the Council of Laodicea forbade them. Then Christians began to use crosses, medals, etc.; and religious emblems, and pictures, crucifixes, etc., multiplied.

Of the time when men first put on sandals to protect the feet history is silent. Egyptian monuments show nobles and priests shod in sandals of leather, palm leaves or papyrus, while soldiers' sandals were of iron or brass. Thongs passing between the great toe and the next and around the heel kept on the sole. These later developed into the upper part of the shoe of our day. In Mexico and in the Orient poor people still wear the sandals

From Egypt the Hebrews brought the shoe. Wealthy people of both sexes wore richly ornamented shoes covering the whole foot. Babylonian, Assyrian, Persian, and other monuments show that kings wore sandals and shoes before the time of Abraham. Isaias mentions " The latchet of their shoes,"[1] and numerous texts of the Old Testament show they were very common.[2]

Sometimes they were of cheap material.[3] But noble Hebrew ladies wore elaborate shoes[4] of violet color,[5] with woven greaves coming up almost to the knees. They were worn walking outside the house, but put off at the door when entering Temple or house, following Moses' example, whom God total to put off his shoes when approaching the burning bush.[6] In Jericho's plains Josue took off his shoes at the angel's orders.[7] Fleeing from Absalom, David took off his shoes as a sign of a penance.[8] Wealthy women wore the costly shoes spoken of in Canticles,[9] which God mentioned to the prophet.[10] Judith wore these beautiful shoes, or sandals, when she cut off Holofernes' head.[11] Afterwards brides presented costly shoes to their betrothed.

Poor Jews of Christ's time wore sandals or shoes made of straw, rushes, etc, tied on with strings, and these are the "poor man's shoes," of the prophet Amos.[12] But shoes were generally made of leather, the latter being placed in the street to be trampled on till tanned. You may see these skins in the streets of Jerusalem to-day trampled over by passing people.

Peculiar customs rose. The wife put on and took off her husband's shoes at the door. The widow, whose brother-in-law would not marry her, "Shall take off his shoe from his foot."[13] Servants and disciples dressed and undressed their master's feet,[14] and carried their shoes after them.[15] As a sign of the contract, the seller gave his shoe to the buyer.[16] After the shoes were removed the feet were washed at the door by the wife, child or servant. But if the master wished to honor his guest he did this himself, following the example of Abraham when the angels visited his tent.[17] To go barefooted was a sign of sorrow, of which the prophet says, "Keep thy foot from being bare."[18]

God forbade the prophet to take off his shoes as a sign of sorrow, when his wife died, and told Isaias to go bare-

---

[1] Isaias v 27.   [2] Jud. x. 4; Matt iii 11, x 10; Mark i 17; vi 9, John i 27; Migne, S. Scripturæ iii 918   [3] Amos ii 6   [4] Jud. x 3   [5] Ezech xvi, 10   [6] Exod. iii 5   [7] Josue v 16   [8] II. Kings xv 30   [9] Cant of Cant vii 1   [10] Ezech. xxiv. 23   [11] Judith x 3, xvi 11   [12] Amos ii 6   [13] Deut. xxv 9, Isaias xx. 2   [14] Mark i 7   [15] Matt iii 11   [16] Ruth iv. 7, 8   [17] Gen xviii. 4.   [18] II. Kings xv. 30; Jeremy ii. 25, Ruth iv 7, 8.

footed. Temple priests always ministered barefooted, and they complained continually of the cold pavements. Thus we see how the shoe figured in Hebrew history.

Some writers hold that Christ went barefooted, others that he wore sandals, still others that he wore shoes. The latter seems the most probable opinion, for he dressed as a noble Jew of his day, and John the Baptist protested he was not fit to loose the "latchets of his shoes." The Jews celebrating the Passover were to wear shoes by order of God himself.[1] This law was strictly followed in the time of Christ. Therefore we conclude that the Lord and his apostles put on their shoes before beginning the Passover. This perhaps is the reason the bishop puts on his shoes in the Church before his other vestments when he is about to pontificate. Sandals and shoes were commonly worn by the early Christians, and Clement of Alexandria[2] severely condemns the men and women who wore highly ornamented ones.[3]

The Jews of the days of Christ wore clothes copied from the Temple vestments or followed Greek and Roman styles. They were clothed in many different garments, because of the changes of climate.[4]

Why did God order the priests to wear drawers? We must go back to those days when paganism spread over the nations, and to which the Hebrews were so addicted. Every Friday pagan priests and people worshiped the goddess Venus with vile ceremonies, for she was the patron of immodest love. Herodotus writes that every woman of Babylon had to worship her by committing adultery once in her life. There she was called Beltis; in Syria she was Astarte, in Greece Athene, in Rome Venus; but she was known by other names, and unmentionable wickedness was committed in her honor. Going up and coming down the stairs from her altars, her votaries lifted up their clothes exposing themselves.[5] As a protest against these public immoral ceremonies, God told Moses to clothe the Hebrew priests, who had to ascend to the high sacrificial altar, in linen drawers, and the custom

[1] Exod xii 11 [2] In Padog Book II., Cap ii [3] See Migne, S Scripturæ ii 1153, 1157, 1158, iii 918; Edersheim, Life of Christ, i 624, 626, gives a description of the clothing Christ wore [4] Geikie, Life of Christ, vol i pp 151 152, 179, 180, etc; Migne, Cursus Comp. S Scripturæ, vol iii p 1025, etc [5] Geikie, Life of Christ, i 26, etc.

spread among the people and has come down to our day.

The Jews of the days of Christ clothed themselves in a long seamless garment like a cassock, which they called the *cutoneth* and the Greeks the *xiton*[1] Josephus writes that it was made of a single piece of cloth without seams, with or without sleeves, and was closed at the neck with a string. The priests always wore it without seams, and this was the seamless robe of Christ.

A modification of it of fine linen worn next the body became the shirt. Made of wool, covering the person from the neck to the feet it was opened in front, but closed with little buttons and gathered at the waist with the girdle. It was of the same form of the priest's cassock of our time. All men of the Orient wear it in our day, and it has the very same form as the clergyman's cassock.

Rulers wore this garment of different colors. That of the high priest was white, and he wore it all the time, putting over it his priestly vestments. This is the reason the Pope's cassock is white, for he is the High Priest of mankind. Jewish Rabbis still wear a white cassock the Day of Atonement.

The Roman emperor's cassock was of brilliant red and this color is seen in the cardinal's red cassock. Kings and members of royal families wore a purple cassock— purple being the mark of authority and dominion. Hence high officials of courts wore purple. Members of royal families dressed in purple even if their dynasty did not sit on the throne Christ, being a Prince of the House of David, highest honored of the Hebrew kings, wore this purple garment. He is often represented in art as clothed in a purple robe, the cutoneth or xiton. This is the reason bishops wear a purple cassock, for that was the color of Christ's cassock at the Last Supper.

The Temple priest's cassock was of linen. But laymen wore a white woolen cassock called the *simehah*. The desert Arabs, who never change, still wear it as an everyday garment This gave rise to the white alb the priest wears at Mass; it was always put on as a sign of gladness at feasts and when celebrating the Passover. Christ and his apostles, it seems probable, were clothed in it at the

---

[1] Farrar, Life of Christ, II, 281; Edersheim, Temple, p 73,

the Last Supper.   This cassock was worn by both sexes at time of Christ.   It was sometimes white or of various colors. It was the nuptial garment mentioned in the Gospel.[1]

Men of the Roman empire wore it covering the whole person.   In the middle ages it was cut short coming down to the knees, and became the frock-coat or "Prince Albert" of our day.   The buttons in the back were used to fasten on the sword when nearly all men went armed. But although the sword has been laid aside the buttons have remained.   The women's cassock became the gown or dress.   The women of the Orient still wear it, having over it a skirt which they raise up and cover their head and upper part of the body with it when they appear in public.[2]

To shield the shoulders from the fierce desert sun they let the ends of the turban fall down on the back behind. You will find the sons of the desert still wearing the garment falling down that way.   The desert heat is so great, and the sunlight reflected from the dry sands so piercing, that the skin would be blistered if not shaded. This is seen in the Scotch cap, sailor hat, and perhaps bands of bishop's miter.

They came to feast with head and upper part of the body protected that way.[3]   It was a relic of the patriarchal period, when their fathers, as shepherd sheiks, pastured their flocks on the borders of the desert.   The Hebrews celebrating religious, civil, and family feast wore it on their shoulders.   After the banquet they took it off.[4]   Rulers and wealthy persons wore these amices made of costly materials.[5]   Sometimes it was made as large as a tunic, and covered the upper part of the body to the knees.   This was the origin of the amice.

When the cincture was first used we know not.   We first find it in the consecration of Aaron's sons to the priesthood[6]   In the house the Hebrews in the days of the Kings laid it off and put it on when they went out.   But by lapse of time the Jews wore it all the time[7]

They wore two kinds of girdles in Asia, one was a sash

[1] Matt xxii 11.   [2] Benedict XIV in his great work, De Missae Sacrificio, Book I, Cap vii to Book II. elaborately treats of the vestments and their mystic meanings   [3] Gen xxvii 27; Psalm xlv 9, Cant of Cant. iv 11.   [4] Ezech. vii 20   [5] IV Kings v 5, Matt x 10; James v 2.   [6] Exod xxix 8.   [7] See Migne, S. Scripturae, iii 908.

about six inches wide, which was fixed with a clasp in front the ends hanging down. It was of leather,[1] wool, linen, or other material. John the Baptist was clothed with a tunic of camel's wool bound up with a leather girdle, such as you see to-day worn by the Bedouin of the deserts. The wealthy wore girdles of wool, linen, or costly material, sometimes of silk woven, embroidered and tied in front or at the side.[2]

Women wore the girdle fastened in front with a buckle, brooch or other ornament,[3] often they were made of costly material.[4] Being wide the folds served as pockets. Arabs stick swords, daggers, etc., in the girdles.[5] These vestments can be seen in the sculptured figures on the great platform of Persepolis where stood the palaces of the great Persian kings before Alexander conquered that country. The girdle survives in the waistbands and belts women wear in our day.

The priestly girdle called the Abnet was a linen band three fingers broad, very long, with tassels adorned with various colored embroidery work.[6] Wound around the body during his ministry, the priest threw the ends over his shoulders as the clergymen of the Oriental Rites still do.[7] Josephus says "the ends were tied in a knot in front, and hung down to the feet," as the celebrant ties the girdle in our day. The men of Palestine still wear the girdle wound around their waist many times.

Girdle and alb are fundamental religious vestments of earth and heaven. The beloved apostle saw the Son of God thus clothed. "And in the midst of the seven golden candlesticks, one like unto the Son of man, clothed with a garment down to the feet and girded about near the paps with a golden girdle."[8] "And the seven angels came out of the temple having the seven plagues, clothed in clean white linen, girded about the breasts with golden girdles."[9] The Church, Bride of the Lamb, thus clothes her clergy at her altars as she is vested in heaven. "And to her it hath been granted that she should clothe herself with fine linen glittering and white. For fine linens are the justifications of saints."[10] Thus all down the ages

---

[1] IV. Kings i 8. [2] Jeremy xlii. 1 [3] Cant vii 3 [4] I. Kings xxv. 13, II. Kings xviii 11, etc [5] II. Kings xx 8. [6] See Migne, lii 908. [7] Exod xxviii 8, xxxix 29 [8] Apoc. i. 13. [9] Apoc. xv 6. [10] Apoc xix 8

the white vestments represent the purity and innocence
of those who minister at our altars.

The tunic called in Hebrew *chaluk* or *kethoneth*, in
Greek *chiton* is found first in history as the garment of
skins God made for Adam and Eve after the fall.[1] When
weaving was invented, it was made of woven wool or
linen and bound round with a girdle. The Temple priest's
tunic was woven without seam, worn next the skin as a
shirt, covering the linen drawers and flowing down to the
knees. The shoes they wore in Moses' day were laced
up to the knees, and youths of both sexes wore long
tunics falling to the ground like a priest's cassock. John's
Greek Gospel says Christ wore a tunic which he calls the
xiton, which was under the seamless garment[2]

The first tunics had no sleeves, but soon short ones
were added, and later they were made to cover the
arms to the wrist Babylonians, Persians, Jews, etc.,
wore the tunic as a shirt, and over it another garment
of more costly material like a cassock.[3]

Rabbis, leaders in Israel and wealthy people of Judea
wore two tunics, the inside one serving as a shirt. The
over tunic was called the *sarbalin*. We find no record,
but it seems reasonable to suppose, that Christ conformed
to this custom and wore two tunics at the Last Supper,
for four times the Gospels mention the two tunics translated "coats." This is perhaps the reason that the bishop
wears two tunics when pontificating. The inside vestment is now called the tunic and the outside one the
dalmatic, because the Dalmatians wore the latter as a
national distinctive garment.[4]

Over the two tunics they wore a large flowing square
garment called the Talith in Hebrew, or Imatian in
Greek. It was one of the oldest garments worn by man,
and is pictured on the monuments of Babylonia, Assyria,
Persia, etc., as a priestly garment the kings vested in
when offering sacrifice.

Wealthy and noble Jews wore it five or six feet wide
and it hung down behind forming a train. At the neck
it was fastened with a clasp In fine weather the front

[1] Gen iii 21   [2] John xix 23   [3] Prov xxxi. 21; Matt x 10; Luke ix 8;
Mark vi 9   [4] Benedict XIV. De Sacrificio Missæ, C. vii n. 6, Migne, Cursus
Completus, S. Scripturæ, v iii 1250

ends were thrown back over the shoulders and hung down the back, these being called wings.[1] Often they threw the two front angles or corners over the left shoulder, and carried the trail on the right arm.

This garment was worn by the Hebrews when leaving Egypt, and we read that they carried the dough of the Passover in their cloaks.[2] The folds of this great mantle or cloak, were often used as a pocket.[3] The poor rolled themselves in its ample folds, folded up their girdle, laid it on a stone to serve as a pillow, thus they slept either on the floor, or on the ground outside—a custom still followed in Palestine and other parts of Asia. For this reason God forbade money-lenders to keep this garment overnight when pledged for a loan.[4] " But thou shall restore it to him presently before the going down of the sun, that he may sleep in his own raiment." [5]

In the translations of the Old Testament, this garment is rendered by the words cloak, mantle, vestments, etc., and is mentioned hundreds of times. At the time of Christ money-lenders got around the law by taking the tunic as a security.[6]

This great cloak, or cope, changed in size and shape by the lapse of time, so that when Christ walked the earth and wore it, it had become the Meil, a garment falling to the knees with holes for the arms and head.

Formed of two parts covering the back and breast, it was fastened on the sides with clasps of gold adorned with jewels.[7] Later, sleeves were added to the garment. Although it belonged to the high priest, by lapse of time noble and famous men wore it.[8] Ezechiel mentions it ornamented with embroidered work.[9] The vestment was worn in the days of the prophets, for Daniel says a modification of it was used as an inside shirt, and the sculptures of Babylonia prove his words.[10]

This was the prophet's mantle the Hebrews named the talith, the Greeks the imatian or elisus. It was a great cloak falling from the shoulders to the ground, and covering the whole person like the cope worn at vespers.[11]

This was the sign of the prophetic office of these seers

---

[1] Aggeus ii. 18 ; Zach. viii. 23 ; II. Kings xv 20   [2] Exod xiii. 34   [3] IV. Kings iv 39   [4] Exod xxii 26.   [5] Deut. xxiv. 13   [6] Matt. v. 40   [7] Exod xxviii 6, 7, etc   [8] Job xxix 14 ; I Kings xviii 41 ; I Kings vi. 14.   [9] Ezech. xxvi. 16.   [10] Dan. iii 21.   [11] Geikie Life of Christ, I. 180, 549

of old who went before the Lord clothed in this garment often made of skins, wandering over Judea, pouring out burning words of the Holy Spirit relating to the Redeemer of whom the world was not worthy.[1] With it Elias, "My God is Jehovah," divided the waters of the Jordan.[2] Often it was made of sackcloth as a sign of penance.[3]

Did Christ wear this prophetic cope at the Last Supper? It was the border of his imatian the woman touched when she was healed.[4] The sick touched his imatian on the shores of Galilee and were cured.[5] In the transfiguration his imatia, translated vestments, became white as snow.[6] When they got through mocking him after the flagellation they put on him his imatia[7] the very vestments the soldiers divided among themselves on Calvary.[8]

The prophet's talith, or in Greek imatian, modified became the Greek sindon, which wealthy Hebrews wore as a large over-tunic often mentioned in the Old Testament[9] and in the Greek Gospels. Often made of fine linen it was worn next the body by the wealthy as a night shirt, and became the shroud. It was the great grave-cloth in which the wealthy Nicodemus and Joseph wrapped the body of the dead Christ.[10]

According to the custom of a noble Jew celebrating the Passover, Christ put on this Prophet's mantle, in Latin the Pluvial, in Greek the imatian, in Hebrew the Taleth,[11] its four corners being covered with embroidery called Ciccilh, "Fringes," to remind them of the Law of Moses. "Speak to the children of Israel, and thou shalt tell them to make to themselves fringes in the corners of their garment, putting in them ribbons of blue. That when they shall see them, they may remember all the commandments of the Lord."[12] This was the origin of the embroideries and decorations of Church vestments. These decorations on our vestments represent Christ, his Passion, etc., to remind the people of the crucifixion, and religious truths.

This great garment covered the whole person, like a cloak, and was about the shape and form of the cope. In

[1] Heb ii 36, 37 [2] B C 896 IV Kings ii 8 [3] Zach xiii 4 [4] Matt ix 20, 21.
[5] Matt. xiv. 36 [6] Matt xvii 2 [7] Matt xxvii 21 [8] Matt xxvii 35 [9] Judges
xiv 12 ; Prov xxi. 24 ; Isaias iii 23 [10] Luke xxiii 53 [11] See Geikie, Life of
Christ, i 567 and ii 386. [12] Numb xv. 38, 39.

this form it is still worn by the Greek, Russian, and Oriental clergy as a chasuble. This was its form in the early Latin Church The deacon had to lift up the garment so the celebrant could put out his hands. But about the twelfth century they cut the sides, because they did not always have a deacon to serve Mass. That has been the form of the chasuble till our day. But as a remnant of the deacon holding up the great chasuble, the altar boys and the ministers at Mass still hold up the chasuble when incensing the altar and at the Consecration. The tunic and dalmatic tied or pinned up during Lent are a survival of that custom of the middle ages.

The people, especially the women of that time, wore a garment like a cloak the Greeks called the Stole and the Romans the Stola.[1] The front was an ornamental band adorned with embroidered work. They often sent this band to friends they wished to honor, who sowed it on their stole. By lapse of time, and because they wore so many other vestments, this band was worn alone and became the stole. As the Hebrews wore this at the Passover and feasts, it came to pass that the clergy of the early Church always wore it during religious functions. This is the stole of to-day which the higher clergy wear in their ministry.

In the Syro-Chaldaic spoken by the common people of Christ's day it was the Arbah Canphoth, "The Four Corners." According to the words of God to Moses it also had fringes. "Thou shalt make strings in the hem at the four corners of thy cloak."[2] The "fringes" or "strings" called ciccith or Zizith were to remind them of the Law. For that reason they were first of blue, the color of the covenant between God and Israel Later Talmudic writers allowed them to be made of white cloth.[3] These had an influence on the embroideries, ornaments, and figures of our vestments.[4]

Two inches from the corner of the garment, a hole was made and seven threads of lamb's wool about half a yard long were passed through and doubled. One thread was then wound seven times round the others and tied. The next was wound nine times and tied, the next eleven

[1] See Geikie, Life of Christ, 1 568 [2] Deut. xxii 12; Numb xv. 38 [3] Talmud, Mem. iv. 1. [4] Geikie, Life of Christ, 1 180

times, the next thirteen times, etc., till seven knots were tied round the threads, making a little string of seven strands, with seven knots hanging down like little tassels This was the origin of the tassels on our stole and manuple. These fringes, surviving in Church vestments and Jewish prayer shawl show us how unchanged have remained the custom which came from God himself through Moses.

The Pharisees used to wear very large "fringes" to attract attention to their great piety and respect for the Law. Lest they might become unclean by touching the body, they had a pocket made in the shawl, wherein they carried them when not at prayer in the synagogue and Temple.[1]

Man is spirit and matter, a living soul in an animated body, and he receives truth through the senses. Therefore God from the beginning taught him through his five senses. God ordered "the fringes" on their vesture to remind them of the law, and every object of Temple and synagogue brought truth to their minds. The early Christians used religious emblems, signs, symbols of the Jewish Church, and St. Augustine[2] tells us these were not forbidden. But the Jewish emblems gradually gave way before the Christian symbols, whence statues, paintings, the sign of the cross, medals, scapularies, beads, etc., may in a way be said to have risen or developed from these Jewish emblems so common at the time of Christ.[3] In the synagogues the writer visited the Jews showed him these fringes, and explained their meanings. He noticed that they held them in their right hands while saying their prayers, to remind them of the Law, as Christians hold their beads.

Vesting in the "prayer shawls," as this vestment is now called but then named tzitzith,[4] the Jews first put it on the head, and then let it fall down on the shoulders, as the celebrant of the Mass puts the amice on his head, and then lets it fall down on the shoulders. Putting it on they said: "Blessed art thou, O Lord our God, King of the Universe, who hast sanctified us with thy commandments, and hast given us the command of the fringes."

[1] See Geikie, Life of Christ, 1 180   [2] Contra Faustum, l. xix n. xvi   [3] St. Augustine, Contra Faustum, l xxii. n ; xci. xcii   [4] Talmud, Succah, vi

The Jewish boy of twelve years is still confirmed by placing on his head and shoulders this prayer shawl, and the Rabbis and officers of the synagogue or Temple imposed their hands on him. This is the Jewish confirmation, the image of the sacrament of confirmation in the Church. By this ceremony the boy becomes of age, takes part in all meetings of the men, and wears the prayer shawl in the synagogues, when praying, and also at the Passover. This ceremony was held at the Temple in the time of Christ, who was thus confirmed when he was in his twelfth year. He remained in the Temple with the men talking and disputing with them for three days. Before this rite, a boy was treated in Israel as a child, after it he was a man. Mary his Mother and Joseph went on their way for three days, men and women traveled in separate groups, and his Mother supposed he was with the men, and Joseph with the women, and that was why they did not miss him.

After being confirmed the Jewish boy makes a speech to the congregation from the synagogue pulpit or rostrum. A boy, confirmed one day the writer visited a synagogue, grew eloquent reciting the glories of the Hebrews, their history, religion, and the influence they exerted on the world, and told how faithful he would be to Judaism The brilliant mind, the blessings of the patriarchs on the race, shone forth in ideas, delivery and enthusiasm. Some of the wealthy Jews ornament the shawl with cloth of gold.

They used to wear around the neck a narrow band which the Greeks of Christ's day called the *xlamos* or *diplois*, and which the Romans named the pallium—both words meaning a coverlet. The ends hung in front or on one side as far as the knees. That of the Roman officers, was sometimes shaped like a cloak being red or purple. This was the purple garment of mockery, called the plaudamentum, with which they clothed Christ after the scourging.[1] Ezechiel mentions this garment as coming in bales to Tyre.[2]

Worn by the wealthy of both sexes, it was wrapped round the body, fastened on the right shoulder with a brooch, or was thrown over the left shoulder, the ends

[1] Matt. xxvii 28, Mark xv. 17.   [2] Ezech. xxvii 24.

20

brought across the back under the right arm, and again thrown over the shoulder. Being the sign of authority. Christ, as Prince of the House of David, we suppose, wore this at the Last Supper.[1] Numerous writers treat of the pallium, but they do not go beyond the early Church, admitting that they cannot find its origin. From most ancient times it was the insignia of the archbishop, primate, or bishop having jurisdiction over other bishops. The Orientals call it the Omophorion. The Pope sends the pallium taken from Peter's tomb to the archbishop as a sign of his authority over the bishops of his province.

Teachers at that time wore over the shoulders this band fastened on the right with a buckle which hung down in front in easy folds.[2] Eusebius of Cæsarea describes a statue of Christ he saw at Panias, called also Cæsarea Philippi, where Christ healed the woman afflicted with an issue of blood.[3] "At the gates of her house, on a raised pedestal, stands a brazen image of a woman on her bended knee, with her hands stretched out before her, like one entreating. Opposite her is the image of a man erect, of the same material, in full Pallium, stretching out his hand to the woman."[4]

St. Augustine writing about Cicero says teachers in the academies wore a pallium,[5] and the philosophers wore it as a sign of their learning.[6] As a teacher in Israel therefore we must conclude that Christ wore a pallium and that this is the reason it became the insignia of the high officials of the Church.

The brooches with which garments were fastened, were often very costly. In the second story of the Cairo museum, on the left at the top of the great stairway in the room devoted to jewelry, you will find gold and silver brooches, rings, etc., ornamented with precious stones, found in Egyptian tombs, and which ornamented the bodies of people who lived long before Moses. The designs are very beautiful and the materials costly.

In the Dublin museum you will find clasps of solid pure gold in the shape of a U, used by the clergy of the early Irish Church to fasten chasuble and cope. Some of

[1] Baronius, l 5 An Ed Rom p 631 and Chardon, Hist des Sacraments, in Migne's Theo Cursus Comp. [2] Geikie, Life of Christ, v 1 p. 567 [3] Luke ix 20, Matt. viii 43, 44 [4] Geikie, Life of Christ, v 1 p 428 [5] Contra Acad l. iii., c viii. [6] De Civitate Dei, l xiv c xx

them must weigh more than two pounds, and they are as bright as the day they were made.

The brooch is still seen in the clasp of the cope. When the brooch developed into the bishop's pectoral cross we do not find. Priests of the early Church wore a simple cross on the breast hanging from the neck with a cord or ribbon. Priests of the Russian and Greek rites still wear them. It is probable that the bishop's cross was developed from these crosses worn in ancient times.

Jews of both sexes carried a handkerchief, either tied to the girdle or hanging from the left arm.[1] They placed it over the face of the dead. In the original Greek it is the *soudarion*, in Latin *sudarium*,[2] meaning "sweatcloth." They tied it into a purse and carried their money in it.[3] They tied the handkerchief round the neck or used it as an apron : the handkerchiefs the apostles wore performed miracles.[4] This was the origin of the neckcloth or cravat of our times. During church services the handkerchief was tied to the left arm, and by lapse of time, it took the color and ornamentations of the vestments, and became the manuple. In the Greek, Sclavonic, Russian and Oriental rites two manuples are worn, one on each arm, between the elbow and wrist, both lying down flat on the arms.

Princes in Israel, and rulers of the ancient world wore a purple garment coming down to their knees. It was sometimes made without sleeves and of the same shape and color of the bishop's rochet. It gave rise to the bishop's rochet and the surplice of our clergy. Being a Prince of the House of David, Christ wore this garment as Daniel saw him in vision,[5] for all members of royalty wore purple in that day, even if their family did not sit on the throne. David's sons were highly honored in Christ's day. The Talmud tells us that they only had a right to sit in the Priests' Court, and that when they came into the sanctuary heralds cried out, " Give honor to the family of David." It seems probable that Christ wore this purple rochet.

In ancient times, people of both sexes tied a string around the head to keep the hair in place. That became

---

[1] IV. Kings v. 23; Isaias iii 18 to 25. [2] John ii. 44; xx. 7. [3] Luke xix. 20.
[4] Acts xix. 12. [5] Dan. x. 2-5.

the fillet you find represented in ancient art. In the days of the patriarchs, a cloth was laid on the head as a protection from the sun and to shade the eyes; falling down on the shoulders it shaded the fierce desert heat. The Bedouin of the desert, Ismael's sons, who never changed since Abraham lived, wear that cloth called Keffyeh,[1] which they keep on the head with two colored fillets of camel's hair about a inch in diameter, wound around the brow. A corps of the Turkish army wear a head-dress of that kind. During the lapse of ages this head covering developed into the hat, and the head-band, with its bow-knot, is a survival of the knotted fillet.

In the days of the patriarchs the head-cloth becoming large, and wound round the head, gave rise to the turban or kerbela of the Orient. When this took place we do not know. Kings and rulers wore elaborate turbans, which later became the king's diadem and crown. Mardochai "shone in royal apparel, to wit of violet and sky-color, wearing a gold crown on his head, and clothed with a cloak of silk and purple."[2] Even the common people were well dressed in that age, as we read that the three Hebrews were thrown, into the fiery furnace, "with their coats, and their caps, and their shoes, and their garments."[3]

After the return from the Babylonian Captivity, the Hebrews shaped the white linen turban into a high miter like that of the high priest.[4] Pontificating on the great feasts of Israel, the high priest wore a magnificent miter of gold cloth encrusted with gems, but on the Day of Atonement he used a simple miter of white linen shaped like the calyx of a flower.[5]

The turban, in Hebrew Megba'ah, in Syro-Chaldaic Mecnepheth, Semitic words meaning "to bind round," according to St. Jerome coming down from earliest history, is still worn in the Orient, Africa, India, etc., where people have not changed since the days of Abraham. The miter of high priest and bishop, the kingly crown and the Pope's tiara are but modifications of it.

While shoes or sandals were left at the door of house

---

[1] Geikie, Life of Christ, i. 179.   [2] Esther viii 15.   [3] Dan. iii 21.   [4] Josephus, Antiq. B. iii., C. vii n. 7; Exod. xxviii 40, xxix 9, xxxix. 26; Bruch. v. 2. [5] See Exod. xxviii. 4, xxix. 9, xxxix. 26, 30; Levit. viii. 13.

and gate of Temple, the turban was always worn during divine services and in the house. To uncover the head is still a sign of disrespect in the Orient. The master of the feast of the Passover wore a large high turban like that of the presiding judge of the Supreme Court of the Jews, and this was copied from the tiara of the high priest. The Machabæan priest-kings put three circles on their miter, making it into the tiara worn by Caiphas at the time of Christ. This is the reason the Pope, high priest of the Church, wears a tiara-miter different from that of other bishops.[1]

Before the Jews reclined at the table to celebrate the Passover, they removed their head-coverings, for they could not wear them while reclining. This is the reason the bishop and clergy remove miter and beretta when going up to the altar during the celebration of Mass.

By lapse of time the miter became more ornamental, and was worn by both sexes of rich or noble families.[2] Kings developed still more elaborate head-coverings, which became the crown of gold adorned with precious stones.

The Rabbi, the Hassan and officers of the synagogue wore black four-cornered caps very like the berettas of our clergy. At present they wear these head-coverings during the services both standing and sitting. In ancient times they wore them only when sitting. These gave rise to the beretta of the clergy, worn when sitting during Mass and church functions.

In France the judges wear similar coverings for the head when on the bench. Judges of other European countries follow rules coming down from time immemorial, they being dressed in long gowns like the priestly cassock.

English magistrates wear wig and silken gown. The latter came in after the Restoration, but the wig or judicial cap dates as far back as the English courts—to the time when the lawyers were priests. Before the wig took its present shape, a small piece of lace, called the coif, was also worn, and later judges cut a hole in the wig so the coif would be seen. At the present time the Lord Chief Justice of England has a round space in his wig

---

[1] See Geikie, Life of Christ, ii. 437.　[2] IV. Kings ix. 30.

covered with black silk where the ancient coif, since left off, used to appear. When pronouncing the death sentence, the English judge covered his coif with a black cap, a ceremony still followed.

At the death of the daughter of James II., courts went into mourning, and the lawyers, called barristers, put on black silk gowns, which they have retained since. They used to give their services freely, but a triangular piece of cloth hanging down behind, like a monk's cowl, formed a pocket into which the clients used to put their fees, when the man of law was not looking, much against the lawyer's will, we may be sure.

The English courts have long since gotten over their grief for the death of the king's daughter, but they are so conservative of old customs, that the judges and barristers still wear the black robes and wig when sitting on "the woolsack," as the bench is called. The barristers, as the lawyers are called, must dress in black when pleading in Canada and the colonies. Peculiar neckties distinguish the English barrister who appears in court from the counsel, the lawyer who prepares the case, and every frill, furbelow and ceremony of olden times are followed; few being able to give origin or reason for the numerous court ceremonies.

Only in the courts of British Columbia do the judges of America wear the wig, but in 1905 a law was passed abolishing it. A few years ago the judges of the U. S. Supreme Court put on the long silk gown, and judges of both federal and state courts are following the example. We have given these details to show how natural it is for man to vest in robes emblematic of his office

But why do bishop, judge and priest cover the head in court and church, while every other man must uncover his head? In ancient times they covered the head as a sign of respect. When Moses approached the fiery bush, God told him to take off his shoes, and Moses "hid his face, for he durst not look at God."[1] To show respect for the holy sanctuary the priests always wore their miters in Temple, during the synagogue prayers, and before they reclined at the Passover table. During first part of Mass, that is from the beginning to the canon which was

---

[1] Exod, iii. 6.

founded on the Jewish Temple services, bishop and priest cover the head with miter and beretta when sitting at Mass. But times and customs have changed since the days of Christ, and to show respect we now take off our hats. But what was the origin of the bishop's ring?

The ring, mentioned thirty-one times in the Old Testament, first a plain band of brass, ivory, bronze, silver, gold or other precious material, is found in many ruins, tombs and monuments of the ancient world. Later it was ornamented with the figure of a god, a scarabæus, a sacred emblem, or a cherished legend, and used as a seal to certify official documents.

Thamar took Juda's ring and staff as a pledge.[1] Pharao took off his ring from his finger and gave it to Joseph to wear as a sign of authority, when he made him his prime minister.[2] Judith wore her rings when she went forth to meet Holofernes.[3] Assuerus gave his official ring to Aman as a sign of authority,[4] and to seal the letters of extermination against the Hebrews. When the king found out the plot, he took the ring from him and gave it to Mardochai who sealed with it the letters revoking the decree[5] Hebrew kings sealed with their official ring their state documents[6] The prophet tells the Hebrews their ornaments of rings and jewels will be taken from them.[7] Solomon writes of the " signet of an emerald in a work of gold,"[8] worn as a ring

The ring often of costly material, was handed down from father to son.[9] Hebrew ladies of the time of Christ had rings set with precious stones, rubies, emeralds, the chrysolite being most common. The art of cutting diamonds was known and diamond rings were worn at that time. In the days of Solon every Greek freeman wore a signet ring of gold, silver or bronze; but the Spartans took pride in a simple plain iron ring. Rings became so common that the Athenians and Lacedemonians made laws against them.

Pliny says the Romans derived the custom of wearing a ring from the Greeks. Florus writes the Etruscans first wore it in Italy, while Livy ascribes it to the Sabines. Gold rings were given later to ambassadors with their

---

[1] Gen xxxviii. 18.　[2] Gen xli 42　[3] Judith x 3　[4] Esther iii 10　[5] Esther viii 8-10　[6] III Kings xxi 8　[7] Isaias iii. 21　[8] Eccle. xxxii 8.　[9] Luke xv 22.

official dress. Senators and judges enjoyed what they called the " jus annuli aurei," (the right of wearing a gold ring) Hannibal sent to Carthage three modii of gold rings taken from the fingers of slain Roman officers.[1] During the Roman empire, the emperors reserved the right of wearing a ring to high officers, magistrates and governors of provinces, and conferred it as a decoration on persons they wished to honor. In the time of Tiberius, who reigned when Christ was put to death, many saved themselves from punishment for breaking the laws on the plea that they wore a ring, and a law was made restricting it to freemen, whose fathers possessed not less than $400,000 worth of property.

Aurelian extended the right to all soldiers, and Justinian to all citizens. The Romans, like the Greeks, Egyptians and Orientals, used to cover their fingers with many costly rings. Martial says Charinus wore ten on each finger, making eighty, and fops had rings for different seasons.

From ancient Egypt, Babylonia, etc., came the custom of engraving on rings images of animals, mottoes, portraits of gods, heroes, etc., and using them as signets and seals. Sometimes they were of immense value, and one the empress Faustina wore was worth $200,000, while Domitia's ring cost $300,000.

High priests, common priests, Levites, Rabbis, leaders in Israel and wealthy people of Judea in the time of Christ wore rings.[2] Did Christ wear a ring? We fail to find any record. But as he conformed to every custom of his people, as he was the Lion of the tribe of Juda, Prince of the House of David and a Leader, we think he followed the universal custom and wore a ring. As we trace all the bishop's vestments back to the Last Supper, we ask where did the bishop's ring come from if not from the same origin as the other vestments? From the beginning of the Church the bishops have worn the episcopal ring. The stone usually is a violet amethyst mentioned three times in the Bible,[3] one of the stones of the high priest's breastplate[4] and as forming one of the foundation stones of the New Jerusalem.[5]

[1] St. Augustine, De Civitate Dei. l. iii., c xix   [2] Edersheim Temple, Sketches of Jewish Life, p. 217. etc   [3] Exod. xxviii 19   [4] Exod. xxxix. 12.   [5] Apoc. xxi. 20.

When preparing for a feast like the Passover, when washing the hands they removed the ring, lest the finger might not be cleaned under the band. As they wore gloves at Passover, they put the ring on over them, because the glove was too small for the ring, and to show their beautiful signet rings, signs of their wealth and authority. This is the reason that the bishop wears his ring over the glove when pontificating. We mentioned the glove, now let us see its origin and history.

The glove as a covering for the hand with a separate sheath for each finger, Homer writes, was worn by Laertes to protect his hands when working in his garden. Xenophon says Cyrus sometimes went without his gloves. In the most ancient times the glove was given as a pledge when concluding a contract, and that gave rise to throwing down the glove as a challenge to a duel. The glove is not mentioned in the Bible, but from other works we learn that in the days of Christ, kings, princes, and leading men of his day wore them, often ornamented with gold embroidery and precious stones.

The Talmud tells us the story of Issachar of Kefar, who was a member of the Jewish Supreme Court which condemned Christ to death. After the ascension he was elected high priest, but when pontificating in the Temple he wore silk gloves, lest he might soil his dainty hands with the blood of the sacrifices. One day, a dispute rose between Herod and his wife whether roasted lamb or kid was the better eating, and they agreed to refer the matter to Issachar, who was a glutton. The latter coming into the throne room waved his hand in a flippant manner at Herod, who ordered his body-guard to strike off his hand, Issachar bribed the guard to cut off his left hand, but when Herod heard it he ordered the other amputated also, as it was with the right he insulted him, and thus he lost both hands which he had raised against Christ. Did Christ wear gloves at the Last Supper? There is no record. But whence came the bishop's gloves if he did not, for the bishops have used them since the apostolic age.

The patriarch shepherds carried a staff, in Hebrew *maggel*, "rod," having a bent crook with which to lead back to the flock the stray sheep,[1] and twenty-seven times

---

[1] Gen xxxii 10, xxxviii. 18-25.

the Old Testament speak of it. The staff was a sign of
power and authority in these days when every object had
a mystic meaning relating to the expected Christ. Jacob
fleeing from his brother when praying for aid said : " with
my staff I passed over this Jordan." [1] The angel who appeared to Gideon carried a staff, as also David did when
he went forth against Goliath.

In Hebrew the word for staff is also *shebet*, " rod,"
" reed," and in Greek *skemtron*, " scepter." The rod of
authority developed into the religious staff of the prophets
and the scepter of the king. [2] Leaders in Israel carried a
staff as a sign of authority. [3] The staff was first made of
wood and that was the kind of staff or rod Moses carried
as a sign of authority and with which he brought the
plagues on Egypt. But the scepter of the Persian king
was of massive gold, [4] and when he inclined it towards a
subject it was a sign of favor and the latter kissed it as a
sign of homage. [5] A carved ivory scepter was discovered
at Nimroud [6] and another in Egyptian ruins. [7]

Patriarchs and prophets with their staff of authority
foretold Christ who was to come into the world with his
divine power, holding his staff, at the Last Supper, and in
the Eucharist give life to human nature dead through
Adam's sin. Let us quote the great bishop of Hippo, St.
Augustine.

" God the Son sent the law of the Old Testament
through his servant Moses, but he himself gave grace.
Look at Eliseus in the great and deep mystery not only
by words but by actions foretelling the future. The son
of his host died. What does this dead boy signify but the
human race dead in Adam ? The news was told the holy
prophet bearing in his prophecy a type of our Lord Jesus
Christ. He sent by his servant his staff and said, ' Go,
put it on the dead child.' He went as an obedient servant.
The prophet knew what he was to do. He put the staff
on the dead boy, but he did not come to life. ' For if
there had been a law given which could have given life,
truly justice should have been by the law.' [8] The Jewish
law could not give life. Then the great prophet came to

[1] Gen xxxii 10   [2] Levit. xxvii 32; Mich. vii 14   [3] Judg v 14; Gen xlix 10;
Numb. xxiv. 17; Psalm xlv. 6 ; Isaias xiv. 5; Amos i 5; Ezech x 11; Wisdom
x. 14, etc.   [4] Esther iv 11; Zenoph, Cyrop. viii. 7, Sec 13   [5] Esther, iv 11, v. 2.
[6] Layard, Nim. and Babyl. 195.   [7] Wilkinson, Anc. Eg. i 276   [8] Galatians iii. 21.

the dead child—the living to the dead. He came and what did he do ? He went up and lay upon the child, and he put his mouth upon his mouth, and his eyes upon his eyes, and his hands upon his hands, and he bowed himself down upon him.[1] 'He,' the Son of God 'debased himself, taking the form of a servant, being made to the likeness of men and in shape found as a man.'[2] 'Who will reform the body of our lowness, made like the body of his glory'[3] Thus in this type of Christ the dead race of mankind brought by Christ back to life was foretold, and the wicked who would be justified. This foretold grace, this is the grace of Christians gained by the Man, the Mediator who suffered, died, rose from the dead, ascended into heaven, led captivity captive and gave gifts to men."[4]

First, it was used as an aid in walking, then to keep the sheep in order, then as sign of Moses' divine power, then in hands of prophets, then as a type of the Law given to Israel. Every Hebrew carried his staff while eating the Passover, as the Lord commanded. "Thus shall you eat it," "gird your reins," "have shoes on your feet, holding staves in your hands"[5] "for it is the Passover of the Lord."[6] Thus stood the Lord and his apostles round the Passover supper table, each holding the staff of patriarchs, prophets and the holy seers of old. The Lord's staff was type of power divine, shown forth by Moses in his Law, and an image of all the prophecies uttered by the Holy Ghost. Law and Prophecy were then about to be fulfilled in the First Mass and in the Crucifixion.

When Christ sent his apostles into Judea before he gave them power over unclean spirits, he told them not to take a staff,[7] but when he gave them that power as exorcists he told them to take their staff.[8] Jews of that time, especially leaders in Israel, always carried these staffs as a sign of their authority, but they were forbidden to take them into the Temple.[9] In the Temple ceremonial of Passover, two long lines of priests held each a staff— one line having gold staffs, those of the other line were of silver, and with them they kept order among the throngs of people. To-day, as a relic of that custom, of-

---

[1] IV. Kings iv 34 [2] Philip ii, 7 [3] Philip iii 21 [4] St Augustine, Sermo xxvi, de Verb. Ps xciv, n. xi [5] In Hebrew maggel, " rod " [6] Exod. xii. 11. [7] Matt. x. 11. [8] Mark vi. 8. [9] Edersheim, Temple, 42.

ficials in the Church of the Holy Sepulchre, Jerusalem, at Easter, have long ornamental staffs, with which they strike the pavement and keep order as they precede the clergy marching round the Tomb of Christ. In France and other countries the beadle has a staff when he goes before the clergy, with which he keeps order during service.

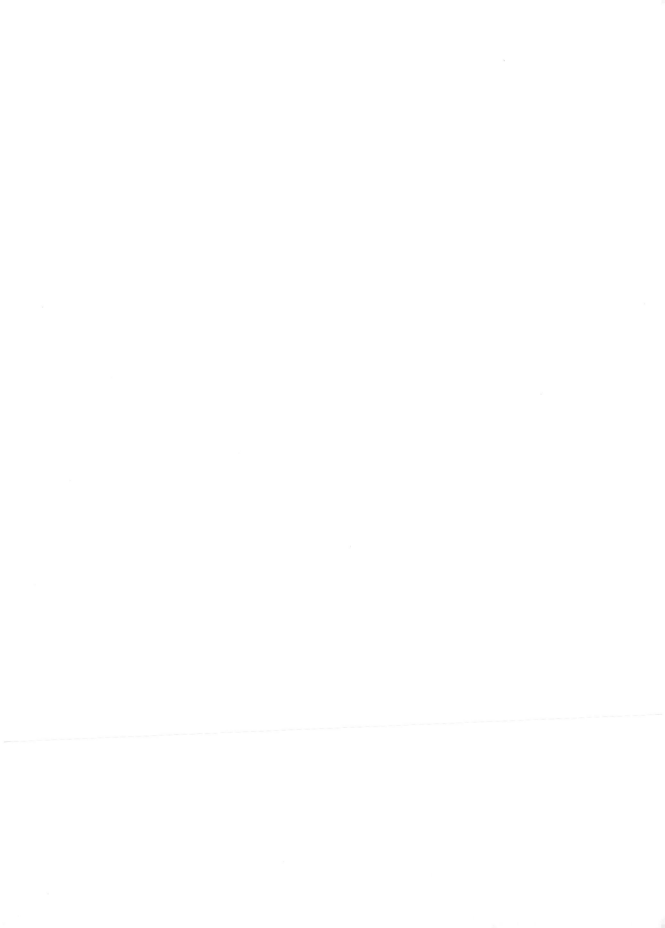

THE FOURTH PART.

HOW CHRIST AND THE APOSTLES SAID THE MASS.

X.—HOW CHRIST AND THE APOSTLES PREPARED FOR THE FIRST MASS.

IF a reporter had been present when the Lord and his apostles prepared for and said the first Mass, with what avidity we would now read the account. But, the Gospels excepted, no details have been recorded, and we must look to the Jewish rites and customs of that epoch.

In Hebrew writings, Temple and synagogue services, in the works of the Fathers, in Catholic and non-Catholic writings relating to the Passover, we find a wealth of lore we now weave together to tell the story of the first Mass. We do not hold that they are absolutely exact, but they are as nearly true as possible after the lapse of centuries.

It was the eve of Passover, the 13th day of the moon of the month of Abib or Nisan,[1] after the spring equinox, corresponding to our 6th of April; in the year A. D. 34; 4088 years after Adam's creation, 788 after Rome's foundation,[2] the ninth year of Pilate's government, when Herod Antipas had ruled Galilee thirty-three years, Pomponius Flaccus, father of the emperor, being ruler of Syria, when Tiberius had sat twenty years on Cæsar's throne, when Joseph Caiphas had pontificated for sixteen years, forty-four years after Herod dedicated his famous Temple, that our story begins. A month before the Jews began these preparations they called the Paraceve.[3] They

[1] Babyl Talmud, Tract Pesachim, c i   [2] Stapfer Palestine, p. 474   [3] Mat. xxvii 62; Mark xv 42, Luke xxiii, 54; John xix. 14, 31, 42.

had fixed the roads leading up to the sacred city, white-
washed the tombs, cleaned the streets, set their houses in
order to receive the great throngs of strangers from all the
nations, who would flock to Jerusalem to celebrate the
Passover. The Law of Moses required every Hebrew
within fifteen miles of the city, who was of age, and free
from legal blemish, "to appear before the Lord" in his
sanctuary on this day they called Haggadah, "Showing
Forth," because every Jew was to come up to Jerusalem
and "show himself" in the Temple as the Lord had commanded.[1] This law bound every Hebrew, who was not
defiled, sick, or had a legal reason for not coming. Those
who could not come this day were to come and be present
at the second Passover held for them a month later.

They divided up into "bands" of ten to twenty members, each bringing his gifts for the feast. Generally the
leader of each "band" brought the lamb on his shoulders
to the Temple. One would buy the wine, another the
flour for the cakes, another the bitter herbs, another the
candles, and the others the food required. This custom
was continued in the early Church, and they brought
gifts each Sunday and placed them on a table in the
sanctuary at the offertory of the Mass, whence the name
"offertory," from the offerings of the people, which in
that day were divided into different parts,—one for the
support of the clergy, another for the maintaining of the
religious buildings, and another for the support of the
poor, the widows and orphans.

In the days of Christ, Jerusalem was much larger than
now, extending south and taking in the large Sion quarter.
The fixed population of the city was about 100,000 inhabitants, whole families living in one small room. But
at Passover nearly 3,000,000 strangers from all the
nations into which the Jews had scattered and engaged
in trade used to come up to the Holy City, according to
the Laws of Moses, to celebrate the feast. They camped
on the hills and filled the valleys all around the sacred
city, covering the country for miles in all directions.

Since Moses' day they had chosen the lamb on the 10th
day of the moon of the lunar month of Abib or Nisan,[2]

---

[1] Exod. xiii. 8; Edersheim. Temple, 183, Life of Christ, I, 229 to 246, 366, 378;
V. II, 479 to 619, etc   [2] Exod xii. 3-6.

and condemned the victim to death.   There was a prophecy in this.   For this year the 10th day fell on Monday, and that day the local Sanhedrin or the Jerusalem Jewish Court, met and handed down a decree to execute the death sentence on Jesus, pronounced a month before by the great national Court of seventy-one judges.[1]

The sentence was to put him to death as soon as they could without rousing the people.   But the prophecies stated and the Temple ceremonial showed that he was to die not that day but on the following Friday   Therefore Christ did not return to Bethany that night, for they would find him in Lazarus' house and kill him.   Where did he hide?

A little below the summit of Olivet, whence he later ascended, was a cave in the dry limestone rock, its mouth then hidden by bushes, where watchmen guarding flocks and watching gardens retired in storms and slept at night.   The cave extended forty feet north and south and was about fifteen feet wide.   In it were four tables, seats, beds, etc.   There the Lord with his apostles spent the three nights before his death.   There he had taught his apostles the Lord's Prayer.   There before they separated after the ascension, they composed the Apostles' Creed.   It is called now the Grotto of the Creed.   In the same inclosure, a little higher up, now stands a large building erected by a French countess, with the Lord's Prayer carved in thirty-five languages of the great nations on its walls.   The first bishops of Jerusalem mention the Grotto of the Creed, many writers visited it, and in the early ages pilgrimages used to be made to it.   A few hundred feet lower rises the church of the Dominus flevit: "The Lord wept," where Jesus wept over Jerusalem. Measuring with instruments, the floor of the church was found to be on a level with the spring of the arch of the Mosque of Omar, so that before his eyes across the Cedron vale, then rose the great buildings of the famous Temple   A little south of the Grotto you can enter the tombs of the Hebrew prophets, who foretold in minute details the Saviour's life and death.   But because they had denounced the Hebrews for their sins, the most of them were killed.   Down deep in the limestone rock, you

[1] John xi. 47-53.

will find half-circle galleries and places for thirty-one bodies ; but they are empty now.

The great throngs were very busy that Monday ; all was turmoil, talk and excitement, for that day they selected the lambs for the Passover. The men of the bands first bought and washed the lamb, and called it " The Lamb of God " as they condemned it to death.

First they washed the victim to image the Passover bath the Lord took with his apostles before the Last Supper. They scented the animal with costly perfume,[1] to foretell the perfume of holiness and good works performed by Jesus. Then they tied the little victim to a colored stake [2] emblematic of Jesus fastened to his bloody cross. This was the way the lamb was prepared from Moses' day to prophesy the future Passion of the " Lamb of God," who was to take away the sins of the world.[3] A hundred and forty times the Old Testament mentions the lamb as a type of Christ, and thirty-four times calls the Lord "the Lamb." [2]

Each morning the Lord, leading his band of twelve apostles, went out of his hiding-place in the Grotto, went down the hill thronged with Jews born of Juda's tribe, and passed the day in the Temple instructing, preaching, healing all diseases, and at nightfall he returned to his hiding-place. The sermons in the Temple, his burning denouncement of the Scribes and Pharisees will be found in the Gospels. The money-changers used to turn into the Temple treasury, as discounts, $380,000 a year, and $45,000 of that went into the pockets of the high priests. When Christ drove them out of the Women's Court, which they disturbed during divine service, he roused the priests to the highest fury. But they feared the people during the day and they could not find him at night on Olivet.

Eve of Passover, of Pentecost, of Day of Atonement were days of fasting and of prayer,[4] and the custom comes down to us in fasting and prayers on the eves of feasts.[5] Therefore Christ with his apostles passed Wednesday in the Grotto in fasting and praying, preparing for

[1] Edersheim, Life of Christ, i 343   [2] Zanolini, De Festis Judæorum, C 4.
[3] John i 29.   [4] Babyl Talmud, Tract Taaneth, "Fasting," pp. 80, 88, 89, etc.
[5] St. Augustine, Enar in Psalm lxxxv. n xxiv.

his death, and that retreat was the model of these retreats people make before ordination or undertaking important works.

From the days of Esdras Thursday was a day of fasting and prayer,[1] because that day Moses began his fast on Sinai before receiving the Ten Commandments and the Law.[2] The Jews, who could not attend the Temple services, fasted in their homes or synagogues for four days before the Passover, taking neither food or drink till sunset.[3]

In memory of the escape of the first-born of the Hebrews when the Angel of death killed the first-born of every Egyptian family the night of the flight from Egyptian bondage, the first-born of every family down the ages kept a still stricter fast on the day of the Passover. This fast the Jews still observe, and their Form of Service of the Passover of our day has the following rubric: "All the first-born fast in commemoration of the deliverance of the first-born of the Israelites when God smote all the first-born of the Egyptians" (p. 3).

Christ and his apostles were therefore obliged to fast, because it was the eve of the feast and because it was Thursday.[4] The Lord was bound by the law of the first-born, and they came to the Last Supper fasting. Therefore in every age coming down from the apostles, Church law and custom have prevailed, that the celebrant of the Mass and those who receive Communion must be fasting, the sick alone excepted. It is still the law in every Oriental church.

Law and custom enforced not only fasting, but directed every Hebrew on the eve of the Day of Atonement and of Passover to take part in the Temple ceremonial of preparation for the feast. There they prayed and confessed their sins, as to-day the people come to the church to confess and to prepare for our feasts. Let us see what Jewish writers say of these preparations we imagine Christ and his apostles attended because they followed every law and custom of their glorious Temple.[5]

[1] Palestine in Days of Christ, p. 381   [2] Babyl Talmud, Baba Kamma, vol 82-1; Edersheim, Life of Christ, ii 291; Levit xvi 29; Joel i 14|; Acts xiii. 2, etc: Judges xx 26, 1 Kings vii 6, etc.   [3] Edersheim, Temple, 300; Zanolini, De Festis Judæorum, C 4   [4] Babyl Talmud, Tract Taanith, cap iv p. 78, etc   [5] See Passover, cap iii pp 95, 97, Tract Taanith, pp 36, 42, 75.

21

A whole Tract of the Talmud [1] devoted to this subject of fasting, gives minute details of the Jewish fasts before great feasts, and in times of public calamities. The details are too numerous to give here. They were also forbidden to do any kind of work, light a fire, or even prepare food, and Jews of our day observe some of these regulations.[2]

This eve, of Passover and of Sabbath was called by Grecian Jews the Paraceve, "preparation."[3] St. Augustine says that in his day Christians called the eve of Easter the "pure supper."[4] The Passover being the greatest of the Jewish feasts, as Easter is the chief Church feast, the Hebrews began the solemn preparations in the Temple and synagogues the evening before—that is, on the eve of the Passover. St. Augustine writes that the eve of Easter, now called Holy Saturday, is the mother of all the eves of the feasts of the Church [5] Let us see what the Talmud says regarding the preparations for the Passover.

"Mishna: The following religious acts may be done during the whole of the day on which they are obligatory: The reading of the Megilla, the Hallel, the sounding of the trumpet, the handling of the Lalub, the prayer at the additional offering, the additional offering, the confession of sin at the sacrificing of the bulls, the confession to be made on bringing the second tithe, the confession of sin by the high-priest on the Day of Atonement, the imposition of hands on the sacrifice, the slaughtering of a sacrifice, the waving of the offering. (In the form of a cross as already explained) the bringing it to the altar, the taking of the handful of flour [6] the burning with insence of the fat of a sacrifice on the altar."[7]

The Talmud goes into minute details of the services and ceremonials of the Jewish church at the time it was written, many of these ceremonies with hardly a change we find in the ceremonies of the Church. We cannot give them all because they would alone fill a large book. But we will here show how they prepared for the Passover on the paraceve, "the preparation."[8]

"On the eve of the Day of Atonement (or of Passover)

[1] Taanith, "Fasting"   [2] Babyl Talmud, cap x , p 224.   [3] Dupreon, Concor S Scripturæ, Paraceve   [4] Sermo ccxxi In Vegel Pas ni   [5] Sermo ccxix in Vigil Paschæ 1   [6] Levit i 15   [7] Babyl. Talmud, Tract Megilla, Cap. ii. 55. [8] See Babyl Talmud, Passover xi. 210.

it is forbidden to eat and drink, to wash, anoint, lace shoes or have sexual intercourse.[1] The one who broke these laws suffered Kareth, "excommunication." Children need not fast, but when one to two years old they must, so as to become accustomed to obey the religious commandments. If one has eaten or drunk through forgetfulness, he must bring a sin-offering; if he has eaten and worked he must bring two. From dawn of day (This was Wednesday of Passion week) they must begin, but a pregnant woman who longs for food, and the sick were allowed to eat a little, the food being given them under medical direction."

To the Temple came the people on the eve of the feast to confess their sins, each bringing different offerings and victims to be sacrificed for different sins.[2] They excited themselves to acts of sorrow and contrition and were truly penitent, many pages are devoted to this subject. Let us take a passage.

"Penance is great, so that it brings redemption. 'And there shall come a Redeemer to Sion, and to them that return from iniquity in Jacob, saith the Lord,"[3] which means, 'Why is the Redeemer come?' Because Jacob has returned from transgression. Penance is great, even the sins that have been done intentionally, are considered as done unintentionally, as it is written, 'Return, O Israel, to the Lord thy God, for thou hast fallen down by thy iniquity.'[4] Penitence is great. 'And when the wicked shall depart from his wickedness, and shall do judgments and justice, he shall live in them.'[5] One is from love, the other from fear. Penitence is great, it causes a man to live long, as it is written, 'he shall live.' The way of the Holy One, blessed be He, are not like the ways of man.[6]

They came into the Temple and confessed their sins to the priests as to-day Christians come to the churches to confession the day before the Easter feast. They humbled themselves before the Eternal of their forefathers, and over them the priests prayed for forgiveness.

"The Rabbis taught: The sins one has confessed on one Day of Atonement, he need not confess on the next Day

---

[1] Deut. viii. 3.   [2] See Edersheim, Temple p. 87.   [3] Isaias lix. 20.   [4] Osee xiv. 2.
[5] Ezechiel xxxiii. 19.   [6] Yomah viii. 136.

of Atonement. This is the case if he has not repeated his sin, but in that case, he should repeat the confession. If without having sinned again, he confessed again, then to him applies the verse, 'As the dog returneth to his vomit, so is the fool that repeateth his folly.'[1] Rabbi ben Jacob however said, 'So much the more he may be praised as it is written,[2] For I know my iniquity, and my sin is always before me.'"[3]

"When he confesses, he must specify his sin, as it is written, ' This people hath sinned a grievous sin, and they have made themselves gods of gold.'"[4] Why then has Moses specified the sin ?

The Rabbis taught the duty of confession is on the eve of the Day of Atonement (and Passover) when it grows dark Still the Rabbis said, one should confess previously to the meal, for if something happened to him at his meal, he will have remained without confession. But although one has confessed before the meal, he should confess again in the evening, and once more the next morning, and in the additional Minchab prayer and the concluding N'ilah prayer.[5]

"At what place in the prayer should he confess? an individual at the end of the prayer, and the reader of the congregation in the middle of the prayer. What shall he say ? He shall begin : ' Thou knowest the secrets of the world.' ' From the depths of the heart.' ' In thy Law it is written thus.' ' Lord of the Universe, not for our merits do we pray Thy mercy.' 'Our transgressions are too numerous to be counted, and our sins too mighty to be told.' 'My God, before I was created, I had not been worthy to be made, and now when I am created, I am the same as before. I am earth during my life, and so much more when I am dead. May it be Thy will that I may sin no more. I am a vessel before Thee full of disgrace and shame.'"

As a sign of sorrow they struck their breasts as the celebrant and his ministers still do at the General Confession at Mass " Lamenting is by striking the breast for thus it is written."[6]

That vast congregation, formed of Jews from fartherest

---

[1] Prov. xxvi 11   [2] Yomah viii 137   [3] Psalm l 5   [4] Exod. xxxii. 31.   [5] Yomah viii. 140, 141.   [6] Isaias xxii 12 ; Luke xviii 23-48.

ends of earth that Wednesday evening, bent their bodies down before the veil closing the dread Holy of Holies, of the Lord of hosts, where formerly, in the form of the Shekina, God Eternal their King dwelled. It was the morning light of Christianity rising over mankind. Silently, walked the Levites with torches lighting the thousands of candles to illuminate the courts with the prayer:

"Blessed art thou, O Lord, King of the Universe, who hast sanctified us by Thy commandments, and ordered us to kindle the Passover light."

They began the evening prayers with the Shema: "Hear, O Israel," etc., and then said the following prayers:

"Thou hast chosen us from all peoples," etc. "O, our God, and the God of our fathers, may our remembrance rise, and come, and be accepted before Thee, with the remembrance of our fathers; of the Messiah the Son of David, thy servant; of Jerusalem the holy city, and of all Thy people, the house of Israel, bringing deliverance and well-being, grace and loving-kindness, mercy, life and peace on this Day of Atonement.[1] Remember us, O Lord, our God, for our well-being; be mindful of us for blessing, and save us unto life; by Thy promise of salvation and mercy spare us, and be gracious unto us. Have mercy on us, and save us, for our eyes are bent on Thee, because thou art a gracious and merciful God and King."

Unseen grace coming from future merits of the Crucified streamed down that night into repenting hearts of Israel's children, rousing them to realize the wickedness of sin. Brighter rose the aurora, the morning light of Christianity, since Moses, coming from the foreknowledge of the true Day of Atonement, that terrible Good Friday of the crucifixion. In the days of which we write, during the Ten Days of Penance, on the New Moon, on the Seven days of Passover, on the eve of the Atonement, great throngs gathered in the Temple, body and soul bowed down before the Holy of Holies, while that cry of anguish poured out the following before the Lord of hosts:

O, Our Father, Our King. } We have sinned before Thee, We have no King but Thee.

[1] Or of the Passover.

O, Our Father, Our King.

Deal with us for Thy name's sake.
Let a happy year begin for us.
Nullify all evil decrees against us.
Nullify the designs of those who hate us.
Make the counsel of our enemies of no effect.
Rid us of every oppressor and adversary.
Close the mouths of our adversaries and accusers.
Of pestilence, sword, famine, captivity and destruction rid
    the children of Thy covenant.
Withhold the plague from Thine inheritance.
Forgive and pardon all our iniquities
Blot out our sins and make them pass away before Thine eyes.
Erase, in Thine abundant mercies, all records of guilt.
Bring us back in perfect repentance unto Thee.
Send perfect healing to the sick of Thy people.
Let Thy remembrance of us be for good.
Write us in the book of happy life.
Inscribe us in the book of redemption and salvation.
Let salvation soon spring forth for us.
Exalt the Horn of Israel Thy people.
Hear our voice, spare us, and have mercy on us.
Open the gates of heaven unto our prayer.
We pray Thee turn us not back empty from Thy presence.

The priestly and Levite choirs formed of 1,000 men sang the first words, " O, our Father, our King," and the vast congregation filling the great Courts sang the forty-three responses. The high priest ended the Litany with these words:

" O, our Father, our King, be gracious unto us, and answer us, for we have no good work of our own, deal with us in charity and kindness and save us

" In the book of life with blessing, peace and good sustenance, may we be remembered and inscribed before thee, we and all thy people, the house of Israel, for a happy life, and for peace. Blessed art Thou, O Lord, who makest peace.

" O, our God, and the God of our fathers, let our prayer come before Thee ; hide not thyself from our supplications, for we are not arrogant and stiff-necked, that we should say before Thee, O Lord, our God, and the God of our fathers, we are not righteous we have sinned ; truly we have sinned.

" We have trespassed ; we have been faithless ; we have robbed ; we have spoken basely ; we have committed iniquity ; we have worked injustice ; we have been presumptuous ; we have done violence ; we have forged lies ;

we have counseled evil; we have spoken falsely; we have scoffed; we have revolted; we have blasphemed; we have acted perversely; we have transgressed; we have been rebellious; we have been stiff-necked; we have done wickedly; we have corrupted ourselves; we have committed abomination; we have gone astray; we have been led astray.

"We have turned aside from Thy commandments and good judgments, and it hath profited us naught. But Thou art just in all that is come upon us, for Thou hast acted truthfully, but we have wrought injustice.

"What shall we say before Thee, O Thou, who dwellest on high, and what shall we recount unto Thee, who abidest in the heavens? dost Thou not know all things, both hidden and revealed?

"Thou knowest the secrets of eternity, and the most hidden mysteries of all living. Thou searchest the innermost recesses, and triest the reins and heart. Naught is concealed from Thee, or hidden from Thine eyes.

"May it then be thy will, O Lord, our God, and the God of our fathers, to forgive us for all our sins, to pardon us for all our iniquities, and to grant us forgiveness for all our transgressions.

For the sin which we have committed before Thee.

Under compulsion or of our own will.
In the hardening of the heart.
Unknowingly.
With the utterance of the lips.
By unchastity.
Openly and secretly.
Knowing and deceitfully.
In speech.
By wronging our neighbor.
By the sinful meditating of the heart.
By associating with impurity.
By confession with the mouth alone.
By despising parents and teachers.
In presumption or in error.
By violence.
By the profanation of the divine Name.
By unclean lips.
By folly of the mouth.
By evil inclination.
Wittingly or unwittingly, etc.

The petitions numbered fifty-four, of which we have given the first twenty. At the end of each petition the high priest prayed in a mournful chanting tone while cries and sobs fills Jehovah's sacred building.

" For all these, O God of forgiveness and pardon, grant us remission."

Did Christ say over his apostles the words of absolution forgiving them their sins, that in the state of grace they might receive the two sacraments of Holy Orders and Communion the next day at the Passover? We find no record. But it is probable, for He forgave the sins of others.[1] These sacraments must now be received in a state of grace. After the resurrection he gave them power to forgive sins, saying, " Whose sins you shall forgive, they are forgiven them; and whose you shall retain they are retained."[2] There was nothing striking or unusual to them in confession of sins, for they had seen multitudes go to confession every eve of Atonement and of Passover whenever they attended the Temple on these days. Christ simply raised the Temple sacramental confession of the old Testament coming down from Moses, to the higher dignity of a sacrament of the New Testament.

The Temple Litany we have given was the origin of the General Confession or Confiteor said at the beginning of Mass, and was the model of the Litanies of the Church. The Great Petition of St. Chrysostom's Liturgy followed to-day by the Greek, Sclavonic and Oriental Christians, resembles this Temple Litany.

The Talmud goes into minute details regarding this general confession in the Temple and Jews followed the custom in the synagogues down to our day.

Confession has been fiercely attacked by people who do not know the Temple customs of the time of Christ. The Jew confessed his sins with sorrow for his wickedness, and he was animated with the love of God when he recited each day the Shema, " Thou shalt love the Lord," etc.[3] Those who had a perfect love of God above all, received forgiveness, because perfect love—called perfect charity— wiped out sin in every age. This was the way patriarchs, holy prophets, priests and saints of the Old Testament received forgiveness of their sins. The Jews of our time do not carry out all these rites regarding confession on the eve of the Passover. But on the Day of Atonement, they

---

[1] Matt. ix. 2; Mark ii 5-9; Luke v. 20, vii. 48   [2] John xx. 23.   [3] Deut. vi. 5.

gather in their synagogues, and observe many of these regulations. Religious communities still tell their faults and their infractions of the Rule before the whole community, or to the superior. But they are forbidden to tell their sins except to a duly authorized priest. Often at prayer meetings members of Protestant denominations tell their sins and the graces they received—the custom coming down from before the reformation.

The exercises in the early Church on Holy Saturday, preparing for Easter, copied from these Temple customs, were very long. St. Augustine tells us that he was so tired after these exercises one Easter that he could only preach a short sermon of only eleven lines.[1]

Priests, Levites, men and women, not only confessed their sins in public in the Temple but asked the others to pray for them, and the high priest and the priest said prayers of absolution over them, as the celebrant of the Mass still says the words of absolution over the people after the general Confession at Mass.

Following this Temple ceremony, the early Christians confessed their sins to the bishop and his twelve priests— forming a court—whence confession is called a tribunal, and the bishop and priests pronounced the words of absolution over them. Before this court, in public, men and women confessed before the congregation their sins, and these so shocked the people that the Church made a law that in future sins must be confessed in private to the bishop and his court. Later the custom obtained of confessing to a priest in private, and thus began our present discipline relating to confession.[2]

The high priest chants in mournful minor key:

" And also for the sins for which we are liable to any of the four death penalties inflicted by the court—stoning, burning, beheading and strangling, for the violation of positive, or for the violation of negative precepts, whether the latter do or do not admit of a remedy by the subsequent fulfilment of a positive command,[3] for all our sins, whether they be or not be manifest to us. Such sins as are mani-

---

[1] St. Augustine, Sermon, 320, die Paschæ See Migne, Cursus Comp S Scripturæ, iii 1052   [2] See Chardon, Histoire des Sacraments, in Migne, Cursus Com S Theologia   [3] A Note in the Liturgy says : " Such for example are the laws forbidding work on the Sabbath, and leaven bread to be eaten on the Passover, to each of them the statement applies,"

fest to us, we have already declared and confessed unto Thee, while such as are not manifest[1] unto us are known to Thee, according to the word that has been spoken. 'The secret things belong unto the Lord, our God, but the things that are revealed belong unto us, and to our children forever,' that we may do all the words of this Law. For thou art the forgiver of Israel, and the pardoner of the tribes of Jeshurun in every generation, and beside Thee we have no king, who pardoneth and forgiveth."

The Temple gates of massive bronze were closed every night, locked, and the keys placed in a recess under a stone in the Chamber of the Beth Ha Moked, "The House of Stones," on which a priest slept. But this Wednesday night the gates were left open, for great crowds were continually passing back and forth. The Courts were filled with people, some standing, some kneeling, some prostrated on the ground, others spent the night bowing down till their foreheads touched the marble pavement. When you enter a church to-day on Easter eve and see the people gathered there in prayer and meditation confessing their sins, you can go back in thought to the Temple of Jehovah and imagine that scene when Jesus Christ with his apostles in his "Father's House"[2] prepared for the Last Supper and the awful scenes of his Passion.

When did Christ and his apostles leave the Temple for the Grotto on Olivet? Did he spend the whole night in the Temple in prayer as many pious Jews did before the Passover? we find no replies to these questions.

The next day, Thursday, at 9 A. M., they sacrificed the lamb with the daily ceremonial and began the sacrifice of the afternoon service, not at 3 P. M. as was the custom on ordinary days, but at 2.30 in order to get ready for the sacrifices of the paschal lambs they were to eat that evening in synagogue and homes of Jerusalem.

At two o'clock that Thursday afternoon, the chief Temple chassan notified the priests stationed on the Temple tower, at the southeast corner of the area, to sound the trumpets[3] to tell the assembled people that they were ready to sacrifice the paschal lambs.[4] At that moment Jesus

[1] That is, forgotten   [2] John 11 16   [3] Edersheim, Temple, 151.   [4] Geikie, Life of Christ, 1. 221, 222 ; 11 p 436.

Christ with his apostles came out of the Grotto, and went down the western slope of Olivet. According to the custom, Jesus, as Master of the band, carried the lamb on his shoulders as he is represented in the Catacombs and in Christian art.

By heart they knew the Psalms of the Temple Hymn-book, and they went down singing what the Jews called *Maaloth*, "the Pilgrims' Psalms." This the Hebrews always did when coming to the great feast of Israel. Christ, the Master, of the "band" intoned the first verse, the apostles responded with the second verse, and thus they went down the Olivet hill praising God in words of his father, the royal prophet David.[1]

"I have lifted up my eyes to the mountains," etc.[2]
"Praise the Lord, for he is good," etc.[3]

They pass on the right Annas' summer-house called the Beth Ini, "House of figs" shaded by two large cedars, with the dovecots, where this avaricious Jew had four shops for the sale of religious articles for the Temple services. There, more than thirty-four years before, the Lord's Mother, Mary, had bought the two pigeons she offered in the Temple the day of her purification.

The path leads down to the north of Gethsemane's walls, crosses the road leading out what is now called St. Stephen's Gate, running down through the Cedron vale, then over the southern slope of Olivet by Bethany down to Jericho. They crossed the bridge the high priests long before had thrown over the Cedron brook, that bridge over which the victims were driven for the Temple sacrifices, and over which they dragged the Lord that midnight after his arrest to fulfil these types.

They ascend the hill east of the Temple area, pass along the road leading to the Golden Gate entering into the sacred inclosure. That part, east of the Temple outside the walls, was then covered with houses belonging to the wealthy Nicodemus, Joseph of Arimathea and Joseph Caiphas the high priest.

They enter the rooms of the Gate where the judges used to hold court, and mount the steps leading up into the Temple area. That gate is now closed, for the prophet

---

[1] Psalms cxx. to cxxxv. [2] Ps. cxx. [3] Ps. cxxxv.

foretold [1] the Lord the Conqueror would enter by it, and the Moslems think some future victor will enter through it and capture the city.

Great multitudes filled the great Temple area, about 1,000 feet square.[2] They had gathered there from all the nations into which their fathers had been exiled since the Babylonian Captivity. There were merchant princes from Africa, strangers from Cyrene, now a part of Tunis, to which Ptolomeus had banished 110,000 of their fathers, members of the Scaramella family bankers of Alexandria, whose fathers had sent the magnificent bronzes of the Nicanor Gate, Jewish writers say was shipwrecked but saved by a miracle; Arab sheiks were seen with venerable white locks of hair hanging from under white turbans; leaders of desert tribes surrounded by their families with dark fillets of camel hair keeping on the turban; Scythian Jews from the north of Asia, garbed in fur of wolf and bear; Assyrian nobles clothed in purple and gold; Greco-Hebrews of noble bearing, instinct with the arts of Javan's sons, with whom they were reared and educated; Israelites from Germany, called by their brethren Askanez Jews; traders from imperial Rome and from Italian cities decked in toga and bejeweled in rare gems —Hebrews from all nations were there that day divided into bands of ten or more men, each leader of the band with a little lamb.[3]

All were talking or walking back and forth in the great cloisters, filling the Chol, mixing with heathens and crowding the Chel, where Israelites alone could enter. They were talking, disputing, arguing about the most minute points of the Law, the Prophecies, the Passover, the Temple and its services. Priests and officers of the Temple passed through the throngs, examining the lambs, and passing seals to leaders, whose lambs they found without blemish.[4]

The most interesting items of news related to the Rabbi Carpenter of Nazareth, who for more than three years had been going around Judea with twelve apostles and seventy-two disciples, followed by great multitudes of people he had healed of various diseases. He claimed to be the Mes-

[1] Ezech xliv 2. [2] Edersheim, Temple, 184. [3] See Geikie, Life of Christ, i. 470.
[4] See Edersheim, Temple, 183; Geikie, Life of Christ, i, 470.

siah foretold by the prophets. But they were not sure.
How many false Messiahs had risen and led them to death?
But, they argued, this man was different He had done
wonders. He had even raised from the dead Eleazar,
whom the Greeks named Lazarus, of Bethany, laid to rest
in the tomb twenty-eight steps down in the rock at
Bethany, after he had been four days dead Did not the
great prophet of David's family, Isaias, say "God himself will come and will save you. Then shall the eyes of
the blind be opened, and the ears of the deaf be un-
stopped Then shall the lame leap as the hart, and the
tongue of the dumb be free " [1]

This new Rabbi of Galilee had denounced the Scribes
and Pharisees, foretold the destruction of the city, the
ruin of the Temple. The priests had ejected him from
the sanctuary because he had driven out the money-
changers from the courts, etc. These were the discussions and the disputes heard on every side among the
vast crowds filling the Temple area

It was nearly half-past three when Christ leading his
band of twelve apostles entered the great Nicanor Gate
of Corinthian bronze. The lamb had been sacrificed, the
incense offered in the Holies, and the priests and Levites
were ready to immolate the paschal lambs. Twenty-four
Levites formed two long lines leading up to the great gate.
One line had gold staves and the other silver staves in their
hands to keep order. Each strikes the pavement with his
staff as a sign of authority, while the chief chazzan cries
out, "People of the Lord, listen, the time for sacrificing
the paschal lamb has arrived in the name of Him who
rests in this holy house." [2]

With two other bands the Lord and his apostles enter
the Priest's Court, Christ carrying the lamb on his
shoulders as leader.[3] To the north of the great altar
with its three ever-burning fires on top, they pass and
Christ lays down the lamb A priest comes forward
and receives the seal the examiner had given them without
the Courts, testifying that the lamb was without blemish.

They pour a chalice of wine on the lamb, emblem of
the Eucharist, uniting Passover and Mass with Temple

[1] Isaias xxxv 4-6 [2] Talmud, Yomah, Appendix. [3] Exod. xxiii. 15, Deut.
xvi. 17; Mishna, Chag. 1, 2, etc

sacrifices. They tie his feet with a cord, the right fore foot to the left hind foot, and the left fore foot to the right hind foot, making with the cord a cross, uniting the lamb with Calvary's cross [1] They wash again the victim with perfumed water, showing forth the odor of miracles of Christ's humanity. They give it a drink of water to prophesy the vinegar and gall they offered the Victim of the cross.[2]

The members of each band now approach, lay their hands on the lamb's head, while the attending priests lay on their hands—all hands are held with thumbs crossed, palms down while they together recite.[3]

" Ah, Jehovah, they have committed iniquity—they have transgressed; they have sinned—Thy people, the house of Israel. Oh, then, Jehovah, cover over, I entreat Thee, cover over their transgressions, and their sins, which they have wickedly committed, transgressed, and sinned before Thee—Thy people, the house of Israel, as it is written in the Law of Moses, saying, " For on that day it shall be covered for you, to make you clean from all your sins, before Jehovah ye shall be cleansed."

They put their hands under the lamb, raise him up as high as their heads, and offer him to the Lord as a victim of their sins. Thus from Moses' day the victims foretold Christ raised up on the cross.[4] Lowering him a little they " wave him " to the north, south, east and west, making with him a cross, to foretell the world's Victim crucified. These two ceremonies were carried out with every offering of Temple and Passover, and are still continued in the Mass, when the celebrant offers the bread and wine.

On the steps of the Nicanor Gate leading up from the Women's Court into the Court of Israel, its great bronze doors given by the Scaramella family of bankers of Alexandria, now swung wide open, stands a choir of 500 Levites, vested in white albs, bound by wide girdles with miters on their heads and the Book of the Psalms in their hands. Their sons stand with them and many have flute, cornet, harp and cymbals in their hands as the great organ with bellows of elephant hide burst forth in diapason melody and the men begin the base, the youths tenor, and the young boys soprano.

---

[1] See Balyl. Talmud, Passover, 255   [2] See Palestine , Edersheim, Life of Christ, i 378 ; Geikie, Life of Christ, etc   [3] See Bayl. Talmud. pp 119, 120, 155. [4] Levit iv, 15, xiv 21, xvi 21, iii 3-8, Edersheim, Temple, 88, 92, 230

In the Priests' Court, stand 500 priests of the rank of Abia, "the eighth," vested in rich robes of cloth of gold, embroidered in white, green, violet, and red, the sacred colors of the sanctuary of the Lord of hosts, God told Moses to make for Aaron and his sons. Miters are on their heads, their brows are bound round with tephilim, phylacteries are on their left arms next the heart, the strap wound round their arm seven times and circle their two fingers, but the feet are bare, for the ground where Abraham offered Isaac is holy.

All turn their backs to the east to mock the pagans worshiping the rising sun, moon and stars. They face the Holies and the Holy of Holies, where the Shekina, the Holy Ghost, once dwelled in their fathers' days. They face to the west, waiting, praying for, and expecting the Messiah, who was foretold to come, end, seal up, and fulfil these sacrificial types. They did not know it, but they faced towards that Calvary, 1,000 feet west, outside the walls, where the next day their Saviour was to die.

The priest drawn for that purpose, robed in red, now comes forward, and with sacrificial gem-incrusted knife he cuts the lamb's throat. Two long lines of priests vested in red robes magnificently embroidered in white, green, purple and red, range from the lamb on the north to the south side of the great altar, the priests of one line having each a gold cos or chalice and the priests of the other line silver chalices in their hands. Each cos was without a pedestal, so they could not be put down lest the blood might coagulate. The nearest priest catches the blood from the lamb's wounded throat in his cos held in his right hand, turns round, passes it into the right hand of the next priest, and takes the empty chalice from him. To do this, each must cross his arms. The one who receives the filled chalice turns around, and in the same way hands it to the next; thus forming a cross with their arms, as dying Jacob blessed Joseph's two sons,[1] the blood passes along that line of priests to the passage on the south leading up to the great altar. Thus the ceremony foretold the sacrifice of the cross.

The last priest of the lines to receive the chalice mounts to the altar up the inclined passage on the south side,

---

[1] Gen. xlviii. 14 to 19.

walks along the balustrade, and on the southeast horn he splashes the blood from below up, then another splash across. He does the same on the northeast, northwest and southwest horns—thus they mark the four horns of the great altar with a bloody cross to foretell Calvary's cross.[1]

Rapidly they go through the ceremonial they practised for a month, for there are thousands of lambs to be sacrificed before sunset. The lamb is now hung up on a hook from the marble pillar, his skin taken off, as the Lord was hung up to a pillar the next day and his skin torn off by the scourges. The entrails and fat are taken out, with the tail salted and burned on the altar as an offering to the Lord. The body of the lamb is rolled in the skin, Christ takes it again on his shoulders, and they pass out, their places being taken by another band.

During this sacrificial ceremony, on the steps of the Nicanor Gate stand 500 Levites who with young men and sons of the tribe and people sing the Hallel.[2] They begin with the Hebrew Hallelu-jah which now we pronounce Alleluia, "Praise Jehovah."

The Levites	Hallelu Jah
The People	Hallelu Jah.
The Levites	Praise, O servants of Jehovah.
The People	Hallelu Jah.
The Levites.	Praise the name of Jehovah.
The People.	Hallelu Jah.
The Levites	When Israel went out of Egypt.
The People.	When Israel went out of Egypt.
The Levites.	The house of Jacob from a barbarous people
The People.	Judea was made his sanctuary, Israel his dominion, etc.

Thus they sang to the end Psalm cxiii., then the next Psalm.

"I have loved because the Lord will hear the voice of my prayer," etc.[3]
"I have believed, therefore have I spoken,"
"But I have been humbled exceedingly," etc.[4]
"O praise the Lord, all ye nations," etc.[5]
"Give praise to the Lord, for he is good," etc.[6]

---

[1] Edersheim, Temple, p 88.   [2] Geikie, Life of Christ, i 373   [3] Psalm cxiv.
[4] Psalm cxv   [5] Psalm cxvi.   [6] Psalm cxvii.

When they came to the twenty-fifth verse of this Psalm its Hebrew words, Anna Adonai hoscihanna, "O Lord, save me: O Lord, give good success," are shouted as Hosanna with a mighty sound from the choirs of priests, Levites and people. This word is sung by the choir at every High Mass, at the Sanctus before the "Lamb of God" is sacrificed.

Hebrew writers tell us this was the great Egyptian Hallel, which differed from the common Hallel formed of Psalms cxix to cxxxv and pointed to five religious truths—the Delivery of the Hebrews from Egypt, the Passage through the Red Sea, the giving of the Law on Sinai, the coming of the Messiah and the general resurrection of the Dead.

The Son of God, carrying the lamb on his shoulders, with his apostles passes through the Women's Court down the Nicanor Gate steps, down into the Chel, down and into the Chol. For the last time leaves his Father's Temple he had visited and worshiped in so often since he had been confirmed at twelve with the laying on of the hands of its priesthood, when he argued with the doctors.[1]

The Temple of Moriah, "Jehovah provides," whose priesthood should have formed the foundations of his Church, had rejected him and condemned him to death. The magnificent ceremonial of the Sanctuary of the Lord foretelling him was to be completed and finished by passing into the Church ceremonies. But the Hebrew priesthood was to end as the prophets had foretold. But he would not leave the world without an official teaching body, else the modern world would have been inferior to the olden days.

He was about to found a priesthood, which was not to pass away like that of Aaron sacrificing suffering victims in the Temple. That new priesthood was to be an eternal order of priests, according to that of Melchisedech, offering him under forms of bread and wine among the nations till the end.

A great bridge then led from Moriah with its Temple to that other, higher and holier hill, Sion, mentioned a hundred and seventy-one times in the Old Testament. Patriarch, prophet and ancient seers of Israel seem to

---

[1] Luke ii 42

22

exhaust words foretelling Sion's glorious future, because there the first Mass was to be offered.   Numerous are the Scripture texts of prophets hundreds of years before foretelling Christ that day leading his apostles to Sion, to say the first Mass and ordain them bishops, that they might sit on their episcopal thrones among the heathens. We will cite only two texts.

"The Lord hath prepared his arm,
    In the sight of all the Gentiles.
Depart ye, go out from thence,
Touch no unclean thing.
Go out of the midst of her.
Be clean you that carry
The vessels of Jehovah.
For Jehovah shall go before you,
And the Lord, the God of Israel,
Will gather you together." [1]

"For the Lord hath chosen Sion,
    He hath chosen it for his dwelling place.
This is my rest forever and ever ;
Here will I dwell, for I have chosen it.
I will clothe her priests with salvation,
And let thy saints rejoice,
The Lord hath sworn the truth to David,
And he will not make it void,
Of the fruit of thy body I will set upon thy throne.
Their children forevermore shall sit upon thy throne." [2]

There was foretold his Church wherein the Prince of the House of David now rests enthroned in our tabernacle and sacrificed by priests according to Melchisedech's order, the patriarchal priesthood of the fathers of our race coming down from Abel and from Adam.

What did Christ do when the Temple priesthood rejected him? He went beyond the Temple ceremonial and Jewish priesthood to the patriarchal Passover, and changed it into the new and eternal sacrifice. He did not found his Church and priesthood on the Temple and its priesthood, for these were to pass away. The Mass with its ceremonial comes directly from the Passover and only indirectly from the Temple, for the latter was but an extension, a development of the ancient Passover Although we find the Temple ceremonies in the Mass and in our Church ceremonial, yet we trace them directly to

[1] Isaias lii. 10.   [2] Psalm cxxxi. 8-14.

the Last Supper which Christ and his apostles held that night as the Hebrew Passover.

The apostles wondered where they were to hold the feast, and while crossing the great bridge they turn to Jesus. 'Whither wilt thou that we go and prepare to eat the pasch?'[1] And he said to Peter and John, 'Go and prepare us the pasch that we may eat.' But they said : 'Whither wilt thou that we prepare?' And he said to them, 'Behold as you go into the city, there shall meet you a man carrying a pitcher of water, follow him into the house, which he entereth, and you shall say to the master of the house, say to him the Master saith, 'My time is near at hand. I will keep the pasch at thy house with my disciples.'[2] 'The Master saith to thee, 'Where is the guest-chamber, where I may eat the pasch with my disciples?' 'And he will show you a large dining-room furnished, and there prepare for us.' And his disciples went their way and came into the city, and they found as he had told them, and they prepared the pasch."[3]

They were crossing the bridge when Jesus sent his two chief apostles on ahead. Herod the Great had built this bridge to replace the one Solomon had stretched across the Tyropœon vale separating Moriah from Sion. In the middle of the valley far below, separating the sacred hills within the Holy City, then ran north and south the Cheesemongers' Street, where farmers gathered on Mondays, Thursdays and feasts to sell their produce. The bridge was of the yellow limestone of Judea, 125 feet over the street, supported by arches $41\frac{1}{2}$ feet wide east and west by 50 feet, the width of the bridge, which was 350 feet long, uniting Moriah and Sion, its eastern end debouching into the southern part of the Temple area. Some of the stones were from 20 to 40 feet long, weighing over 109 tons. The writer measured one of the stones laid by Solomon in the Temple foundations near where this bridge ended, and found it $17\frac{1}{2}$ long and three feet high—how far it extended into the wall he could not tell.[4] The broken eastern abutment of the fallen bridge is now called "Robinson's Arch."

[1] Mark xiv 12   [2] Matt. xxvi. 18   [3] Luke xxii 11 ; Mark xiv. 16   [4] See Edersheim, Temple, p 19.

Peter and John hurried ahead, crossed the bridge to David Street, turned south, passed Annas' and Caiphas' palaces, and near the Sion Gate they met the man with a pitcher of the "Water of Precept," for the Passover. The man, whose name is not given by any writer, had drawn that water from a well dug deep down in the lime-stone rock at the eastern end of a bridge the high priests had stretched over the Cedron brook a little south of Gethsemane where the well may still be seen.

The man was bringing that water to the Cenacle to mix with the flour for the Passover cakes. To him they told the Master's message, then they followed him to the tomb of David, and told the keeper of the Cenacle what the Lord had directed them to say.

Jerusalem belonged to all the people of Israel. The line dividing the lands of Juda's tribe from the Benja-mites passed through the center of the Temple, and con-tinued westward till it divided Calvary at the spot where next day stood the cross. This division was made so no tribe could claim the Holy City as its own property. Whence no one owned a house in Jerusalem, for it be-longed to all the tribes.[1] The families who lived in the houses had only the right of occupation. They were for-bidden to rent a house, and dwelling-houses and lands were given by lot. At the Passover, every house was open to the strangers, no one was ever refused bed and board at this time, and hospitality was boundless during the feasts.[2] The man who would refuse a Passover pil-grim the use of his house would expose his family to the execration of the whole population.[3]

The celebrated Chamber over the tombs of the kings, the Greeks called Anageon, the Hebrews Aliyah, mean-ing "High," or "Beautiful," and the Romans, the Cenacle, "The Banquet Hall." St. Luke's Greek Gospel has the words : "And he will show you the great Cenacle fur-nished, there prepare."[4] The word is *estromenon* "fur-nished," and the words mean the same as what we say when we speak of "a furnished house" ready to be oc-cupied. The Cenacle or upper chamber had the Bema or

---

[1] Talmud, Yomah, 12a.   [2] See Migne, Cursus Comp. S. Scripturæ, v. ii. 918, 1172, etc   [3] Edersheim, Temple, p 17; Life of Christ, ii. p. 484; Acts xii, 13; Geikie, Life of Christ, ii 116, 484, 578.   [4] Luke xxii 12.

sanctuary for the synagogue services, the Aaron with the sacred Scrolls, the hanging lamb before the Law, the candles on the ark, the seven-branched candlestick, the pulpit, the table in the middle of the chamber, the couches on which to recline and all things required for the great feast of Israel.

The Cenacle was filled with people preparing for the feast, and according to the custom, entering the two apostles said: Shalom Lachem, "Peace to you,"[1] or "Peace be with this house" and the people replied: "May your heart be enlarged." This was the Marahaba of the Hebrews, the Alaic of the Talmud, the Shelama of the ancient days of Melchisedech and Abraham, the name the former called Sion, Salem, "Peace," the greeting of friends as we say: "How do you do?" They used to greet each other with the words: "Peace be with you," as the pontificating bishop says to the people, or "The Lord be with you," as the priest says seven times during Mass sending the Holy Spirit to the people with his seven-fold gifts,[2]—the greetings going back, in sentiment at least, to the days when the great high priest Melchisedech founded Jerusalem.

To the keeper of the Cenacle the apostles delivered the Master's message. Christ was the Prince of the House of David, heir of the great kings sleeping in the rocky tombs beneath, and the palace belonged to his family. Through his Mother he was the direct representative of David's royal family, had the highest title to the building and that was the reason that the Cenacle was given him in which to celebrate the feast with his apostles.

All in the place gather round the two apostles, for this day of the Passover, stranger was more honored than the master of the house. For days they had been preparing for the great feast. They had cleaned and washed the floors of the great Cenacle Hall, wherein synagogue Sabbath and feasts had been celebrated since Herod had built the great Chamber over the tombs of Juda's famous kings. Peter and John, following their Master's words, "And there prepare for us,"[3] went to work helping in the Passover preparations.[4]

[1] Judges xix 20 [2] Isaias ii. 2. [3] Luke xxii 12; Mark xiv. 15. [4] Geikie, Life of Christ, i. 132 to 207; ii. 434 to 475, etc.

The Master, surrounded by his ten apostles, soon came
with the sacrificed, skinned lamb, rolled in its skin on his
shoulders, while the others carried the flour, wine, bitter
herbs, salt, vinegar, apples, nuts, almonds, candles and
things required for the feast. At the door the Lord
gave the lamb's skin to the keeper of the Cenacle, according to the custom.[1]

They laid the lamb on a table, and drove a stick of pomegranate wood, called *mechna*,[2] through his body, along the
backbone and through the tendons of his hind feet.
Carefully they open out the chest, as butchers still sometimes do, and place another stick of the same wood into the
tendons and small bones of the forefeet, opening out the
body so it will better roast.[3]

They are very careful not to break a bone, or they will
be punished with thirty-nine stripes.[4] This was the way
the lamb was crucified down the ages since Moses' day
to prophesy the body of the dead crucified Christ hanging by the nails through his feet and hands The Jews
not wishing to see such a striking emblem of the dead
Christ, left these details out of the Talmud. But the
early writers mention the crucified lamb and how it was
prepared.

Carefully they carry the lamb out into the yard, and
place it in the earthenware oven shaped like ancient round
beehive, and filled with burning charcoal. They rested
the lamb entirely on his cross because Jesus the next day
hung entirely from the nails. If any part of the lamb
touched the sides or door of the oven it was cut off as
being unclean.[5]

One stood by and turned the lamb, so the flesh might be
well roasted. The fire penetrates all parts, as the fire of
the Holy Ghost filled Christ, inspiring him with the love
of all mankind, moving him to die for our salvation. The
roasted, skinned lamb looked when done like the dead
body of Christ, his skin torn off with scourges, his wounds
yellow with dried serum. When he lay dead his body
looked as though it had been roasted. Thus was the
victim of the Passover prepared, sacrificed, skinned, cru-

[1] See Edersheim, Life of Christ, 492-505, for description of Last Supper
[2] Talmud, Pesachim, vii 12. [3] Justin Martyr, Dialog Cum Trypho Maimon
etc., Geikie, Life of Christ, i 206, etc. [4] Exod xii. 46. [5] Exod. xii 9, 11 Parap.
xxxv. 13, etc.

cified, roasted and eaten, down the ages, to foretell the
Lord condemned to death, arrested, scourged, crucified
and partaken in the Eucharist.

With the "water of precept," the man had drawn
from the deep well in the Cedron valley, the women mix
flour and make a dough they call the Mazzoth. They
roll the mass as thin as possible into four cakes called
ashishah, each as large as a dinner-plate. They imprint
in them with their fingers five holes, *challoth*, as they
thought to make them bake better, not knowing they
foretold the five wounds in the Lord's body when he was
dead.[1]

Perhaps these five finger-marks of the Passover cakes
give rise to the figures on our altar-breads. The best
examples we now see of these unleaven cakes are the altar
breads used in churches of the Latin Rite. Biscuits
"twice baked," crackers, etc., are made somewhat like
the unleaven bread and have designs like these ancient
cakes.

They prepare the three tables and the table linens, for
three cloths were spread over the cross table, the ends
hanging down to the floor, as you will see the ends of the
upper of the three altar cloths hangs down.

They get ready the candlesticks for the beeswax
candles, for no religious services was ever carried out in
Israel without these candles to remind them of the Messiah foretold to come and enlighten them with his teachings. Some not going deeply into Jewish rites think the
candles on our altars came from the Catacombs. But the
early Christians of Rome when using martyrs' tombs as
altars placed the candles on them because it was the
custom at the Jewish Passover and because they were
used at the Last Supper.

When the four cakes are baked, they anoint them with
olive oil in the form of the Greek cross, according to the
ancient custom, to make them emblematic of the expected
Messiah, in Hebrew "The Anointed," in Greek "The
Christ." These cakes were made generally the day before,
each of the four cakes being called *kiccar*, "circle." One
cake called the *challah*, "tithe of the dough," or *mata-
noth* they sent to the Temple priests as an offering. The

---

[1] Migne, Cursus Com S Scripturæ, n. 1335, 1045.

other three cakes they sprinkled with incense [1] to represent the Lord's body prepared with incense for the tomb.

They mix sage, raisins, chestnuts, figs, apples, vinegar,
etc, which they pound in a mortar and form into a
kind of salad they called the *chaseroth*, to remind them
of the mortar their fathers were forced to make in Egypt
under the Pharaohs. This is the way the dish is prepared
in our day. They used also eggs, Zis Sadai, and meat to
remind them of the Leviathan, "the elephant," and the
Behemoth" [2] Many strange fictions the Talmud gives
of these animals [3]

They prepare the couches round the tables for the
members of the "band," called *mesabbim*, "the recliners,"
and get ready all things required for this great feast of
Israel, of which Moses wrote: "Butter of the herd, and
milk of the sheep, with the fat of lambs, and of the rams,
of the breed of Basan, and goats, with the marrow of
wheat, and might drink the purest blood of the grape." [4]

On the table they place terra cotta lamps, [5] and beeswax candles, for the feast takes place at night, and they
must have light to read the words of the Passover Seder,
"Section" They decorate the table with vases of flowers,
and these are still continued in the candles and decorations of our altars. [6] Two flagons, one of wine, the other
of water, are on a small table on the left of the Master's
place, but on your right, for the Master faced the congregation, this table being in memory of the gold table in
the Holies of the Temple, on which rested the twelve
cakes and twelve gold flasks of the wine of proposition.

They adorn the walls of the Cenacle with green bows,
palm branches, and costly curtains, in remembrance of
the thirteen veils of the Temple. On the floor they spread
the rare rugs of Persia, with carpets cover the stone floor. [7]
They set the table with the *bachelimnaim* "beautiful
vases " or "dishes," but before the Master's place is a large
plate for the three cakes, and another for the *chasoreth*

With fire from the ever-burning lamp, hanging before
the Holy Scrolls, the Pentateuch, which the Jews call the

---

[1] Edersheim, Temple, 333 ; Zanolini, De Festis Judæorum, C 4 note   [2] Job
in 8, xl 20 ; Isaias xxvii 1, etc   [3] See Migne, Cursus Comp S Scripturæ, m.
873-1071   [4] Deut. xxxii. 14.   [5] Migne, Cursus Completus, S Scripturæ, in 1061.
[6] Migne, Cursus Compl. S Scripturæ, m. 806.   [7] Zanolini, De Festis Jud., C. 4,
p. 41

Torah, "The Law," they light the lamps of the seven-branched candlestick in the Bema, the candles on the table, and the other candles round the room. This is the reason that candles burn on the walls of a church during its dedication ceremonies.[1] They light each candle with the words:

"Blessed art thou, O Lord our God, King of the Universe, who hast sanctified us by thy commandments, and hast commanded us to kindle the festival lights"

How many candles did they light? After sundown each Friday of Sabbath eve, and on the Passover they lighted six lamps or candles. To each lamp or candle they held out the hands and prayed for the repose of the souls of the dead. The Jews of that day piously believed that while the candles of Sabbath and feast burned, God allowed the souls in purgatory to cool themselves in cold water, remaining there while the candles burned.[2] We conclude therefore that six wax candles burned at the Last Supper, and these are continued in the six candles of Pontifical and High Mass.

The women lighted lamps and candles in that day, because, as the Jews say, the men were occupied with the preparations outside, while the women prepared within. They give another queer reason the reader may accept or not. When Eve offered Adam the apple and he refused to eat, she struck him and beat him with rods till he agreed to eat the forbidden fruit, which brought such misfortunes on the race. Therefore women had to light the lights as a sign of the prophesied Seed of the woman, who would come to enlighten the world with his teachings.[3] The women covered the table with its three linen cloths, chalices and dishes. On one dish they put the three cakes of unfermented bread, one in memory of the manna of their fathers, the second cake to remind them of the double portion which fell on the Sabbath, and the third was for the Passover feast.[4]

According to immemorial custom copied from the Temple, each took a bath before beginning the Passover. The bath was emblematic of innocence of soul required

---

[1] Edersheim, Life of Christ, ii 165, 445, etc. [2] Zanolini, Disp et Sectis Jud, Cap I in Note [3] Zanolini, De Festis Judæorum, C I., Note 4 See Edersheim, Life of Christ, ii 150 to 160. [4] Ibidem, Note 3.

to eat the Lamb in Communion, and prophetic of Christian baptism. The Rabbis of that time practised three kinds of bathing, for the Wilderness bath using five and a half gallons of water, taking the Jerusalem bath with eight and a half gallons and the Sepphoris, "The Legal Bath," with sometimes sixty gallons. Stone jars, called *metretes*, translated in the King James Bible as "firkins," held the water." [1]

This was the reason that Jesus said at supper, "He that is washed needeth but to wash his feet, but is clean wholly: and you are clean, but not all. For he knew who would betray him." [2] Their feet had become soiled in walking over the floors, and by a play of words Christ applied the bath to the innocence of soul all had, but Judas with murder in his mind, for he had made an agreement with the priests to deliver up to them his Master that they might inflict on him a horrible death.

The Passover began at Ben aharbaim, "Between the two vespers," according to the words of God to Moses, giving place and time, "In the place, which the Lord shall choose that his name may dwell there, thou shalt immolate the Passover in the evening, at the going down of the sun, at which time thou camest out of Egypt." [3] The Hebrew has "between the two vespers."

What is the meaning of "the first" and "the second" vespers? The Jews of that time called the afternoon, that is after three o'clock, when the lamb was sacrificed, the "first vespers," and in our Gospel the words are translated "evening." [4] During this "first vespers," the Lord fed the multitude with the miraculous loaves and fishes, and in the "second vespers" he went to pray. Writers disagree regarding the exact time when the "second" vespers began, but the most probable opinion is that of Rabbi Aben Esra, quoted in the Talmud, that it was between sunset and darkness, that is, in the gloaming these second vespers began. The first night of the Passover, therefore when darkness fell on the earth, the Jews began the Passover prayers in the synagogues in the time of Christ. The Jews of our day do not begin the Passover till it is dark. Now let us see these prayers and ceremonies in the Cenacle.

---

[1] John ii. 6. [2] John xiii. 10, 11. [3] Deut. xvi 5, 6. [4] Matt. xiv. 15-23.

XI.—THE CEREMONIES AND PRAYERS OF THE FIRST MASS TO THE END OF THE PREFACE.

On the high tower at the southeast corner of the sacred area now stands the chief Temple chassan or porter, with a silver trumpet in his hands watching the sun setting behind the western hills.

Gazing intently on the sky, when he sees the first star, he blows a loud blast, emblematic of the coming of the expected Messiah, and all the people in the country start for the city. When he sees the second star he blows again, the sound signifying God's providence over the world, and all the people go home. When he sees the third star he sounds again to remind them of the trumpet tone of the Last Judgment and then the Passover has begun, "between the two vespers."

Thus when darkness deepens, they began the synagogue services, the evening prayers with Psalm, petition, versicle, response, the reading of the Old Testament relating to the feast,—the services we described when treating of the synagogue.

Sabbaths, Mondays and Thursdays they held these services with special devotions in Temple and synagogue, and they were prolonged so that the Passover lasted till nearly midnight.[1] This year the Passover fell on Thursday and therefore they had special devotions with the full synagogue service.

The Temple hassan, then called the chassan, first saw the evening star the Greeks called Hesperos, the Romans Venus, or any bright star, and that time they called vespers, "evening" and from that Temple time of prayer came the Vesper service of the Catholic Church.

In desert wanderings, the ram's horn called the people to prayer, but by lapse of time this was replaced by the silver trumpet, and all Temple services were regulated

---

[1] Talmud, Baracoth xii. 2, etc.

347

by the trumpet's tone. We read in the Babylonian Talmud the following.[1]

"Mishna. In the Temple they never blew less than twenty-one times a day, nor oftener than forty-eight times. They daily blew the trumpet twenty-one times, thrice at the gates, nine times at the daily morning offering, and nine times at the daily evening offering. When additional offerings were brought, they blew nine times more. On the eve of the Sabbath they blew six times more, thrice to interdict the people from doing work, and thrice to separate the holy day from the work day. But on the eve of the Sabbath or during a festival, they blew forty-eight times; thrice at the opening of the gates, thrice at the upper gate, thrice at the lower gate, thrice at the drawing of water, thrice over the altar, nine times at the daily morning offering, nine times at the daily evening offering, nine times at the additional offerings, thrice to interdict the people from doing work, and thrice to separate the holy day from the work day."

We have given this quotation to show how the trumpet tone sounding over the sacred city from the Temple tower regulated the movements of Passover preparation. This was the way the priests had notified the multitudes that Thursday afternoon, that they were ready to sacrifice the paschal lambs. The sound rang out again for the last time that evening "between the two vespers" when the watchers saw the third star.

At that moment Christ with his apostles, disciples, and the crowds which followed him, ascended the stone steps on the outside leading to the Cenacle, walked over the stone roof of the adjoining building, turned to the left and entered the holy historic room. Passing through the door, each touches the Muzuzzah, the little box hanging on the right door jamb.[2] Each recites the following prayer written on the enclosed parchment:

"May the Lord keep thy coming in and thy going out from henceforth and forever."[3]

They always said this prayer entering Temple or synagogue to remind them of the blood of the paschal lamb on the door-posts of their fathers the night the Hebrews

[1] Tract Succah, "Booths," 85   [2] Deut iv. 9, xi. 13-21; Edersheim, life of Christ, I, 76; Talmud, Josephus, etc   [3] Psalm cxx 8.

were delivered from Egyptian slavery, when they became a nation through the sacrifice of the paschal lamb. Christians take holy water at the church door and cross themselves with a prayer, to remind them of their delivery through baptism from the bondage of the demon.

They pass by the table prepared in the middle of the room and walk towards the Bema or sanctuary where the synagogue services are to be held. According to the Temple custom the lowest in dignity goes first, then the others in order according to rank, last coming the Prince of the House of David. From this Jewish processional came the custom found in all the Christian Rites, the lowest in dignity marches first and the highest or the celebrant comes last.

The immolated lamb of Abel and of the antediluvian patriarchs, the sacrifices of Abraham, Isaac and Jacob, the rivers of blood reddening the Temple, the ceremonial of the synagogue, the mystic meanings of the Hebrew religion, the prophetic words of the great men of the Old Testament are about to be fulfilled, sealed up and accomplished in the awful Tragedy of Calvary the next day. Then the Temple will have fulfilled its mission, and in thirty-six years Titus with his Roman armies will take the city and destroy that sanctuary[1] But by the providence of God, the Temple ceremonial with all its symbolic rites had been introduced into the synagogue, and Christ was about to set his sacred seal, the sanction of his Divinity, on these synagogue and Temple rites, and incorporate them into the everlasting ceremonial of the Euchatistic Sacrifice. Whence, while the Temple building passed away, its striking and imposing ceremonial comes down to us two forms, one in the synagogue the other in the Mass The Temple ceremonies were loaded with type, image, and figure of the long-looked-for Messiah—every movement of its ministers and every object told of Him to come in the future, as now in the Mass every ceremony and object shows us that he came and fulfilled them.

They began the Passover with the synagogue service, Christ acting as the Rabbi or leader of the congregation. The words of the Liturgy were sung in chant, response, versicle and prayer, as in the early Church[2] when there

[1] Dan ix ; Josephus, Jewish Wars vi 4, 5   [2] S Augustine, ix. De Decim Chor.

was a bishop in every city with his twelve priests, images of Christ with his twelve apostles at the Last Supper.

"Without doubt," says St. Augustine, "that is especially to be done, which can be proved by Scripture, as the singing of hymns and Psalms, because we have the documents, example and commands of the Lord regarding these things."[1]

Numerous quotations from the Fathers and writers of the early Church show that the Mass was always sung by the bishop and priests. Ages afterwards, when Christians had multiplied, a priest was placed over a church as pastor. Often having no ministers to aid him the custom obtained of saying a low Mass.

The Last Supper was therefore a pontifical High Mass with Christ as the Celebrant, assisted by the apostles. To-day, when the bishop pontificates with his ministers, with choir and clergy assisting, he says the Mass more according to the Last Supper than when the priest says a low Mass. Thus the bishops have better preserved the customs and rites of the early Church.

When the bishop pontificates surrounded by his ministers, waited on by all, when the whole external ceremonial seems to refer to him, when his honors look to lift him into dignities higher that should be given any man, let the reader go back in thought to that Cenacle, that night we are describing, when the Celebrant of the Mass was the Word made flesh. There all the ceremonial of the Mass find its origin and completeness.

As God acts in the highest, Christ said the first Mass therefore not as simple priest, but as "the Pastor and Bishop of our souls."[2] As a Bishop he pontificated, that night and consecrated the apostles bishops so they might say the Mass with him, and that they might consecrate bishops in the churches they were to establish.

When they went forth into the nations, when they formed a band of converts, they consecrated bishops and placed one over every church. Therefore in the early ages every church had a bishop. These ordained twelve priests forming the presbytery of the diocese, an image of the apostolic college, and later these priests became the cathedral chapter. When the priesthood rose out of the

---

[1] Opera omnia, Mellier's Edition, Paris, 1850, Vol. 28 p, 521.   [2] I. Peter, ii. 25.

episcopate we do not find.   But centuries later the monks were ordained priests

St Augustine says that Christ at the Passover celebrated the evening prayers of the first day of unleaven bread.[1]   This was the synagogue service we will give

The Lord himself revealed the very place of the Last Supper, the Sion mount, the graces of Communion, the spiritual nourishment of souls among the nations   Isaias, Israel's greatest prophet, uttered these words : " And the Lord of hosts shall make unto all people in this mountain a feast of fat things, a feast of wine, of fat things full of marrow, of wine purified from the lees."[2]

The chains of pagan errors, the bondage of heathen sacrifices he will destroy, the Mass will take the place of pagan worship, says the prophet in the next verse: " And he shall destroy in this mountain the face of the bond with which all people were tied, and the web that the demon began over all nations   He shall cast down death headlong forever " etc[3]

Now let us penetrate into the deep meaning of this prophecy

The word Isaias uses for mountain is *har*, " a hill " ; the word translated " Lord " is Jehovah, and that for hosts is *tsaba*, " warfare," " service," " a disciplined army."   The word translated feast is *mishteh*, " drinking," " a feast," with the bread and wine the elements of the Last Supper and the Mass.   The word translated " death," " which he will cast down headlong forever,"[4] is the Hebrew *muth*, " a violent death," " a murder,"[5] the demon brought on mankind because of Adam's sin ; it is the word God used when he forbade under penalty of death, our first parents to eat of the forbidden fruit.[6]   The Hebrew word translated " victory " is *netsach*, " prominence," " pre-eminence " foretelling the power of the prophesied Prince of Peace about to celebrate the Last Supper.

The first part of the Last Supper, that is the synagogue prayers, took place within the Bema ; the " chancel " or " sanctuary " ; the name is still used for sanctuary by the Greek and Oriental Christians.   This Cenacle sanctuary was approached by steps, as steps lead up to the altar

[1] Ibidem, tom 41, p 242   [2] Isaias xxv. 6   [3] Isaias xxv 7, 8   [4] Ibidem, 8. [5] Numb xxxv 31   [6] Gen iii 3, 4

railing in a church. How many steps were there? We do not know. The Bema of the Cenacle is now nearly three feet higher than the floor of the nave. St. Augustine twice uses the word Bema for sanctuary. To the Manicheans he wrote, "I used to ask you in those days what was the reason you used to celebrate the Lord's Passover generally with a lukewarm or hardly any celebration, with no watchings, no long fasting, no festive solemnity, while the day Manichæus was killed, your Bema, approached by five steps, is adorned with precious linens put before the worshipers in which you show him such honors."[1]

The Saviour with his apostles enter the sanctuary for celebration of the evening prayers prescribed before the Passover Supper. The seventy-two disciples and the Lord's converts gather in the nave of the Cenacle to take part in the service before they separate into "bands" to celebrate the feast.

We must remember that the Jewish Church, with its Temple and synagogue, its Old Testament, its religious rites coming down from Moses and the patriarchs, its traditions and sole pure worship of God amid the pagan rites, was the true spouse of Jesus Christ[2] The sacramentals of the Jewish Church we have described did not of themselves give grace. They were only images of the foretold glories and greater graces of the Christian sacraments. These Hebrew sacramentals Christ raised up to be the materials of the seven sacraments of the New Law. The grace and salvation of the Hebrew people depended on the pious dispositions of the worshipers, *ex opere operantis*, while the sacraments of the Church of themselves produce their effects in the soul if the receiver place no obstacle, *ex opere operato*.

The Talmud tells the time, the prayers and the ceremonial of the Passover before they sat at the table.[3] They always began the Passover with the synagogue prayers. This was Thursday, when special services were held in all the synagogues; this was the evening of the Passover; this was a time of special devotions in all the realms of Jewry,

---

[1] S. Augustine Contra Epist. Manichaei, L I. n. ix. [2] S Thomas in q 8, Art 5 ad. 3 etc. [3] Baracoth, Palestine in the Time of Christ, p 386 . Geikie, Life of Christ, i p 204 , Edersheim, Life of Christ ; Talmud, Magilla, etc.

when each band of Jews had ts own leader who led the services.

Let us see how the Son of God, the Word made flesh, the Memra, Logos, " Wisdom," carried out the first part of the Mass. It was foretold, that according to the synagogue custom of his time, as Jews still do in our day, that he would select seven men to aid him in the ceremonial.

" Wisdom hath built himself a house, he hath hewn out seven pillars. He hath slain his victims, mingled his wine and set forth his table. He hath sent his maids to invite to the tower, and to the halls of the city Whosoever is a little one let him come to me. And to the unwise he said, ' Come and eat my bread and drink the wine I have prepared.' " [1]

What was the house Wisdom the Divine Word was to "build" but the Church Universal? What were the victims he had " slain " but the paschal lamb then roasting in the oven? What was the " tower " foretold but the Cenacle rising from Sion's heights? What was the foretold " bread and wine " but that we have described ?

Christ therefore acting as Rabbi about to lead in the synagogue service, chose seven men to aid him. Who were these? history is silent. Peter, leader of the apostolic band, to whom after the resurrection the Lord gave full power to feed and govern his lambfolds and sheepfolds, as the Gospel tells in the original Greek,[2] perhaps waited on him at his right. James and John were Temple priests. The priest was always given the place of honor in the synagogue, perhaps they stood on the right and left of the Lord. Who were the two acting as deacons of honor and the two masters of ceremonies? we do not know. It seems that these seven officials of the synagogue were types of, or gave rise to, the assistant priest, deacon, subdeacon, deacons of honor, and masters of ceremony of the pontifical Mass. We only throw this out as a suggestion, as these officials are found in all Rites when the bishop pontificates, as in the early Church the archpriest, archdeacon and chief subdeacon, "pillars," of the diocese, attended the bishop when he said Mass.

Often the feast was held in the nave of the synagogue

1 Prov. ix. 1-5.   2 John xxi. 15-17.

23

building, or in a room attached, but never in the sanctuary itself. The sanctuary of the Cenacle was an inclosed place separated from the great room by a railing copied after the Temple railing separating the Holies from the Priest's Court. In this sanctuary the prayers were said, after which they reclined at the tables set in the large room called the Cenacle, the arrangement being like a church and its sanctuary.

First they silently meditate on the law relating to the Tephillin, the Greeks called Philacteries,[1] each saying: "He commanded us to lay the Tephillin upon the hand, as a memorial of His outstretched arm, opposite the heart to indicate the duty of subjecting the longings and designs of our heart to his service, blessed be He ; and upon the the head, over against the brain, thereby teaching that the mind, whose seat is the brain, together with all senses and faculties, are to be subjected to His services, blessed be He, etc."

Each places his Tephillah on his arm saying : " Blessed art thou, O Lord our God, King of the universe, who hast sanctified us by thy commandments, and hast commanded us to lay the Tephillin. Winding the Retsuah, "leather strap," around the arm and fingers, they say:

" And I will betroth thee unto me forever, yea, I will betroth thee unto me in justice, and in judgment, and in lovingkindness, and in mercy, I will even betroth thee unto me in faithfulness, and thou shalt know the Lord." Putting on the Tephillah on the forehead.

"Blessed art thou, O Lord our God, King of the Universe, who hast sanctified us by thy commandments, and hast given us command concerning the precept of the Tephillin. Blessed be His name, whose glorious kingdom is for ever and ever."

They meditate on the mystery of the Tallith, "Prayer-shawl," saying each in a low voice.

" I am here enwrapping myself in this fringed robe, in fulfilment of the command of my Creator, as it is written in the Law : 'Thou shalt make strings in the hem at the four corners of thy cloak.'[2] And even as I cover myself

---

[1] Geikie, Life of Christ, i. 181, 214 ; ii. 121, 293. See Edersheim, Life of Christ, i. 277 ; Matt xxiii 5 ; Luke viii 44 ; Numb xv. 88 ; Deut xxii 12 ; Palestine, 397, Sketches, 221 to 224, etc. [2] Deut. xxii. 12.

with the Tallith in this world, so may my soul deserve to be clothed with a beauteous spiritual robe in the world to come, in the garden of Eden, Amen." Putting it on they say : "Blessed art thou, O Lord our God, King of the universe, who hast sanctified us with thy commandments, and hast commanded us to enwrap ourselves in the fringed garment."

They first put the Tallith on their heads, then let it fall down on their shoulders the way the celebrant puts on the amice. The Jews still put on the prayer-shawls in this way.

The common belief then was that when the Messiah would come he would gather the patriarchs and all the members of the Jewish people to a great feast the prophet had foretold : "And the Lord of hosts shall make unto all people, on this mountain, a feast of fat things, a feast of wine, of fat things full of marrow, of wine purified from the lees." [1]

The Rabbis held the most wild and exaggerated ideas regarding these words prophetic of the Last Supper. All animals used for food would be there. The Leviathan,[2] the Behemoth[3] with the gigantic bird Jochani.[4] And the wine the Messiah shall use shall be made of grapes kept from the foundations of the world.

From the days of the prophets came down a tradition, crystallized into Jewish writings of the time of Christ, that the Messiah would robe himself in seven vestments —the first of honor and glory at creation,[5] of majesty at the Red Sea,[6] of strength when giving the Law, or Torah on Sinai :[7] of white, when he would blot out Israel's sins :[8] of zeal when he avenged them of their enemies,[9] of justice when he would be revealed,[10] and of red when he would take vengeance on Edom." This last was the vision of the Lord the prophet saw when Jesus sweated blood in Gethsemane.[11]

The commentary continues : "But the garment with which He will clothe the Messiah, its splendors will extend from one end of the world to the other, as it is written; "As a bridegroom priestly in headgear."[12] And

[1] Isaias xxv. 6. [2] Talmud, B. Bath. 75a. [3] Ibidem, Pirke, d Eliez. II etc. [4] B Bath. 73b Bekhor, 57b. [5] Psalm civ. 1 [6] Psalm xcii [7] xcii. 1 [8] Dan. viii. 14 [9] Isaias lix. 17. [10] Isaias lix 20. [11] Isaias lxiii 1 to 4. [12] Isaias lxi. 10.

Israel will be astounded at his light, and will say: " Blessed the hour in which the Messiah cometh. Blessed the womb whence he issued. Blessed the generation that shall see him. Blessed the eye worthy to behold him.

" The opening of his lips is blessing and peace. His speech is a quieting of the spirit. Glory and majesty are in his vestments, and confidence and quietness in his words, and on his tongue compassion and forgiveness. His prayer is a sweetly-smelling odor, and his supplication holiness and purity. Happy Israel that these are reserved for you," etc.[1] The revelations coming down not only in the Bible but in sacred words of prophet, seer and holy ones of Hebrew race are about to be fulfilled in the Messiah, the Grecian Jews called Epxomenos, " The Coming One."

The synagogue services were not only sung by the Rabbi and his ministers, but the people also took part in the congregational singing. There was a night foretold by Israel's great prophet, when the Lord Messiah would come and sing the Passover service. In the original Hebrew it is " You shall have a song as in the night of the solemn Festival,[2] and joy of heart as when one goeth with a pipe, to come into mountain of the Lord (Sion), to the mighty One of Israel (Christ). And the Lord shall make his glorious (*hod*, 'beautiful,') voice: (*gol*, sound,) to be heard."[3] The latter part of this chapter shows that the prophet foresaw Christ chanting the Last Supper service. Numberless proofs force us to believe that the Last Supper was a pontifical High Mass sung by the Lord, his apostles and the people taking part in congregational singing.

We said that the word Isaias uses is the Hebrew *chag*,[3] " a sacred dance," which is translated " solemn festival " in our Bible. Was there a dance at the Last Supper, as we understand the word? Certainly not. Why then did the prophet prophesy a dance? Let the reader observe a Pontifical High Mass while the bishop with his deacon, subdeacon, deacons of honor and ministers, robed in glorious vestments go through the ceremonial. The organ plays, the priests chant, the choir sings, and the

---

[1] Pesiqta ed Ruber, p 149 a. b. [2] Chag, " A holy dance." [3] Isaias xxx, 29-30.

worshiping laity fill the building. Bishop and clergy, trained for years in the service, each pass back and forth, follow rules, observe forms and rites, carry out ceremonies proper to their office, resembling in a way the movements of a dance, and thus the prophet described the Last Supper. Whence St. Augustine says:[1] "You hear the singers, let us hear the dancers, understand the customs of the dancers with the movement of their members. Desire is driven out, charity takes its place." He compares the Mass to a holy dance following the Jewish idea that the Temple, Passover, and synagogue worship was a solemn festival of joy unto the Lord. The word chag, "solemnity" is used in the Old Testament a number of times for the Passover.[2]

They are about to begin the synagogue prayers in the Cenacle, as was the custom at that time. "For what purpose should the Kiddush be recited in the synagogue? In order to afford the guests, who eat, drink and sleep in the synagogues, an opportunity to hear it. Samuel thus holds to his theory that the duty of hearing the Kiddush recited can be only acquitted in the place where the person takes his meals."[3]

The Lord gave special directions regarding the vestments they were to wear during the Egyptian Passover, "And thus shall you eat it, you shall gird your reins, and you shall have shoes on your feet, holding staves in your hands."[4] By lapse of time these developed into the Passover vestments. The Lord was clothed in purple for he was the Prince of David's dynasty. Without removing his purple cassock he clothed himself in the vestments of a Rabbi, while the seven apostles vested in sacred Passover robes. Every vestment was embroidered in white, red, green and violet, the colors of the Temple, as was then the custom.

Having robed themselves in the vestments we described in a former chapter, Christ, with his seven apostles beside him, comes to the steps leading up to the ark, the Aaron or Tevah, "the chest," or "Hechal," called the Little Temple," containing the sacred Books of Moses.

[1] Sermo cccxi in Nat Cyp M in vii   [2] Psalms lxxiii. 4, lxxxi ; Isaias xxx. 29; II Esdras viii 18, Ezech xlvi 11; Zach. xix. 10, 18, 19.   [3] Babyl Talmud, Cap X., p. 212.   [4] Exod xii 11.

There they stand, and put hands together, eyes on the floor as become suppliants in the presence of their God and Creator. These were the customary postures of prayer in the time of Christ,[1] as still seen at the beginning of Mass. First they bow deeply down before the Holy Scrolls in the ark, as the celebrant of the Mass bows down before the altar.[2] Thus they began the synagogue prayers always said before the celebration of the Passover.

According to the Temple custom they recite the Versicle and the Psalm—the Master beginning, the ministers responding.

" I will go into the altar of God, to God who giveth joy to my youth.

" Judge me, O God, and distinguish my cause from the nation that is not holy," etc.[3]

Christ beginning and the apostles responding, thus they recited the whole Psalm. In the Liturgy St. Peter composed at Antioch, still followed by the Maronites, they follow this custom of Temple and Cenacle, beginning this Psalm when entering the sanctuary. But the celebrant of the Latin Mass says it at the foot of the altar.

" I will go into the altar of God, etc.

" Bless ye the Lord, who is to be blessed.

" Blessed is the Lord, who is to be blessed for ever and ever.

" Blessed, praised, glorified, exalted and extolled, be the name of the supreme King of kings, the Holy One, blessed be he, who is the first and the last, and beside him there is no God. Exalt ye him that rideth upon the heavens by his name Jah, and rejoice before him. His name is exalted above all blessing and praise. Blessed be his name whose glorious kingdom is for ever and ever. Let the name of the Lord be blessed from this time forth and for evermore.

" Blessed art thou, O Lord, our God, king of the Universe, who formest light, and createst darkness, who makest peace and createst all things

" How goodly are thy tents, O Jacob, and thy dwelling-place, O Israel! As for me, in the abundance of thy

---

[1] Edersheim, Temple, 127.   [2] Geikie, Life of Christ, i , 167 to 190, Migne, Cursus Completus, S. Scripturæ iii. 1242.   [3] Psalm xlii.

loving-kindness, I will come into thy house. I will worship toward thy holy Temple in the fear of thee Lord, I have loved the habitation of thy house, and the place where thy glory dwelleth I will worship and bow down. I will bend the knee before the Lord, my Maker. May my prayers unto thee, O Lord, be in an acceptable time. O God, in the abundance of thy loving-kindness answer me in the truth of thy salvation."

Filled with sorrow for their sins, like the penitent hosts of Israel on the eve of the Day of the Atonement, they strike their breasts, as the Talmud tells us, " They shall strike on the breast lamenting. Clapping is done with the hands, and striking is done with the feet." [1] It is evident that from this Temple and synagogue custom came the ceremony of striking the breast at the Confiteor, " the General Confession," during Mass.

This was the custom from the beginning of the Church. " Who does penance is mad with himself. For if he is not sincere, why is the breast struck ? Why do you do it if you are not mad ? When therefore you strike your breast, you are mad in your heart that you may satisfy your Lord, and thus may these words be understood. " Be angry and sin not." [2] "And the publican standing afar off would not so much as lift up his eyes to heaven, but struck his breast saying : " O God, be merciful to me a sinner." [3] Striking the breast is the sorrow of the heart What does the stroke on the breast mean ? " O God, be merciful to me a sinner." And what was the sentence of the Lord ? " Amen I say unto you, that publican went down to his house justified rather than the other." [4] This great doctor tells us that when the people heard the General Confession at Mass they struck their breasts. [5] He says that in his time the bishop and clergy struck their breasts at the Confession. Did Christ and his apostles, following this Temple ceremony, strike their breasts as the clergy and people still do at the beginning of Mass? We find no record.

After the prayers at the foot of the staircase, Christ with his two ministers went up to the ark and kissed

[1] Tract Ebel Babyl Talmud, p. 37   [2] Psalm iv 5 Sermo xix in Ps 1 n 11
[3] Luke xviii 13   [4] Luke xviii 14, St Augustine Enar ii in Ps xxxi n xi
[5] St Augustine, Enar in Ps cxii. n. i, Enar in Ps cxxxvii n. 11 , De Discipline Christiana, n xi , etc.

the place where the holy Scrolls rested,—that was a synagogue ceremony, a sign of their love of the Law. This
the celebrant of the Mass now does.

The Lord takes the censer, puts incense on the burning
coals with blessing, and with an apostle on each side of
him, bows deeply down before the holy Scrolls of Moses
and the Prophets, the Torah and the Heptorath. First
he incenses the Torah in the middle, then on each side
where rest the other sacred Books of the Old Testament.[1]
While offering incense, they recited the words of the
Psalm said in the Temple since David's day.

" Let my prayer be directed as incense in thy sight,
the lifting up of my hands as evening sacrifice. Set a
watch, O Lord, before my mouth, and a door round about
my lips. Incline not my heart to evil words, to make
excuse in sins with men that work iniquity, and I will
not communicate with the choicest of them." etc.[2]

Handing the censer to one of the apostles at the right
side of the ark the latter incenses him as the Rabbi, then
they go to the middle, bow deeply down before the holy
Scrolls, and return to the floor of the Bema.

The ceremony of incensing the Scrolls, and Rolls of
the Prophets and ark in the synagogue, was in memory
of the incense offered in the Holies of the Temple before
the sacrifice of the lamb twice a day, at nine and three
o'clock, with the Psalm we have given. This ceremony
without a change is carried out at the High Mass.

When Israel fought against the Amalecites, Moses
held up his hands—hands and body forming a cross—
foretelling the crucifixion. While he held them that way
the Hebrews prevailed. When he tired, and let his
hands fall, Amalec overcame. Aaron and Hur held up
his hands, and the battle of Raphidim was gained.[3] God
commanded Moses to write the history of this battle in a
book, because it foretold that at a future day the Lord
on Calvary would stretch out his hands, nailed to the
Cross, in superhuman patience till his death, in which he
conquered mankind's enemy the demon.[4]

When saying the Temple prayers the high priest held
out his hands like Moses blessing the people. The

[1] See Edersheim, Temple, 139 to 141, etc   [2] Psalm cxl.   [3] Exod xvii 8 to 15.
[4] See Babyl Talmud, Taanith iv.

Talmud tells us, "At three periods of the year the priests should raise their hands at each prayer, and during such periods there are days when this is done four times during the day, viz: during the morning, and additional, the afternoon and the closing prayers. In all the four prayers, mentioned above, the priests are to raise up their hands." [1]

Did Christ hold out his hands with his body forming a cross, as he stretched out his hands when he was crucified, as the celebrant of the Mass holds his hands? The Talmud says they held out their hands this way in Temple and synagogue prayers, and that they were forbidden to hold them higher than the Phylactery on their brow. Isaias foretelling Christ celebrating the Last Supper says, "And he shall spread forth his hands in the midst of them as he that swimmeth spreads forth his hands to swim." [2] We conclude therefore that Christ stretched out his hands during the prayers as now the celebrant of the Mass holds his hands during the prayers.

The following prayers almost word for word are taken from the Old Testament. The word Selah, given seventy-one times in the Psalms and prophetic books, is found only in Hebrew poetic works and at the end of a verse. The Jewish writers say it means "forever and ever," or "in the world to come." It is rendered in the Latin Mass: "Per omnia sæcula sæculorum, For ever and ever," or "Through the ages of ages." The Church Fathers and many writers have treated the subject. Some think it means that the music should stop, that the tone should be changed, or the instruments taken up. But it seems to be a sign to raise up the hands in prayer, although the rabbinical writers lead by tradition as given above offer the most reasonable meaning. The Lord and his apostles continue the prayers as follows.

"Blessed be Thou, O Lord, King of the Universe, who formest the light, and createst darkness, who maketh peace and createst every thing, who in mercy doth give light to the earth, and to those who dwell on it, and in thy goodness day by day reneweth the works of creation. Blessed be the Lord our God for the glory of His handiwork and for the lightgiving lights which He made for

[1] Talmud Tract, Taanith, Fasting, Gemara, 81.   [2] Isaias xxv. 11.

His praise. Selah, Blessed be the Lord our God, who hath formed the lights.

" With great love hast Thou loved us, O Lord, our God, and with much overflowing pity hast Thou pitied us, our Father, and our King. For the sake of our fathers, who trusted in Thee, Thou taughtest them the statutes of life; have mercy on us and teach us. Enlighten our eyes in Thy law, cause our hearts to cleave to Thy commandments, unite our hearts to love and fear Thy name, and we shall not be put to shame forever and ever. For Thou art a God who preparest salvation, and thou hast chosen us from all nations and tongues, and in truth Thou hast brought us near to Thy great name—Selah— that we may lovingly praise Thee and thy Oneness. Blessed be the Lord, who in love chose His people Israel."

To each prayer the apostles replied Amen, " Let it be so." The first prayer was said in the morning and gave rise to the prayer for peace in the Christian Liturgies the second prayer was added at the evening service.

" The prayer Sch'mone Esre : " Eighteen Benedictions," was drawn up in the years 348–342 before Christ. The Jews say Esdras was its author.[1] But some believed that the 14th and 17th petitions were added later. The whole petition was spoken in a low tone by the congregation and allowed by the Rabbi. Three times a day every Israelite repeated it after he had recited the Sch'ma, " Hear," morning and evening. During these prayers the congregation stood immovable, faced towards the shrine, feet close together, mind fixed in devotion. At the beginning and end of the first and sixteenth Benediction, all bent the knee, and bowed their heads down towards the earth. It seems that this is the reason the congregation in our churches stand during the Gospel, and bend the knee at the end.[2]

THE EIGHTEEN BENEDICTIONS.

" Be Thou praised, O Lord our God, the God of our fathers, the God of Abraham, of Isaac and of Jacob, the great, mighty and dreadful God, the Supreme Being, Dispenser of benefits and of favors, and the Creator of all

---

[1] See Cohen, p. 191; Jos. V. I. p. 39, V. II. 262, etc.   [2] See Geikie, Life of Christ, V 1. p. 183.

things. Thou rememberest the piety of the Patriarchs, and Thou wilt send a Deliverer to their children to glorify thy name, to show forth Thy love, O King, our help, our strength. Be Thou praised, O Lord, the shield of Abraham.

"Thou livest forever, Almighty Lord. Thou dost raise the dead, Thou art almighty to help. Thou dost make the winds to blow and the rain to fall. (This was said only in time of bad weather from the Feast of Tabernacles to the Passover.) Thou dost sustain all that live by Thy grace. Thou dost raise the dead of Thy great mercy. Thou dost uphold those who fall. Thou dost heal the sick. Thou dost free the prisoners and dost keep Thy promises to those who sleep in the earth. Who is mighty like unto Thee, O Lord? Who can be compared to Thee? O our King, it is Thou who killest and makest alive; from Thee comes all our help. Thou wilt fulfil Thy promise to raise the dead. Praise be Thou, O Lord, who raisest the dead.

"Thou art holy. Thy Saints glorify Thee day by day. Selah. Praised be Thou, O Lord, the Holy God.

"Thou givest man wisdom, and fillest him with understanding. Praised be Thou, O Lord, the Dispenser of wisdom.

"Bring us back to thy law, O our Father, bring us back, O King, into Thy service, bring us back to Thee by true repentance. Praised be Thou, O Lord, who dost receive our repentance.

"Pardon us, O our Father, for we have sinned. Absolve us, O our King, for we have offended against Thee. Thou art a God, who dost pardon and absolve. Praised be Thou, O Lord, who of Thy mercy dost pardon many times and forever.

"Look on our misery, O Lord, and be Thou our Defender. Deliver us quickly for Thy glory, for Thou art an Almighty Deliverer. Praised be Thou, O Lord the Deliverer of Israel.

"Heal us, O Lord, and we shall be healed. Help us and we shall be helped. Thou art the object of our praise. Wilt Thou therefore bring effectual healing for all our ills? Thou art the King Almighty, our true Physician, full of mercy. Praised be Thou, O Lord, who healest the sick of the children of Thy people.

"O Lord our God, bless this year and these harvests, give dew and rain (these words were added in winter), give thy blessing to the ground. Satisfy us with thy goodness, and make this year as the good years. Praised be Thou, O Lord, who blesseth the years.

"Sound the trumpet of deliverance, lift up the standard which will gather together the dispersed of our nation and bring us all quickly again from the ends of the earth. Praised be Thou, O Lord, who gathereth together the outcasts of Israel.

"Let our judges be restored as before, and our magistrates, as in the times past. Deliver us from afflictions and anguish. Reign Thou over us, O Lord, by thy grace and mercy, and let not Thy judgments come upon us. Praised be Thou, O Lord, who lovest truth and justice.

"Let the slanderers be put to shame, let all the workers of iniquity and the rebellious be destroyed, let the might of the proud be humbled. Praised be Thou, O Lord, who doth trample on Thine enemies, and abase the proud. (This was said twice.)

"Let Thy mercy, O Lord, shine on the upright, the humble, the rulers of Thy people Israel, and may the teachers be favorable to the pious strangers among us, and to us all. Grant a good reward to those who sincerely trust in Thy name, that our lot may be cast among them in the world to come, that our hope be not deceived. We also put our trust in Thee. Praised be Thou, O Lord, who art the hope and the confidence of the faithful.

"Return Thou in thy mercy to Thy city Jerusalem. Make it Thine abode, as Thou hast promised. Let it be built again in our days. Let it never be destroyed. Restore thou quickly the throne of David. Praised be Thou, O Lord, who dost rebuild Jerusalem."

These relate to the destruction of the Holy City when the Israelites were carried away to Babylon. On the Feast of the 9th of the month of Ab, the following words were added :

"O Lord, our God, comfort those who mourn for Jerusalem and Sion. Have pity on this city which is filled with mourning, desolation, and contempt. She bears the grief of the children she has lost. Her palaces are broken down, her glory is passed away. She is overthrown,

desolate and without inhabitants.   She is forsaken, her
head is covered like a barren woman who has borne no
children.   The legions of the enemy have laid her waste,
the idolators have taken possession of her.   They have
slain thy people Israel.   They have slaughtered without
pity the saints of the Most High.   Therefore Sion weeps
with bitter tears, and Jerusalem lifts up her voice.   My
heart, my heart bleeds for these martyrs ; my bowels, my
bowels are torn for these massacres.   But Thou, my God
who hast consumed this city with fire, Thou wilt rebuild
it by fire, for thus it is written, Zach. ii. 5, " For I saith
the Lord, will be unto her a wall of fire round about, and
I will be the glory in the midst thereof.

" Cause the stem of David to spring quickly forth, and
make it glorious by Thy strength, for in Thee do we hope
all the day.   Praised be Thou, O Lord, who dost make
Thy salvation glorious.

" Hear our supplications, O Lord, our God, protect us,
have pity on us.   Hear our prayers in Thy loving-kindness, for Thou art the God who heareth prayers and supplications.   Send us not away, O our King, until Thou
hast heard us, Thou dost graciously receive the prayers of
Thy people Israel.   Praised be Thou, O Lord, who heareth
prayers.

" Let thy people Israel, and their prayers be acceptable
to Thee.   Restore thou the service in the courts of Thy
house.   Of Thy favor, receive the offerings of Israel, and
their prayers, and let the worship of Thy people be ever
acceptable to Thee.   May our eyes see the day when Thou
in Thy mercy will return to Sion.   Praised be Thou, O
Lord, who will establish Thy dwelling-place in Sion.

" We confess that Thou art the Lord our God, and the
God of our fathers for ever and ever.   Thou art the rock
of our life, the shield of our salvation from generation to
generation.   Blessing and praise be to Thy great and
holy name, for the life which Thou hast given us, for our
souls which Thou doth sustain, for the daily miracles
which Thou doth work in our behalf, for the wonderful
loving-kindness with which Thou dost surround us at all
times—in the morning, at mid-day, and in the evening.
O God of all goodness, Thy mercy is infinite, Thy faithfulness fails not.   We hope in Thee forever.   For all

these Thy benefits let Thy name be praised forever and ever. Let all that live praise Thee. Selah. Let them praise Thy name in sincerity. Praised be Thou, O Lord, Thy name alone is good, and Thou alone art worthy to be praised.

"O our Father, let peace and prosperity, Thy blessing, Thy favor, Thy grace and mercy be on us, and on all Thy people Israel. Bless us all with the light of thy face, for it is by this light, O Lord our God, that Thou hast given us an eternal law, the love of justice and uprightness, blessing, mercy, life, peace. May it please Thee to bless Thy people Israel at all times, and in all places, and to give them peace. Praised be Thou, O Lord, who giveth peace to Thy people Israel.

" The breath of every living being shall bless Thy name, O Lord, our God, and the spirit of all flesh shall continually glorify and exalt Thy memorial, O our King, from everlasting to everlasting Thou art God, and besides Thee we have no King, who redeemeth, saveth, setteth free and delivereth, who supporteth, and hath mercy in all times of trouble and distress, yea we have no King but Thee.

" He is God of the first and of the last, the God of all creatures, the Lord of all generations, who is extolled with many praises, and guideth the world with loving-kindness, and his creatures with tender mercies. The Lord slumbereth not, nor sleepeth; he arouses the sleepers, and awakeneth the slumberers. He maketh the dumb to speak, looseneth the bound, supporteth the falling and raiseth up the bowed.

" To Thee alone we give thanks. Though our mouths were full of song as the sea, and our tongues of exultation as the multitude of its waves, and our lips of praise as the wide-extended firmament, though our eyes shone with light like the sun and moon, and our hands were spread forth like the eagles of heaven, and our feet were swift as hinds, we should still be unable to thank Thee, and bless Thy name, O Lord, our God, and God of our fathers, for one thousandth, or one ten-thousandth part of the bounties which Thou hast bestowed on our fathers, and upon us

" Thou didst redeem us from Egypt, O Lord our God, and didst release us from the house of bondage; during famine Thou didst feed us, and didst sustain us in plenty, from the sword thou didst rescue us, from pestilence Thou didst save us, and from sore and lasting disease Thou didst deliver us. Hitherto thy tender mercies have helped us, and thy loving-kindness has not left us, forsake us not, O Lord, our God, forever.

"Therefore, the limbs which thou hast spread forth upon us, and the spirit and breath which thou hast breathed into our nostrils, and the tongue which thou hast set in our mouths, lo, they shall thank, bless, praise, glorify, extol, revere, hallow and assign Kingship to thy name, O our King. For every mouth shall give thanks unto thee, and every tongue shall swear unto thee, every knee shall bow to thee, and whatsoever is lofty shall prostrate itself before thee, all hearts shall fear thee, and all the inward parts and reins shall sing unto thy name, according to the word that is written: 'All my bones shall say, Lord who is like unto thee?'[1]

"Praised be thy name forever, O our King, the great and holy God, and King in heaven and earth. For unto thee, O Lord, our God, and God of our fathers, song and praise are becoming; hymn and psalm, strength and dominion, victory, greatness and might, renown and glory, holiness and sovereignty, blessing and thankgiving, from henceforth, ever and forever. Blessed art thou, O Lord, God, and King, great in praises, God of thanksgivings, Lord of wonders, who makest choice of song and psalm, O King, and God, the life of all worlds.

"O Lord, open thou my lips, and my mouth shall declare thy praise.

"Blessed art thou, O Lord, our God, and God of our fathers, God of Abraham, God of Isaac, and God of Jacob, the great, mighty and revered God, the most high God, who bestowest loving-kindness and poscessest all things, who remembered the pious deeds of the patriarchs, and in love wilt bring a Redeemer to their children's children for thy name's sake.

"We will sanctify thy name in thy world, even as they sanctify it in the highest heavens, as it is written by the hand of thy prophet "And they called one to the other and said:

[1] Psalm xxxiv. 10.

"Holy, holy, holy, is the Lord of hosts, the whole earth is full of his glory.[1]

" Those over against them say, Blessed—

" Blessed be the glory of the Lord from his place.

" And in the Holy Words it is written saying:

" The Lord shall reign forever, thy God, O Sion, unto all generations. Praise ye the Lord.

"Unto all generations we will declare thy greatness, and unto all eternity we will proclaim thy holiness, and thy praise, O our God, shall not depart from our mouth forever, for thou, art a great and holy God and King. Blessed art thou, O Lord the holy God.

" Quickly cause the offspring of David thy servant to flourish, and let his horn be exalted by thy salvation, because we wait for thy salvation all the day. Blessed art thou, O Lord, who causest the horn of salvation to flourish.

" Our God, and the God of our fathers, may our remembrance rise, come and be accepted before thee with the remembrance of our fathers, of the Messiah the Son of David thy servant, of Jerusalem thy holy city, and of all thy people, the house of Israel, bringing deliverance and well-being, peace and loving-kindness, mercy and peace on this day of the Feast of the Unleaven Bread."

They go up the steps to the ark, and deeply bow down before the Law. They open the ark and reverently take out the Scrolls of the Law, all together saying:

" And it came to pass when the ark set forward, that Moses said, ' Rise up, O Lord, and thine enemies shall be scattered, and they that hate thee shall flee before thee,'[2] ' For out of Sion shall go forth the Law, and the word of the Lord from Jerusalem.'[3] Blessed be he who in his holiness gave the Law to his people Israel."

As Leader, the Lord takes the Scroll of the Law saying:

" Magnify the Lord with me, and let us exalt his name together.

" Thine, O Lord, is the greatness, and the power, and the glory, and the victory, and the majesty, for all that is in heaven and on the earth is thine. Thine, O Lord, is

---

[1] Isaias vi 3   [2] Numb. x 85.   [3] Isaias ii. 3.

the kingdom, and the supremacy as head over all. Exalt
ye the Lord our God, and worship at his holy mount, for
the Lord our God is holy

"May the Father of mercy have mercy on the people
that have been borne by him. May he remember the
covenant with the patriarchs, deliver our souls from evil
hours, check the evil inclination in them that have been
carried by him, grant us grace of an everlasting deliverance, and in the attribute of his goodness, fill our desires
by salvation and mercy.

They place the Scrolls on the reading desk, and the
Lord unrolls them till he comes to the place to be read,
saying:

"And may his kingdom be soon revealed, and made
visible to us, and may he be gracious to the house of
Israel, granting them grace, kindness, mercy and favor,
and let us say Amen Ascribe all of you greatness unto
our God and render honor to the law."

"Blessed be he who in his holiness gave the Law to
his people Israel. The Law of the Lord is perfect re-
storing the soul, the testimony of the Lord is faithful,
making wise the simple. The precepts of the Lord are
right, rejoicing the heart. The commandment of the
Lord is pure, enlightening the eyes. The Lord will give
strength to his people The Lord will bless his people
with peace. As for God, his way is perfect. The word
of the Lord is tried. He is a shield to all them that
trust in him."

Those called to read say: "Bless ye the Lord, who is
to be blessed," while all the others reply, "Blessed be the
Lord, who is to be blessed for ever and ever." The others
reply.

"Blessed art thou, O Lord, our God, King of the Universe, who hast chosen us from all peoples, and hast given
us thy Law. Blessed art thou, O Lord, who givest the
Law.

Mondays and Thursdays three sections of the Law
were read. But on the Passover and feasts, they read
seven sections, with two sections from the Prophets,
making the nine lessons, like the nine Lessons of Matins.
If a priest or Levite were present in the congregation, he
read the last section in honor of the priesthood of Aaron

24

and of the tribe of Levi. James and John were of the priestly family, and perhaps they stood next the Master, as the deacon and subdeacon stand by the bishop,[1] and read the last sections.

They read the parts of the Scriptures relating to the feast as the Epistle is now read in our churches. This custom Hebrew writers trace back to the times of David and Samuel. Each of the men came up and read a part, one standing by and pointing out to him the words, so he would not miss any part. After reading his part, the reader kissed the sacred Scrolls at the place where he began to read. This is why the celebrant kisses the Gospel after reading it. In the synagogues of our day they wipe the sacred text with the corner of the prayer shawl and kiss this.

Who were the nine apostles who read that day we know not. As Rabbi leading the service, Christ first read the whole text, as the celebrant now does at Mass. Did one stand by and translate the Hebrew text into the Syro-Chaldaic spoken that day in Judea? we know not.[2] Unrolling the Scrolls till they come to the history of the Passover called the Megillah, they say " Blessed be He, who in his holiness gave the Law to his people Israel."

THE MEGILLAH[3]

"And the Lord spoke to Moses and Aaron, in the land of Egypt. This month shall be to you the beginning of months, it shall be the first in the months of the year. Speak ye to the whole assembly of the children of Israel, and say to them :

" On the tenth day of this month, let every man take a lamb by their families and houses. But if the number be less than may suffice to eat the lamb, he shall take unto himself his neighbor that joineth to his house, according to the number of souls, which may be enough to eat the lamb. And it shall be a lamb without blemish, a male of one year, according to which rite you shall take a kid. And you shall keep it till the fourteenth of this month, and the whole multitude shall sacrifice it in the

---

[1] See Geikie, Life of Christ, i 184; ii 581, etc. [2] See Babyl. Talmud, Megilla, Cap. ix. p 85–87. [3] Exodus xii.

evening. And they shall take of the blood thereof, and put it on both the side-posts, and on the upper door-posts of the house wherein they shall eat it.

"And they shall eat the flesh that night roasted at the fire, and unleavened bread with wild lettuce. You shall not eat thereof anything raw, and boiled in water, but only roasted at the fire. You shall eat the head with the feet and entrails thereof Neither shall there remain anything of it until morning. If there be anything left, you shall burn it with fire. And thus you shall eat it, you shall gird your reins, holding staves in your hands, and you shall eat in haste, for it is the Phase, that is the Passage of the Lord.

"And I will pass through the land of Egypt that night, and will kill every first-born in the land of Egypt, both man and beast, and against all the gods of Egypt I will execute judgments. I am the Lord. And the blood shall be to you for a sign in the houses where you shall be, and I shall see the blood and shall pass over you, and the plague shall not be on you to destroy you, when I shall strike the land of Egypt.

"And this day shall be for a memorial for you, and you shall keep it a feast to the Lord in your generations, for an everlasting observance. Seven days shall you eat unleavened bread. On the first day there shall be no leaven in your houses, whosoever shall eat anything leavened from the first day until the seventh day shall perish out of Israel. The first day shall be holy and solemn, and the seventh day shall be kept with the like solemnity, you shall do no work in them, except those things that belong to eating And you shall observe the feast of the unleaven bread for in this same day I will bring you out of the land of Egypt and you shall keep this day in your generations by perpetual observances.

"The first month, the fourteenth day of the month, in the evening, you shall eat unleavened bread until the one and twentieth day in the evening Seven days there shall not be found any leaven in your houses, he that shall eat leaven bread his soul shall perish out of the assembly of Israel, whether he be born or a stranger in the land You shall not eat anything leaven, in all your habitations you shall eat unleavened bread.

"And Moses called all the ancients of the children of Israel and said to them, "Go and take a lamb by your families, and sacrifice the Phase. And dip a bunch of hyssop in the blood that is at the door, and sprinkle the transom of the door therewith and, both the door-cheeks; let none of you go out of the door of his house till morning. For the Lord will pass through striking the Egyptians, and when he shall see the blood on the transom and on both the posts he will pass over the door of the house and not suffer the destroyer to come into your house, and to hurt you.

"Thou shalt keep this thing as a law for thee and thy children forever. And when you have entered into the land, which the Lord will give you, as he hath promised, you shall observe these ceremonies. And when your children shall say to you, "What is the meaning of this service?" You shall say to them, "It is the victim of the passage of the Lord, when he passed over the houses of the children of Israel, striking the Egyptians and saving our houses," And the people bowing themselves adored.

"And the children of Israel going forth did as the Lord had commanded Moses and Aaron. And it came to pass at midnight the Lord slew every first-born in the land of Egypt, from the first-born of Pharao, who sat on the throne, unto the first-born captive man that was in the prison and all the first-born of cattle.

"And Pharao arose in the night, and all his servants, and all Egypt and there arose a great cry in Egypt, for there was not a house wherein there lay not one dead And Pharao calling Moses and Aaron in the night said, Arise and go forth from among my people, you and the children of Israel ; go sacrifice to the Lord, as you say you sacrifice to the Lord in due season."

Did the Son of God, leading in this solemn synagogue service, explain in a sermon to the congregation that eating the lamb with the bread and drinking the wine from patriarchal times foretold Calvary and the Eucharist? We know not; history is silent on the details of that Last Supper. But his sermon in the synagogue of Capharnaum, had prepared them for the change he was about to make in the Passover. We beg the indulgence of the reader and give his words[1] as the Gospel of this, the first Mass.

"I am the bread of life. Your fathers did eat manna in the desert, and they died. This is the bread descending down from heaven, that if any one eat of it he may not die. I am the living bread, which came down from heaven. If any man eat of this bread he shall live forever: and the bread which I will give, is my flesh for the life of the world. The Jews therefore debated among themselves saying: "How can this man give us his flesh to eat?"

"Then Jesus said to them. 'Amen, amen I say to you: Unless you eat the flesh of the Son of man, and drink his blood, you shall not have life in you. He that eateth my flesh and drinketh my blood hath everlasting life, and I will raise him up on the last day. For my flesh is meat indeed, and my blood is drink indeed. He that eateth my flesh, and drinketh my blood abideth in me and I in him

"As the living Father hath sent me, and I live by the Father, so he that eateth me the same shall live by me. This is the bread that came down from heaven. Not as your fathers did eat manna and died. He that eateth this bread shall live forever.'

"These things he said teaching in the synagogue in Capharnaum.[2]

When they read the Scriptures in the Temple or synagogue the clergy stood, while the congregation sat. That is the reason the celebrant and ministers stand and the people sit during the reading of the Epistle in all the Christian Rites. But when they said the Shema, the Jewish Creed, either in the synagogue or in private they always stood. Perhaps this is the reason we stand during the Creed. The congregation rises and stands while all recite the Jewish Creed.

The Jewish Creed was the Shema, which the Jews now pronounce Sh'ma: "Hear," the opening word. The prayer is composed of Moses' words,[3] and was the Creed of the Hebrew church protesting against paganism, with its multitude of gods and vile worship. Twice a day in Temple and synagogue this Creed was sung long before

[1] John vi. [2] John vi. 51-60. [3] Deut. vi. 4-9, and xi. 13-21, with Numb. xv. 37-41

Christ as the Talmud says.[1] It was also recited during the
morning and evening prayers by every male at his bed-
side, with his phylacteries on, standing beside his couch.
This prayer every orthodox Jew still says wearing his
phylacteries on brow and arm.

After the unity of the Godhead comes the love of God
above all, which Christian writers call charity, which
forgives sin when the sacraments cannot be received. By
and through this love the Saints of the Old Testament
saved their souls through God's foreknowledge of Christ's
atonement.

While reciting this Temple Creed, at what precise time
in the prayer we cannot find out, they brought in the
roasted lamb and laid it on the table, as the chief victim
of patriarchal and of the Temple worship. Who brought
in the lamb? It was becoming for a Temple priest to
bring in its victim, to link together patriarchs, Temple,
synagogue, Last Supper and Eucharist. James was a
Temple priest. He was, as we explained, the quasi deacon
of the Last Supper, while his brother John acted as the
subdeacon. The deacon during Mass represents the
Catholic Church while the subdeacon typifies the Jewish
Church.

It was just and right therefore that James, a Temple
priest, might bring in the lamb at this Passover which
was to fulfil the Passovers celebrated down the ages,
for now the great yearly feast was about to pass into the
eternal Passover, the Eucharistic Sacrifice the great Antitype of them all.

While singing the Creed, James went to the credence
table where with the wine and water rested on its cross
the roasted lamb. He takes up the plate on which it
rests, passes by where the Lord and his ministers are in
the sanctuary, bows deeply down before his Lord and
Master, and goes to the table in the middle of the Cenacle.
On the table he spreads a linen cloth, on that lays the
dish with the lamb, returns into the sanctuary, bows to
the Lord, and sits in his place beside his Master.

To-day that very ceremony is seen at every High Mass
while the Creed is sung. The deacon bows to the celebrant
goes to the credence table, takes the burse with its cor-

---

[1] Ber. i. 3.

poral, bows to the celebrant, goes and spreads the corporal on the altar, returns, bows to the celebrant and sits in his place

But the Shema, or Creed of the Jewish Church would not suffice for the Christian Church because new elements, the Divinity of Christ, the doctrine of the Holy Spirit, baptism, and other truths had been added to the Hebrew religion.

After the coming of the Holy Ghost, the apostles gathered in the Grotto on Olivet, where they had hid with their Master from Monday till that Thursday afternoon before the crucifixion. There they formed what is now called the Apostles' Creed, each one forming, it is said, one of its doctrines. This Creed, a little modified by ancient councils when its articles had been attacked, became the Creed now sung at every High Mass as the Jewish Creed was sung at the Last Supper.

THE SHEMA.

DEUT VI 4-9

" Hear, O Israel, the Lord our God is one Lord. Thou shalt love the Lord thy God, with thy whole heart and with thy whole soul and with thy whole strength. And these words which I command thee this day shall be in thy heart. And thou shalt tell them to thy children, and thou shalt meditate on them sitting in thy house and walking on thy journey, sleeping and rising. And thou shalt bind them as a sign on thy hand, and they shall be, and shall move between thy eyes. And thou shalt write them in the entry and on the doors of thy house "[1]

DEUT XI. 13-21.

"If then you obey my commandments, which I command you this day, that you love the Lord your God, and serve him with all your heart and with all your soul, he will give to your land the early rain, and the latter rain, that you may gather in your corn, and your wine and your oil, and your hay out of the fields to feed your cattle, and that you may eat and be filled. Beware lest perhaps your heart be deceived and you depart from the Lord

[1] See Edersheim, Life of Christ, i. 268.

and serve strange gods and adore them; and the Lord
being angry, shut up heaven that the rain come not down,
and the earth yield not her fruit, and you perish quickly
from the excellent land, which the Lord will give you.
Lay up these my words in your hearts and minds, and
hang them for a sign on your hands, and place them between your eyes. Teach your children that they may
meditate on them when thou sittest in thy house, and
when thou walkest on the way, and when thou liest down
and risest up. Thou shalt write them on the posts, and
the doors of thy house. That thy days may be multiplied, and the days of thy children in the land which the
Lord swore to thy fathers that he would give them as
long as the heavens hangeth over the earth.

NUMB. XV. 37-41

"The Lord said also to Moses: Speak to the children
of Israel and thou shall tell them to make to themselves
fringes in the corners of their garments putting in them
ribands of blue. That when they shall see them, they
shall remember all the commandments of the Lord and
not follow their own thoughts and eyes, going astray after
diverse things. But rather being mindful of the precepts
of the Lord, they may do them and be holy to their God."[1]

Christ: "Hear, O Israel the Lord our God the Lord is
One.

Apostles: "One is our God, great is our Lord: holy is
his name.

Christ: "Magnify the Lord with me and let us exalt his
name together. Thine, O Lord, is the greatness, and the
power, and the glory, and the victory, and the majesty,
for all that is in heaven and on earth is thine. Thine, O
Lord, is the kingdom, and the supremacy as head over all.
Exalt ye the Lord our God, and worship at his footstool,
holy is he. Exalt ye the Lord our God; and worship at
his holy mount, for the Lord our God is holy.

"Be thou blessed, O our Rock, our King and Redeemer,
Creator of holy beings, praised be thy name forever. O
our King, Creator of ministering spirits, all of whom stand
in the heights of the universe, and proclaim with awe in
unison aloud the words of the living God, and everlast-

---

[1] Beracoth, Chapter I.

ing King. All of them are beloved, pure and mighty, all of them in dread and awe do the will of their Master, and all of them open their mouths in holiness and purity, with song and a psalm, while they bless praise, glorify, reverence, sanctify and ascribe sovereignty. The name of the Divine King, the great, mighty and dreaded One, holy is he. And they take upon themselves the yoke of the kingdom of heaven one from another, and give sanction to one another to hallow their Creator in tranquil joy of spirit, with pure speech, and holy melody, they all respond in unison and exclaim with awe:

"Holy, holy, holy, is the Lord of hosts, the whole earth is full of his glory." [1]

"And the Ophanim and the holy Chayoth,[2] with the noises of great rushing, upraising themselves toward the Seraphim, thus over against them they offer praise and say:

"Blessed be the glory of the Lord from his place."

These synagogue services brought the First Mass to the end of the preface in our Latin Mass.

This Temple and synagogue prayer, little changed, comes down to our day in the Preface of the Mass. Thus far and no farther the synagogue brought the Mass as we see it to-day in the Latin Liturgy, as far as the end of the Preface. Therefore the Mass in the Roman Rite follows the general outlines of the Temple worship Moses established. He led the Hebrews in sight of the Promised Land but did not himself enter. When from Nebo's summit be saw Palestine to the west stretched out before him, he had fulfilled his mission and then he died. The Jew comes in sight of the supernatural wonders of the Mass with its Consecration and Eucharistic Sacrifice. A greater than Moses, was foretold to come to lead the world into the Christian faith.

When the Lord and his seven ministers had finished the synagogue services, they sat within the Bema or sanctuary as the bishop sits on his throne surrounded by his ministers during the first part of the mass.[3]

Then the Lord and his ministers rose from their seats, deeply bowed down before the Torah, "the Law," then

---

[1] Isaias vi 3 [2] These Hebrew names of the Seraphim and Cherubim are not found in the Bible [3] See St Thomas, Sum Theol, 3 22; 3 ad 3, etc.

marched from the sanctuary to the table in the middle of the Cenacle. Following the Temple rite they march before him according to their dignity, as the clergy still go before the bishop up to the altar, figuring the patriarchs, prophets, priests, and holy men of the ancient world who went before Christ to prepare for his coming in personage, prophecy and ceremonial. This is the reason that in all Church ceremonials the celebrant comes last, that the bishop goes up to the altar from his throne at the offertory of the Mass.

Clothed in sacred vestments we described, each carrying his staff, they march to the table as the Lord had commanded them to eat the Passover lamb: " And thus shall you eat it, you shall gird your reins, and shall have shoes on your feet, holding staves in your hands."[1] First the five apostles who had acted as his ministers went, then the seven who had read the seven sections of the Law, and lastly came the Prince of the House of David clothed in royal purple and vestments of cloth of gold, embroidered in white, red, green and violet—the sacred colors of the Temple of the Lord of hosts.

The rule was that each one should take part in the evening worship before celebrating the Passover, and up to this time the Cenacle was filled with the seventy-two disciples and the people he had converted who had followed him from Galilee to attend the Passover—men and women being separated by a low balustrade down the center of the room.

But as the law laid down that not less that ten or more than twenty persons could form a band to celebrate the Passover, all withdrew and left him alone with his apostles forming a band of thirteen.[2] The others formed into " bands " and held their Passover in the various rooms into which the Cenacle buildings were divided.[3]

[1] Exod. xii. 11   [2] Geikie, Life of Christ. i 191 to 210, 445 to 475.   [3] Ibidem, vol ii. 120; Luke viii. 1; Edersheim, Life of Christ, i 572.

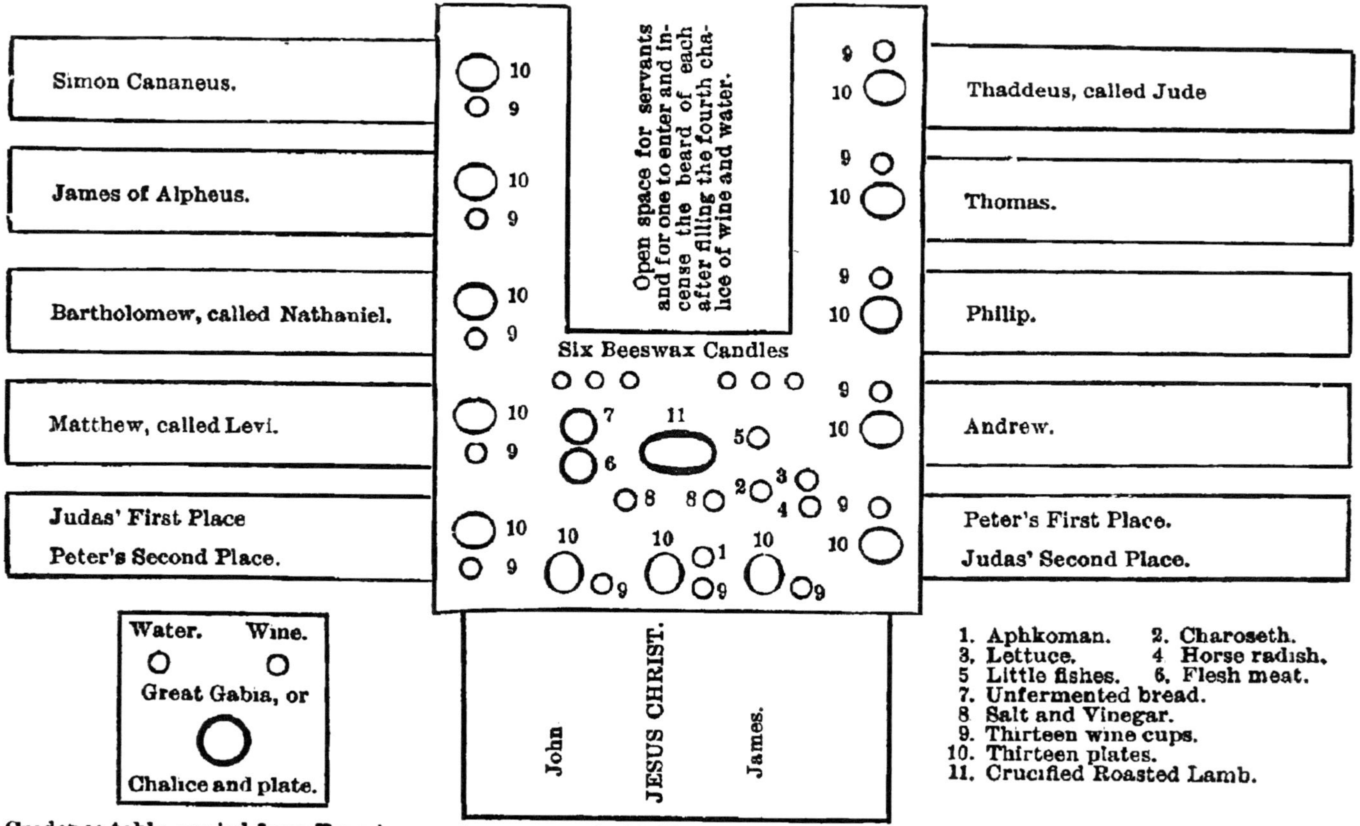

This is a diagram showing the arrangement of tables at the Last Supper.

Top row of names (apostles on one side):

Simon Cananeus.

James of Alpheus.

Bartholomew, called Nathaniel.

Matthew, called Levi.

Judas' First Place
Peter's Second Place.

Credence table (upper left):

Credence table, copied from Temple
Table of Proposition Bread

Water.   Wine.
O   O
Great Gabia, or
O
Chalice and plate.

Center:

John

JESUS CHRIST.

James.

Six Beeswax Candles

Open space for servants
and for one to enter and incense the beard of each
after filling the fourth chalice of wine and water.

Bottom row of names (apostles on other side):

Peter's First Place.
Judas' Second Place.

Andrew.

Philip.

Thomas.

Thaddeus, called Jude

Legend:

1. Aphikoman.   2. Charoseth.
3. Lettuce.   4. Horse radish.
5. Little fishes. 6. Flesh meat.
7. Unfermented bread.
8. Salt and Vinegar.
9. Thirteen wine cups.
10. Thirteen plates.
11. Crucified Roasted Lamb.

Caption (lower):

Arrangement of tables, couches, positions of Christ and apostles during first part
of Last Supper. After the lamb was eaten its remains were removed and they
began the Feast of Unleaven Bread which Christ changed into the Mass.

Thaddeus, called Jude

Thomas

Philip

Andrew

Judas

The Aphikoman was the unleaven bread on the plate before Christ and which he consecrated.

The great chalice was filled with wine mixed with water.

In the early Church they said Mass facing the people. Later they went to the other side of the table, so the celebrant's back was towards the congregation, and thus custom obtains in our day

Open space for servants and for one to enter and incense the beard of each after filling the fourth chalice of wine and water.

Six Beeswax Candles

Great Chalice

Aphikoman

James

JESUS CHRIST

John.

Simon Canaaneus.

James of Alpheus

Bartholomew, called Nathaniel

Matthew, called Levi

Peter

Water   Wine.

Credence table, copied from Temple Table of Proposition Bread.

Arrangement of tables, couches, positions of Christ and the apostles beginning second section of the Last Supper, called the Feast of the Unleaven Bread,

XII.—THE PRAYERS AND CEREMONIES OF THE CANON OF THE FIRST MASS.

CLOTHED in sacred vestments we described, cinctures binding up their loins, shoes on their feet, turbans on their heads, staffs in their hands, the Lord and his apostles came to the table to eat the Passover according to the rites God laid down through Moses for their fathers [1]

As they could not well hold their staffs while reclining, they hand them to the servants, as the bishop hands his crosier to one of his ministers before ascending to the altar, to sacrifice and eat the real Lamb of God in the Eucharist. They did not wear the turbans reclining at the table, and we suppose they removed them, as the bishop puts off his miter before going up to the altar.

Before the Bema or sanctuary, in the middle of the Cenacle, three tables had been prepared; arranged in the form of a U, one across the ends of the other two, so the servants could come in between and wait on the guests. These tables the Romans called the Triclinium, "Three Beds." [2]

The tables for Passover were always covered with linen table-cloths, the cross table having three covers, and the ends of the upper cloth hung down to the floor,[3] as seen in our churches in the three linen altar cloths, the upper one hanging down at the ends of the altar.

The master who presided at a feast, who was called the architriclinus,[4] "the master of the three beds," reclined at the middle of the cross table, his place being called the *medius*: "the middle." He had at his right hand, in the place called the *summus*: "the highest," one of his relatives or his dearest friend, and on his left, in the *immus*, "the lowest," another friend. Celebrating the

---

[1] Exod xii 11. [2] Edersheim, Life of Christ, II 115, 491 ; Geikie, Life of Christ, ii 114, Smith's Dic. of Bible, Feasts, etc. [3] Talmud, Babyl , c. x p 211, etc.
[4] John ii. 8-9.

Passover, in order to image the high priest, with his Sagan beside him in Temple ceremony, the master placed beside him on his right a prominent Rabbi, "the president of the synagogue," or one he wished to honor.

Sometimes the couches or divans were quite wide, and friend reposed next to friend, their heads over the table, left elbow resting on the cushion, feet extended out nearly touching the floor. Thus resting near each other, side by side, they talked to one another in a low tone and exchanged confidences.

A large couch was parallel with the cross table, and nine small couches had their heads to the two tables for the other apostles. In the middle of the large couch, at the head table, the Lord reposed with his dearest friends. Who were these? In Gospel history, Peter, James and John are given as Jesus' dearest friends. First called Simon, Christ changed his name to Peter, "the Rock," the corner-stone of his Church, and he is always given first as the prince of the apostles. Twenty-three times Matthew mentions him, nineteen times Mark gives his name, twenty times Luke writes of him in his Gospel, and John thirty times, while in the history of the infant Church—the Acts has fifty-five verses with his name.

James and John, sons of Zebedeus, fishermen of Galilee, were of the family of Aaron and therefore Temple priests. So say some writers. Nineteen times James' name is found in the Gospels and the Acts, but his brother John does not mention him; he was appointed, some say, by Christ himself as the first bishop of Jerusalem. Famed even among Jews and pagans for his holiness, the Jews killed him, and their great historian Josephus says the calamities of the awful siege and destruction of Temple and city by the Romans under Titus was a visitation of God on the Jews because of James' martyrdom.

John, "the Pious," youngest of the apostolic band, was loved of Jesus above the others, because he was a virgin, and into his care he gave his Mother. From his seat at Ephesus John ruled the churches in Asia. He wrote his Gospel to defend Christ's Divinity, attacked by early heretics. Nineteen times we find his name in Gospel, and Acts. He does not give his own name, but refers to himself as "that disciple whom Jesus loved"

These three Jesus held in highest esteem because of what they represented in his future Church. Peter, first bishop of Rome, imaged that long line of Pontiffs who taught the world religion. James, the first apostle to have a fixed seat, first bishop of Jerusalem, first to form a liturgy, first bishop to die a martyr, represented the bishops of the world. John imaged the Jewish Church, the Temple with its sacrifices, the synagogue with its services, the patriarchal fathers of the nations, the prophets with their inspired words and writings in the Old Testament, the whole Hebrew religion and history.

Therefore when Christ raised the dead girl,[1] when he was transfigured on Tabor, when he entered into the awful sorrows of Gethsemane, when he showed his powers as God, when he suffered in the garden, he called these three—Peter, James and John—to be with him.[2] Therefore we conclude he called them beside him when he celebrated the Last Supper.

Thus it came to pass that the Lord with Peter, James and John reclined at the cross table facing the other apostles reclining at the outside of the two parallel tables facing each other. The early Church carefully copying every detail of that feast placed the bishop behind the altar, where he said Mass facing the people. There was the bishop's throne, in the apse of the cathedral, as to-day you will find it in St. John Lateran, the Pope's cathedral, Rome, and in ancient cathedrals, a custom still followed by Oriental Christians. The apostles reposing on the outside of the parallel tables facing each other, gave rise to the cathedral stalls, and the seats for the clergy in our sanctuary.

Resting near the Lord on his right was Peter, his chief, as to-day the assistant priest is beside the pontificating bishop, as the Sagan was beside the Temple high priest when he sacrificed. At his right was James waiting on the Master, as to-day you see the deacon beside the bishop at his right. On the other side was John, as the sub-deacon is at the bishop's left.

As they repose on the couches, Jesus faces James, his back is turned towards John, and thus it was easy for the latter to lay his head on Jesus' breast beside him, and ask

[1] Luke viii. 51.   [2] Matt. xxvi. 37.

in whispered confidence who the traitor was, and for the
Lord to dip the bit of bread into the Charoseth, or salad,
and hand it to Judas at the other side of James.

On the cross table before the reclining Lord and his
"band" of apostles burned the six Passover beeswax
candles, with the different dishes we have described.
Before him was the crucified roasted lamb resting still on
his cross, the striking image of Him who was to be crucified
the next day. The Lord, as Master of the Passover, was
to carve "the Body of the Lamb," to cut portions of the
flesh for each, that the victim called since it was chosen
Monday as "The Lamb of God," might so strikingly foretell him whom John the Baptist called "the Lamb of
God who was to take away the sins of the world."[1]   He
was to give himself to them in Communion to fulfil the
patriarchal and Temple image—the sacrificed lamb.

Down the ages from the days of Adam and of Abel the
lamb was sacrificed and eaten as a type of the Redeemer
in patriarchal, prophetic sacrifice and ceremonial with all
ther mystic and symbolic meanings.   Therefore, he who
was the true "Lamb of God," the great Antitype to whom
all pointed was to give himself to them in the Eucharist,
that as the body was nourished by the lamb's flesh in the
Old Testament, so Christian souls might be nourished by
the Body and Blood of the true Lamb of God, Christ.
For if he were not really present in the Eucharist—in
Communion, then the types of the Jewish Church would
never have been fulfilled, the shadow would never have
its reality, and God himself would have deceived mankind.

Ever onward, upward, higher, strive human souls.   The
deepest instincts of our very reason is to tend towards
truth and perfection eternal in God.   The dream and
aspiration of our race is towards heaven, towards union
with God in eternal bliss beyond the skies.   Union with
the Deity!   What but this can satisfy the instinctive
everlasting cravings of our souls?   Now the God-man is
about to fulfil the types, to satisfy that soul-hunger, that
craving natural to us all.   He who was about to die for
mankind would give himself to us, give his whole self,

---

[1] John i. 29; Talmud, Babyl., Pesachim, x. 3; Geikie, Life of Christ, i 391;
ii. 447.

his Body, Blood, soul, Divinity, that the millions of the redeemed might nourish their spiritual life on him, the only font of the supernatural, sole bond of union between God and mankind. The roasted lamb of the Old Testament with all its mystic ceremonial was united with the bread and wine of the New Testament, about to be changed into his Body and Blood. Therefore when they came to the table, looking back on the past filled with type and emblem of this great Supper, and glancing into the future, into the other life of heaven, when all would be fulfilled, Christ uttered the deep sentiments of his loving heart.

" With desire have I desired to eat this Pasch with you before I suffer. For I say to you, that from this time I will not eat it, till it be fulfilled in the kingdom of God." [1]

With deep desire he wished to fulfil the meanings of the Passover, that as he had united the Godhead with our humanity in his one personality of the Divine Son, that he might unite himself to every member of his Church in Communion, and thus bind himself in closest union possible to every one of the members of his Church, and thus satisfy the longings of our nature for union with the Deity.

As in Temple and in times of prophets and patriarchs, every object, every ceremony was emblematic in the Passover. In type, image, emblem, religious objects and Scripture, God had revealed the future to their fathers. Prophecy and mystery and history hidden in Passover from far beyond historic days were now about to be fulfilled, revealed, finished, completed, sanctified, unfolded, and find the reasons of their revelation. They were to be blessed by the Son of God himself. Till then only shadows they were to pass into the substance they so wonderfully foretold.

We will therefore ask the reader's indulgence, and again recall the mysticism of Passover. Before the Lord's place in the middle of the cross table, on a large dish, the sacrificed, skinned, roasted lamb rested on his cross. Down from prehistoric times, from beyond the deluge it had come, it was prepared and eaten at Easter each year

---

[1] Luke xxii. 15.

to foretell, far better than any words, preaching, or writing the Lord soon to be, arrested, tried, condemned, scourged, crucified, dead, covered with yellow serum oozing out. His body skinned in scourgings, when he was dead looked as though he had been roasted, to show that he, filled with unseen fire of the Shekina, the Holy Spirit inspiring him with love, was to die to redeem us and be eaten as "the Lamb of God" in the Eucharist.

The three unleaven cakes of wheaten flour mixed with water, oil and incense, anointed with a cross, with five finger holes, and baked with fire, foretold the Lord's body, with its five wounds, broken in his Passion, as it were baked in the fire of the Shekina, anointed by the Holy Ghost, the real Manna Christians eat in Communion. The wine in the cruet was an emblem of his blood poured out in his sufferings for mankind's sins.

The bitter herbs imaged that bitter slavery their fathers suffered in Egypt, and the bitter habits of sin, which enslave Christian souls. Wine soured becomes vinegar, the pleasures of life represented by wine are soured by sin and wicked habits, which bind the soul in demoniac slavery.

The flesh meat representing the Leviathan, the hippopotamus of the Nile, was emblematic of Egypt to the Jew, and typical of the demon to the Christian. The beast is given in Job afflicted by a terrible skin disease brought on him by the demon. Job could not understand in his innocence why he was so afflicted, but he represented the future Christ in his patience suffering the awful scourgings in Pilate's Forum. The Leviathan to the Jewish mind was the emblem of Egypt, their fathers' enemy, but the Christian sees in this beast the demon, whom not Job but Christ conquered.[1] Whence God spoke to Job:

"Canst thou draw out the Leviathan with a hook, or canst thou tie his tongue with a cord?" that is put a bridle in his mouth and subdue him? for a greater personage than Job, the Messiah, was to come and rescue mankind from the devil's slavery. The flesh meat also reminded them of the elephant they named the behemoth, "large beast," typical of Babylonia, where for seventy years their fathers were enslaved, and was emblematic of

---

[1] Job iii. 8; Migne, Cursus Comp. S. Scripturæ, iii. 978.

the Old Serpent, who from Eden's gates had enslaved Adam's race, and whom Christ was to conquer in his death.

At the Passover the master who presided used a larger chalice called the mezrak, because at the end of the banquet he offered his chalice to each guest, "and they all drank from it,"[1] as a sign of friendship before they parted. Law and custom prescribed that each one should drink not less than four cups of wine. Women, weak persons and the children could not always take four full chalices of pure wine, and in prehistoric days, they mixed the wine with water, that they might take the four "legal cups." This is the reason that water is mixed with the wine at Mass, which some writers say foretold the water flowing from the side of the dead Christ.

The Prince of David's dynasty that night used a large silver chalice, the famous Gabia, "Chalice," his forefathers foretold the Messiah would use, according to David's word's: "I will take the chalice of salvation, and I will call on the name of the Lord."[2]

A curious tradition of the Jews at that time stated, that this was the chalice Noe used when he blessed the white races in their father Japheth and cursed Ham's children in Canaan.[3] His son Sem, named Melchisedech, used it when he offered bread and wine, and blessed the Hebrews in their father Abraham.[4] It had been handed down to the Hebrew kings. When Babylonians sacked the city, it was lost. But in the twelfth year before Christ, when Herod began to build the Temple, it was found in the ruins, and for safe keeping placed in the Cenacle. Let the reader judge himself the truth of these statements. Of it Ven. Bede writes—the Martyry he mentions being then the ruins of Pilate's palace and Golgotha Calvary.

"In the street leading from the Martyry to Golgotha, was a shrine, which covered the Lord's Chalice, and through the grating they used to touch and kiss it. The chalice was of silver, and had two handles, and in it was the sponge which was offered the Lord from which to drink."[5]

---

[1] Mark xiv 23.   [2] Psalm cxv 13, etc   [3] Gen. ix 21-27   [4] Gen. xiv 18, etc.
[5] De Locis Sacris, Cap 2

25

This chalice was therefore like "a loving cup," having two handles so the guests could take it in their hands when drinking—this ceremony being the last token of their love and esteem for the master of the feast, at whose hospitable table they had feasted. When the Lord consecrated this the last or fourth cup of wine and passed it to his apostles, he fulfilled the meaning of the ancient rite of the goblet of love and friendship of the Passover.

With the great Chalice was a silver plate, belonging to the set Melchisedech used when he offered bread and wine. This paten held the three cakes of unfermented bread. Chalice and plate were covered with napkins as the sacred vessels are covered on our altars. At each apostle's place was a small goblet or chalice called a cos or sepil. Following the Jewish rite the early Christians used more than one chalice, till abuses rose and our present discipline began.

Near the end of the cross table, on the Master's left, was a small table copied after the Temple golden table on which the priests each Sabbath placed the proposition bread and wine before the Lord.[1] At Passover, on this table they placed the chalice the master used, the plate holding the three cakes of unleaven bread and the two flagons holding wine and water.[2] Therefore we suppose that on this table rested the ancient historic Gabia, "Chalice," with its silver plate holding the three cakes and the two vessels, one of wine the other of water. After the master breaks the Aphikomen into two halves, one half is returned to this table, the other lay on the table before the master. These two parts of the middle cake are referred to frequently during the ceremonies.

At Passover the master's friends, or the "standing men" of the synagogue filled the chalices of the guests with wine and mixed it with water from this flagon, and also used this water to wash their hands. To-day in the sanctuary beside the altar, stands the credence table, coming from the Temple, whereon at High Mass you see the chalice, the paten, or little plate, with the bread, these being covered as during the Passover, and beside them the cruets of wine and water.[3] Peter, James and John

[1] Talmud, Hagaga, 53.   [2] See St. Thomas Sum 3a Q 74, A. 6–8. etc.   [3] See Geikie, Life of Christ, ii. 191, 514, etc.

acting as "standing men" of the Jewish Church, perhaps poured the wine and water into the chalice for the Lord. To-day the assistant priest stands beside the bishop, while the deacon and subdeacon prepare and pour the wine and water into the chalice.

The oldest part of the Passover was the ceremonial at the table when they ate the lamb's flesh, and the feast of unleaven bread when they took the bread and wine with prayer, Psalm and anthem. The synagogue services or evening prayers were added after the Babylonian Captivity, but this service at the table came down from the patriarchs, or from Moses and the prophets.

The synagogue service was sung in a loud tone, while the table Seder was recited in a lower voice. The synagogue worship brought the Passover to the end of what we call the Preface of the Mass. During this first part of the Mass, the celebrant sings in a loud tone, while he recites the Canon in a low voice. Why is this? Some writers say the Canon is thus said in a low voice because of the persecutions of the Roman empire, and that then they said Mass in secret places and in a low voice lest enemies might hear them.

But enemies would have heard the first part of the Mass which was always sung from the beginning when possible. The Orientals, not disturbed by Roman persecutions, sang the Mass from apostolic days, and therefore this does not seem a valid reason why the Canon is recited in a low tone. This Canon, found only in the Latin Liturgy, the Mass St. Peter established at Rome, is the most sacred part of the Mass, and corresponds to the sacred Seder of the Passover the Jews said at the table in a lower voice. St. Peter, leader of the apostolic band therefore established the Latin Liturgy with its Canon more according to the Jewish Passover Rite than the other apostles, who established Liturgies of the Mass in different languages.

Two intervals of rest divide the Passover Seder into three sessions. They claim one section foretold the sufferings of the Messiah, the second the sufferings in hell, and the third the wars against Gog "The Mountain," "The High," and Magog, his country, foretold to fight against Israel. He was a figure of that Anti-Christ prophesied to fight against Christians towards the end of the world.[1]

Each person celebrating the Passover held the scroll of the Liturgy in his hands, and read the service with the master, the latter leading. Therefore each apostle held his scroll or book of the Passover Liturgy in his hands, and with Christ recited the prayers. For this reason the priest when being ordained, or the bishop at his consecration, says the Mass with the ordaining or pontificating bishop.

When they came to the table they reclined on the couches, recalling their fathers' freedom after the Egyptian slavery, and emblematic of the rest of mankind from the trials and troubles of the Old Testament. Thus they began that part of the Passover Liturgy which corresponds to the Canon of the Latin Mass. In remembrance of this reclining position, when the celebrant begins the Canon with these words: "Thee therefore most merciful Father," etc., he raises up his hands, brings them down on the edge of the altar table, and bends deeply down, resting the ends of his fingers on the edge of the table in memory of Christ and his apostles reclining at the Last Supper.

The Gospels give only words and incidents which did not belong to the Passover—the Lord's words, the washing of the feet, the prophecy of Judas' treason, the Consecration, the Communion, the words of warning, the promise to pray for Peter against the demon's wiles—these did not belong to the Jewish feast, and they are given in the Gospels.

Why were not all the details of the First Mass given? Because they would have been superfluous. Every Jew celebrated the Passover. He had reclined at the table since he was confirmed at twelve; he knew the ceremonial and the Liturgy of Passover, and it would have been useless to fill the Gospels with the Liturgy and Ceremonial, for all Hebrews, as well as most pagans, knew or could learn all about the Passover.

Can the Passover of the days of Christ be laid before the reader? We give the rite as we saw it celebrated in

[1] See Zanolini De Festis Judæorum, C i Note 6. We refer the reader to this work, to Benedict XIV De Festis D N Jesu Christi, Cursus Comp S. Scripturæ, and to various Jewish writers, the Talmud, Lives of Christ, etc., for numerous details of the following pages.

Jerusalem, and place Christ as leader of this band of twelve apostles   We do not say that the following is absolutely correct, but it is as near the Last Supper as it is possible to reconstruct it after the lapse of nearly twenty centuries.

The Greek Gospels say "he reclined " at the table, our Bible says he "sat down." "And when the hour was come he reclined, and the twelve apostles with him."[1]

The Liturgy of the Passover, formed of prayers, Psalms, chants, anthems, directions, rubrics, etc., were the foundations on which the apostles, apostolic men and great saints formed the fifty-four different Liturgies of the Mass   The most famous, the Roman Rite, established by Peter in the Eternal City, and with little change comes down to us under the name of the Latin or Roman Mass.

The Jews call these services at the table the Seder, " Section," to distinguish it from the synagogue prayers and services already given, and which were said in the Bema or sanctuary.   Whence did this Passover Liturgy, or Seder, arise?   Some Jewish writers say Moses is its author; others that Moses laid the foundation, and that the prophets and great men of Israel added to it; but all agree that it took its rise way back in times immemorial, beyond the Babylonian Captivity.   The Palestine Jew has hardly changed an iota of his religion since these far-off days, and he spurns the idea of any important additions to the Seder since the prophets lived.   Nothing equals the conservatism of the Jerusalem Hebrew regarding his faith.[2]   We will give the fourteen Divisions of the Hebrew Passover Liturgy, under different headings, with free translations modern Jews give of these Hebrew Headings.

---

[1] Luke xxii 14   [2] See Edersheim, Life of Christ, I. 438, II. 137, 138 , Geikie, Life of Christ, etc.

THE LITURGY OF THE LORD'S LAST SUPPER.

SANCTIFICATION OF THE PASSOVER.

1. THE KADDESC, "SANCTIFY." (SAY THE SANCTIFI-
CATION.)

They pour the wine into the chalices, mix it with water, saying this prayer, as a blessing over the wine:

"Blessed art thou, O Eternal, our God, King of the Universe, Creator of the fruit of the vine.

"Blessed art thou, O Eternal, our God, Sovereign of the Universe, who hath chosen us from among all people, and didst exalt us above all nations, and didst sanctify us with thy commandments; and with love thou has given us, O Eternal, our God, solemn days for joyous festivals, and seasons for gladness, this day of the Feast of unleaven bread, the season of our freedom, a holy convocation, a memorial of the departure from Egypt. For thou has chosen and sanctified us above all people; and holy festivals thou has caused us to inherit, with love, and favor, joy and gladness, O Eternal, who sanctifieth Israel and the seasons.

"Blessed art thou, O Eternal, our God, King of the Universe, who hath preserved us alive, sustained us, and brought us to enjoy this season."

They drink the first goblet of wine. While washing the hands the rubric states that they are not to say the blessing.

2. URCHATZ, "WASH." (WASH THE HANDS.)

After drinking the first cup of wine, all rise and wash their hands. Before, during and after the Passover, they washed their hands. Following this rite the celebrant of the Mass washes his before, twice during, and after Mass. Then they again reclined and began the Supper.[1]

[1] Edersheim, Life of Christ, II 9, 10, 152, 205, 215 For rules for washing of hands see Geikie, Life of Christ, I 207, 451, Talmud, etc.

3 CARPAS " THE PARSLEY." (TAKE THE PARSLEY.)

Jesus takes the parsley the Scripture calls the "bitter herbs," dips it into the vinegar, and hands a portion to each. Holding it in their hands, all together say :
" Blessed art thou, O Lord our God, King of the Universe, Creator of the fruit of the earth."

4. JACHATZ, " DRAWING FORTH " (BREAK THE MIDDLE CAKE.)

Jesus uncovers the three cakes of Passover, which lay on the plate on the credence table, covered with a napkin. " Drawing forth," he takes the middle cake and breaks it into two equal parts, as the celebrant of the Mass breaks the Host into two equal parts after the Consecration. The smaller half he lays again on the plate, hiding it under a napkin till toward the end of the feast.

This part of the middle cake was called the Aphikuman, which they pronounced Ophikoman : " the heavenly manna," " the heavenly bread," " Food of Angels," and reminded them of the manna falling from heaven to feed their fathers in the desert. It was so sacred it was hidden till near the end of the feast. This the prophets ordered to show that the mysteries of the Mass were hidden in the Passover. Following this rite the bread and wine are always covered after being offered on our altar. Half the Ophikoman was covered on the table with the other cakes, the other half was covered with the prayer shawl, as we will later describe.

5. MAGGHID, " SHOWING " (SAYS THE SERVICE).

The Master uncovers the cake of unleaven bread and holds up the dish with the cake. With eyes uplifted to heaven they say this prayer, which seems to have come from the days of the Babylonian Captivity, when the prophets foretold and Israel hoped they would return to their country.
" Behold this is the bread of affliction our fathers ate in the Land of Egypt. Let all who are hungry enter and eat thereof. At present we celebrate it in here, but next year we hope to celebrate it in the land of Israel. This

year we are servants, but next year we hope to be free-men in the land of Israel."

They fill again the chalices with wine from the large cruet on the credence table and mix it with water. They cover the chalices with napkins, as they had covered the bread.

6. ROCHTZA, "WASH." (ALL AT TABLE WASH HANDS.)

They wash their hands again lest they might have become soiled. The Passover services prescribed this second washing of the hands before taking the food from the common dishes with the fingers, for they did not use table knives and forks in the days of which we write. They were very careful to follow the Law regarding washing.[1]

They hold up the unleaven bread while the youngest asks the question. When he finishes they lay it on the table. Then they explain the meanings of the ceremony, following the directions God gave Moses." "And when your children shall say to you: What is the meaning of this service? You shall say to them. It is the victim of the passage of the Lord, when he passed over the houses of the children of Israel in Egypt striking the Egyptians and saving our house."[2] The Passover rubric says. "The youngest in the company asks," etc. John therefore asked the question.

"Wherefore is this night distinguished from all other nights? On all other nights we eat either leavened or un-leavened bread, but on this night only unleaven; on any other nights we may eat any kind of herbs, but on this night only bitter herbs; on all other nights we do not dip even once, but on this night twice; on all other nights we eat or drink either sitting or reclining, but on this night we all recline?"

7. MOTZI MATZA, "BRING FORTH THE BREAD," (BREAK THE CAKE).

The Master makes a sign to bring the dish on the credence table with the two cakes of unfermented bread to him. He takes the cakes and shows them to the one

---

[1] Levit. xv. and xvi. [2] Exod. xii. 26-27.

who asks the questions; when the paschal lamb is mentioned, he points to it; when the wine is mentioned all take up their cups of wine and hold them in their hands. Reading from the Liturgy all together they answer John's questions.

" Because we were slaves to Pharaoh in Egypt, and the Eternal our God brought us forth from thence with a mighty hand, the outstretched hand of the Most High, blessed be he. Had he not brought our ancestors from Egypt, we, and our children, and our children's children, would have continued in bondage to the Pharaohs in Egypt. Therefore, although we are all wise, all of us men of understanding and experience, all of us having knowledge of the Law, nevertheless it is incumbent on us to discourse of the departure from Egypt, and all who largely discourse on the departure from Egypt are looked on as worthy of praise."

A little more than a page of this part of the Liturgy is written in the language, form and style of the Talmud, giving the names and ideas of famous Rabbis who lived in the middle of the second century after Christ. These parts were evidently added about this epoch. We are not certain regarding some minor portions immediately following, as internal evidence seems to hint that they did not exist at the time of Christ; but we give them to let the reader judge for himself. The words, " It is said," refer to Bible statements, but there are no quotation marks in the Liturgy.

" Blessed be the Omnipotent, blessed is he who hath given his Law to his people Israel, blessed be he whose Law speaketh distinctly of four children of different dispositions, viz: the *wicked*, the *simple*, and *he who hath not the capacity to inquire.*

" The wise son thus expresses himself: What mean these statutes and judgments, which the Lord our God has commanded us? Then shalt thou instruct him in all the laws of the Passover, also that we must not have a dessert brought to the table after the paschal lamb.

" The wicked son expresses himself thus What mean you by this service? By the expression " you " it is clear he does not include himself, and as he hath withdrawn himself from the collective body of the nation, it is proper that thou retort on him, and therefore answer him thus, This is done because of that which the Eternal did for me, when I went from Egypt, i. e. for me, but not for him, for had he been there, he would not have been thought worthy to be redeemed.

"The simple son artlessly observes, What is this? Then shalt thou answer him : For with a strong hand the Eternal brought us out of Egypt, from the house of bondage.

"But as for him who hath not the capacity to inquire, thou must begin to discourse, as it is said, And thou shalt show thy son that day saying, This is done because of that which the Eternal did for me, when I went forth from Egypt.

"Possibly you may think that he (the father) is bound to explain this from the first day of the month, Nisan, therefore it is said on that day, yet as it says on that day, it might be inferred that it must be whilst it is day, but as it is said, This is done because of that, etc, from which it is to be inferred at no other time, but when the unleavened cake and bitter herbs are placed before thee.

"Our ancestors were anciently idolaters, but at present the Lord hath brought us near to his service, as it is said : And Joshua said unto all the people, thus saith the Eternal, the God of Israel, your ancestors dwelled on the other side of the River (Euphrates) in old time, even Terah, the father of Abraham, and the father of Nachor, and served other gods.

"And I took your father Abraham from the other side of the flood, and led him through all the land of Canaan, and multiplied his seed, and gave him Isaac, and I gave unto Isaac, Jacob and Esau, and I gave unto Esau mount Seir for his possession, but Jacob and his children went down into Egypt.

"Blessed be he who strictly preserveth his promise unto Israel, blessed be the Most Holy who premeditated the end of the captivity, that he might perform what he had promised to our father Abraham between the parts." (Note in the Liturgy.) "The covenant made with Abraham when he was commanded to divide the heifer, goat and ram, through which a smoking furnace and flaming lamp passed, by which the covenant was made between God and Abraham, and is therefore called the covenant made between the parts," as is said: And he said unto Abraham, Know for certain, that thy seed shall be strangers in a land that is not theirs, and shall serve them, and they shall afflict them four hundred years. And also that a nation, whom they shall serve will I judge, and they shall afterwards go forth with great substance.

"Lift up the cup of wine and say:

" And it is this same promise which hath been the support of our ancestors and of us also, for not one only hath risen up against us, but in every generation there are some who rise up against us to annihilate us, but the Most High, blessed be he, hath delivered us out of their hand.

" Set the cup on the table again.

" Search and inquire what Laban,[1] the Syrian intended to do to our father Jacob, for Pharaoh decreed the destruction of the males only, but Laban intended to root out the whole, as is said: A Syrian hath nearly caused my father to perish, and he went down into Egypt, and sojourned there with few persons, and there became a great, mighty, and populous nation.

" And he went down into Egypt, compelled thereto by the word of God, and sojourned there, by which we are taught that he did not go down to settle there, but only to sojourn, as is said: And they (Joseph's brethren) said unto Pharaoh, To sojourn in the land we are come, for thy servants have no pasture for their flocks, for the famine is sore in the land of Canaan, now therefore we pray thee let thy servants dwell in the land of Goshen.

" With few persons, as it is said: With threescore and ten souls, thy ancestors went down into Egypt, and now the Eternal, thy God, hath made them as the stars of heaven for multitude.

" And he there became a nation, by which we are informed that the children of Israel were distinguished even in Egypt as a peculiar people.

" Great and mighty, as it is said: And the children of Israel were fruitful and increased abundantly, and

[1] Gen. xxvii; Gen xxxi.

waxed exceedingly mighty and the land was filled with them.

"And populous, as it is said: I have caused thee to multiply as the vegetation of the field, and thou becomest considerable and great and adorned with many beauties, thy breasts are formed, and thy hair grown, yet thou art naked and bare.

"And the Egyptians ill-treated us, afflicted us, and laid heavy bondage upon us. And the Egyptians ill-treated us, as it is said: Come let us deal wisely with them, lest they multiply, and it come to pass if there chance to be a war, that they might go over to our enemies, fight against us, and so get them out of the land.

"And they afflicted us, as it is said: And they set over them taskmasters to afflict them with their burdens, and they built for Pharaoh store cities, even Pithom and Raamses. And they laid heavy bondage upon us, as it is said: And the Egyptians made the children of Israel serve with rigor.

"And we cried unto the Eternal, the God of our ancestors, the Eternal heard our voice, and observed our affliction, our labor and our oppression.

"And we cried to the Eternal, the God of our ancestors as it is said: And it came to pass in the course of time, that the king of Egypt died, and the children of Israel sighed by reason of their bondage, and they cried and their cry ascended unto God, by reason of their bondage.

"And the Eternal heard our voice as it is said: And God heard their groaning, and remembered his covenant with Abraham, Isaac and with Jacob.

"And he saw our affliction, this denotes their being denied the company of their wives to prevent propagation as it is said: And God looked on the children of Israel, and God had knowledge of their affliction.

"And our grievousness, this denotes the destruction of the male children, as it is said, Every son that is born ye shall cast into the river, but every daughter you shall save alive.

"And our oppression, this denotes fatigue, as it is said: And I have also seen the oppression with which the Egyptians harass them.

"And the Eternal brought us forth from Egypt with a strong hand, and with an outstretched arm, with terror and with signs and wonders.

"And the Eternal brought us forth from Egypt not by means of an angel, nor by means of a seraph, nor by means of a messenger, but the Most High, blessed be he, Himself is his glory, as it is said: And I will pass through the land of Egypt this night, and I will smite all the first-born in the land of Egypt, both of man and beast, and on all the gods of Egypt will I execute judgment, I am the Eternal."

"And I will pass through the land of Egypt, I myself and not an angel, and I will smite all the first-born, I myself, and no seraph, and on all the gods of Egypt, I will execute judgment, I myself, and not a messenger, I am the Eternal, I am He and no other.

"With a strong hand, this denotes the murrain, as it is said: Behold the hand of the Eternal will be upon thy cattle, which are in the field, upon thy houses, upon the asses, upon the oxen, and upon the sheep, a very grievous murrain.

"And with an outstretched arm, this denotes the sword, as it is said elsewhere on such an occasion: And a drawn sword in his hand stretched out over Jerusalem.

"And with great terror, this denotes the appearance of the Divine Presence, as is said: For God assayed to go and take unto him a nation from the midst of another nation, by proofs, signs and wonders, by war and a mighty hand, by an outstretched arm, and great terror, according to all that the Eternal, your God, did for you in Egypt, before your eyes.

"And with prodigies, this denotes the miracles performed with the rod, as it is said: And thou shalt take this rod in thy hand, wherewith thou shalt do the prodigies.

"And with wonders, this denotes the plague of blood, as is said: And I will do wonders in the heavens, and on earth, blood and fire and ascending pillars of smoke.

"It may also be explained thus : 'With a strong' hand denotes two plagues; 'with an outstretched arm,' two plagues 'with great terror,' two plagues; 'with prodigies,' two plagues; 'with wonders,' two plagues.

"There are ten plagues which the Most High, blessed be He, brought on the Egyptians in Egypt, viz:

BLOOD,	FROGS,
VERMIN,	MURRAIN,
A MIXTURE,	NOXIOUS BEASTS,
BOILS,	HAIL,
LOCUSTS,	DARKNESS,

and

THE SLAYING OF THE FIRST-BORN.

When each plague is mentioned the Jews of our day let fall a drop of wine on the floor. The reader will notice that the killing of the first-born makes eleven plagues, and that the slaying of the first-born in Egypt is given as a special category in itself, for it was the last and greatest punishment God inflicted on Egypt. Thus it stands out alone because it foretold the killing of the Virgin's First-born on Calvary.

"What abundant favors hath the Omnipresent conferred on us!

"For if he had but brought us forth from Egypt, and had not inflicted justice upon the Egyptians, it would have been sufficient.

"If he had inflicted justice upon them, and had not executed judgment upon their gods, it would have been sufficient.

"If he had not executed judgment on their gods, and had not slain their first-born it would have been sufficient.

"If he had slain their first-born, and had not bestowed their wealth on us, it would have been sufficient.

"If he had given us their wealth, and had not divided the sea for us, it would have been sufficient.

"If he had divided the sea, and had not caused us to pass through on dry land, it would have been sufficient.

"If he had caused us to pass through the dry land, and had not plunged our oppressors in the midst thereof, it would have been sufficient.

"If he had plunged our oppressors in the midst thereof, and had not supplied us with the necessaries in the wilderness, forty years, it would have been sufficient.

"If he had supplied us with the necessaries in the

wilderness forty years, and had not fed us with manna,
it would have been sufficient.

"If he had fed us with manna, and had not given us
the Sabbath, it would have been sufficient.

"If he had given us the Sabbath, and had not brought
us to Mount Sinai, it would have been sufficient.

"If he had brought us near to Mount Sinai, and had
not given us his law, it would have been sufficient.

"If he had given us the law and had not brought us to
the land of Israel, it would have been sufficient.

"If he had brought us to the land of Israel, and had
not built the Temple, it would have been sufficient.

"How much then are we indebted for the manifold
favors the Omnipresent conferred on us?   He brought us
forth from Egypt, executed judgment on the Egyptians,
and on their gods, slew their first-born, gave us their
wealth, divided the sea for us, caused us to pass through
on dry land, plunged our oppressors in the midst thereof,
supplied us with the necessaries in the wilderness forty
years, gave us manna to eat, gave us the Sabbath, brought
us near to Mount Sinai, gave us the law, brought us into
the land of Israel, built the chosen holy Temple for us to
make atonement for our sins.

"Whosoever doth not make mention of the three
things used on the Passover, hath not done his duty and
these are they, the paschal lamb and the bitter herbs, the
unleaven cake.

"The paschal lamb, which our ancestors ate during the
existence of the holy Temple, what did it denote?   It
denoted that the Most Holy, blessed be he, passed over our
fathers' houses in Egypt, as is said: And ye shall say it
is the Lord's Passover, because he passed over the houses
of the children of Israel in Egypt, when he smote the
Egyptians, and delivered our houses, and the people
bowed their heads and worshipped."

The Master takes up the cakes in the dish lying on the
table, shows them to the apostles as a memorial of their
freedom and continues the Liturgy.

"These unleavened cakes, wherefore do we eat them?
Because there was not sufficient time for the dough of
our ancestors to leaven, before the Holy Supreme King
of kings, blessed is he, appeared to them and redeemed

them as is said : And they baked unleaven cakes of the dough, which they brought forth out of Egypt, for it was not leavened, because they were thrust out of Egypt, and could not tarry, neither had they made any provision for themselves."

Now the Master takes the lettuce, with the green top of the horse-radish, and shows it to the company as a memorial of the Egyptian slavery while he continues.

"This bitter herb, why do we eat it? Because the Egyptians embittered the lives of our ancestors in Egypt, as is said : And they embittered their lives with cruel bondage, in brick, mortar and in all manner of labor in the field, all their labor was imposed on them with rigor.

"Therefore it is incumbent on every Israelite, in every generation, to look on himself, as if he had actually gone forth from Egypt as it is said : And thou shalt declare unto thy son on that day, saying, This is done because of that which the Eternal did for me, when I came forth from Egypt. It was not our ancestors only that the Most Holy, blessed be he, redeemed from Egypt, but we also did he redeem with them ; as is said : And he brought us forth from thence, that he might bring us to the land which he swore to our fathers"

They drink the wine and the service continues

"Therefore we are in duty bound to thank, praise, adore, glorify, extol, honor, bless, exalt, and reverence him, who wrought all the miracles for our ancestors and us. For he brought us forth from bondage to freedom, from sorrow to joy, from mourning into holidays, from darkness to great light, and from slavery to redemption, and therefore let us chant unto him a new song, Hallelu-Jah, "Praise Jehovah."

"Blessed art thou, O Eternal, our God! Sovereign of the Universe, who has redeemed us and our ancestors from Egypt; and didst cause us to attain the enjoyment of this night, to eat therein unleavened cakes and bitter herbs. O Eternal! our God, and the God of our fore-fathers, mayest thou cause us to attain other solemn festivals and seasons, which approach us, that we may rejoice in the building of thy city, and exult in thy service, and that we may there eat of the sacrifices and paschal lambs, whose blood shall be sprinkled on the horns of thine altar, that they may be acceptable : then we will give thanks to thee with a new song for our deliverance and redemption. Blessed art thou, O Eternal, who redeemed Israel.

THE LITTLE HALLEL.

They sing the Psalms composing what was then called the Little Hallel. The Master began, the others responded.

Christ. " Praise the Lord, ye children.

Apostles. " Praise ye the name of the Lord, etc. (Psalm cxii.)

Christ. " When Israel went out of Egypt.

Apostles. " The house of Jacob, from a barbarous people, etc. (Ps. cxiii.)

This was named the Little Hallel to distinguish it from the Great Hallel, which will be found later in the Passover, the latter being sung in the Temple and during the processions coming up to the great Jewish Festivals. Members of the School of Shamai stopped at the end of Psalm cxiii., but the strict Pharisees sang other Psalms and then held the first recess.

8. MAROR, " BITTER." (EAT THE BITTER HERBS.)

He takes the bitter herbs, the lettuce, dips them in the vinegar, rolls them around a portion of the Embamma also called the Charoseth, the salad, formed of apples, almonds, fruits, etc., and hands a portion to each, saying

" Blessed art thou, O Lord, our God, King of the Universe, who hast sanctified us with thy commandments, and hast commanded us to eat the bitter herbs."

While saying this prayer they eat the bitter herbs recalling the bitter slavery of their fathers in Egypt, and shadowing forth the bitter slavery of sin and the repentance of Christians filled with sorrow preparing for Communion by confession.

During the preceding ceremonial half of the broken Aphikoman rested with the two other cakes covered with a napkin on the little plate before the Master. Jesus now uncovers the plate, takes half of this cake, breaks off twelve pieces and hands one to each of the apostles while they say together :

26

" Blessed art thou, O Eternal, our God, King of the Universe, who bringeth forth bread from the earth. Blessed art thou, O Lord, King of the Universe, who hast sanctified us with thy commandments, and hast commanded us to eat unleaven cakes."

Each dipped his piece of bread into the dish of Charoseth, typical of the bitter slavery of their race in Egypt, and with the Master ate the portion as a sign of friendship towards their leader. The rite continues in our day. If you eat bread with a Bedouin of the Orient, it is a sign of a contract of love and friendship between you and him, and he will protect you with his life. Taking from him the portion, and eating it with him, showed how the apostles loved their Master.

9. CHERECH " ENROLLING " (EAT THE HORSE-RADISH.)

Christ takes the third or under cake lying under the half of the broken Aphikoman, breaks off thirteen pieces, rolls them in the horse-radish, eats his piece, and hands a portion to each of the apostles as a sign of friendship and in memory of the Temple Sanctuary with all its sacrifices and ceremonies. While eating these portions they say:

"Thus Hillel did during the time the holy Temple stood. He took the unleaven cake and bitter herb, and ate them together, that he might perform what is said: "With unleaven cakes and bitter herbs shall they eat it." [1]

Jewish writers say this word Hillel comes from the Hebrew Aillel, "The Elder," and refers to Esdras, who led the Hebrews back from the Babylonian Captivity. But some hold that it refers to the famous Hillel Hazzakeh, so celebrated in Jewish history, who flourished about the time of the first Herod, and who died before Christ's birth. The latter Hillel was born in Babylonia and came when a youth to Jerusalem to attend the famous schools which then flourished in Judea. Too poor to pay for his education, he listened at a window where, one day he fell asleep and was found covered with snow, and they admitted him as a free scholar. He became the most learned of the Scribes, was made Nasi, " President " of

---

[1] Exod. xii. 8.

the Sanhedrin for life. He gathered up the traditions now found in the Talmud, and formed a liberal school in opposition to that of his contemporary Shammai, the latter being very rigid. Another Hillel who flourished in the fourth century after Christ reformed the Jewish calendar.

Eating this bread of friendship dipped into the Charoseth of Egyptian bondage, eating to remind them of their freedom, eating as a bond of love between them and their Master, the Lord spoke warning words, prophetic words foretelling the basest betrayal of all human history.

"And whilst they were eating he said: 'Amen, I say to you that one of you is about to betray me.' And they being very much troubled began every one to say: 'Is it I, Lord?'

"But he answering said: 'He that dippeth his hand with me in the dish the same shall betray me. The Son of man indeed goeth as it is written of him, but woe to that man by whom the Son of man shall be betrayed. It were better for that man if he had not been born' And Judas that betrayed him answering said: 'Is it I, Rabbi?' He said to him, 'Thou hast said it.'"[1] "And he said to them, 'One of the twelve who dippeth his hand with me in the dish.'"[2]

Replying to Judas' question he said: "Thou hast said it," as much as to say, "It is you." The Greek of St. Mark's Gospel has not 'Judas that betrayed' him as given in our translation, but, 'Judas betraying him,' which shows that the traitor all along had meditated the betrayal, and that it was not an after-thought. The words, "It were better for that man if he had not been born," is a quotation from the Book of Henoch, a prophetic and peculiar book much used by the Jews of that day and which foretold the betrayal.

The Passover was always a time of rejoicing; mirth, gladness and joy reigned round the table, but the Lord's words filled them with consternation. "Is it I?" each one asked himself. Sadness setted down on the "band." They began to talk among themselves and ask who would be so base as to betray the Master they so loved.

The time came now to take the third chalice of wine,

[1] Matt. xxvi. 21-25. [2] Mark xiv. 20.

and they fill the cups with wine from the great cruet and mix with water from the flagon saying while filling each chalice:

"Blessed art thou, O Lord, King of the Universe, Creator of the fruit of the vine."

Custom immemorial, and Passover rubric directed each guest to drink four goblets or chalices of wine. They had taken two and this was the third The Gospels tell us what here happened.

"And having taken the chalice, he gave thanks and said, 'Take and divide it among you. For I say to you that I will not drink of the fruit of the vine till the kingdom of God come."[1]

The Gospels give the very words of the Jewish Liturgy : "the fruit of the vine." In these days they made wine of different fruits. But wine of the grape "of the vine" was alone used at Passover. Christ's words show us that this was the wine of the grape used at the Last Supper, and from that day wine made from grapes has been always used at Mass, and no other wine is valid.

He said he would not drink it till he took it in his Father's kingdom, the Church he established through his death. While hanging on the cross, the soldiers offered him vinegar mixed with gall, but he refused it because he was a Nazarene forbidden wine or vinegar.[2]

He drank from the fourth chalice after he said this, but he did not contradict himself, for it was not wine but his consecrated Blood, and this was why he spoke these words. A change of substance took place at the Consecration, and he called their attention to it. If this change of substance did not and does not take place, at the Last Supper and at every Mass, the wine was only a type and figure of his blood. The Churches therefore which believe not in the Real Presence are no higher or no nearer the supernatural than the Jewish Church.

Christ excepted, all drank from the great chalice with the words given above. Then they washed their hands saying:

"Blessed art thou, O Lord, our God, King of the Universe, who hast sanctified us with thy commandments, and hast commanded us to wash the hands."

[1] Matt. xxvi 27, 29; Mark xiv 25; Luke xxii 16, 18. [2] Deut. xxix 6; Numb. vi 3,

Two feasts were celebrated at the Passover, one that of the Passover proper, the other of unleaven bread.[1] One was the Legal the other the Common Supper. The first supper that night fulfilled, with the death of Christ, all types and bloody sacrifices of the Old Testament, while the feast of unleaven bread began the New Testament. The first, the strict Passover, wherein the lamb was eaten, was held for only one night, for Christ was sacrificed only once on the cross. But the feast of unleaven bread which then began lasted for a week ended with an octave. The octave signifying completeness, typified eternity in heaven and was emblematic of the Mass where Christ is sacrificed day by day on our altars by priests of the eternal order of Melchisedech.[2]

When they had finished eating the lamb with the bitter herbs with the different Passover foods and had drank the three cups of wine, our Lord and his apostles said the following thanksgiving prayer ending the First Supper:

Christ. " Brethren, let us give thanks.

Apostles. " Blessed be the name of the Eternal from henceforth and forevermore.

Christ. " We will bless our God of whose bounty we have been satisfied.

Apostles. " Blessed be our God of whose bounty we have been satisfied and through whose goodness we live."

They carefully gather up the bones and remains of the lamb, remove and burn them, to foretell how the body of the dead Lord was the next day taken down from the cross and buried before sundown.

The Passover supper then ended and the recess began. Christ was about to confer two sacraments on the members of his band. He took the sacramentals of the Old Testament, the signs and ceremonies of the Jewish Church, and raised them to the dignity of two great sacraments of the New Testament. Holy Orders and Communion were to be the very soul and heart of his future Church, and he would now confer them on his apostles. But first he gave them a sensible sign of the innocence of soul and purity of heart required in all who would receive these ordinances.

" And when supper was done, the devil having put

[1] Zanolini, De Fest Jud   [2] Psalm cix. 4

into the heart of Judas, the son of Simon, the Iscariot, to betray him, knowing that the Father had given all things into his hands and that he came from God and goeth to God.

" He riseth from supper, and layeth aside his garments, and having taken a towel (called luntith, " towel," used at bath) he girdeth himself. After that he poureth water into a basin, and began to wash the feet of the disciples, and to wipe them with the towel wherewith he was girded (He come first to Peter his chief.') He cometh therefore to Simon Peter. And Peter saith to him, " Lord, dost thou wash my feet ? " Jesus answered and said to him. " What I do thou knowest not now, but thou shalt know hereafter.' Peter saith to him : " Thou shalt never wsah my feet." Jesus answered him : " If I wash thee not, thou shalt have no part with me." Simon Peter saith to him, " Lord, not only my feet, but also my hands and my head." Jesus saith to him : " He that is washed needeth not but to wash his feet, but is clean wholly. And you are clean, but not all." For he knew who he was that would betray him, therefore he said : " You are not all clean." '

Washing, emblem of baptism, the Lord used to show them the innocence of soul required for their ordination and first Communion, which Judas did not have. They had all taken the Passover or legal bath, but their bare feet were soiled walking over the floors, and by words and acts Christ showed again the betrayal.

" Then after he had washed their feet, and taken his garments, having sat down again ' he said to them : " Know you what I have done to you? You call me Master and Lord, and you say well, for so I am. If I, then, being Lord and Master, have washed your feet, you also ought to wash one another's feet. For I have given you an example, that as I have done to you, so you do also. Amen, amen, I say to you, The servant is not greater than his lord, neither is the apostle greater than He that sent him. If you know these things you shall be blessed if you do them."

" I speak not of you all, I know whom I have chosen,

¹ Geikie, Life of Christ, ii 440 ³ See Migne, Cursus Comp S Scripturæ, iii 1155, John xiii. 4 to 11. ⁵ The Greek text says " having again reclined "

but that the Scripture may be fulfilled : " He that eateth bread with me shall lift his heel against me."[1] At present I tell you before it comes to pass, that when it shall come to pass you may believe that I am the Messiah.[2]

Christ knew the Temple was to be destroyed, that its priesthood was to pass away, that another priesthood foretold according to the order of Melchisedech was to rise over the world, be eternal and sacrifice him in Eucharistic Offering. This was the burden of prophetic words of the Old Testament, of Passover ceremonial, of Temple worship and of proposition bread and wine.

The High Priest of eternity was not to stay always here in our world of sufferings and sorrows, but after finishing the work his Father gave him to do, man's redemption, to return to heaven. Would he leave the world without a divinely ordained priesthood ? Then mankind would be worse off than before he came, for there would be no sacrifice, no religious body of men who could speak with divine authority. The world required a priesthood.

He would give the world priests to sacrifice him in truth and reality, as the Temple priests had sacrificed him in type and figure. He was about to offer himself, his life, his Body, Blood, soul and Divinity at that table, and complete that offering on the cross the next day. But he must show the apostles how to sacrifice him at the Last Supper, that they might do the same in the Mass. They must take part with him in his first Mass, that the Last Supper might be united with every other Mass down the ages till the world ends.

What order did he raise them to ? Did he make them priests or bishops ? If he made them simple priests, they could not have ordained other priests, and with their death the priesthood would have died. The Jewish priesthood was to end with the destruction of the Temple, the sacrifices of the ancient religions were gradually to cease, and without a priesthood the Christian world would have been left without a divinely appointed body of religious teachers.

Acting as a Bishop—in his highest order, he consecrated them bishops of equal rank giving them religious power,

[1] Psalm xl. 7-10 , Osee xli. 3.   [2] John xlii. 4-19.

that with him they might take part in his Eucharistic Sacrifice, as the bishop being consecrated takes part with the consecrating bishop, that thus they might ordain priests, and consecrate bishops in the churches they would found.

What rite did he follow? The ancient ceremony of Temple and Synagogue. Therefore at least in external rite the apostles saw nothing new or strange in their ordination. God does nothing abruptly, and Christ came not to condemn but to fulfil the ancient Hebrew rites. But the apostles did not know the full meaning of the ceremonies till the Holy Ghost came on Pentecost.

The Temple high priest, the Hebrew priest, the king, the magistrate, the Rabbi, the guests at Passover were anointed on head and hand with holy oil, and hands laid on them when inducted into their offices. This was the ceremonial which had come down in Israel from remotest days, and the Jews called this laying on of hands the Semichal.[1]

Jacob imposed his hands in form of across on Joseph's two sons.[2] Moses laid his hands on Josue, when giving him power as general over the hosts of Hebrews with grace to conquer the Promised Land.[3] Jewish physicians anointed the sick with oil, which Rabbi Simeon says was mixed with wine, the ceremonial usually taking place on the Sabbath.[4] The Talmud in many places mentions this anointing.[5]

Not less than three Rabbis could ordain a Rabbi in the days of Christ. This was the custom in the early Church, when three bishops consecrated a bishop. When the custom fell into disuse, Pope Anecletus, the third from Peter, forbade a bishop consecrated by less than three bishops. That has been the discipline down till our day.

First, we conclude Christ consecrated the holy oils, for the holy oils of the Temple were hallowed by the high priest before being used, say learned writers, who also hold that since the Last Supper the holy oils are conse-

[1] Edersheim, Life of Christ, ii 210 ; Sketches of Jewish Life, 276, 280, 282 , Geikie, Life of Christ, ii 679; Farrar, Life of Christ, ii. 579 , Babylonian Talmud, passim, etc [2] Gen xlviii 13 [3] Deut. xxxiv. 9 [4] Talmud in Hor. v ii 415 [5] Geikie, Life of Christ, ii 608 , Edersheim, Temple 71 ; Life of Christ, 555, 382. etc., Sketches of Jewish Life, 281, 282.

crated on Holy Thursday in all Christian rites. Down from the apostolic days come the custom St. Favain, Bishop of Rome from 236 to 240, writes[1] that after Christ had washed the apostles' feet, he showed them how to mix the oil and consecrate the holy chrism.[2] Christian Lupus states Pope Sylvester[3] teaches that Christ established the rite of blessing the oils. In every Oriental rite they bless the oils on Holy Thursday. The Greeks, Sclavonic and other Eastern Christians mix the chrism with thirty-two different perfumes, imparting an intensely sweet smell.

In the form of a cross they laid their hands on the head of the high priest, priest, rabbi, magistrate, and on every official of church and state.[4] They anointed the the heads of the guests with oil during the Passover.[5] They put the oil on the head in the form of a cross, or Greek cross.[6] This is the reason that clergymen are ordained in all Christian rites with oil and the imposition of hands in the form of a cross.

We must conclude, although we find no record, that Christ ordained his apostles with holy oil and imposed his hands on them, as the Lord laid down the rite in Moses' day.[7] This rite of consecrating bishop and priest with holy oil and imposition of hands, comes therefore down to us from the Temple, the synagogue, and the Last Supper.

The guests held their scrolls of the Passover Service, and followed the leader, with him pronouncing the words. He ordained them therefore, for he wished them to take part with him in the first Mass. According to the Last Supper, and apostolic custom, the clergyman about to be ordained a priest or consecrated a bishop, says the words of the Mass with the bishop.

Laying his hands on their heads, did he say : " Receive ye the Holy Ghost "? Did he place on their heads and shoulders the Holy Scrolls of Moses' five books with the prophetic and historic books of the Old Testament taken from the Aaron in the sanctuary? Did the holy oil flow on their beards as it had on Aaron's, when Moses conse-

---

[1] Tomb 1 Concil Epist. I   [2] Migne, Cursus Comp S Theologiæ De Olio Sacro   [3] Lib. Pont., born A D. 270   [4] Edersheim, Temple, 71 ; Sketches, 281. 282. Life of Christ, II 554, etc.   [5] Geikie, Life of Christ, I. 549 ; II 382, 555   [6] Geikie, Life of Christ, II. 579 ; Farrar's Life of Christ, II 183.   [7] Exod. xxix.

crated him? History hints not on these. They were now bishops to take part with him in the First Mass, to immolate and offer him in Eucharistic sacrifice. Only after the resurrection did he give them power to forgive sins.[1] The power of sacrifice related to his real Body and Blood. The forgiveness of sins was to be exercised on his mystic body, the members of his Church.

The full powers of the Episcopate imprinted its character in their souls, but the graces of Holy Orders lay dormant in them, for he had not yet suffered, sin was not atoned, mankind was not yet redeemed. Pentecost, the fiery Shekina, the Holy Ghost, came in the cloud, tongues of red burning flame filled the apostles with the graces of the apostolate and episcopate, completed graces of the Holy Orders they had received at the Last Supper. But the Lord reminded them of the powers he had given them to act as his agents, his ministers to the world.

"Amen, amen, I say to you, he that receiveth whomsoever I sendeth, receiveth me, and he that receiveth me, receiveth him that sent me. When Jesus had said these things, he was troubled in spirit, and protested and said, Amen, amen, I say to you that one of you will betray me,"[2] Why was he troubled in spirit at this solemn ordination of the apostles? Because he knew that he had ordained Judas with murder in his heart. He had imposed his holy hands on and raised to the apostolic college the meanest man of human history.

They were now the first bishops of the Catholic Church, bearing the fulness of the episcopal order, with its imprint on their souls lifting them to the highest spiritual power a creature can receive, giving them a power even the heavenly spirits can never exercise. But they did not feel the fires of love of God and man lifting them to the heights of the supernatural no one ever feels who has not received Holy Orders. The change in the Passover rite was hardly perceptible to their eye. It differed little from each Passover they had attended since they were boys of thirteen.

But towards the end of the Passover, after the Communion, he warned them as to the dangers of pride and

[1] John xx. 23.   [2] John xiii. 20, 21.

vanity and tyranny, the special temptations of rulers, flattered by their subjects. He told them he had made them officials of his Church to offer the Eucharist and sit on episcopal thrones as judges over his people, as since the bishops sit on their episcopal thrones.

" And you are they who have continued with me in my temptations. And I appoint to you, as my father hath appointed to me, a kingdom. That you may eat and drink at my table in my kingdom, and may sit upon thrones, judging the twelve tribes of Israel.[1]

He made them his agents to act for him in saving souls, and in offering his Sacrifice. The agent binds the one who appoints him. Thus the apostles were clothed with the spiritual powers of Christ. Of this he reminded them when he said :

" Amen, amen, I say to you, he that receiveth whomsoever I send, receiveth me, and he that receiveth me receiveth him that sent me." [2]

The Son of God pontificating as the Great Bishop of the world thus raised the apostles from laymen to be bishops, that they might take part with him in the first Mass, and that he might show them how to consecrate bishops after he had gone from earth to the glories of his Father. The words " Do this in memory of me " related then not only to the Mass but to the ordination and the consecration of the clergy in every age and country.

Three orders we find typified in the Gospels,—the Papacy in Peter, the bishops in the apostles, and the diocesan priests in the seventy-two disciples. These three are the foundations of the Church. All other orders or bodies of religious ordained to the priesthood are accidental, came later—the apostolic age did not have them, the Church could exist without them. But when the diocesan priesthood, represented by the seventy-two disciples, separated from the episcopate, represented by the apostles, and became an order of simple priests different from the bishops, we do not find All signs seem to indicate that it was about the time the deacons were ordained.[3] These are the priests belonging to the diocese who serve under the bishop and act as pastors, assistants,

[1] Luke xxii. 28–30   [2] John xiii 20,   [3] Acts vi ; Philip i. 1 ; 1 Tim iii. 8-12.

etc. The religious orders were founded by famous men —nearly all being saints,—during the middle ages, or many centuries after the apostolic age.

The time between the two suppers was thus taken up with the ordination rites, the second supper, the feast of unleaven bread, then began, wherein the reader will find more solemn ceremonies, holier prayers, deeper devotion, for it related more strictly to the Eucharistic Sacrifice.

10. HORECH SULCKAN "SET THE TABLE." (BRING THE MEAT
TO THE TABLE, EAT AND BE JOYFUL.)

Now they set the table for the feast of unleaven bread. The preceding ceremonies recalled the history of the patriarchs, the delivery of the Hebrews from the Egyptian bondage, the giving of the Law on.Sinai, the story of their nation, their providential mission among the pagans, and pointed to the crucifixion to take place the next day.

The Passover proper ended, or rather developed into the feast of unleaven bread, which now began and lasted till the 21st day of the moon, that is for a week, and ended with a great feast on the octave. The Passover was celebrated only once, the feast which followed was celebrated for a week, each night it was held with holy solemnity, for it foretold the Mass which takes place not once, but continues down the ages, lasting till the end, offered by priests of the eternal order of Melchisedech. The octave typifies eternity with God in the other world. Therefore not to the Passover, strictly speaking, which foretold the death of Christ, but to the feast of unleaven bread we must look for the origin of the ceremonial of the Mass.

11. TZAPHUN "THE HIDDEN." (TAKE THE PIECE OF THE
MIDDLE CAKE FIRST BROKEN OFF AND EAT
A SMALL PART THEREOF.)

Christ uncovers the half of the broken middle cake, which he had broken into two equal parts at the beginning of the Passover Seder, and which up to this time had been lying before him covered with a napkin, as the paten lies on the altar covered with the purificator during Mass. Taking in his hands this half of the Aphikoman, he breaks off a particle, and eats it in memory of the paschal lamb they had just eaten. Then he breaks off a particle for each guest and lays it in the left palm of each. This was the way the celebrant of the Mass in the early Church gave Communion. The other half of the Aphikoman was concealed from the beginning, that is covered with a napkin. The hiding of this piece came down from Moses or the prophets to foretell that the Mass was hidden in the Passover rite. Later they hid the other half of the Aphikoman with a more solemn ceremony we will soon describe.

12. BARECH, "BLESS." (SAY THE GRACE AFTER MEALS.)

Each apostle receives his particle of bread, saying, "Blessed art thou, O Lord, King of the Universe, who bringeth forth bread from the earth." Then they eat the particles of bread.

The Menachot Table (page 37) shows how the Temple sacrifices were offered with movements forming a cross. As the Temple ceremonial was an extension of the patriarchal Passover, or as the latter was a compendium of the former, long before Christ, the precise epoch we cannot find, the Hebrews offered the bread and wine with these movements of the Temple ceremonial.

The master of the feast, one after the other raised up first the bread and wine, then they offered them to God with prayer. Then he lowered them. The Hebrews called these movements the Teruma. Before placing on the table the plate of bread or the chalice full of wine, the master moved them from him to the west, the move being called *molish*, then towards him, to the east, called *umeul*, towards the south, to his left, the action being the *mahale*, and then to his right, to the north, the rite being the *morul*, then he laid the vessels of bread and wine on the table.

While raising or lowering the bread and wine, the "standing men" and officials near the master put their hands under and touched the vessel, while the prayer was said dedicating the sacrifice to God. The reason was this. In the Temple the animals were thus offered alive, and it required a number of priests to raise up the victims, especially when large, and to move them high up in the air to the four points of the compass. But at Passover women were forbidden to touch the vessels of bread and wine during the offering, because they could not officiate in the Temple, and lest evil might be suspected if they took part with the master.[1]

The Jews before Christ supposed that the Temple sacrifices were raised up and thus offered to God as sacrifices for sins, but they did not see that these two movements of the victims, as well as of the bread and wine of Temple and at Passover foretold how Christ would be raised up on his cross, and taken down for burial. They also write that the four movements, to the west, east, south and north, signified that the sacrifices were offered for all the nations living in the four quarters of the world. But the Christian sees that the rite foretold the cross on which the world's Victim was to be later sacrificed.

With these movements coming down from Temple and Passover, the bread and wine are offered during the offertory of the Mass, and the deacon touches the paten holding the bread and the chalice of the wine as the Temple priests and " standing men " did in Temple and Passover.

Every victim in the Temple was thus offered by the Jewish priesthood, which was later to demand the death of Christ. Then with the one who brought the victim, they placed their hands on the animal's head, palms down, and placed Israel's sins, the sins of his family, or the sins of the one for whom he offered the sacrifice on the victim. In this way at Passover the master of the feast, after offering the bread and wine, spread out his hands over them, and placed his sins on them. Now let us see what Christ and the apostles did at this part of the Last Supper. No record has come down directly relating to this ceremony, and we can only give the religious custom as we find it among the Jews of that epoch, as we see it now in the Mass.

The Lord carefully following every rite and custom of

[1] See Zanolini, De Festis Judæorum. c. iv , etc.

Passover in his day, uncovered the Aphikoman on the silver plate and raising up the paten, he offered the bread to his Eternal Father.   James at his right, we suppose, touching the plate.   Then he moved it the four points of the compass, making a cross as the celebrant of the Mass does, and then laid it on the table.

One of the apostles, perhaps James, at his right, filled the great Chalice, the Gabia, with wine.   Another apostle, —was it John?—mixed the wine with water as the subdeacon does at a high Mass, and the Lord offered the chalice of wine with the Temple ceremonial we have given, as to-day the wine is offered during Mass by raising, lowering and making with it a cross.

After offering the bread and wine did Christ spread out his hands over them according to the Temple rite after offering the victims?   Was it at this time that he offered his life Body and Blood as the Victim of the sins of all men?   The celebrant at Mass, just before the Consecration, holds out his hands over the bread and wine according to the Temple ceremony, and we conclude Christ did the same, but we do not find the exact time of the Passover when this was done.   Then they hid the Aphikoman on the little plate.

The Jews of our day hide half of the Aphikoman in different ways.   In this country they often put it under a little cushion, on which they lay the left elbow in memory of the reclining position of the time of Christ. In Jerusalem the writer saw the master of the feast cover the plate with a napkin.   Emely Beaufort [1] says, that after the boy asked the question: " What is the meaning of these ceremonies," etc.   " The master laid a white cloth over the boy's shoulders, and removing the coverings from the table, he took one of the large cakes of the Passover bread, till then hidden, and breaking it in half, tied it into the end of the cloth, and slung it over the shoulder of the youngest boy, who kept it for ten minutes, and then passed it to the next, and so on—all continuing to recite from the books without stopping."

We conclude therefore that Christ hid the Aphikoman on the paten, in the end of the prayer-shawl, which was of the form and size of our benediction veil, and placed

---

[1] " In Egyptian Sepulchres and Syrian Shrines."

it on the shoulders of St. John, the youngest, who held it up before his eyes till after the Consecration. At a low Mass the paten, covered with the purificator, lies partly under the corporal. Some of the Jews of our day cover the bread in this way.

The youngest at the table held the plate before him covered with the prayer-shawl on his shoulders. It was he who asked the questions, " Wherefore is this night distinguished from all other nights," etc. John was the youngest of the apostolic band, and we suppose therefore he held the hidden Aphikoman before his face so he could not see his Master. What did John in this ancient Passover ceremony typify ? In his Gospel,[1] John tells us that when they heard the Lord had risen, he and Peter ran to the tomb. Let us see what these apostles represented, in the words of one of the early Popes :

" Those disciples ran the fastest, who loved him, Christ, more than the others, namely Peter and John. The two ran, but John ran faster than Peter. The first came to the tomb, but did not dare to enter. Peter, who was behind, came and entered. What, brethren, did this mean ? are we to believe that this minute Gospel description has no mysteries ? By no means. John would not have said he outran, but did not enter, unless he believed there was a mystery hidden. What did John signify but the Synagogue, and what Peter, but the Church."[2]

John represented Jewish Church, Temple and synagogue with their services, the Jewish people and their stubborn conservatism. John behind his Master holds the silver plate with the Aphikoman, " The heavenly manna," " the bread of angels," up before his eyes, blinding him so he cannot see his Lord, for the Jewish people would not see in Jesus their Messiah. They did not believe his words said in their synagogue when he promised the Eucharist, his Body and Blood, " I am the living bread which came down from heaven. This is the bread which came down from heaven. Not as your fathers did eat manna and died."[3] Let the reader see the whole of John vi.

Therefore from apostolic times the subdeacon, at a high Mass and when the bishop pontificates, holds the paten

---

[1] John, xx. 4-6.   [2] St. Gregory, Hom. xxii. in Evang. of John's Gospel
[3] John vi. 51, 59.

covered with the end of the benediction veil up before
his eyes behind the celebrant, imaging the Hebrews who
rejected their Messiah and who still persist in their
blindness.

Now begins the Temple ceremonial of incensing the
bread and wine. On burning coals in the censer, little
differing from the censer of our day, the Master puts the
incense He swings the censer to the four points of the
compass over the bread and wine, as the incense was
offered in the Temple, repeating the words of the Psalm
over that bread and wine offered each Sabbath in the
Holies.

" Let my prayer be directed as incense in thy sight, the
lifting up of my hands as evening sacrifice. Set a watch,
O Lord, before my mouth, and a door round about my
lips. Incline not my heart to evil words to make excuse
in sins." [1]

A servant takes the censer and incenses the beard of
each, beginning with the Lord, then going to each apostle
according to his dignity. Did he swing the censer once
or more? History is silent. To do that he went into the
space between the tables, passing from one to another as
the servers at Mass incenses the celebrant and members
of the clergy in the choir, after the offertory.[2]

Then they washed their hands lest they might have
become soiled during the recess and preceding ceremony.
Did they say the words of the Psalm, " I will wash my
hands among the innocent," etc.,[3] the celebrant of the
Mass now says while washing his hands? We cannot
find a record.

THE LITURGY CONTINUED.

" Blessed art thou, O Lord, our God, King of the Universe, who feedeth the whole world with thy goodness,
and with grace, kindness and mercy, giveth food to every
creature, for his mercy endureth forever. And as his
abundant goodness has never been deficient towards us,
so may we never be in want of sustenance, for ever and
ever, for the sake of his great name, for he is the God
who feedeth and sustaineth all, and dealeth beneficently

---

[1] Psalm cxl. [2] See p. 211, 212 [3] Psalm xxv. 6 to end

27

with all, and provideth food for all the creatures that he created. Blessed art thou, O Lord, who giveth food to all.

"We will give thanks to thee, O Lord, our God, for having caused our forefathers to inhabit this desirable land, and because thou hast brought us forth from the land of Egypt, and redeemed us from the house of bondage, and for thy covenant, which thou hast sealed in our flesh, for the Law which thou hast taught us, and for the statutes which thou hast made known to us, and for the life, and kindness, and mercy, which thou hast graciously bestowed on us, and for the food wherewith thou dost feed and sustain us continually every day and hour."

"And for all these things, O Lord, we will give thanks to thee, and praise thee. Blessed be thy name continually in the mouth of every living creature forever and ever, as it is written: When thou hast eaten and art satisfied, then shall thou bless the Lord thy God for the good land, which he hath given thee Blessed art thou, O Lord, for the land and for the food."

"O Lord, our God, we beseech thee, have compassion on thy people Israel, on Jerusalem thy city, on Sion the residence of thy glory, and on the great and holy house of David thine own anointed, and on the great and holy house, which is called by thy name. Thou art our God, Father, Pastor and Feeder, our Maintainer, Supporter and Enlarger. Enlarge us speedily from all our troubles, and suffer us not, O Lord, our God, to stand in need of the gifts of mankind, nor their loan, but let us depend on thy full, open and extensive hand, so that we may not be put to shame nor ever be confounded"

"O God, and the God of our fathers, wilt thou cause our prayers to ascend, and come, approach, be seen, accepted, heard, and thought on, and be remembered in remembrance of us, and in remembrance of our fathers, in remembrance of thine anointed Messiah, the son of David, thy servant, and in remembrance of Jerusalem, thy holy city, and in commemoration of all thy people, the house of Israel before thee to a good issue, with favor, with grace, with mercy, to life and peace on this day of the Feast of Unleaven Bread O Lord, our God, remember us thereon for good, visit us with a blessing, and save us to enjoy life, and with the word of salvation and mercy, have compassion and be gracious to us. O have mercy on us and save us, for our eyes are continually toward thee, for thou, O God, art a merciful and gracious King."

The following prayer was evidently composed when the Jews were in captivity in Babylon:

" O build Jerusalem, the holy city, speedily in our days. Blessed art thou, O Lord, who in thy mercy buildeth Jerusalem. Amen. Blessed art thou, O Lord, our God, King, Strength, Creator, Redeemer and Sanctifier of Jacob, our Pastor, the Shepherd of Israel, the beneficent King, who dealeth beneficently with all, for he hath been, is, and ever will be daily beneficent towards us. He hath dealt bountifully with us, as he doth now, and ever will be, granting us grace, favor, mercy, enlargement, deliverance, prosperity, blessing, salvation, consolation, maintenance and sustenance; and may we never want mercy, and a peaceable life with every good. May he who is most merciful reign over us for ever and ever. May he who is most merciful, be praised in heaven and on earth. May he who is most merciful, be adored throughout all generations; be eternally glorified amidst us, and be honored amongst us to all eternity. May he who is most merciful, maintain us with honor. May he who is most merciful break the yoke of captivity from our neck, and lead us securely to our land. May he who is most merciful send us abundant blessing in this house, and on this table on which we have eaten. May he who is most merciful, send us Elijah, the prophet of blessed memory to bring us good tidings of salvation and consolation."

Elijah, "My God is Jehovah," translated into the Greek as Elias, was foretold to come and prepare the way before the Messiah.[1] The Jews of that time had mixed up the prophecies relating to this great prophet-recluse who lived in the desert in the days of the wicked kings of Juda. John the Baptist lived like him and came in his spirit preaching penance and baptizing. He pointed out Jesus the Prophet of Nazareth, supposed son of Joseph, as the Messiah and the true "Lamb of God." During the transfiguration, Elias representing the prophets came in person, and Moses representing the Torah or Law with

[1] Malach iv. 5.

all its Temple ceremonial came, and these the two greatest
men of old appeared on Tabor's heights, one each side of
the Messiah, showing that all prophecy and all the Law
were fulfilled in Jesus

When the Jews at Passover mention Elijah they place
a cup of wine on the doorstep for Elias and say these
words of Psalm lxxviii. 6-7 :

" Pour out thy wrath upon the nations that have not
known thee, and upon the kingdoms that have not called
upon thy name, because they have devoured Jacob and
have laid waste his place."

At the Passover on Sion, Jerusalem, a woman filled the
cup, opened the door, and placed it on the doorstep.
Jewish writers say this has been a part of the Passover
from most ancient times, and that it related to the Babylonian captivity. The Palestine Jews still expect the
Redeemer, the strict Hebrews of other lands are divided
on the question, but the reformed synagogue hardly look
for his coming

During the Passover at the time of Christ, they prayed
to the saints of the Old Testament, the patriarchal fathers
of their race. The Talmud says : " Whence do we deduce
that we should mention the patriarchs in the prayer?
Because it is written "O ye seed of Abraham his servant,
ye sons of Jacob his chosen. With thy arm thou hast
redeemed thy people the children of Jacob and of Joseph." [1]
Following these prayers to the great and holy men of
Israel, when forming the Liturgies of the Mass, the
apostles mentioned the names of the early saints and
martyrs written on the dyptics, and later their names
were incorporated into the Canon of the Latin Mass.

" May he who is merciful bless my honored father, the
master of this house, my honored mother, the mistress of
this house, their children, and all belonging to them, us
and all belonging to us, as our ancestors, Abraham, Isaac
and Jacob were blessed with all and every good, thus may
he bless us altogether with a complete blessing, and let
us say Amen. May they in heaven show forth our merit
for a peaceable preservation, and may we receive a blessing
from the Lord and justice from the God of our salvation,

[1] Talmud Babyl. Magilla C II. 26, 47, etc. The Talmud here quotes these
words as being in Psalm civ. 6, which is a mistake.

and may we find grace and good understanding in the sight of God and man."

"May he who is most merciful cause us to inherit the day that is entirely good. May he who is most merciful make us worthy to behold the day of the Messiah, and eternal life in the future state. He giveth salvation to his king, and showeth mercy to his anointed, to David and his Seed forever. May he who maketh peace in his high heavens grant peace to us and to all Israel, and say ye Amen.

"Fear the Lord all ye his saints, for there is no want to those who fear him. The young lions do lack and suffer hunger, but those who seek the Lord shall not want anything. Praise ye the Lord, for he is good, for his mercy endureth forever. Thou openest thy hand and satisfieth the desires of every living thing. Blessed is the man who will trust in the Lord, and the Lord will be his trust. Blessed art thou, O Lord, our God, King of the Universe, Creator of the fruit of the earth."

13. HALLEL, "PRAISE."

(Finish the Hallel).

This Antiphon having been said they then all sing the Hallel composed of the following Psalms. Hallel is a contraction of Halleluia, "Praise Jehovah. It is Alleluia in our Liturgies.

Psalm cxiii. (bis), " When Israel went out of Egypt, etc.
    "   cxiv.   " I have loved, because the Lord, etc.
    "   cxv.   " I have believed, therefore I have, etc.
    "   cxvi.   " O praise the Lord, all ye nations, etc.
    "   cxvii.   "Give praise to the Lord, for he is good," etc.

In these Psalms the apostles could see the wonderful prophecies of Christ, the Last Supper, and his death. When they came to the words " What shall I render to the Lord for all the things that he has rendered to me? I will take the chalice of salvation, and I will call upon the name of the Lord,"[1] we suppose that then Christ took the chalice in his hands, as we do just after the Consecra-

---

[1] Psalm cxv 12-13.

tion of the Host in the Latin Liturgy. Psalm cxvii. is given in the Liturgy of the Passover thus, the Master saying the first part of the verse, the others replying:

> " Give praise to the Lord; for he is good:
> For his mercy endureth forever.
> Let Israel now say that he is good,
> That his mercy endureth forever.
> Let the house of Aaron now say,
> That his mercy endureth forever.
> Let them that fear the Lord say,
> That his mercy endureth forever," etc.

In Psalm cxvii. 22, the words " The stone which the builders rejected, the same is become the head of the corner," etc., foretold his official rejection by the Jewish Priesthood the Sunday before in the Temple, and his rejection by the whole people the next day in Pilate's Hall. Jesus referred to this in his instructions in the Temple.[1] When they come to the words of Psalm cxvii. 25, 26, Christ sang one line and the apostles repeated the same words after him.

Christ. " O Lord, Hosanna.
Apostles. " O Lord, Hosanna.
Christ. " O Lord, send now prosperity, we beseech thee.
Apostles. " O Lord, send now prosperity, we beseech thee.
" Blessed is he that cometh in the name of the Lord," etc.

The word Hosanna is a contraction of the Syro-Chaldaic of the Hebrew, Anna Adonai hoschihanna, " Save us now, we beseech thee." This gave rise to the same word Hosanna at the end of the Preface in the Latin Mass, and to words of the same nature in the other Liturgies. Then follows the Prayer of the

14. NIRTZA, " MAY IT BE ACCEPTED."

(The service thus performed will be acceptable to God.)

" All thy work, O Lord, shall praise thee, thy pious servants, with the righteous who perform thy will, and

[1] Matt xxi 42; Luke xx. 17.

thy people, the house of Israel with joyful song shall give thee thanks, bless, praise, glorify, extol, reverence, sanctify, and acknowledge thy kingly name, O our King, for to thee it is proper to offer thanksgiving, and pleasant to sing praise to thy name, for thou art God from everlasting to everlasting."

Melchisedech's chalice, the cos-ha-berachah,[1] "The cup of blessing," the fourth cup of wine mixed with water of the Jewish ceremonial, covered with a napkin, stands before the Messiah.[2] Lying between it and the edge of the table was the silver plate holding the half cake of unleaven bread which had been hidden the Aphikoman still covered with a linen cloth. These were not partaken till the master of the feast had explained the whole ceremonial of the Passover, and we suppose the Lord pointed out their mystic meanings.

The Aphikoman, "The heavenly bread or manna," of every Passover, reminded them of the desert manna on which their fathers had lived for forty years, and that was the fondest memory of the nation. "As Moses brought down manna so the Messiah would bring down a more wonderful food,"[3] "God made manna to descend for them in which was all manner of tastes. The young tasted bread, the old honey, and the children oil."[4] Teachings had come down from the prophets that when the Messiah came he would repeat the wonders of the manna. The Rabbis taught "As the first Saviour, Moses, the deliverer from Egyptian bondage, caused manna to fall from heaven for Israel, so the second Saviour, the Messiah, will also cause manna to descend for them once more, for it is written, "There will be abundance of grain in the land.""[5] Thus they interpreted the prophecies of the Eucharist the only-begotten Son was about to fulfil in the Aphikoman and change the shadow into the reality.[6]

The Passover rite in the days of Christ, still observed by strict Jews of the Orient, is as follows. The master of the feast makes a sign to the boy holding the hidden plate with the Aphikoman, who brings it to him.

[1] Farrar, ii. 291 [2] The wines of Judea are described in Edersheim, Life of Christ, ii. 208, and Geikie, Life of Christ, i. 450–573. [3] Edersheim, Life of Christ, i. 176. [4] Talmud explained by Lightfoot, Hor Heb iii 304. [5] Nork, 174 [6] See Zanolini, Disputat de Festis Judæorum, Benedict XIV. De Festis Dom. N. Jesus Christi et B. M. Virgin, col. 144, 659, Migne Edition

The master uncovers it, breaks off a piece which he eats. Then he breaks off a piece for each and lays it on the guest's left palm. The guests take the pieces of bread between thumb and index finger and put them in their mouths. The master drinks the wine from the chalice, then hands it around to the guests, who all drink from it. They thus take the bread and wine in memory of Noe, Melchisedech and the proposition bread and wine of the Temple. This ends the feast, and they are forbidden to eat or drink anything after this, even a dessert is forbidden.[1] The Gospel narrative and Consecration words according to the Roman rite show that Christ carefully followed the Jewish custom and the Passover rule.

"Jesus took bread, and blessing, broke and gave to them."[2] "And having taken the chalice, giving thanks, he gave it to them, and they all drank of it."[3]

THE CONSECRATION.

"Taking it in his holy and venerable hands, and with eyes uplifted to thee, O God, his Father, giving thanks to thee, He ✠ blessed, He ✠ broke and He ✠ gave to his disciples saying: Take ye all of this:

FOR THIS IS MY BODY.

"which is given for you. Do this for a commemoration of me."[4]

It was the Aphikoman in his hands, over which he pronounced these words. He breaks off a piece for each and lays the Particle in the left palm of each apostle, for that was the Passover rite. The apostles take It with right thumb and index finger and place It in the mouth. This was the way Communion was given in the early Church, and women covered the left palm with a linen napkin. The Oriental Churches still give Communion this way.

At Passover the master of the feast took his large chalice in his hands, raised it up with a thanksgiving prayer, drank from it, and passed it round to the guests, as a loving cup and a bond of friendship between them. And they all drank as a sign of esteem, friendship, and love of the master at whose hospitable table they had

---

[1] See Talmud   [2] Matt. xxvi. 27.   [3] Mark xiv. 23.   [4] Luke xxii. 19.

celebrated the Passover. The Gospel and the Latin Rite show us that Christ followed this Jewish custom

"In like manner, after he had supped, taking this goodly chalice in his holy and venerable hands, also giving thanks to thee,[1] he gave to them saying, Drink ye all of this:

" FOR THIS IS THE CHALICE OF MY BLOOD OF THE NEW AND ETERNAL TESTAMENT, THE MYSTERY OF FAITH, WHICH WILL BE SHED FOR YOU AND FOR MANY UNTO THE REMISSION OF SINS.

"As often as you do this you shall do it in my memory. And I say to you, I will not drink from henceforth of this fruit of the vine, until that day when I shall drink it new with you in the kingdom of my Father."[2]

Following the Passover custom fundamental to the feast, for Christ broke no religious rite or ancient ordinance, he first partook of the chalice himself as the celebrant of the Mass always does. Then he passed the chalice to each of the apostles. "And they all drank from it." In the early Church the chalice was thus passed to all who received Communion till abuses forced a change of discipline

The first three Gospels give the words of Consecration.[3] St. John omits them, for in his sixth chapter, he had given the words of Christ regarding the Real Presence.

What mean the words "The New and Eternal Testament and the Mystery of Faith?" A testament is a will bequeathing property, and is not valid till the person who makes it dies Christ refers to his death on the morrow, when the Passover of the Hebrews will end, when the New and eternal Testament will begin with the glories of the redeemed. No one can believe in the Real Presence without faith, a gift of God, and even to those with faith it is a mystery of faith

Did a long interval of prayer and praise intervene between the Consecration and Communion? This we find in every Christian Liturgy of the Mass. But the Gospel words seem to imply that immediately after the words he gave Communion to the apostles.

[1] Matt. xxvi 27. [2] Matt. xxvi 29 [3] Matt. xxvi 28; Mark. xiv. 22; Luke xxii. 19-20

But human worldly elements were still the motives of their actions, and they began to dispute about the first and chief places they were to occupy in the Holy Orders to which he elevated them in his Kingdom, the Church, of which he had made them bishops and apostles.

"And there was also a strife amongst them, which of them should seem to be the greater. And he said to them: 'The kings of the Gentiles lord it over them, and they that have power over them are called beneficent. But you not so, but he that is greatest among you, let him be as the least; and he that is the leader as he that serveth.

"For which is the greater, he that reclineth at the table or he that serveth? Is not he that reclineth at the table? but I am in the midst of you as he that serveth, and you are they who have continued with me in my temptations.

"And I appointed to you, as my Father hath appointed to me, a kingdom. That you may eat and drink at my table in my kingdom, and may sit upon thrones judging the twelve tribes of Israel."[1]

He alludes to his kingdom, the Catholic Church, which was to spread over the world, interpenetrating all governments, boundless as the human race. But he, the King, was not to reign here in this world, but mid the unnumbered spirits and redeemed souls of heaven to be bought by the cross on the morrow. When a king is away, his prime minister administers the laws, and rules for him in his absence. Would he be so foolish as to leave his kingdom to anarchy? Would that be the act of a wise statesman? He provided for the future. He turned to his chief apostle Peter, and promised the power he gave him after the resurrection, when he appeared as the lone Personage on the shores of Galilee. He gave then to Peter power to: "Feed his lambfolds, to govern his lambfolds, to feed his sheepfolds," as John tells us in his Greek Gospel.[2] To Peter now he says:

"Simon, Simon, behold Satan hath desired to have you, that he may sift you as wheat. But I have prayed for thee, that thy faith fail not, and thou being once converted, confirm thy brethren."[3]

Peter thought he was very strong in faith and devotion

[1] Luke xxii. 24-31.   [2] John xxi 15 to 17.   [3] Luke xxii 31, 32.

to his Master. But he was to learn a lesson of human weakness when not upheld by the Holy Spirit. Therefore the Lord told him he would deny him three times before the next morning. Only after the Holy Ghost came down on them did they understand all the Master's words, acts and the lessons of that their last Passover.

After Communion they sang the Thanksgiving Hymn given in the Jewish Liturgy. They sang it like a Litany; Christ singing the first versicles, the apostles responding: " For His mercy endureth forever."

O, give thanks to the Lord for he is good :
O, give thanks to the God of gods :
O, give thanks to the Lord of lords :
To him who alone doeth great wonders :
To him who by wisdom made the heavens :
To him who stretched out the earth above the waters :
To him who made great lights :
The sun to rule by day :
The moon and stars to rule by night :
To him who smote Egypt in their first-born :
And brought out Israel from among them :
With a strong hand and outstretched arm :
To him who divided the Red Sea :
And made Israel to pass through the midst of it :
But overthrew Pharao and his host in the Red Sea :
To him who led his people through the wilderness :
To him who smote great kings :
And slew famous kings :
Sihon king of the Amorites :
And Og king of Bashan :
And gave their lands for an heritage :
Even an heritage unto Israel his servant :
Who remembered us in our low estate :
And hath redeemed us from our enemies :
Who giveth food to all flesh :
O, give thanks to the God of heaven :

For His mercy endureth forever.

"The breath of all living bless Thy name, O Lord, our God, the spirit of all flesh continually glorify and extol thy memorial. O, our King, thou art God from eternity to eternity. Besides thee we acknowledge neither king, redeemer or saviour. Thou redeemest, deliverest, maintainest, and hast compassion on us in all times of trouble and distress, we have no other king but thee. Thou art God of the first and God of the last, the God of all creatures, the Lord of all productions, thou art adored with all manner of praise, who governeth the Universe with tenderness, and thy creatures with mercy. Behold the Lord neither slumbereth nor sleepeth, but rouseth those who sleep, awakeneth those who slumber, causeth the dumb to speak, looseneth those that are bound, supporteth the fallen, and raiseth those who droop, and therefore thee alone we adore. Although our mouths were filled with melodious songs as the drops of the sea, our tongues with shouting as the roaring billows thereof, our lips with praise like the wide extended firmament, our eyes with sparkling brightness like the sun and moon, our hands extended like the towering eagles, and our feet as the hinds for swiftness, we nevertheless are incapable of rendering sufficient thanks unto thee, O Lord, our God, and the God of our fathers, or to bless thy name, for one of the innumerable benefits which thou hast conferred on us and on our ancestors. For thou, O Lord, our God, didst redeem us from Egypt, and release us from the house of bondage, in the time of famine thou didst sustain us, and in plenty thou didst nourish us. Thou didst deliver us from the sword, saved us from pestilence, and from many sore and heavy diseases thou didst withdraw us. Hitherto thy tender mercies have supported us, and thy kindness has not forsaken us. O, Lord our God, forsake us not in the future. Therefore the members of which thou hast formed us, the spirit and soul which thou hast breathed into us, and the tongue which thou hast placed in our mouths, lo! they shall worship, bless, praise, glorify, extol, reverence, sanctify and ascribe sovereign power unto thy name. O, our King, every mouth shall adore thee, and every tongue shall swear to thee, and every knee shall bend to thee, every reasonable being shall worship thee, every heart shall revere thee, the inward parts and reins shall sing praise to thy name, as it is written, all my bones shall say, O Lord, who is like unto thee? who delivereth the weak from him who is too strong for him, the poor and needy from their oppressor. Who is like unto thee? Who is equal to thee? Who can be compared unto thee? great, mighty and tremendous God, most high God, possessor of heaven and earth. We praise, adore, glorify and bless thy name, so saith David.

" Bless the Lord, O my soul, and all that is within me, bless his holy name.

" O God, who are mighty in thy strength, who art great by thy glorious name, mighty for ever, tremendous by thy fearful acts. The King who sitteth on the high and exalted throne, inhabiting eternity, most exalted and holy is his name, as it is written: Rejoice in the Lord, O ye righteous, for praise is becoming to the just. With the mouth of the upright thou shalt be praised, with the lips of the righteous blessed, with the tongue of the pious extolled, by a choir of saints thou shalt be sanctified

" And in the congregation of many thousands of thy people the house of Israel shall glorify thy name, O our King, through all generations, for such is the duty of every created being towards thee, O Lord, our God, and the God of our forefathers, to render thanks, to praise, to extol, to glorify, to exalt, to ascribe glory, to bless, to magnify, and to adore thee, with all the songs and praises of thy servant David, the son of Jesse.

" May thy name be praised for ever, our King, the Almighty, the King great and holy in heaven and on earth, for to thee, O Lord, our God, and the God of our fathers, belongeth song, praise, hymns and psalms, might and dominion, victory and power, greatness, adoration, holiness and majesty, blessings and thanksgivings; these are thine from henceforth to everlasting. Blessed art thou, O Lord, Almighty King, great with praises. Almighty to be adored, the Lord of wonders, who hath accepted songs of psalmody, King Almighty who livest eternally."

They sing the following Hymn.[1] Some Jewish writers say it was composed in the Middle Ages, others hold it comes from the prophets: nobody knows its author. Did it foretell Christ arrested at midnight near the Winepress, Gethsemane?

[1] Mark xiv, 26.

AND THUS IT CAME TO PASS AT MIDNIGHT.

THEN thou didst perform abundant miracles in the night.
In the beginning of the first watch of this night,
The just professor of God (Abraham) conquered when he
    divided his company at night.
        And it came to pass at midnight.

Thou didst threaten the king of Gerar with death in a dream
    by night,
Thou didst terrify the Syrian in the dead of the night.
And Israel wrestled with an angel and overcame him in the
    night.
        And it came to pass at midnight.

The first-born of the Egyptians thou didst crush at midnight.
Their strength found them not when they rose at night.
The swift army of the prince of Haroshet thou didst tread
    down with the stars of the night.
        And it came to pass at midnight.

The blasphemer who imagined to lift up his head against thy
    beautiful habitation, thou didst frustrate by the number
    of his slain in the night.
The idol Bel and its statue were overthrown in the darkness of
    the night,
To the meritorious man the secret was revealed in the vision
    of the night.
        And it came to pass at midnight.

He who got drunk with holy vessels (Balshassar) was slain at
    night,
He who was delivered from the den of lions interpreted the
    dreadful dreams of the night.
The Agagite cherished enmity and wrote letters at night.
        And it came to pass at midnight.

Thou didst awaken all thy conquering power against him by
    disturbing the sleep of the king in the night,
Thou wilt tread the winepress (Gethsemane) when saying to
    the watchman, What of the night?
Let the watchman (Israel) say aloud, The morning is come
    after night,
        And it came to pass at midnight.

O, may the day draw nigh that is neither day nor night,
O, thou Most High make known that under thee belongeth the
    day and also the night,
Appoint watchmen to thy city (Jerusalem) all day and all
    night,

O, illuminate as the splendor of the day, the darkness of the night.

And it came to pass at midnight.

On the second night, that is the first night of unleaven bread, the following is said :

And ye shall say this is the sacrifice of the Passover,
Thou didst wonderfully show forth thy mighty power of the Passover.
Above all solemn feasts thou didst exalt the Passover.
Thou didst reveal to the Oriental (Abraham) the miracles wrought in the midst of the night of the Passover.
And ye shall say this is the sacrifice of the Passover.

Thou didst appear to him in the heat of the day on the Passover.
He entertained the Angels with unleavened cakes on the Passover.
And he ran to the herd as a memorial of the offerings of the Passover.
And ye shall say this is the sacrifice of the Passover.

The inhabitants of Sodom provoked God to anger and they were consumed by fire on the Passover.
Lot was delivered who baked cakes for the Passover.
Thou didst sweep the land of Moph and Noph, when thou didst pass through on the Passover.
And ye shall say this is the sacrifice of the Passover.

O Lord, thou didst wound the head of the first-born on the night of the observation of the Passover.
O Omnipotent! yet thou didst pass over the first-born son (Israel) being marked with the blood of the sacrifice of the Passover.
And ye shall say this is the sacrifice of the Passover.

The strong and fortified city (Jericho) was surrendered in the season of the Passover.
Midian was destroyed by the cake of barley bread, like the offering of the omer of barley on the Passover.
The mighty men of Pull and Lud were destroyed with burning fire on the Passover.
And ye shall say this is the sacrifice of the Passover.

The king abode yet in Nob this day, till the time of the Passover.
The part of the hand wrote the destruction of the foundation of the Babylonian empire on the Passover.
Even the time when the watch was set and the table prepared on the Passover.
And ye shall say this is the sacrifice of the Passover.

Esther gathered the congregation to fast three days on the
    Passover.
The sworn enemy (Haman)[1] thou didst cause to be executed on
    a gallows fifty cubits high, on the Passover.
These two things shalt thou bring in a moment on Utz on the
    Passover.
Thy hand will then be exalted as on the night whereon was
    sanctified the Festival of the Passover.
And ye shall say this is the sacrifice of the Passover."

The Passover ended   They were all now bishops.   All
had received Communion.   Some writers seem to think
that Judas left before the end of the feast and that he
did not receive the Eucharist.   But this is a mistake, for
the law strictly commanded every male Hebrew, not
prevented by good reasons to be present, and forbade him
to leave the table before he had fulfilled all its rites and
ceremonies.   If Judas left before the supper was over he
would have been under Kareth, " Cut off," " Excommunicated."

Judas (twelve of this name are mentioned in the Bible.
Two of the apostles were called Judas, the other being
Judas Thaddeus) Iscariot was thus called from the
little village to the south of Hebron where he was born,
mentioned only once in the Old Testament in the Carioth
of Josue,[2] the name being a Hebrew word meaning " The
man of murder " or " of extermination."   Thus was his
betrayal foretold in the name of the village of his birth.
He was a miser, loved money more than he did his Lord,
had been acting as a spy for Joseph Caiphas his uncle,
the high priest, and had promised the officials of the
Temple to show Christ's place of prayer in Gethsemane.
This archtraitor had for days been scheming with his
uncle Caiphas, his cousin Sarah, the latter's daughter,
and the Temple officials for the betrayal of the Master.
Let us see how the Lord treated Judas.

At the end of the Passover, the master used to dip
bread into the charoseth and hand it to his dearest
friend, as a special mark of love, friendship and esteem.
When John asked his master in confidence, who would
betray him, Jesus dipped the morsel into the dish typical
of Egyptian bondage, and handed it to Judas as a special

[1] Translated in our Bible Aman, Esther iii   [2] Josue. xv 25.

and a public mark of friendship for Judas, although he knew his murderous designs.[1] Thus the God-man, who taught men to love their enemies, handed the betrayer the sop of friendship to show he held no feeling of hatred towards him, and to give the world an example of full forgiveness of his enemy.

"When Jesus had said these things, he was troubled in spirit, and he protested and said, 'Amen, amen, I say to you that one of you will betray me.' The disciples therefore looked upon one another doubting of whom he spoke. Now there was leaning on Jesus' bosom one of his disciples whom Jesus loved. Simon Peter therefore beckoned to him and said to him, 'Who is it of whom he speaketh?' He therefore leaning on the breast of Jesus saith to him, 'Lord, who is it,' Jesus answered, 'He it is to whom I shall reach bread dipped.' And when he had dipped the bread he gave it to Judas Iscariot, the son of Simon. And after the morsel Satan entered into him. And Jesus said to him: 'That which thou do, do quickly.' Now no man at the table knew for what intent he said this to him. For some thought because Judas had the purse, that Jesus said, 'Buy those things which we have need of for the festival day,' or that he should give something to the poor. He therefore having received the morsel went out immediately. And it was night."[2]

The feast of unleaven bread lasted for a week, each "band" of Jews brought to the place where they celebrated the supper the eatables required, and the apostles supposed that the Lord sent Judas to buy these things for the next supper in the booths of the Holy City which were always open during eight Passover nights.

Down to his uncle Joseph Caiphas went that basest man of human history to get the money they promised him to show them the Master's place of prayer. The Lord had now offered as a sacrifice himself, his Body and Blood as a Victim for the world's sins and to fulfil all the figures and types of the Jewish religion. Therefore the shades of his Passion began to close over him. But when Judas had gone he preached these burning words of love, of unity, of sublime principles to the eleven

[1] Edersheim, Life of Christ, ii. 509, 511.   [2] John xiii. 21-30.

28

apostles as his last sermon before his death. Then a little before the midnight hour, with his band he passed out the Sion Gate, crossed the Tyropœon vale, went through Ophel, passed the Cedron and entered Gethsemane and the awful sufferings of his Passion we have described in the book The Tragedy of Calvary.

THE END.

INDEX.

435

CPSIA information can be obtained at www.ICGtesting.com
Printed in the USA
LVOW062017120313

323921LV00022B/1240/P